BACK TO BASICS

The Traditionalist Movement
That Is Sweeping
Grass-Roots America

BURTON YALE PINES

William Morrow and Company, Inc.
New York   1982

Library of Congress Cataloging in Publication Data

Pines, Burton Yale.
  Back to basics.

  Includes index.
  1. United States—Moral conditions.   2. Conservatism—United States.   I. Title.
HN59.2.P53   306'.0973   82–2106
ISBN 0–688–01117–9   AACR2

Printed in the United States of America

First Edition

1 2 3 4 5 6 7 8 9 10

BOOK DESIGN BY BERNARD SCHLEIFER

To

My grandparents Samuel and Lena Kaplan,

immigrants who came to this country

and thus gave me the privilege

of being born American.

ACKNOWLEDGMENTS

I AM DEEPLY INDEBTED to scores of people for helping with this study. Without the encouragement of Irving Kristol and Richard Clurman, for example, I doubt that I would have had the confidence to begin what turned out to be an eighteen-month effort of research and writing. That I was able to devote full time to the task is due in very great part to the generosity of the American Enterprise Institute, which named me its resident journalist. AEI provided a stipend, research funds, a Washington office and the opportunity to associate with its very distinguished and intellectually provocative staff. To AEI President William Baroody, Jr., I indeed owe a great debt, as I do to Phillip Marcus and the trustees of the Institute for Educational Affairs, which provided a major grant for my work. For their early and continued support, I also am extremely grateful to R. Randolph Richardson and Leslie Lenkowsky. *Time* magazine Managing Editor Ray Cave not only allowed me to take a leave of absence from my post as an associate editor of the publication, but then kindly extended the leave when I needed more time.

The research task was greatly eased by the generosity of those who submitted to interviews, patiently answered my questions and gave me much of the information cited in the book. Particular thanks go to Stephen Wesley of Cardinal Ritter Prep School in St. Louis; Bud and Marion Clark of the Basic Education Leadership Conference; Arthur Levine of the Carnegie Endowment, Jerry Gaff of Project GEM and Bruno Manno of the National Catholic Education Association in Washington, D.C.; Rosemary Thomson and Elizabeth Clark of Stop-ERA in Illinois; Edwin

Feulner, Jr., of the Heritage Foundation; New Right leaders Paul Weyrich, Howard Phillips, Terry Dolan, Connie Marshner and Ed McAteer; the staffs and students of Wheaton College and Fuller Theological Seminary; Richard Gottier and David Clark of CBN University; Ronald Godwin and Cal Thomas of Moral Majority, Inc.; David Fogel of the University of Illinois (Chicago Circle Campus); the Economics Department of the University of Minnesota; members of Washington's Carlton Group; Frank Chew at the University of Southern California; Judy DiSario at the American Council on Education; Russell Vlaanderen and Chris Pipho of the Education Commission of the States; Pro-family advocates Sam and Beth Skousen of Warren, Michigan, and George and Mary Schroeder of Little Rock; Timothy Smith of Johns Hopkins University; Leonard Theberge of the Media Institute; Harold Deakins of Illinois Power Company; and John Kramer of the Pennsylvania Sentencing Commission.

My colleagues at AEI indulged my enthusiasm for the information I was finding, allowed me to test my ideas on them, endured what must have been painfully tedious monologues at lunch in the AEI dining room and—above all—helped educate me. In particular, I want to thank Michael Novak, Robert Nisbet, Jeane Kirkpatrick, Walter Berns, Steve Miller, Mike Malbin, Howard Penniman, Ben Wattenberg, Karlyn Keene, Marvin Kosters, Anne Brunsdale, Robert Woodson, Thomas Johnson, Ed Somensatto, John Cooper, Jerry Hyman, John Kessell and Tom Mann.

Critical to the making of this study were my research assistant Fred Mann; my secretary at AEI, Randa Murphy; AEI librarians Evelyn Caldwell and Brigid Shea; and AEI's Jim Barnes. In an earlier day, it would have been appropriate to thank one's dedicated and harried typist. Alas, in this era, my gratitude (and respect) instead goes to my Savin 950 Veritext word processor— loyal, efficient and uncomplaining.

I owe a great debt to Harvey Ginsberg, whose deft editing of my manuscript and whose willingness to challenge some of my ideas substantially improved the final product.

In conclusion, very deep and special gratitude is due two extraordinary individuals:

To George L. Mosse, the distinguished historian from whom, during seven years as an undergraduate and graduate student at the University of Wisconsin, I acquired the tools of research, some ability to analyze concepts and a respect for the power of ideas; the excitement of his classes and the intellectual rigor of his legendary seminars are legacies from which I have been drawing abundantly during my entire professional life.

To Helene Sue Brenner, my patient, supportive, indulgent, forgiving and loving wife, who endured endlessly yet another one of the tidbits of information which I had gathered during my research, was willing (even appeared eager) to reread again a chapter revision, was lavish with her encouragement and held my hand when I was certain that I had run into a research or writing dead end.

To those above and to scores of others who helped in this project, I offer my thanks. They have aided me as much as they could, and now the responsibility for the contents of the book I must bear alone.

CONTENTS

INTRODUCTION: Back to Basics   13

1: Daring to Fight

I. A Free Enterprise Counteroffensive   31

II. Evangelizing for Capitalism   50

III. Battling the Leviathan   66

IV. Back to Classroom Basics   99

V. Rallying Around the Family   130

VI. Legions of Homemakers   155

2: A New Traditionalist Mood

VII. Faith of Our Fathers   183

VIII. Vengeance and Just Deserts   209

IX. Tomorrow's Traditionalists   226

3: A War of Ideas

X. Arsenal of Ideas   245

XI. The New Right   273

XII. Conclusion: The Traditionalist Challenge   308

NOTES   333

INDEX   341

INTRODUCTION:
BACK TO BASICS

HIS HAND ON THE family Bible, his beaming wife at his side, the day bright and unseasonably warm and his countrymen in the tens of millions watching by television, Ronald Reagan repeated an oath taken by only thirty-eight other men in American history. Was the nation, on this January morning, inaugurating a new President or a new era? Had Reagan's surprisingly decisive election victory eleven weeks earlier been a personal triumph over a pathetically discredited Jimmy Carter? Or had it been a conscious rejection of a whole set of ideas, outlooks, attitudes, mindsets and policies which for nearly two generations had dominated the United States? Put another way, would the Reagan election be a 1932 or a 1952? Would it become analagous to Franklin Roosevelt's landslide victory which ushered in the age of the New Deal, or analagous to Dwight Eisenhower's landslide which, though a thundering tribute to a wartime hero, left the nation's course fundamentally unchanged?

From the start, the incoming President behaved as if he was ushering in a new era. His sweep of all but six states (and the District of Columbia) and the Republican capture of the Senate had stunned political analysts. "Tidal Wave," is what the liberal *Washington Post* called it in an editorial-page headline. The editorial then asserted that "something of gigantic proportions happened." Idaho's Frank Church, one of the most prominent of the liberal Democratic senators defeated in reelection bids, could only say: "The conservatives are in charge now." And seasoned political analyst David Broder, in the space of a single article, managed to call the Reagan win "the sharpest turn to the right in a generation," "the start of a new era" and "the biggest power shift in Washington since 1952."

When Reagan moved into the White House, he did so with commanding self-assurance and generosity, calling courteously on congressional leaders, flattering the Washington political and power establishment and signaling sharply that he had no intention of abandoning principles which he had been championing for nearly two decades. Shortly after his inaugural, he exclaimed to a cheering, adoring conservative gathering: "Fellow citizens, fellow conservatives, our time is now. Our moment has arrived." In quick measure, he froze the federal payroll and began hacking away at the jungle of regulations strangling the U.S. economy. Within just months, he surprised veteran observers by slashing the federal budget and winning congressional approval of a sweeping, multi-year, across-the-board tax cut.

Surprise was predictable. For ever so long, analysts and pundits had been scoffing at, even ridiculing, the very notion that policies such as those being pushed by Reagan had any chance of becoming law. Smugly these experts could list all those things that a President could *not* do, reciting with barely a pause for breath "untouchable" budget items, programs that could not be abolished, tax policies that could never gain public and Capitol Hill backing, regulatory agencies that could not be tamed and a Congress that could not be led. Yet here was Reagan, proving them wrong, demonstrating, in fact, that it could be done.

What had happened? What had changed on the American political landscape? The answer, in part, is the President himself —his personality, administrative skills and rare talent for articulating the reasons for and purposes of his programs. The answer, in part also, is the politically astute team assembled for his administration. Mostly, however, the answer seems to be a happy confluence at that rare historical moment of a right man in a right place at a right time. And what is making this time right is the resurgence, across a broad national front and in many critical sectors of life, of American traditionalism. A new era indeed seems at hand, a traditionalist era marked dramatically by a return to basics. Ronald Reagan did not start it but, as candidate and President, he has been riding its crest as it promises to become one of the century's most powerful movements—certainly the most powerful since the New Deal rewrote the nation's basic political equations. Though not beginning as a political phenomenon, the traditionalist resurgence had enough political impact in the 1980 elections to account for the margins of victory in perhaps dozens of electoral battles. Mainly, however, the traditionalist resurgence is nonpolitical, a phenomenon profoundly affecting Americans' personal lives and how they define and assess public policy issues. It is a definition, moreover, leaving little room for liberalism.

After a long, confident reign, after dominating all aspects of American life, after watching its values, attitudes and even methods become conventional wisdom, American liberalism is crumbling. When Reagan, in his February 1981 budget-slashing address to Congress, turned to the liberal Democrats and asked if they had a better alternative to his program, there was only silence—a persistent silence confirming that liberals no longer seem to have an alternative in which they believe.

So thorough and sudden is liberalism's collapse that had it occurred in Imperial China, chroniclers would have written confidently of the Liberal Dynasty losing the Mandate of Heaven—that universally perceived attribute which gave regimes legitimacy and assured them popular support. Inevitably, however, misfortunes would erode that popular backing, thus allowing one rival faction or another to depose the rulers. Imperial wisemen would explain the change by proclaiming that heaven's mandate had been withdrawn and was being transferred to a new dynasty.

In today's America, the heavenly mandate has shifted from a faltering Liberal Dynasty to a vigorous, resurgent Traditionalist Dynasty. Across the nation, in numbers beyond tallying, Americans have been mobilizing—some for more than a decade, others for just a few years—against liberalism and in support of traditional values. They are brushing aside many of the intellectual and moral concepts not only taken for granted as the 1970's were ending, but which also provided the dominant liberal rationale and justification for the nation's public policies since the 1930's.

Resurgent traditionalism is most dynamic at the grass roots, in life's very private, yet most critical sectors. There, legions of Americans are going back to basics in education, back to Scripture and spirituality in religion, back to trusting the free enterprise system, back to appreciating the nuclear family. They are speaking out, signing on with groups like Stop-ERA and the Moral Majority, backing candidates and exchanging newsletters. Reinforcing and guiding them is a torrent of studies from proliferating and expanding conservative research institutes and think tanks and the writings of the enormously influential group of intellectuals known as neoconservatives.

This book is a journey through traditionalist America in search of the forces creating the back to basics sea change which the Reagan Administration, though not initiating, has focused and harnessed politically and from which it benefits. Encountered on this journey are the enormous frustrations of traditional Americans who have felt themselves increasingly assaulted by their society's predominantly liberal ethos and its often open contempt for traditional values. Encountered too are the responses to the assault, countless separate and independent responses which in the aggregate are reshaping the contours of the political landscape.

This study, while comprehensive, is not definitive. The journey skips many byways, and even a major route or two. Some traditionalist organizations, vigorous and successful, are ignored, some scholars are uncited and some fine programs are overlooked. In method, this study attempts to marry the academic researcher's respect for the authoritative printed document with the journalist's confidence in the person-to-person interview and eyewitness, on-site reporting.

The journey's milestones are the study's chapters, each more or less dealing with a critical sector of American society now churning with traditionalist resurgence. The journey's landmarks are the dozens of heroes encountered along the way. Some are major figures in the traditionalist movement, like neoconservative Irving Kristol, *Family Protection Report* editor Connaught Marshner, Eagle Forum founder Phyllis Schlafly and Moral Majority President Jerry Falwell. Most of the heroes, however, are ordinary folk with low public profiles, like Principal Stephen Wesley of Cardinal Ritter Prep, Stop-ERA's Rosemary Thomson, Methodist minister Ray Sells, Sam and Beth Skousen of Michigan's Pro-Family Coalition and the feisty officers of the Illinois Power Company.

By and large, these folks are startled by what they have been doing, surprised to find themselves on the cutting edge of a traditionalist—or, for that matter, any—resurgence. They are not veterans of political movements or issues-oriented organizations. For most of them, it turns out, community activity had meant little more than a good attendance record at the Kiwanis Club and

P.T.A., an annual weekend outing with the Boy Scouts and selling raffle tickets or baking pies for the church bazaar. They are private, hard-working people who have become activists only reluctantly—and altruistically. Unlike those liberal activists who end up on public payrolls working for or administering the very programs which they advocated, traditionalists seldom benefit directly or personally from the causes for which they battle. Rather than having been drawn into the fray, therefore, they have been pushed into it by a liberalism which has been careening out of control since the late 1960's. At first, traditionalists scarcely responded. Only gradually did their frustration mount, moving from annoyance to anger to outrage and, finally, to determination to take a stand. Liberalism's excesses, in effect, pushed them right up to the brink until they felt that they had no choice but to say, "Enough!"

In each sector, for each community, the brink has come at different times and in different ways. For most, the process has been incremental. For others, a single jolting event or development has exposed regnant liberalism, or those acting in its name, as having gone too far.

For some business leaders, the final step up to the brink was the congressional attempt to create a Consumer Protection Agency, a new super-bureaucracy with authority to interfere in a marketplace already choking from government regulations and regulators. For parents and employers, it was the shocking spectacle of local public high schools graduating near-illiterates. For homemakers, it was the sight of extremists seizing control of the feminist movement and ramming through an ultraradical agenda purporting to reflect the views of all American women. For Fundamentalist preachers, it was the Carter Administration's attempt to use the Internal Revenue Service to intimidate private Christian schools. For Establishment intellectuals, it was the dawning realization that liberal policies and policy-makers were crippling the nation's economy and ignoring its military needs. For devout Christians and Jews, it was the aggressive anti-religious secularism (commonly called "secular humanism") of those in control of schools, courts and other key social institutions.

These all represented brinks of sorts which traditional Americans balked at approaching and whose specter galvanized vast numbers into unaccustomed action. They went into action originally as discrete groups and to a considerable degree remain

quite independent of one another. Those pushing for a basics
school curriculum may be completely unaware of the nearby
women's group fighting ratification of the Equal Rights Amendment. The new evangelicals may not notice the neighborhood
association protesting the clinic which performs abortions on
fifteen-year-olds without requiring parental consent or even
notification. And certainly those intellectuals, academics and
business executives who are increasingly committed to a stronger
national defense and an unfettered free enterprise system are
total strangers to those humbler folk mainly concerned with education, family matters, open homosexuality and other social issues. These two broad strata, in fact, rarely communicate, and
when they try, they often have trouble understanding each
other's language.

What all these groups share and what transforms their individual actions into a semblance of a movement is the similar
way that they have responded to being pushed to the brink. They
have reacted by reacting, by trying to recapture a precious value
or quality which they believe has been lost. Their doing so is not
without precedent. "Human history," writes Irving Kristol, "read
in a certain way, can be seen as full of critical moments when
human beings deliberately turned the clock back. The Reforma-
tion, properly understood, was just such a moment, and so was
the codification of the Talmud in post-exile Judaism." Often,
what seems intellectually and spiritually "new," continues Kristol, is "nothing more than a novel way of turning the clock
back."[1]

Settling on a label for this broad-based reassertion of fading
or lost values presents problems. In some respects, it is a "rightist" phenomenon. Yet this term is inappropriately too political
for some members of the movement. While the Moral Majority
and other New Right groups indeed are "rightist" in a political
sense, there is nothing particularly political about the back to
basics movement in education, the quest for spirituality in religion or the pro-family movement.

As a label, "conservative" fits better than "rightist." Many of
the sinews binding the movement's parts are basic conservative
tenets, such as affirming authority, discipline, a moral order with
a hierarchy of values, standards and individual duties balancing
individual rights. Central to the movement is another fundamental conservative principle: reverence for society's organic institu-

tions of family, religion and community. Central also is conservatism's recognition that individuals' unequal abilities result invariably in unequal achievements. Within the traditionalist movement, there is complete acceptance, moreover, of conservatism's doctrine upholding the individual's right to own and use property and of the concept linking personal liberty with economic freedom. Such freedom, however, is tempered by the solid conservative virtues of hard work, thrift and deferral of immediate pleasures for the sake of future rewards, a future not always measured in terms of this lifetime or even of this world.

Traditionalist groups further share a conservative abhorrence of utopian schemes and of liberalism's near-total faith in human reason's ability to construct the perfect society. Suspicious of human nature and such claims for the power of reason, conservatives are willing to adjust and rearrange institutions only slightly. They especially oppose liberal-style bulldozing broad swaths through the social structure. Writes historian Gertrude Himmelfarb: "The conservative is more passive in political and social matters because he prefers the evils he knows to those he does not know—but can well imagine. He has no confidence that change will be for the better."[2] And to change for the worse breaches trust in what Conservative Founding Father Edmund Burke called the partnership of the living with past and future generations. For the conservative, this means that social institutions are merely entrusted to each generation for safekeeping for its heirs.

Though these conservative principles are widely embraced by traditionalist groups, "conservatism" still is not quite a broad enough umbrella to gather beneath it the entire movement. The ranks of the abortion foes, for instance, contain public figures closely identified with "liberal" positions on other matters. There is nothing particularly conservative, moreover, about concern for national defense; liberals too have cared (and generally still do) deeply about it. And the New Right seems singularly unconservative when boasting of its intention to revolutionize the nation's political institutions. Several neoconservatives, meanwhile, protest strongly that they are not conservative at all. Social analyst Michael Novak, for one, prefers being called "neoliberal" if he is to be labeled.

Perhaps no single label can perfectly fit each group and individual examined by this study. To impose one merely may compound what public opinion expert Everett Ladd, Jr., calls "the long-standing American penchant for obfuscating terminology."[3] Obfuscation is indeed a problem. At a Conservative Caucus conference in late 1980, an exasperated district chairman complained that, "I'm a conservative but don't know any longer what a conservative is. I'm so confused. Everyone now is claiming to be a conservative."

Yet there is great value in a rubric that manages to convey in shorthand the essence of a phenomenon. And one term does come fairly close to capturing a sense of the concerns, motivations and goals of the movement now sweeping America. It is a term which additionally provides a banner around which the movement's varied parts can gather. More than "rightist" and more than "conservative," what the U.S. is witnessing is a "traditionalist" resurgence. Ask those involved what they seek and often, without prompting, they reply, "traditional values." And those who happen not to volunteer the term seem comfortable with it when offered. It is less political than "rightist" and less ideological than "conservative." Augmenting rather than contradicting these two other, closely related terms, "traditionalist" conveys warmth, a sense of the tried and the true, of familiar roads on safe journeys and of means that once worked, principles that once proved sound and methods that once shepherded the nation through earlier troubled times.

"Traditional" also manages to reach just beyond "conservative" to grasp the peculiarly American—a faith in conquering frontiers and building better societies, in political democracy and market capitalism, in a federal system that protects the residual powers of the states and local communities and in public ritual that enthusiastically celebrates patriotism. It is the struggle on behalf of this traditionalism that is providing a bond for what in most respects remain quite separate phenomena. By marching in the same general direction along a common front, they constitute a loose, informal movement that is changing the way that America poses and answers questions of public policy.

How powerful is the traditionalist resurgence? Though it is too early to tell for sure, public opinion survey data cited throughout this study indicate that it is strong and growing stronger. It is unlikely, however, that traditionalist groups constitute a national majority. They need not. The public policy agenda is not set by majorities but by vocal, articulate minorities competing for the minds, affections, loyalties and backing of the huge, un-committed majority. For decades, the traditionalist stayed on the sidelines in this competition. The reason, writes historian James Hitchcock, is that the traditionalist is "usually taken by surprise when his beliefs are challenged. He finds it amazing and incomprehensible when values which to him are so obviously correct are questioned." While the liberals thus monopolized the public platform, commanding the megaphone for communicating with the grass roots, the traditionalist, says Hitchcock, tended "to alternate passivity with grouching, waiting for someone else to erect and man the barricades."[4]

What eventually has brought reluctant traditionalists to the barricades is fear that their nation, communities and families are more seriously threatened than at any time in memory. At fault, in part, are external factors, such as OPEC oil price increases, Moscow's military buildup, the predictable self-doubts following the collapse of American strategy in Indochina and the relative erosion of U.S. global economic power as other economies have expanded. But at fault too, say traditionalists, is a liberalism that has spun out of control and is impinging on life's most critical arcas.

With their wide conservative streak, of course, traditionalists always have been antagonistic to liberalism. Its rationalism leaves too little room for the romantic and mysterious, its secularism seems to deny the spiritual and its almost arrogant optimism not only makes it blind to inherent human limitations and frailties but also tempts it to prescribe social cures whose side effects are worse than the malady.

In the face of liberalism, traditionalists were accustomed, as Hitchcock notes, to do barely more than "grouch." In the late 1960's, however, demons of sorts seemed to possess American liberalism, distorting its judgment, radicalizing its methods and goals and driving it to ugly excesses. This was too much not only for traditionalists but also for many mainline, old-guard liberals, who reacted in horror. "All about us canvas tore and cables parted," bewailed Democratic Senator Daniel Patrick Moynihan. "A new kind of liberalism spread through our party like a plague," said political scientist Jeane Kirkpatrick, a founder of the liberal Coalition for a Democratic Majority and later Ronald Reagan's cabinet-ranking ambassador to the United Nations. Sociologist Daniel Bell, meanwhile, spoke of his dismay with a "liberalism in which issues such as equality, racism, imperialism and the like took precedence over other values like liberty and free enterprise."5

The transformation is indeed startling. Where historic, classical liberalism had aimed at protecting the individual from capricious authority, it now fathers intrusive government. Where it had fostered proscriptive laws, setting bounds and limits, it now legislates prescriptively, confident that the state knows better than the individual what is best for him. It is this contemporary liberalism—known variously as the New Left or the New Politics —which spawns forced busing, affirmative action, hiring and enrollment quotas, reverse discrimination and occupational safety rules mandating the shape of toilet seats.

In refusing to acknowledge that nature, history and fate stamp humans with real differences, liberalism pushes with increasing aggressiveness for equality. Where once this had meant equality of opportunity, it now means equality of results. Trusted no longer, apparently, is America's unique meritocratic tradition that for generations has rewarded achievement and fostered social mobility. To end what it regards as sexual inequality, liberalism forces public schools to integrate sports activities sexually and to abolish such single-gender groups as male glee clubs. In the name of equality, the American Civil Liberties Union and other very liberal groups have launched a campaign to prevent intelligence exams from being used to determine qualifications for a college, job or promotion. Pushing current liberalism's concept of pure equality to a perverse, but logical extreme is the Connecticut consumer affairs advocate who argued that individuals and firms whose names begin with "A" enjoy an unfair competitive advantage because they appear in telephone books and similar directories ahead of those whose names start with other initials. To remedy this, the consumerist proposed that the telephone company randomly mix listings in the Yellow Pages or reverse them every other year by putting "Z" at the front.

In no area probably is intrusive liberalism more annoying and costly than the economy. Since the late 1960's, its rhetoric has grown ever more hostile not only to capitalism but to industrialization and technology as well. Completely forgotten, it seems, is liberalism's proud legacy as *the* ideological and political champion of a free market and economic growth. Now "no growth" seems its ideology, "Small is Beautiful" its motto and a bureau-cratic Leviathan its omniscient coordinator of economic activity. As a result, enterprises groan under an enormous load of government regulation. Instead of promoting policies for creating new wealth, liberalism delights in redistributing existing wealth through massive welfare programs financed by high taxes, inflation and a soaring national debt. So high have liberalism's tax rates climbed that they seem designed deliberately to penalize hard work, incentive and risk-taking. This leads economist George Gilder to conclude, in *Wealth and Poverty,* that liberalism now assumes "that wealth can be taken for granted rather than produced by toil and thrift; that life is supposed to be easy and uncomplex; that its inevitable scarcities, setbacks and frustrations are the fault of malevolent others."

While the new liberalism has been restricting freedom in the marketplace, it has been equally energetic in loosening social restraints. Under attack have been the traditional mores and standards which check individual behavior and punish wrongdoings. Through "values clarification" courses inserted into school curriculums by liberal educators, youngsters are being taught, to many parents' horror, what is known as situational ethics. This teaches that just about all values are equal and that there are very few right or wrong answers. Outside the classroom, liberals have been using the courts and legislatures to advance individuals' claims against those of social institutions. Little does it matter, apparently, that newfound rights of criminals are at the expense of society's right to protection from lawlessness, that newfound rights of children are at the expense of parents' rights to raise their offspring and that newfound rights of pornographers are at the expense of the community's right to propriety and decency.

Concern for individual rights, of course, is hardly new to liberalism; it always has had highest priority. Liberalism indeed was born in the late eighteenth century's struggle against the authority of State, Church and tradition. Yet liberals always had accepted boundaries to individual rights. American philosopher John Dewey and his early twentieth-century liberal colleagues, explains historian Oscar Handlin, never sought to dismantle all restraints but rather expected that "free speech would promote sober discussion, [that] enlightened divorce laws would strengthen the family; and equal opportunity would bring merit to the fore."[6] Alien to these liberals of an earlier era would have been contemporary liberalism's unyielding, absolutist reading of the Bill of Rights that enshrines individual liberties as the premier—even sole—right deserving protection by political institutions.

It is such a reading that allows liberals to transform the First Amendment from a shield protecting religious practice from state harassment to a weapon of militant secularism. In liberals' hands, for example, First Amendment strictures on Church-State relations are being used to bar student religious groups from meeting on public university campuses and children from saying voluntary prayers, reading the Bible or even singing Christmas carols in their public classrooms. Freedom of speech now has come to mean, moreover, that states cannot require pupils to pledge allegiance to the American flag.

In foreign and national security matters, new liberalism is shockingly soft. American liberalism always has harbored a small pacifist, appeasement and even pro-Soviet wing sharing outlook and goals with the Marxist left. But mainstream liberalism was steely spined in foreign and military affairs, particularly during the generation following World War II. This has changed dramatically. A near-decade of liberal-inspired anemic defense budgets has allowed the Soviets to match or surpass the U.S. in just about every critical category of military capability. In what policy analyst M. Stanton Evans calls "an intense display of national masochism," moreover, liberals emasculated the FBI and CIA, particularly their abilities to counter Soviet espionage and related operations. U.S. intelligence agencies have become so unreliable, in fact, that allies have balked at cooperating with them and at sharing data.

Ignoring the Kremlin's nonstop arms buildup, liberals seemed oblivious to the mounting Soviet military threat. Typical was the simplistic trust with which Jimmy Carter and key lieutenants, such as Secretary of State Cyrus Vance and U.N. Ambassador Andrew Young, viewed Moscow. They behaved and conducted U.S. policy as if they had read no history or had lost their nerve. A naive idealism somehow had replaced the tough appreciation of global realities with which liberalism, a generation before, had responded firmly to Soviet provocations in Berlin, South Korea, Cuba and Indochina.

Accounting in part for liberals' broad retreat on the foreign policy front has been the gusher of works by far-left academics who imaginatively have been revising post-World War II history.

Through a kind of alchemy, these Revisionists, as they are called, have transformed the Soviet Union from the aggressor which swallowed the Baltic states and Eastern and most of Central Europe into an innocent, misunderstood and shamefully wronged party. Contrasting with this Soviet-whitewash are the dark colors with which Revisionists paint the United States; no longer is it an arsenal of democracy ready to sacrifice youth and resources to halt totalitarian aggression. Instead, Washington emerges as an evil, imperialist power responsible for much of the world's misery. Moving backward from the immediate past, Revisionists seem determined to demonstrate that the U.S. has been a demonic force from its earliest days. In their works, the Founding Fathers become racists, while the heroic conquering of the West and opening of the frontier are "unmasked" as exercises in genocide—comparable, presumably, with Nazi Germany's Final Solution.

In the face of such Orwellian rewriting of history, liberals by and large have remained inexplicably silent or responded apologetically by repudiating their earlier tough-minded policies. They also have been operating with an insidious double standard which accords special treatment to Communist states. Indeed, the same liberal-dominated American Political Science Association which canceled a Chicago meeting as a protest to Illinois' failure to ratify the Equal Rights Amendment, notes Oscar Handlin, did not hesitate sending members to a conference in Moscow, where there is little equality and fewer rights. The double standard further allows liberalism to overlook repression and brutality in mainland China, Libya, Iraq and other favorite leftist regimes, while protesting indignantly human rights violations in rightist states such as the Shah's Iran, South Africa, Taiwan and Nicaragua.

Liberalism's excesses alone probably would have roused quiescent traditionalists eventually and sent them scampering to the barricades. What made this a certainty was the eruption in the mid-to-late 1960's of the counterculture, a short-lived but enormously influential movement whose outrageous radicalism, while aimed at liberals as much as at traditionalists, tremendously influenced liberalism, spawning many of its most anti-traditional ideas. Comprised mainly of youth, the counterculture was almost classically adolescent in its rebellion against the adult world—though it attracted adult camp followers, particularly in the fashionably liberal enclaves of Manhattan, Georgetown, Beverly Hills and university campuses. Exactly what triggered the counterculture is a subject for another study. Yet a major contributing factor surely was the record-breaking numbers of restless, rebellious middle-class youngsters in the bulging baby-boom cohort as they reached adolescence. As if this were not enough, this cohort began challenging adult authority precisely at the moment when the adult world was hardly able to uphold its norms because of a near-paralysis coming from agonizing self-doubts over the enduring U.S. military involvement in Southeast Asia.

Lacking much of a positive program or anything beyond short-term goals, the counterculture is best defined by what it opposed—tradition, history, technology, modernity, America, patriotism, ambition, careers, rationalism and sexual restraint. As do nearly all adolescents, counterculturists mainly revolted against authority and rules, notably those enforcing traditional rites of passage into adulthood. It is this which almost surely accounts for the counterculture's vehemence in denouncing the "repressive" nuclear family, the "authoritarian" performance-based educational system which measures achievement by grades and the "immoral" conscription by the state of able-bodied youth to serve national interests. Structures and obligations unquestioningly accepted by traditionalists, therefore, were viciously ridiculed and massively defied.

A good deal of the counterculture was theater, designed to be outrageous and offend the hard-working middle class for whom the movement displayed naked contempt. Foul language and obscene gestures were standard fare, as was open use of marijuana, hashish and hallucinogenics like LSD. By their courtroom behavior, the so-called Chicago Eight defendants sought to make a mockery of the criminal justice system—and largely succeeded—during their 1970 trial for conspiring to incite riot at Chicago's 1968 Democratic National Convention. By open sexuality and glorification of communal living, counterculturists demonstrated contempt for traditional social norms. Reviewing the period, sociologist Robert Nisbet writes: "I think it would be difficult to find a single decade in the history of Western culture when so much barbarism—so much calculated onslaught against culture and convention in any form, and so much sheer degradation of both culture and the individual—passed into print, into music, into art, and onto the American stage as the decade of the

1960's." What was launched in that decade, concludes Nisbet, was "an all-out nihilism against culture."7

Liberalism today is tainted by this nihilism, and much of the liberal movement has been captured by the counterculture New Left and New Politics. Though mainline, classical liberals have been protesting that they remain the authentic incarnation of the liberal tradition, the radicals clearly dominate. Disgusted by this, a significant group of intellectuals has bolted liberalism, defecting to the right and becoming the neoconservatives. Other mainline liberals keep struggling to wrest control of liberalism's political and ideological turf back from the radicals. Whether they ultimately succeed is an open question. In the meantime, the perverse, distorted figure into which liberalism has transmogrified and the influence which it has had on American life so terrify traditionalists—of all sorts, in all areas—that they at last are sounding the tocsin, manning the barricades, charging into battle and daring to fight.

1

DARING TO FIGHT

I

A FREE
ENTERPRISE
COUNTEROFFENSIVE

"THIS IS WAR," declared Cornell Maier, the feisty boss of Kaiser Aluminum and Chemical Corporation. Under assault is the free enterprise system which, he warned, "can't survive in this country unless those of us who should be defending the system, who should be improving it, fight to save it."

Maier's call to action and that of other businessmen began echoing across the United States in the late 1970's—before American business had a friend in the White House, before free enterprise conservatives descended on Washington, before supply-side economics became fashionable. The numbers speaking out were not great, yet they signaled a changing mood. Businessmen's self-confidence was mounting and they were ready again to defend capitalism. Addressing a 1979 meeting in Des Moines, Willard Butcher, the president of New York's Chase Manhattan Bank, stressed that the business community's sole critical task was "to go public. We must take our message into American homes."

And indeed they have. So doing, they have launched a free enterprise counteroffensive that is helping transform the nation's economic mood, making quite plausible the Reagan Administration's argument that America's economic recovery depends on business rather than government, on entrepreneurs rather than bureaucrats, on private savings and investments rather than on public spending. In speaking out, businessmen have ended a very long period of silence. Once again, basic free enterprise has champions in America's boardrooms.

At the nation's grass roots, in a torrent of pamphlets, books, advertisements, films, lectures, discussion groups and even games and quizzes, the free enterprise system is being explained and promoted. Profit is not a four-letter word, blue-collar groups are learning. Government is a major cause of inflation and economic distress, they are being told. And lagging investment eventually leads to a flagging economy. Not all the message, obviously, sinks in; yet some of it does. And this is creating sympathy for and understanding of national policies based on a reborn faith in capitalism.

This pugnacity represents a seismic shift in attitude and behavior contrasting sharply with most of the 1970's. Then, businessmen painfully bore with almost universal silence a steady barrage of assaults. Complained a 1980 Kaiser Aluminum booklet: "An entire generation of chief executives has operated with the premise that if you take care of the bottom line, everything else will take care of itself." Reflecting on those years, Michael Kort, a onetime student radical activist, has written: "Poor 'Mr. Businessman' received no mercy; he was guilty of worshiping the golden calf instead of turning on to genuine love, peace and natural food."[1] What is needed, quipped Herbert Stein, former chairman of the Council of Economic Advisers and now resident scholar at the American Enterprise Institute, is a "businessmen's liberation movement . . . and a businessmen's liberation day . . . and a businessmen's liberation rally in Washington, attended by thousands of businessmen shouting and carrying signs."

The decade-long anti-business offensive has taken a toll. Polls reveal that while just about every major American institution has suffered a drop in public esteem in the 1970's, none has fallen so precipitously as business. From 1966 to 1979, for example, a Louis Harris survey shows that individuals expressing "a great deal of confidence" in leaders of major companies plummeted from 55 percent to 18 percent. In that same period, confidence in the military fell "only" from 61 percent to 29 percent and in the executive branch of the federal government from 41 percent to 17 percent. Part of the dramatic business drop probably is explained by the public's outrage at the increased cost of energy and the simplistic tendency to blame this on gas and oil companies. But part of the plunge clearly must be attributed to the anti-business, even anti-industrial mood of the counterculture.

It is something of an irony that while business as an institution has been plunging in the polls, the free enterprise system itself earns relatively high marks. Most Americans, for instance, reply negatively when pollsters ask if "the free enterprise system benefits the few." According to a *Los Angeles Times* poll in late 1979, 75 percent of the respondents felt "our system of business and industry is basically sound." The trouble is that though most Americans support the system, many do not understand it. When invited to estimate, for instance, how much a typical manufacturing company keeps as profit out of every dollar collected from its customers, Americans on the average guess about fifteen to seventeen cents. Yet the actual profit is only five cents.[2] When a group of considerably above average high school students is asked to identify the Federal Reserve, one third have responded that it is a branch of the National Guard which helps businesses in a disaster area. Misunderstandings about the economy's operation breeds suspicion about business and prompts the public to look to government rather than the marketplace for solutions to economic problems.

Combating such economic illiteracy is a top priority in the free enterprise counteroffensive. There is little agreement on which weapon is most powerful or what kind of campaign is most effective; nor is there much coordination among business allies. What is clear, however, is that an increasing share of the business community is expending resources and talent to change the public's view of economic matters. Writes Randall Poe, a staffer at the Conference Board, a corporate-sponsored research group: "Despite the risks and dangers, the feelings that companies of all sizes must stand up and speak out is now widespread. The only real debate is over how often to speak out, where and in what tone."

For some firms, the battle is best fought with a weapon they best know: advertising. Taking to newspapers and magazines (the copy is too controversial for television), companies have begun advocating specific solutions to pressing public problems. This shatters a powerful taboo. Business long has run "institutional" ads—low-profile, soft-sell copy which instead of promoting a specific product portrays the firm as a good citizen. Here, the aim is to create a reservoir of kindly feelings about the company. Quite another thing is the new advocacy advertising. Its strong positions on controversial issues risk antagonizing readers. Yet a growing number of firms are accepting the risk. In a 1979 survey, the Association of National Advertisers found a significant increase "in the number of [companies] discussing public issues in advertising." In two years, the share of polled firms engaging in such advertising jumped from 11.7 percent to 21 percent.

These advertisers reach a receptive audience. The Opinion Research Corporation discovered in a 1980 poll that 60 percent of the public approves of businesses using "paid advertising to present their point of view on controversial public issues;" 68 percent find such advertising very believable or fairly believable. What is more impressive, 57 percent say that the ads changed their minds on the issue and an astounding 25 percent actually profess to have been inspired by the ads to write a letter on the matter to a public official.

The granddaddy of advocacy advertising is Warner & Swasey, a Cleveland manufacturer. Since 1936, it has run more than 1,200 issues ads championing, among other things, the virtues of individualism and the evils of excessive government. Typical of its ad headlines are: THE GREATEST WAR ON POVERTY IS A SUCCESSFUL CORPORATION, and HOW MUCH FEDERAL AID DID THE PILGRIMS GET? For decades, Warner & Swasey was just about unique. Then, in 1970, Mobil Oil Corporation bought its first *New York Times* op-ed page space and inaugurated advocacy advertising's modern era. Explains Herbert Schmertz, Mobil vice-president of public affairs and key strategist of the ambitious campaign: "Corporations are not in business to manipulate public opinion. But if their livelihood is threatened— or if they perceive a threat to the national welfare in some proposed government action—they should speak out."

That is what Mobil has been doing. Since its first issues ad calling for more public transportation (a somewhat odd stance for an oil firm), its thoughtful and sometimes pugnacious statements have been appearing regularly in *The New York Times* and a half-dozen other leading national newspapers. At the same time, its "Observations" columns reach a wide audience through Sunday supplements. Mobil topics range from issues on the economy to the right of corporate free speech; mostly, however, it addresses energy questions. When NBC's New York affiliate, for example, telecast a five-part series in 1976 on gasoline supplies and prices that Mobil, with good reason, felt was an unfair attack on the U.S. oil industry, the firm countered quickly. Within weeks, it crafted what is acclaimed an advocacy advertising classic. Under the headline "What ever happened to fair play?" were seventeen tiny hatchets, each introducing a key paragraph recounting an NBC "hatchet job" against the energy industry. At the same time, Mobil offered to buy thirty minutes from the TV station to "present additional information" on the subject covered by the telecasts. The NBC affiliate refused. By then, however, the "hatchet job" ad was attracting wide attention, including stories in *Time* and *Newsweek*. Notes Mobil's Schmertz: "We had also heard that NBC, the parent network, planned to syndicate segments of the gasoline series to its stations across the country. We made sure that each one received a copy of our ad—and NBC never did syndicate the segments." Now into its second decade, Mobil's advocacy campaign shows no sign of abating and claims about one fourth of the firm's more than $20 million public affairs budget.

Along with Mobil, at least a dozen other firms now regularly run advocacy advertising campaigns. SmithKline Corporation has featured full-page discussions by prominent Americans and experts on issues of general national interest. Chase Manhattan Bank has run a series attacking excessive government regulation and federal budget deficits and arguing that tax laws should be changed to allow corporations to invest more money in new equipment and research and development. Bethlehem Steel Corporation, the nation's second-largest steel maker, turned to advocacy in 1976, cutting back on its traditional institutional advertising. "It had become obvious to us that if we didn't speak up, no one else would present our side of the issues," William Latshaw, the firm's advertising manager, later told *Saturday Review*. [3]

Bethlehem's campaign had a triple aim: to influence government decisions and public opinion leaders; to make the steel manufacturer a recognized leader in the national discussion of critical issues; and to defend the corporation as an institution. For two years, the firm ran a series of hard-hitting ads in the nation's most important newspapers and magazines. An early topic was capital formation. "What will it take to make jobs for your children?" read the ad headline. Bethlehem's answer: *"money."* But, asked the ad, *"Where will that money come from?"* Bethlehem's response: from earnings to be invested in new factories and expanded operation. The problem, continued the text, is that "under present federal tax laws" the government takes so large a share of future company earnings, that little remains for investment.

To remedy this, Bethlehem called for something that was to become a centerpiece of Reagan supply-side economics. What is needed, said the ads, is a reform of federal taxes "to help lower barriers to capital formation." Readers were told that if they agree with the company, they should urge their senators and congressmen to back four specific measures that would benefit corporations and spur capital formation. The ad was tightly written and at times quite technical. Latshaw later told S. Prakash Sethi, director of the Center for Research in Business and Social Policy at the University of Texas (Dallas), that Bethlehem realized that the term "capital formation" hardly "turns people on;" still, he said, the term belonged in the ad copy because "it is a very important part of our business."

Using a similar format, the steel company blasted excessive government regulation. One ad carried the headline: "Steel must comply with 5,600 regulations from 27 federal agencies. It's a wonder we get anything done." Other ads addressed energy conservation, the high cost of environmental controls, business concentration and steel imports. Some ads contained cut-out forms on which readers could write messages to their elected representatives or Jimmy Carter. And they did. During the peak of the write-in, 5,000 Bethlehem-prompted letters a week inundated the White House. Beyond this measurable impact, the Bethlehem campaign probably has played some role in alerting the public to pressing economic issues and hence in changing its attitudes.

A slightly different advocacy strategy is employed by W.R. Grace and Company, the multibillion-dollar shipping, chemical and oil exploration conglomerate. It favors short, concentrated bursts on specific topics. It launched its first advocacy campaign in 1978, focusing on just one target: slicing the capital gains tax in half. In just four months, it helped mobilize public and congressional opinion and forced Jimmy Carter to sign a measure that he would have loved never to have seen hit his desk.

The advocacy drive was ordered by the firm's boss, J. Peter Grace. Horrified by Carter's call at the start of 1978 for a *hike* in the capital gains tax, Grace vowed to do something to convince Washington and the rest of the country that a cut, not a boost, was needed. He commissioned a study of the matter, including an analysis of tax rates in other industrial nations. This yielded a forty-nine-page report bearing the tongue-numbing title, "The Disincentivization of America," but made the powerful case that the nation's businesses have been sorely overburdened by taxation. The study found, for example, that while Americans were forking over a 49 percent top tax on earnings from long-term investments, the Belgians, French, Japanese, Dutch and West Germans were paying exactly . . . ZERO.

Grace orchestrated a two-front war. Members of Congress, business executives and the country's top editors received letters arguing for lower taxes. At the same time, the battle was carried to the public through a series of advocacy ads in ten influential newspapers. These ads blithely ignored just about every accepted trick for capturing reader attention. Instead of lively, graphic attention-grabbers, there were simply unrelenting columns of type; but they made, as it turned out, a convincing case. There was "a deliberate strategy to present information . . . in a somewhat crude form," a Grace executive told S. Prakash Sethi. The last thing Grace wanted, he said, "was any kind of 'Madison Avenue' slickness."

The ads' appearance was synchronized with the tempo of the congressional tax debate. From the start, Capitol Hill had greeted Carter's call for higher taxes coolly, and a number of legislators had introduced bills to lower levies. Grace added to this momentum. For example, the firm boldly locked horns with Carter after he had told a June 26, 1978, press conference that he opposed trimming capital gains taxes. Neither the American people nor he, stated the President, would "tolerate a plan that provides huge tax windfalls for millionaires and two bits for the average American." Grace responded with a widely praised ad proclaiming, "you don't have to be a millionaire to have a stake in the capital gains debate." The text explained that "nearly two thirds of total capital gains were being earned by individuals with an annual income under $50,000." Most of those who would benefit from a capital gains tax cut, therefore, hardly would be the millionaires whom Carter had excoriated. The ad had enormous impact; more than 100 supportive letters a day began pouring into Grace's New York headquarters; at least 106 newspapers published stories about Grace's push for a tax cut; and scores of legislators wrote the company backing its stance.

When a very reluctant Jimmy Carter eventually signed the Revenue Act of 1978 on November 6, what he was making into law was not the capital gains hike that he had sought, but rather a sharp cut in the maximum rate from 49 percent to 28 percent.

This was an extraordinary victory for a broad-based tax-cutting movement of which W. R. Grace's advocacy advertising campaign was part. Three years later, Grace again mobilized for the same cause, though this time the firm was backing the White House. Grace went back into print with full-page ads in three dailies to urge Congress and the nation to give Ronald Reagan his proposed across-the-board cuts in individual income tax rates.

For growing numbers of corporate executives, speaking out means literally that—not advocacy ads or TV commercials, but directly addressing the public and the press. Not long ago, notes a U.S. Chamber of Commerce aide, "a good corporate public relations man was the guy who got the boss out the back door when reporters were crowding around the front." Businessmen are realizing, however, that they can no longer afford to be press-shy. Says Thomas Finch, chairman of Thomasville Furniture Industries in Thomasville, North Carolina: "We simply can't tell the press: 'No comment.' At one time, we could, but now we've got to be able to respond to questions that come up in newspapers and TV. If not, we're going to get clobbered everywhere."

When businessmen first started opening their mouths, however, many stuck their feet in them. They became tongue-tied, confused, irritated. A number of them concluded that they needed help and turned to a handful of professionals, most with journalistic or broadcasting backgrounds, who were running courses on personal communication skills. That original handful has grown to more than 100 "media consultancy" organizations. They range considerably in size, from the lone moonlighting TV producer who has one or two clients to giants like J. Walter Thompson, Communispond, MediaCom, Burson-Marsteller and the U.S. Chamber of Commerce. Hundreds if not thousands of executives yearly are now learning how to handle themselves skillfully in TV interviews, before congressional committees and shareholder meetings, on televised panels and, adds Communispond's Ted Fuller, "if someone throws a microphone in their face." The typical course lasts one or two days and, in 1981, cost from $300 to $2,000 per day.

One of the most demanding courses is offered by former television station executive Charles Crutchfield of Charlotte, North Carolina. The name of his firm just about says it all about his philosophy; it is called—"Talk-Back! Associates." Like most other consultants, Crutchfield emphasizes interview training. "What are the interviewers' objectives?" he tells his clients to ask themselves. "Why do they ask negative and embarrassing questions, why do they seem to leave out of the broadcast the most important points made?" With one of Crutchfield's staffers playing the unrelenting reporter, the participants are videotaped while being interviewed. A replay allows the executive to see how he looks and sounds. Some have been so embarrassed by their early performances that they have fled the room.

Crutchfield relishes such moments, for they make his point about the hazards of dealing with journalists. He quickly assures his clients, however, that "we can combat the problems." He tells the businessmen that they can take command of an interview. When answering a reporter's questions, he advises, "put the important facts up front so that if the film is edited and only the first forty seconds are used, as often happens, you will have made your point." He particularly enjoys preparing his clients for abrasive reporters. Mike Wallace of CBS regularly is used as an example because, says Crutchfield, "he is so vitriolic." Crutchfield tells his clients that "there is a way to beat the Mike Wallaces at their own game, a way to respond to negative or personally embarrassing questions." The trick is, he says, "to 'bridge' from a negative question to a positive answer," to find an opportunity even in a hostile query to say something favorable about the firm. He warns clients that "nothing is off the record, so do not start spilling your gut just because the cameras have stopped rolling; do not try to be a comedian, because the odds are that the humor will backfire; do not wear loud ties, bold plaids, herringbone or houndstooth-pattern clothes for a TV interview, because they could detract from what you are saying."

Other consultants are less earthy than Crutchfield but use generally similar techniques. Just about all of them try to throw their clients off balance to illustrate the importance of retaining self-control. At a session of the Chamber of Commerce's Communicator Workshops, for instance, a participant suddenly was asked why his firm had sold property which it earlier had used as a chemical dump. The angry executive exploded, sharply saying that the matter was "no longer my problem." Technically he might have been correct. But when he saw the videotape replay, he recognized that his answer was a disaster; it clearly was not the image that he wanted to project on the evening news. Ted Fuller of Communispond recalls a training program for four senior officers of a major chemical company. Shocked at how much inside information he had about them and their firm, they demanded to know where he had obtained it. "Where do you think '20/20' gets information for its questions?" Fuller retorted. "You ask around; you call the ad department, the accounting department, a branch office. The information is all there for the getting."

No company is too big to turn to a consultant for help. Charles Crutchfield's clients have included Exxon, Cannon Mills, Southern Bell Telephone and Duke Power Company. Other consultants have coached executives from General Motors, Bristol-Myers, Pittsburgh Plate Glass, Armco Steel, Mobil Oil, Caterpillar Tractor and Union Carbide. The training sessions almost always get kudos from their alumni. Calls to dozens of corporate executives find example after example of businessmen grateful that they invested time and money in the course. Many said that the lessons came in very handy when they later found themselves dealing with the press in tough situations. Recalls Duke Power Company President William Lee: "I've used the training I received from Charles Crutchfield scores of times—on "Good Morning, America," Walter Cronkite's show, the local news. And I was interviewed on site at Three Mile Island. I certainly learned to handle off-the-wall, unfair questions." Says Ted Fuller: "Most of our clients are ready to go out there and knock heads with anybody."

Two cases, a half-continent apart, best typify the emerging breed of combative businessmen. One is Kaiser Aluminum's bout with network television. The other is Illinois Power Company's challenge to CBS-TV's credibility. Their stories are landmarks in the traditionalist resurgence, signifying an end to a long era of passivity.

Cornell Maier did not plan to get into a battle with the major broadcast networks. All he intended in 1978 was to purchase television time to broadcast short public interest commercials like those Kaiser had been running in newspapers and magazines for two years. The point of this was to increase public understanding of basic economic issues. But he, like Illinois Power Company the following year, ran up against the communications media's deep (and perhaps subconscious) hostility to business. The result has been one of the most dramatic confrontations in businessmen's new drive to tell the story of the free enterprise system.

For his TV spots, Maier focused on three topics that he and his aides felt adversely affect the nation's economic health: lack of a national energy program, impact of government red tape and threats to the free enterprise system. Typical was the thirty-second commercial depicting an American eagle behind bars, with an off-camera announcer asking, "Is free enterprise an endangered species? How much government regulation is enough? Is business bad just because it is big?" The ad ended with the announcer declaring that "whatever your views, let your elected representatives know."

The text of this ad and others prepared by the firm seemed tame enough. Kaiser simply raised questions; it offered no answers, took no stance. By no means could they be regarded as "advocacy advertising." Thus, Maier was astonished when all three national networks refused to sell Kaiser air time for the commercials. CBS said that "public affairs are the sole province of CBS News." ABC argued that it could not accept ads "saying 'write your congressman.'" And NBC maintained that the commercials would "clearly violate the Fairness Doctrine by opening a discussion on an issue of public importance." Kaiser's first instinct was to find a way to accommodate the networks. Explains Ronald Rhody, the firm's corporate vice-president for public relations and advertising: "We were so interested in getting these commercials on the air that we decided to modify them in the hopes of satisfying some of the networks' objections." But even after substantial revisions, complains Rhody, the networks' answers still were: "No! You cannot run them."

Maier complained publicly that he did not see what is "wrong, objectionable, controversial or unacceptable about encouraging people to become involved with the government." He was horrified that the networks felt that it was not "positive" to encourage people to contact their elected representatives. What particularly infuriated Maier was CBS's attitude. The network had told a Kaiser representative: "Where do these guys get off thinking they have a right to express an opinion on these points?"

Rather than take his fight to the courts or the Federal Communications Commission, where, Maier says, it could have been tied up for four or five years, he went directly to the public—a tactic that he was to employ in future battles. He placed full-page

ads in six of the nation's most influential newspapers. In heavy
typeface, a headline asked: "Can a corporation speak its mind in
public?" The ad then described what it branded the network's
censoring of Kaiser's commercials and concluded by suggesting:
"If you believe a free exchange of ideas is as important now as
it ever has been, write your elected representatives or write us at
Kaiser Aluminum."

The response delighted Maier. Kaiser received more than
2,000 letters, with 96 percent backing the company. Meanwhile,
Representative Lionel Van Deerlin, a California Democrat,
scheduled hearings on the matter before his House Communications Subcommittee. The panel called officials from the three
networks and heard from Maier. While in the capital, the Kaiser
boss also pleaded his case at lunch with ten senators. On a local
Washington radio show, Maier explained: "All we're saying is
that there ought to be fair access to television and somebody
besides the television networks ought to help decide what those
rules are."

In the months following, Maier and other top Kaiser officials
spoke out frequently on the matter, apparently with measurable
impact. Of some 400 commercial television stations surveyed in
mid-1980 by the Television Bureau of Advertising, 89 percent
said that they now would accept advocacy or opinion advertising.
That was up markedly from 50 percent in a similar poll taken in
1975. When the 1980 sampling asked specifically if the stations
would air Kaiser's "Free Enterprise" ad, 78 percent said yes. The
public also backs Kaiser. A national survey conducted in July
1980 by Princeton's Opinion Research Corporation found that
85 percent of the respondents feel that "companies should be
allowed to use television to speak out on public policy issues."
This is up from 72 percent in just two years. This message is not
lost on the TV networks. Both ABC and NBC modified their
positions and began accepting Kaiser's issue commercials in
1980.

In the midst of his struggle with the networks over public
interest commercials, Maier found himself embattled with ABC
over quite a different issue. On the April 3, 1980, telecast of the
network's "20/20" program, a segment entitled "Hot Wire"
focused on the alleged hazards of aluminum wiring. It described
a number of fires thought to have been caused by such materials,
citing Kaiser by name several times. The topic covered by the

broadcast is extremely technical and complex, too complex, Kaiser argues, for a relatively short program. What angered Maier most was that the tone, innuendo and structure of the segment amounted to an implicit indictment of Kaiser. The reporter's boast that the program was the result of a "seven-month undercover investigation" immediately set up a good-guy/bad-guy situation. And during the segment's first minutes, the reporter said that his investigation "supports the conclusion that something may be very wrong."

Maier was enraged by the broadcast and decided, he says, "to raise hell and to play to win." Within weeks, ABC's top officers had received a scathing letter from Kaiser's attorneys denouncing several "Hot Wire" statements as "blatantly untrue, misleading and unfair." Concludes the letter: "The entire segment, including advance advertising and teasers, was intended by word, picture, inflection and composition to create a false and defamatory picture." As such, Kaiser demanded that ABC "retract the entire program."

At the same time, Maier was calling for Congress to convene hearings on the matter and asking the Federal Communications Commission, under its "personal attack" doctrine, to compel ABC to provide facilities and time for Kaiser to tell its side of the story. Relying again on newspapers to deliver a wallop, Kaiser ran a full-page ad in sixteen dailies in ten cities. Under the bold headline "Trial by Television," Kaiser outlined its grievances. "We have been advised by many to ignore the '20/20' attack on the basis that you can't fight the network, and to prevent further harassment," stated the ad. "We will not allow ourselves to be maligned or misrepresented by any group—even television." At the bottom of the page, Kaiser encouraged readers who were "upset by the unfairness of 'Trial by Television' " to write their elected officials or Kaiser. Thousands did so. In addition, Maier received calls from officers of dozens of firms cheering him on and offering their support. Says Maier: "On this matter, a lot of companies have begun coming out of the closet."

For six months, Kaiser kept up the pressure. As 1980 was ending, victory seemed in sight; ABC consented to give Kaiser four minutes of free air time to rebut "Hot Wire." Maier was jubilant. In his spacious twenty-second-floor office at Kaiser headquarters in Oakland, California, he declared: "Getting the time from ABC is more important than the rebuttal we broadcast.

It has never happened before. That's an admission on ABC's part that we weren't treated fairly. That could have an impact on all TV broadcasting. We raised hell and ABC knew that we were not going to give up." Though Kaiser and ABC continued to disagree over details of when the rebuttal was to be aired, the free time offer by the network was a major victory in the fight against what has been widely regarded as journalism's, particularly television's, anti-business bias.

Anti-business bias and the new determination of businessmen to speak out are also at the heart of the epic battle between little Illinois Power Company and giant CBS. The Decatur-based utility firm was building a nuclear power plant at nearby Clinton. Construction delays and cost overruns attracted the attention, in late 1979, of America's Number 1 television investigative organization: CBS' "60 Minutes." The program's planners decided to produce a segment on Illinois Power that would coincide with hearings on the utility's request that it be granted a 14 percent rate hike by the Illinois Commerce Commission.

When contacted by Paul Loewenwarter, a "60 Minutes" producer, Illinois Power officers decided to cooperate fully with the network. They knew that they were having problems at Clinton and that costs were running far over original projections. But they also knew that cost overruns were typical for nuclear power construction projects. Confident that they had nothing to hide, Illinois Power executives made themselves available for lengthy interviews with Loewenwarter and reporter Harry Reasoner. Says Harold Deakins, Illinois Power's manager of public affairs: "We turned CBS loose on the grounds. They circulated among the workers and could talk to anyone they liked. That was the only way that we were going to get the facts out. Otherwise, the only thing that we were going to get would be a camera shot through the front gates and a statement that Illinois Power refused to talk. So we gave them carte blanche."

Illinois Power imposed only one condition, that it be allowed to film whatever the TV crew did. CBS consented. Several factors prompted Illinois Power to make this unusual request. For one thing, the utility was pretty excited about being visited by big-time TV celebrities from New York. "When a prestigious program comes into Decatur, it creates a tremendous amount of interest," recalls Deakins. "We wanted to film that event and later show it to our employees." Illinois Power was so upbeat about the visit that it even devoted a special ten-page edition of *Hi-Lines,* its employee magazine, to the activities of the "60 Minutes" crew; on its cover was Harry Reasoner.

There was another reason, however, why the utility wanted to record CBS at work. Deakins had been called by officers of several companies who had heard about the impending "60 Minutes" visit to Illinois Power. They described what he calls "personal experience horror stories" about the program's unbalanced reporting. He thus decided that "it was only prudent to take some precautions and record what was going to transpire." He was right.

On the evening of November 25, 1979, there probably were few Illinois Power Company employees not tuned in to "60 Minutes." Not only had Illinois Power publicized the upcoming program, but the network had promoted it heavily throughout the central Illinois region served by the utility. "Everyone was hyped up anticipating the show," recalls Deakins. Were they worried? "No," he says. "By the time that we had finished with CBS, we felt that there was no way that this story could go wrong. We gave them everything they asked for. I figured that we were going to get blasted because our costs increased on the Clinton project, but I was sure they would explain why and give our side of the story."

It was thus with mounting shock—even horror—that Illinois executives watched Harry Reasoner's episode unfold on their TV screens. Entitled "Who Pays? You Do," the program amounted to an indictment of Illinois Power. Among the most devastating points made against the firm, were that: Cost overruns at Clinton ran "well ahead of the pack" of "other plants of similar design;" the company used an inexperienced general contractor to build the nuclear power plant; the utility set for itself wildly optimistic and unrealistic deadlines; and the utility was asking its customers to swallow a 14 percent hike in their electric bills to pay for the overruns. CBS even introduced a sinister note. An interview with a former Illinois Power employee showed only his silhouette, disguised his voice and kept his identity secret. Implying that Illinois Power, somehow, would retaliate against private citizens who criticize the company, Reasoner told the estimated 27 million viewers that this mysterious witness "fears retribution if his identity becomes known."

Illinois Power was badly shaken by the program. So was the public. The next morning, the firm's telephones began ringing off their cradles. Calls poured in from irate owners of the company's stock, angered customers and demoralized employees. Soon after the New York Stock Exchange opened, more than 10,000 shares of Illinois Power were traded and final volume exceeded by more than three times that of any other day in the utility's history. Within days, the company had been attacked or criticized on newspaper editorial pages throughout its region. What made this so painful was that Illinois Power executives were firmly convinced that "60 Minutes" had been unconscionably unfair.

The problem was, how to respond to "60 Minutes"? The utility felt woefully out of the network's league and decided against directly attacking the broadcasting Goliath. What it could do, however, was repair, or at least limit, the most serious damage —its bruised reputation among its employees, customers and shareholders. Deakins and his staff concluded that their best material was their film footage of the CBS crew in action. Working nearly day and night for almost a week in the studio which Illinois Power uses to produce employee training films, Deakins's team prepared a unique and powerful rebuttal: a videotape, mimicking the "60 Minutes" format, that shows what appeared on the network and also what Loewenwarter and his colleagues edited out. In addition, the rebuttal corrects CBS errors.

As in "60 Minutes," a ticking stopwatch opens the rebuttal. On screen is the fresh face of Howard Rowe. This young member of Deakins's staff uncannily imitates the style and cadence of the CBS program. He begins: "What happens when a major TV network comes to town to do a news feature on the power company? Plenty! And not much of it is very pleasant, as we learned when Illinois Power became the target on . . . '60 Minutes.'" For the next forty-two minutes, Rowe presents the incisive Illinois Power rebuttal. Each time that he interrupts the original CBS broadcast to make a correction or an observation, the case builds inexorably for Illinois Power's assertion that it had been wronged.

Item: Rowe says that the cost overruns at Clinton were not, as Reasoner had claimed, "well ahead of the pack," and then shows, on film, an Illinois Power executive telling Reasoner exactly that and citing figures to back up the statement. Reasoner ignored this.

Item: Rowe explains that the utility's timetable does not, as Reasoner had claimed, require doing "some jobs in record time." That Reasoner should have known this is clear from the videotape of the CBS visit. In it, a utility executive is seen giving Reasoner a careful and detailed explanation of the complex construction timetables that leave no doubt that nothing was being attempted "in record time."

Item: Rowe questions CBS's motive in creating a "theatrical" setting by disguising the voice and using only a silhouette when interviewing the former Illinois Power employee. Observes Rowe: "Based on what was said, the identity of 'Mr. X' was fairly obvious to the supervisory staff at Clinton. The implication is that Illinois Power has some sort of goon squad, that runs around the country, to 'put the heat' on former Clinton workers."

Item: Rowe discredits the CBS assertion that the project at Clinton was the first such undertaking by the general contractor used by Illinois Power.

Item: Rowe points out that the man whom Reasoner described as the "sharpest critic" of Illinois Power had, in fact, dubious credibility. He had fabricated his professional credentials and was not even allowed by the Illinois Commerce Commission "to testify as an expert." Not only was such information available from the Commission, explains Rowe, but "60 Minutes" knew about it before broadcasting its program on Illinois Power.

Concluding the rebuttal, Rowe comments with dismay that "those of us who clung to the notion of fairness and accuracy by programs such as '60 Minutes' were disappointed." Adds Harold Deakins privately: "CBS had its script written before its people showed up. Their coming here was a charade to get us on the videotape. What I have trouble figuring out is why the hell they bothered to ask us the questions."

As soon as Deakins and his staff finished producing the rebuttal, they started making videotape copies. On December 3, 1979, just eight days after the "60 Minutes" broadcast, the rebuttal was running nonstop on TV sets at Illinois Power facilities. At the headquarters building, for example, groups of seventy-five employees were brought into the auditorium to see the film. It was the same story at plants and customer service offices all over the central Illinois area. And when employees were not watching the rebuttal, the TV sets were moved into the front of the utility's local offices so that customers, coming to pay their bills, could see it. Word soon spread around central Illinois towns that Illinois Power had a dynamite show. Crowds began packing the utility's offices just to see the rebuttal; some even cheered the screen as Howard Rowe made point after point against CBS.

Deakins sent videotapes to the area's newspapers and radio and television stations. This prompted favorable news coverage and just about erased the negative impression of the original "60 Minutes" broadcast. Tapes of the rebuttal also were shown at utility trade conferences, and requests for the videotape began pouring into the Decatur headquarters from all across the country and even from overseas. The utility has been duplicating the rebuttal for anyone mailing in a blank videotape cassette. Dow Chemical Company and other firms have obtained scores of the tapes and distributed them to colleges and to business and journalism schools. Other companies have provided them to Rotary Clubs and similar service organizations for showings at meetings. In Washington, the Media Institute has played the videotapes for members of Congress and their staffs. In all, by early 1981, an estimated 4,000 copies of the rebuttal were in circulation, permitting hundreds of thousands, if not millions, of Americans to see CBS's treatment of the utility.

How was CBS reacting to this? Its vice-president and director of public affairs broadcasts, Robert Chandler, sent Illinois Power a five-page letter seven weeks after the utility started distributing the rebuttal. In it, Chandler conceded that the telecast had been "inaccurate in two respects" and promised to broadcast corrections on the air. That it did about a week later, when it admitted that only one fourth of the 14 percent rate hike obtained by Illinois Power was related to the Clinton project; in the original "60 Minutes" broadcast, the network had very strongly implied that the entire boost was due to Clinton. The network also retracted its statement that the Illinois Commerce Commission staff had opposed the rate increase; in fact, the staff backed most of the boost.

As for the other issues raised by Illinois Power, Chandler flatly stated that the videotape failed to persuade "us that our story was unfair or . . . inaccurate." Though the remainder of the long letter attempts to refute most of Illinois Power's rebuttal, it overlooks many key charges raised by the utility. A week later, in a fifteen-page "analysis" of the CBS letter, Illinois Power once again methodically rebutted the network's assertions. The network has ignored this second rebuttal. Illinois Power's intention, however, has not been to force a wholesale retraction from CBS. The utility simply has wanted to correct the public record for its employees, customers and stockholders. To do this, Illinois Power has been willing to speak out. The enormous demand for copies of the rebuttal testifies to the public's readiness to hear the business side of stories. Indeed, more than two years after the "60 Minutes" broadcast, Illinois Power was still getting requests for videotape copies.

II

EVANGELIZING FOR CAPITALISM

BUSINESSMEN'S MOST AMBITIOUS defense of capitalism is also the most basic: economic education. And they are going at it with evangelical zeal. They have become increasingly convinced of the strong correlation between people's attitudes toward business and the amount of correct economic information they have. "There's just a phenomenal body of research showing that if you can deal with economic ignorance, then people become more market-oriented," says Calvin Kent, head of Baylor University's Center of Private Enterprise and Entrepreneurship and former president of the National Association of Economic Educators. "The private enterprise system does not have to be defended; it only has to be understood."

Taking this to heart, countless executives across the country have begun teaching their employees and the general public the fundamental concepts of the free market economy. The precise impact of these efforts remains a matter of debate, and not all programs are equally well structured or executed. Yet the very number that now exist and are being started and the enthusiasm for them are a revealing barometer of businessmen's determination to do something to nurture broad-based support for the free enterprise system.

These efforts are now particularly necessary, says J. Clayburn LaForce, dean of U.C.L.A.'s graduate school of management. For most of the nineteenth and early twentieth centuries, he explains, performers in the economy "needed only to pursue their own immediate economic interests" to make the system work. In those days of "an unencumbered economy," participants did not need to understand how the overall process functioned. Today, notes LaForce, the situation is far different because regulation, high taxation and other forces are undermining the free marketplace. As a result, the players in the economic game must know something about the schema and rules which keep it functioning smoothly. The task, writes LaForce: is to "teach principles which *accurately* and *consistently* explain how our decentralized, seemingly uncontrolled and uncoordinated economic system coordinates and controls human action."

Economic education in itself is nothing new. For years, American corporations have been underwriting some sort of programs, usually through their public relations departments. There was a boomlet of these in the 1950's, typified by the establishment of the New York-based Joint Council on Economic Education. The emphasis then was on polishing capitalism's image and explaining the operation of key capitalist institutions, such as the stock market. But in the face of the counterculture, corporate leaders retreated, defensively hunkering down. There were exceptions, like Armstrong Cork, Central Illinois Public Service and Pacific Gas and Electric companies, but by and large, corporate economic education efforts idled until the mid-1970's. Then they dramatically started increasing in numbers and widened in scope. A catalogue of programs compiled in 1977 by the National Association of Manufacturers contained about 150 listings; two years later, the total had doubled. Since then, it surely has doubled again. So fast are programs proliferating that most experts have abandoned trying to keep count.

Why the new boom? Justin Dart's experience provides part of the answer. For years, Dart focused primarily on his enormously demanding business interests. He forged the multibillion-dollar Dart Industries that counted, among its subsidiaries, West Bend Electric Products, Tupperware and Duracell Batteries, and then, in 1980, swallowed the giant Kraft Corporation, which led the conglomerate to change its name to Dart & Kraft. While building this business empire, Dart's interest in public affairs was spurred by his close friendship with Ronald Reagan during and after the future President's two terms as California governor. Dart's horizon further expanded in the mid-1970's when he became active in the Business Roundtable, a high-powered organization comprised of the heads of the nation's 200 top companies. From his

work in Roundtable projects, Dart concluded that the free enterprise system was just not getting adequate public support. This
appalled him. "A house is burning down," he declared, "and if
we don't do something about it, it's going to burn all the way
down. So let's get busy and do something."

For Dart, doing "something" has meant becoming an economic education evangelist. He figures that the more a person
knows about economics, the better he will feel about corporations. To test this, he launched a pilot program at his company's
factory in West Bend, Wisconsin. This program since has been
expanded and extended to most of Dart's 70,000 employees in
89 U.S. plants. Using posters, leaflets stuffed into pay envelopes,
contests, films, group discussions and short presentations shown
on TV sets in the cafeteria, the firm informs its employees about
such issues as inflation, national health care, Social Security,
wage-price guidelines, the federal budget and productivity. From
the start, Dart has tailored this program for those made uneasy
by typical classroom procedures. Explains Steven Rhodes, a Dart
public affairs executive who joined the Reagan White House staff:
"We wanted to reach those not necessarily interested in receiving
the message. We wanted to change their attitudes. So we have
kept reading material to a minimum and call our program economic 'information' rather than 'education.' "

Dart's aim, as he explains it, is to get the American workers
"to vote for a person not because he is a Democrat or a Republican, but because he's promised to keep his cotton-picking hands
out of their pockets so that inflation may be curbed and the
ever-rising cost of government may be controlled." Rather than
deny that this amounts to advocacy, Dart asserts that "advocacy
of all the things we don't believe in is going on all the time." Like
any other inspired evangelist, Dart takes to the trail to carry the
message of economic education to his fellow businessmen. He
and his staff have become familiar faces at meetings and conferences across the nation, where they urge firms to launch their own
economic information programs. In 1980 alone, Dart made several dozen speaking trips. More than 500 corporations have contacted his staff for information about establishing programs and
dozens of corporate executives have visited Dart plants to see the
programs in operation. Queries about them, meanwhile, also
pour in from colleges and chambers of commerce.

Justin Dart, though perhaps the most fervent, is not the only economic education evangelist. Others include Joseph Coors of Coors, Jay Van Andel of Amway, S. Bruce Smart, Jr., of the Continental Group and Paul Oreffice of Dow Chemical. The economic education programs that they and their fellow executives sponsor are as diverse as the corporations themselves. Some aim at employees, some at the local community and still others at both. While a number attempt to cover the spectrum of economic concerns, many deal mainly with issues particularly relevant to the sponsoring firms. For example, though the Central Illinois Public Service Company, a Springfield-based utility, offers a wide selection of topics and films through its speakers bureau, its two most frequent presentations deal with energy problems.

Companies of any size can launch a program. Its 250 employees, for example, make Metal Bellows Corporation of Sharon, Massachusetts, a relatively small firm. Yet it conducts an economic education project that includes monthly employee discussions of public affairs and a regular public issues newsletter. Some of the employees have become so motivated by what they have learned that they signed up as community activists; one group, for example, helped collect signatures on a petition calling for tax cuts. The most ambitious programs, of course, are at large companies. Coors Industries, the famous Colorado-based brewer, sponsors a continuous employee program of film and slide presentations, plant posters and banners, pamphlets, speakers, bulletin board notices and letters to employees from the firm's senior executives. An aim of the program is to defang the word "profit." Says a Coors officer: "We must develop greater public awareness of the true nature of profit and what it means to our future." Another aim is to relate business to individual well-being. Coors even sponsored an essay contest on the topic, "What has the American business system done for me and my family?" The top prize: a Hawaiian vacation for two. Meanwhile, autos around the company's plants have begun sporting bumper stickers with a slogan inspired by a Coors worker: FREE ENTERPRISE—IT WORKS WHEN WE DO.

Because many employees expressed interest in learning more about the economy than the introductory program offered, Coors added what it calls "an economic consciousness-raising program." This allows employees on their own time to attend a series of ten discussion groups, each lasting one hour, which focus on the economic roots of everyday problems such as government regulation, taxes, productivity and—naturally—inflation. Even this series is not enough for some Coors workers; they continue meeting informally after the ten segments are concluded. With materials provided by Coors, they have begun to study relatively advanced economic concepts.

At Dow Chemical Company, Carl Shafer of the public affairs department directs an economic education program as ambitious as that at Coors. Dow encourages employees to attend a four-hour "Business Money Workshop." A major aim of the program, the firm candidly admits, is to "demonstrate the superiority of the American free enterprise system and the imminent dangers of government socialistic programs. [It is to] increase employee and voter awareness that: As more government regulations and taxes emerge, our unique American system is an endangered species." At the start of its program, Dow tests participants on their knowledge of basic economic issues, particularly those affecting the company. Sample question: "How much capital does the chemical industry have to invest to create one job?" Much of the workshop consists of movie and slide presentations, during which a specially trained Dow employee leads discussion of economic topics. The workshop's last segment addresses the critical economic concept of trade-offs, using as a theme Milton Friedman's famous aphorism, "There is no free lunch." At this time, of course, lunch is served by Dow.

The chemical firm also provides groups all across the country with films whose themes extol free enterprise. One movie, produced by Dow in cooperation with Amway Corporation, compares the U.S. economic system with socialist and Communist systems. Another dramatizes how the avalanche of government regulation and laws is burying the U.S. economy and individual initiative. Available also from Dow is Illinois Power Company's rebuttal of "60 Minutes." Especially popular is "The Inflation File," a film produced by World Research, Inc., a conservative San Diego think tank. Using a whodunit plot framework, it portrays the travails of a supersleuth in pre-Reagan days trying to track down the causes of inflation; he finds the culprit's trail leading (surprise!) straight to the White House and Washington's mismanagement of the money supply.

For company executives who want to start an economic education program, a great deal of help is available. Officers at Dart and Coors eagerly provide practical advice, as do officials of two of the nation's major business associations, the U.S. Chamber of Commerce and the National Association of Manufacturers. The most active of the economic education midwives is probably the Center for the Study of Private Enterprise, affiliated with the University of Southern California's Graduate School of Business. The founder of the Center was economist Arthur Laffer, one of supply-side economics' leading gurus.

The Center churns out a prodigious variety of handbooks, guides and how-to-do-its for prospective founders of economic education programs. A "procedures guide," for example, explains that "employees are the citizens with whom companies have the most direct and continuing contact" and can be "reached directly, effectively, and *at a minimum cost* through posters, company publications, payroll stuffers and group meetings." The Center calculates that programs only cost between $1.00 and $5.00 per employee, plus the time of the firm's officers. In great detail, the guide describes how to establish a program and addresses some of the most commonly posed questions. Example: Will organized labor create problems? No, says the guide, "all reports indicate that unions support the program; in some cases their stewards have participated as discussion leaders."

Outlining a typical six-month program, the guide suggests "one topic per month, four posters per topic, one brainteaser puzzle a month, one contest with prizes a month." Leaving little to chance, the Center even supplies samples of posters, puzzles, contests and leaflets for prospective sponsors of economic education drives. Their themes read like cue cards for Reagan economics. One poster in the kit proclaims, "Free people and free enterprise are inseparable, you can't have one without the other." A flier to be stuffed into pay envelopes advises, "Profit is the incentive that motivates people (investors) and companies to take financial risks." Another warns that "we're becoming the fastest undeveloping country in the world." This flier urges the employee to tell his elected representative to support "tax incentives for investors [and to reduce] excessive government regulation so that business can use more of its money for new plant and equipment."

How effective is economic education? Some may have limited impact. Even a veteran of the movement like Dow Chemical's Carl Shafer criticizes programs for being "educational gobbledygook" because they fail to present "the business point of view." As an example, he points to a film, underwritten by a giant petroleum firm, which strongly endorses the adversarial role of labor unions. Shafer also notes that with economic education booming, a number of films are being produced less to promote capitalism than to make a profit. (Such motives, however, are not exactly alien to the free enterprise tradition.) A more common problem is one that corporate economic information programs share with other pedagogical efforts: motivating students and fighting boredom. Then there is the matter of credibility; in a few instances, firms find that employees dismiss as "propaganda" the posters, bulletin board notices and films.

Despite these problems, corporate economic education programs generally earn high marks, and there is considerable cumulative impact from the blizzard of leaflets and posters and from the thousands of film presentations and discussions. From all this, a message must be getting through, and some of that must be sinking in. A venerable, battle-scarred Chicago politician used to counsel: "If you toss enough clay against the wall, some is bound to stick." And economic education is sticking. This is clear from the tests given employees both before and after economic education programs. The results indicate very positive gains, particularly in changed attitudes on economic issues.

Dart's programs, for example, were thoroughly analyzed by U.S.C.'s Center for the Study of Private Enterprise in June 1980. Employees were surveyed, and half of those responding said that they were made more or much more aware of economic issues because of the economic information program. In a test of their knowledge, about 45 percent knew that the average U.S. manufacturer earns about five cents profit on every dollar; this is a vast improvement over the responses recorded in national polls. In terms of affecting attitudes, an impressive 98 percent of the Dart respondents (100 percent at some plants) felt that "the opportunity of business to earn profits is essential for the survival of the American private enterprise system."

The Dart program also has heightened employee interest in the economy. Of those polled, 43 percent said that the program has prompted them to more frequently "discuss economic issues;" about the same percentage "read more" on economics. One eighth of the employees said that they have been highly motivated to take more interest in economic matters. This is a major payoff. According to Jonathan Gutman, who conducted the study at Dart, even if only a small share of workers become "very actively involved, they start talking to and motivating others." Observes James Lindberg, a Dart senior executive: "We only have to change a few percentages. We're not looking for a large change. If we hit 10 percent, we've really hit the jackpot." Economic information's impact, moreover, ripples beyond factory gates. Gutman's survey found that 45 percent of the respondents were taking the Dart materials home to be read by family members.

Economic education's biggest potential payoff is to be found in the formal classroom. A number of companies and organizations already have been trying to influence how economics is taught in the nation's schools. The Joint Council on Economic Education, for example, has been promoting its Developmental Economics Education Program since 1964, and it now is used by nearly 600 school systems and reaches 10 million students. It is the country's largest economic education program, and claims, among other things, a 25 percent improvement in student "understanding of the role of profits." It has not been until recent years, however, that public schools have become a main target of corporate economic educators. Activity on this front has been quickening so much that it has earned a prized left-handed compliment; it has been attacked by Ralph Nader. In a report entitled "Hucksters in the Classroom," a Naderite organization denounces economic education programs as being little more than propaganda for the corporate view of the world.

In a sense, propaganda is precisely economic education's aim —although the corporations underwriting the programs wince at such a description of their efforts. It is propaganda in the sense of a much-needed antidote to the anti-capitalist bias which, in many cases, infuses the public education system. It is propaganda too in the sense of aggressively presenting elementary and secondary school students with a sympathetic treatment of the traditional American economy.

A sure way of getting into the school system is via the teachers. This is what the Continental Group (formerly Continental Can Company) was aiming at in 1974 when it launched a pilot program in Hopewell, Virginia. "If teachers provide misinformation [about the economy], the fault lies with those of us who are the custodians of the system," said Holmes Brown, then Continental's director of community and educational relations. Working with the Virginia State Education Commission, Continental taught a group of high school teachers how American business operates. Many of the classroom discussions were conducted by business executives. After the pilot program's first series of classes, Brown says that he saw an "amazing effect on the attitude of the teachers toward business and toward our economic system." The pilot was pronounced a success and Continental ambitiously expanded the program. Today it flourishes at dozens of colleges and universities, influencing high school teachers' attitudes toward economic matters. In return, the teachers earn advanced academic credits. The program is now run by the Institute for Applied Economics, a group founded for that purpose in 1978 by Continental and a dozen other firms. Heading it is Holmes Brown.

Films, games and other materials provided by business groups are getting their messages into the classroom. The U.S. Chamber of Commerce, for example, distributes thousands of its "Economics for Young Americans" kits to schools, while the American Telephone and Telegraph Company offers games for use in social science courses. The Joint Council on Economic Education's catalogue lists a wide selection of movies, manuals and test materials pegged to all grade levels.

The most professionally designed product is "The People on Market Street," a seven-episode movie created by the Los Angeles-based Foundation for Research in Economics and Education (FREE) and produced by the Walt Disney Educational Media Company. U.C.L.A. economics professors Armen Alchian and Douglas Shetler wrote the technical economics portions of the movies. Most of the series' $600,000 cost was underwritten by individual and corporate grants; though schools pay $2,500 for the film, this expenditure often is picked up by local companies and business groups. Each of the film's episodes deals with a basic economic concept; one explains scarcity and planning, others address demand, supply and wages and production. By mid-1981, more than 300 sets of this series were in schools across the country.

Extensive testing of students both before and after they see "The People on Market Street" convinces FREE of the project's positive impact. Depending on the topic, the tests reveal pro-business attitudes increasing from 14 percent to 44 percent. Says

Victor Tabbush, FREE's vice-president: "Student's attitudes have been changed. After the film, they perceive the middleman to be more productive than they did before it. They also learn to regard government economic controls as folly and central planning as pernicious." The most dramatic shift is students' new understanding that "property rights can be exchanged so that both parties are better off." Before viewing the film series, only 13 percent understood this basic capitalist concept, compared to 69 percent after the film.[1] The insight allows the student to see through the so-called "zero sum" argument advanced by radical environmentalists, socialists and some liberals. Its thesis is that the economy cannot grow and thus one party gains economically only at the expense of another. To "equalize" economic resources, zero sum advocates want massive government programs to redistribute society's wealth. In contrast to this stagnant view, free enterprisers insist that the economy can indeed expand and, as it does so, all society's members can, to some extent, increase their wealth—though not to the same extent and not at the expense of each other. The critical point which students thus seem to be getting from FREE's movie series is: Under capitalism, everyone gains.

A similar message is central to another business entry into the classroom: *Our Economy,* a junior high school economics textbook. Commissioned by the San Francisco-based Foundation for Teaching Economics, the book consists of a series of case studies through which the authors, from the University of the Pacific, illustrate how a free market functions. The chapter entitled "From Canvas to Cut-offs: The Jeans Story," for example, describes how Levi Strauss invented blue jeans and how they are produced today. The product is followed from cotton fields to factory to retail counter. At each stage, relevant economic principles are introduced, with emphasis on the book's underlying theme that capitalism fosters production rather than redistribution. *Our Economy* has been more warmly received than the typical new textbook. Only one year after its 1979 publication, it was being used in fifty school districts in twenty-seven states, including such major systems as Los Angeles, Oklahoma City, Minneapolis, Atlanta and Baltimore.

At colleges and universities, interest in business and the economy has been booming without direct prompting from the corporate community. Enrollments in undergraduate business courses are breaking records nearly everywhere, while acceptance at a business graduate school is the hottest ticket on campus. This reflects, of course, the demands of a tight job market in which business training is seen as the best route to a high-paying and secure career. Yet there is one campus pro-business boomlet for which U.S. corporations can take credit. In a testimony to corporate America's mounting determination to do something to support capitalism, specifically endowed or funded chairs in free enterprise are proliferating rapidly.

A few years ago, almost none existed; by mid-1981, there were at least three dozen. At Appalachian State University in Boone, North Carolina, for example, media consultant Charles Crutchfield and other North Carolina businessmen have founded the Center for the Study of Private Enterprise. Funding is provided by a dozen corporations, including Gulf Oil, R. J. Reynolds and Reader's Digest, and the American Bar Association. At Texas A & M, the Center for Education and Research in Free Enterprise's 1981 budget of $750,000 was underwritten by some five-dozen contributors, including $5,000 grants from Exxon and Texas Instruments and $500 from the National Secretaries Association.

Most free enterprise chairs and centers are at relatively small colleges and universities or those of somewhat less than top rank. But chairs also have been established at Purdue, the University of Wisconsin's Madison campus, Kent State and Loyola of Chicago. And their numbers inch upward every year. Michael Mescon, who holds the Chair of Private Enterprise at Georgia State University and is universally regarded as the father of the movement, constantly receives letters from colleges seeking information about establishing such chairs. Inquiries even have come from abroad.

Academic eyebrows often are raised at chairs specifically labeled "free enterprise." Such explicit advocacy, it is argued, is inappropriate at colleges; moreover, hiring chair holders for the purpose of propagating a particular viewpoint violates, at least in spirit, academia's commitment to the free pursuit of knowledge. Indeed, some of the chairs exist specifically to disseminate pro-capitalist concepts. The founders of the free enterprise chair at Alabama's Birmingham-Southern College, for instance, candidly state that because "in the mid-twentieth century, America has leaned so far in the direction of collectivist solutions to all social problems that it is second nature for students to think in terms of governmental answers to any questions of an economic, political or sociological nature . . . the university should attempt to break the intellectual concrete which supports this atmosphere."

The free enterprise chairs are centers bubbling with enormous activity promoting the free enterprise system. They schedule countless seminars and workshops for students, faculty members, high school teachers and residents of the surrounding community. The center at Baylor University sponsors an annual "Free Enterprise Week;" Loyola holds retreats for high school students; Wisconsin runs a program to improve journalists' understanding of business; and Texas A & M convenes an annual summer American Economy Institute at which public high school teachers study business and the economy. Texas A & M also works with a local school district to inject "economic/free enterprise concepts" into the entire curriculum, from kindergarten through twelfth grade. Baylor's Center of Private Enterprise and Entrepreneurship, meanwhile, has organized hundreds of workshops for school teachers and private groups, like the Texas Bankers Association, who have requested training on economic issues. In late 1980, for example, the Baylor Center's Calvin Kent taught fifty-five kindergarten teachers how to convey economic concepts to their young pupils.

At Vanderbilt, local high school teachers frequently turn to the free enterprise center for background information, on subjects like inflation, that they can use in their classrooms. "Our materials provide many perspectives; not just ours," explains Charles Myers, head of the Vanderbilt Center. "But I have worked with plenty of teachers who'd go into the classroom with a nonideological approach and come out with the students believing that there is no better system than the American market economy."

An extremely visible campus pro-capitalist activity is Students In Free Enterprise. Its 6,000 members at 150 colleges and universities are surely the most vocal backers of the American economic system at colleges and universities. The organization's declared goal is "to help young Americans come to their senses before it is too late [by speaking] up for our American Free Enterprise and Incentive System." Local chapters distribute leaflets, plaster bulletin boards, bring conservative lecturers to campus and set up information tables—all promoting the free enterprise system. With backing from a couple dozen corporations (Champion Spark Plug, Chase Manhattan Bank, Dart & Kraft, H. J. Heinz, Ralston Purina and Westinghouse, among others), the organization sponsors an annual national contest which, if nothing else, ignites enormous hoopla for capitalism. To compete for the prizes (first place is worth $2,500 to the winning school), chapters develop programs and products boosting free enterprise. Some have been very serious, such as a program for teaching economics to high schoolers. Others reflect typical campus exuberance. T-shirts have been emblazoned with the slogan "There Ain't No Such Thing as a Free Lunch;" bumper stickers have proclaimed, "Honk if you're a capitalist;" jingles celebrating capitalism have been set to disco tunes and played on local radio stations.

In enthusiasm, the Students In Free Enterprise rival Kaiser Aluminum's Cornell Maier, the team at Illinois Power, the advocacy advertisers and the economic educators. They all are struggling on the same side, against the same enemy. Taken together, they are a new phenomenon—new in their mounting numbers, the fronts on which they fight, the weapons they employ and the confidence they bring to battle. They are, in short, waging a full-blown counteroffensive against the counterculture legacy, making a dramatic stand for one of America's most fundamental traditional values, a free market economy. By waging their battle in public, and for the minds of this public, they have helped alert their fellow citizens to the free enterprise system's imperiled state. That they have been gaining ground is clear from surveys and simple, anecdotal observations of the way American attitudes are changing. It is clear too from the widespread support for the free enterprise philosophy that Ronald Reagan and the other newly elected conservatives have brought to Washington.

Yet free enterprise's foes remain legion. They are found, for example, in the still powerful no-growth movement, which masks its hostility to capitalism by preaching the alleged evils of industrial expansion and increased individual consumption. Environmentalists and other well-intentioned Americans are particularly susceptible to such honey rhetoric and, perhaps unwittingly, swell anti-capitalist ranks. They are to be found, for instance, sponsoring the so-called "Big Business Day" of April 17, 1980, an event billed as a nationwide attack on big business. Though it received little public support, its backers were an impressive roll call of contemporary liberalism. Among them were John Kenneth Galbraith, Robert Heilbroner, Ed Asner, Rabbi Marc Tanenbaum, Arthur Schlesinger, Jr., the Consumer Federation of America and the Newspaper Guild. The goal of this no-growth movement is passage into law of a "Corporate Democracy Act." It proposes a myriad of new regulations and requirements that would deprive corporate managers of the right to run their businesses and thus add enormous new burdens to the economy.

Free enterprise's most formidable foes are found in two of the nation's most important institutions: the church and the communications media. A powerful anti-capitalist network has penetrated a number of the nation's leading religious organizations, particularly self-proclaimed social activist groups within mainline Protestant denominations. The National Council of Churches and its affiliate, the Interfaith Center on Corporate Responsibility, are guided by radical Christian and radical Marxist thinking. A favorite theme is that capitalism is evil and exploitative, while socialism brings secular salvation. A 1975 conference sponsored by the N.C.C. declared that "a basic contradiction exists between the capitalist system and biblical justice, mercy, stewardship, service, community and self-giving love."[2] So outraged by this statement was *Christianity Today,* the country's leading evangelical journal, that it riposted sharply, "What other system do you advocate? Where is there evidence of a better system?"

Evidence appears beside the point for anti-capitalists entrenched in many critical church positions, just as it seems to be for many of the nation's most powerful image-makers. Indeed, while leftist clergy attack capitalism from the pulpit, Hollywood assaults it from the TV set. Ben Stein's study *The View From Sunset Boulevard* reveals that many Hollywood producers and writers are openly hostile to capitalism and business. To them, big business and the Mafia are closely connected. Is it thus surprising that these producers and writers turn out television plots that typically darkly portray businessmen—as greedy, malevolent, corrupt? In an interview with Stein, James Brooks, the executive producer of the "Mary Tyler Moore Show," said of businessmen: "They're all sons of bitches, they're all cannibals."

Brooks's Hollywood colleagues apparently agree. From its detailed analysis of 200 prime-time shows on the three major

networks during the 1979–80 season, the Washington-based
Media Institute finds that "two out of three businessmen on
television are portrayed as foolish, greedy or evil. Almost half of
all work activities performed by businessmen involve illegal acts.
Most characters who run big businesses are portrayed as criminals." Almost never, says the report, are businessmen depicted
making positive contributions to society. States the study: "In
'Barnaby Jones,' a coffee importer fronts for a group of violent
revolutionaries. In 'Vegas,' a wealthy hotel owner, about to de-
fault on a $50 million note, casually plans and oversees several
murders." And then there is J. R. Ewing of "Dallas" who, says the
report, "revels in crimes ranging from illegal land deals and
political dirty tricks to prostitution."

Television news reporting also betrays an anti-business mind-
set. One TV newsman, announcing that a major bank had boosted its interest charges, remarked that it was a rate that previously
had been imposed only by Mafia loan sharks. In his analysis of
CBS-TV's coverage of inflation news, meanwhile, Tom Bethell,
Washington editor of *Harper's,* discovered that about three
fourths of all stories broadcast in 1978 and 1979 actually ex-
onerated the real culprit of inflation: government. Instead, notes
Bethell, "the accusatory finger" was pointed at profits.[3] So long
as the media remain hostile to or ignorant of business, it is going
to be very difficult for the public to understand the free enterprise
system.

It also will be difficult because of businessmen's own behavior. In one of his most-quoted statements, Winston Churchill
quipped: "The trouble with capitalism is capitalists."[4] Too often,
businessmen are poor free enterprisers and the public sees this.
To prod good capitalist behavior, the Council for a Competitive
Economy, recently established in Washington to fight for a freer
marketplace, awards "roses" in its monthly newsletter to those
companies which "lend support to the free, competitive economy." And "raspberries" are given to those who "undermine it."
More raspberries generally are dispensed than roses. A typical
month, for instance, saw raspberries going to "General Motors
Chairman Roger B. Smith for endorsing the suggestion that the
federal government negotiate with the Japanese to limit auto
imports," and to "John Nevin, president of Firestone Tire &
Rubber Company for his support of restrictions on rubber imports to 'protect' the American industry." Roses went to the

Texas Farm Bureau for telling its members to "rediscover free enterprise" and to the Hospital Corporation of America for "endorsing competition in health care."

Continued silence, above all, remains corporate America's deepest self-inflicted wound. Despite the new willingness to take a stand, those doing so are in a minority. Kaiser Aluminum President Cornell Maier concedes: "I'm still disappointed that more companies aren't speaking out. On many matters, they are still too shy." He is amazed at how many of his colleagues say to him: "What you're doing is great! But you know, we can't do it because our company is in a different situation and has a different problem." He retorts: "They don't have a 'different' problem. We all have 'different' problems. They're just afraid of offending customers or unions or congressmen or the governor or any number of groups. I just think that the issue is damn important and that we all have to speak out." If increasing numbers do so, they will deprive the opponents of the free marketplace of their long monopoly of the arena in which ideas compete. Capitalism now at least and at last has vocal champions, point troops in a new counteroffensive. For this counteroffensive to succeed, the Cornell Maiers, Illinois Powers, advocacy advertisers and economic educators will need business community reinforcements.

III

BATTLING
THE
LEVIATHAN

CONSUMER PROTECTION ACT. The name seemed unbeatable. Who could be against it? The name resonated with righteousness and virtue. Indeed, the first time a bill to establish a Consumer Protection Agency reached the floor of the House of Representatives, it carried by one of those rare lopsided margins that make analysis superfluous—344 to 14.

That was in 1971, and consumerism was becoming an unstoppable juggernaut with the Naderites manning its controls. There was thus little reason to doubt that the pending Consumer Protection Act (CPA) would become law in very short time and that a new cabinet-level agency soon would be intervening, ostensibly on behalf of consumers, in the deliberations of almost every government agency but the FBI and CIA. Yet the CPA never made it. The measure kept bumping into obstacles. It got bogged down in the Senate, or tied up conference committee, or blocked by the threats of a presidential veto, and each time that it was reintroduced by its sponsors, the ranks of its backers thinned a bit. Finally, in 1978, CPA failed even to carry a majority in the House and was buried, probably for good.

The unbeatable had been beaten. Victory had gone to a new and unique coalition of free market champions who, in the long battle against CPA, had swelled in numbers and mastered once-alien techniques of organization. At the start, only a handful had been audacious (perhaps, it was said, foolish) enough to stand up to CPA and the powerful symbolism of its name. They were a disparate, disorganized band. But they also were desperate. To them, CPA was the last straw, the final pail of sand about to be tossed into the nation's economic gears. Imminent passage of the bill seemed proof that the federal government had become a Leviathan out of control, addicted to interfering in the market-place through a myriad of regulations that were strangling the nation's industry and commerce with red tape.

In the years since the defeat of the CPA, this Leviathan has been in retreat. Its most dramatic setbacks have been coming at the eager hands of Reagan aides determined to prove that their boss has meant it when he promises to get government off citizens' backs. Federal agencies are being dismantled or whittled down, while whole sets of regulations are being abolished or redefined. With Washington's mood now overtly hostile to government meddling of any kind, the burden of proof has shifted to those advocating an expanded federal role in the economy or elsewhere. No longer is it assumed that government does it best —an assumption that long nourished the growth of the gargantuan bureaucracy.

The Reagan Administration clearly bolsters the capital's new mood, but it did not create it. In an important sense, the White House has inherited and profits from a legacy—a very-much-alive legacy—born in the successful struggle against the Consumer Protection Act. That victory, in defiance of the odds, gave the business community the confidence that it could take on the Leviathan, an attitude making business one of the most important engines of the traditionalist resurgence. Since CPA, the business community has been waging war on many fronts, and those engaged in the war frequently discuss what they are doing in battlefield terms. They talk of moving from defense to offense, of strategy and tactics, of mobilizing support and of launching counteroffensives. And even before the Reagan Administration swept into Washington, the tide of war shifted dramatically in their favor. Still a bit incredulous at how much had changed by the time of Reagan's inaugural, Cliff Massa, then with the National Association of Manufacturers, said that "if someone who had taken part in our efforts in the mid-1970's had gone away then and returned at the start of the new decade, he would think that he was experiencing a time warp. So different does the world now look. So much improved is our position."

This improvement came none too soon. By just about any measure, government in the United States was mushrooming out of control as the 1970's ended. Government had become the nation's fastest-growing enterprise and biggest employer. When Jimmy Carter entered office, for example, one of every 75 Americans had a job with the executive branch of the federal government, compared to one in 493 in 1891 and one in 4,000 when George Washington was inaugurated in 1790. And these job-holders were doing well, earning in 1980 an average of 28 percent more than workers in the economy's private sector. To pay for this government explosion, taxes soared, growing much faster than even the cost of living. In 1979, taxes paid by Americans were 5.4 times greater than they were in 1960, although living costs had increased in that period "only" 2.4 times. Even this enormous tax bite could not cover the government's tab. To make up the difference, Washington went on a borrowing binge, pushing up the federal debt faster than Jack's beanstalk. While it increased at what was then a dizzy 50 percent in the quarter-century following World War II (rising from $260 billion to $382 billion), during just the next ten years the debt skyrocketed about 300 percent and was nearing an almost mind-numbing trillion dollars at the end of 1980.

A vivid measure of government growth is the *Federal Register,* a journal which is updated daily to record the rules, regulations, announcements and proclamations issued by all branches of the federal government. In 1953, the *Register* totalled 8,912 pages; by 1970, it was bulging at 20,036 pages. That was slim compared to the typical *Register* of the late 1970's: 60,000 pages and more.

This expansion of governmental activity has produced anthologies of horror stories about bureaucratic misdeeds. Many would be amusing were they not taking such a pathetic toll. Americans, and businessmen in particular, seldom can turn around without bumping into a regulator from one of the government's alphabet agencies: OSHA, ERISA, EPA, OFCCP, EEOC and dozens more. Few agencies are as reviled as the Occupational Safety and Health Administration (OSHA), established in 1970. It is the author of that now-notorious rule mandating the shape of toilet seats (they must have an open front). It has required that trucks and other heavy-duty vehicles be equipped with loud back-up horns and that, at the same time, workers wear hearing-protection devices. The trouble is that these devices muffle the warning from the backup horns.

Then there is the Federal Meat Inspection Service, which had ordered a food company to make an opening in its conveyor belt so that inspectors could take out samples of sausage for testing. Enter OSHA; it declared the opening a safety hazard and demanded that it be closed. Each agency threatened to shut the plant unless it complied with each's own ruling. How could a businessman hope to comply, much less understand what government wants? Inconsistency also plagued a steel-maker that was forced to install scrubbing equipment to clean gaseous emissions at one of its plants. The 1,020 horsepower motor which ran the scrubbers, however, spewed out more undesirable gases per hour than the scrubbers removed. Net result of the regulation: a dirtier environment.

Adding to the pain of regulation is often the patronizing attitude of the regulator. One OSHA pamphlet (no longer in circulation) treated the American farmer—one of the nation's most savvy breeds—like a dummy. It lectured: "Be careful when you are handling animals. Tired or hungry or frightened cattle can bolt and trample you. Be patient, talk softly around cows. If they are upset, don't go into the pen with them. Be careful that you don't fall into manure pits. These pits are very dangerous." Often, tenacious enforcement of irrelevant regulations betrays the bureaucracy's tunnel vision. Example: A company was fined because its employees were not wearing life vests while working on a bridge over a channel—even though the water had been diverted from the channel during construction. Example: A miner was served with a citation because he was not carrying a two-way radio—even though the mine was a one-man operation and there was no one for the miner to contact with a radio.

The agencies spewing out such regulations are very costly. Murray Weidenbaum, who was director of the Center for the Study of American Business at Washington University in St. Louis before becoming chairman of the Council of Economic Advisors in the Reagan Administration, estimates that the nation now pays more than $100 billion annually for regulations. Compliance with government requirements, for example, has significantly increased the cost of new cars. Weidenbaum figures that the sticker on the average 1978 model was $666 higher due to regulations; by 1985, this regulatory surcharge will be close to $1,200. Because the mandated safety and environmental features add to a car's weight, fuel consumption is increased. In fact, regulations probably boosted the nation's 1979 gasoline bill by $3 billion.

Prospective homeowners also feel regulation's pinch. A 1980 government report stated that "as much as 20 percent of new housing costs may result from regulatory and procedural excesses."[1]

These are just the quantifiable costs of the regulatory burden. There are others. *The Wall Street Journal* reported that government rules "frequently caused management to take its eye off the ball. Managers were forced to spend more time worrying about what the government might do next. Top executives kept commuting to Washington. Plant supervisors were holding meetings on who should fill out this or that form and how they could comply with some new wrinkle in safety regulations."[2] Said Weidenbaum before taking his new post: "It is difficult to overestimate the rapid expansion of government involvement in private enterprise now occurring in the U.S. The regulators must be consulted on practically every aspect of business activity—where to set up a business, who can be hired, how to operate the business, what to sell, who[m] to sell it to and, of course, how much of the proceeds to keep."[3]

The only major enterprise apparently immune to regulatory overload is the womb of many of the rules. Claiming a "special relationship" with its employees, Congress excludes itself from OSHA oversight, Fair Labor Standards and Equal Employment Opportunity rules and, of course, from forced contributions to the Social Security fund.

A major casualty of this government intrusion has been the nation's economic efficiency. Coal-mining productivity, for instance, had been rising at 5.8 percent annually for a decade until 1969, when tough mine-safety legislation was enacted. Then productivity began sliding by about 3.2 percent annually for most of the following decade. Though an extreme case, coal mining reflects the fate of the entire economy. Each time regulations delay construction of a new plant or create new paper work (estimated by a national commission to cost up to $100 billion annually) or prevent the hiring of the best-qualified workers, productivity suffers.[4] Observes University of Chicago economist Yale Brozen: "Regulatory excess accounts for almost half of the decline in productivity growth." This decline has been substantial, plummeting from a healthy 3.2 percent annual rate of increase in the two decades after World War II to an anemic 1.6 percent annually between 1967 and 1977. Since then, the numbers have been even worse, with productivity actually dropping 0.4 percent in 1980 and more than that in the year's final quarter. Falling productivity, it is widely agreed, is an underlying cause of persistently high inflation.

A Consumer Protection Agency would have added to these woes. It would have been more than just another regulatory body. Independent of the White House and enjoying very broad powers, it was to be a mega-regulator, with almost no bounds to its authority. According to the CPA's charter, its purpose was nothing short of promoting "protection of consumers with respect to safety, quality, purity, potency, healthfulness, durability, performance, repairability, effectiveness, dependability and cost of any real or personal property or tangible or intangible goods, service or credit." To accomplish this, it would have had the power to challenge any other agency's actions and even haul it into court. The State Department, therefore, could have been sued for negotiating a sugar or coffee trade agreement if the CPA felt that the pact could adversely affect consumer prices. In sum, the CPA could paralyze government operations and prolong the already time-consuming, costly bureaucratic decision-making process.

These dangers were obscured at first blush by the sheer attractiveness of creating an agency to help the consumer. Thus, CPA attracted an intimidatingly impressive list of backers: Organized labor, consumer and environmental groups, prominent senators and representatives and even a handful of major corporations like Atlantic Richfield Company and Levi-Strauss. It thus was an act of courage for the 400 members of the business community in Washington who decided to oppose the measure as it began moving through congressional committees and inching toward floor votes. This coalition's main assets were a determination to hang tough and a recognition that they had to hang together. So unique was its cohesiveness, in fact, that the CPA battle is the subject of case studies by Harvard Business School and Michigan State University's Graduate School of Business Administration.

A key strategist in this battle was Emmett Hines, Jr., the Washington representative of the Armstrong Cork Company, who headed the coalition's steering committee during the fight's critical final years. Reflecting on the struggle, Hines stresses "the extraordinary importance of all-out opposition as a strategy, as opposed to trying to ameliorate, revise or amend an inherently bad bill." Hines maintains that the "kill the bill" policy generated a far more dynamic support, especially at the grass roots. At times, a few of the coalition's members wanted to compromise and strike a deal with the CPA advocates. Their feeling was, says Hines, to "take a bill now with some amendments we can live with. If we don't, next year a far worse bill will be shot through Congress." The itchy members, however, were pressured to stay in line by Hines and others on the steering committee.

Such cooperation was almost unprecedented. Business interests historically have feuded with each other in Washington much more than they have cooperated. Rivalries exist, for instance, between associations competing for the same members. Bitter disagreements have erupted, moreover, between those representing basically different interests, such as the generally mom-and-pop size operations found in the National Federation of Independent Business versus the giant industrial concerns affiliated with the National Association of Manufacturers. Individual industries, meanwhile, often find themselves on opposing sides of issues. Certainly the trucking industry and the retailers, for example, do not view interstate transportation rate policies in the same light.

Then there is the Business Roundtable, a group of corporate giants whose leaders, according to a Roundtable member, often have been "more interested in being seen walking in or out of the White House than in representing business's interests." In the anti-CPA coalition, just about all of these forces—the lions and the sheep, the foxes and the hens—bedded down together. This prompted the ultraliberal weekly *The Nation* to complain in 1979 that "for the American business community, the battle over government regulation had begun to assume the dimensions of a class struggle."[5]

During this struggle, the key business "class" participants were:

¶ The U.S. Chamber of Commerce, whose 97,000 members in 1981 included 1,321 trade associations and 2,726 state and local chambers. It functioned as the coalition's secretariat, printing and processing the endless mailings and organizing, by state and congressional district, packets containing clippings of newspaper articles, cartoons and editorials opposing the CPA. These were presented to senators and representatives as proof that tne bill was widely opposed at the grass roots.

¶ The National Association of Manufacturers, a 14,000-member organization comprised mainly of relatively large industrial concerns. In addition to the critical task of rallying its powerful membership against the CPA, it underwrote the cost of the large meetings of the full coalition's hundreds of members.

¶ The Business Roundtable, a relatively new and exclusive group of about 200 heads of the nation's largest companies. It brought top corporate leaders to Washington to lobby against the bill and raised funds for costly opinion surveys and legal analysis of the CPA.

¶ The National Federation of Independent Business, whose new activism and a membership roll of more than 600,000 firms gave it enormous clout in every congressional district. Using computerized tally sheets, it monitored the stances on CPA of each of the 435 representatives and 100 senators.

With rare single-mindedness, the coalition's members worked to dclay the bill and use the time won to convince the public and its elected representatives that a Consumer Protection Agency would pose great dangers. The coalition used almost every delaying tactic dear to wily Washington parliamentarians. It prolonged hearings on other bills so that congressional committees would not have time to get to the CPA. It produced a seemingly endless parade of witnesses when CPA hearings finally did convene. It wrote more than forty speeches for senators who filibustered against the CPA. And it helped preparc more than 500 amendments that could be tacked on to the CPA should the filibusters fail (they did not).

With the time gained, the coalition also mobilized the grassroots pressure that it ultimately focused on Washington with laser precision. Two business associations, for example, hired public relations firms to write sample editorials opposing the CPA; these were then sent to small newspapers around the country, as were canned articles highlighting the CPA's defects. When newspapers published this material, as scores did, the articles and editorials were clipped and sent to those congressmen representing the newspapers' areas. The National Association of Manufacturers, meanwhile, distributed a leaflet warning that the CPA "permanently federalizes and subsidizes the consumer movement as conceived by Ralph Nader." And the Grocery Manufacturers of America, in what it called a "businessmen's responsiveness kit," denounced the CPA as the "Nader Enabling Act." This trade group urged its members to alert their congressmen to this "most serious threat to free enterprise and orderly government ever to be proposed in Congress."

Capitol Hill got the message. Not only were congressmen receiving the Chamber of Commerce packets, but they were visited constantly by businessmen from their districts who typically had come to Washington on some other matter and then were urged by the anti-CPA coalition to call on their elected representatives to tell them to vote against the bill. Capitol Hill was also deluged by anti-CPA mail, some of it from shareholders of companies (such as General Foods and Procter and Gamble) which organized letter-writing drives.

Explains James "Mike" McKevitt, the gruff former G.O.P. congressman from Colorado who heads the Washington office of the National Federation of Independent Business: "We have our membership broken down by ZIP codes, counties, congressional districts. We have identified people who personally know their congressman. They've contributed to his campaign or have worked in the campaign or are related to his kids' godparents or are on a first-name basis with him or something like that. We had them contact him and plead with him not to vote for the CPA. We'd get a foreman or a vice-president from a plant in the congressman's district and they would call him. In this whole struggle, we built the best defensive coalition that this town's ever seen. And it was a lot of fun too." In the end, muses Emmett Hines, what it came down to is the way the system usually works; it is a matter of "who shouts the loudest and works the hardest."

In the battle over the Consumer Protection Act, these honors go to the business coalition. Each time the CPA reached the House floor for a vote, support ebbed. From that lopsided 344 to 14 in CPA's favor in 1971, the margin melted to 239 to 94 in 1974, 208 to 199 in 1975 and finally, in 1978, to only 189 in favor with 227 opposed. This defeat was final. The House had long been the CPA's staunchest backer, and when it abandoned the measure, there was no chance of revival. States Professor George Schwartz in his Michigan State University case study of the matter: This defeat "must be regarded as one of the biggest victories ever won by business opponents of proposed legislation."

It was more than that. It was the business community's Gettysburg, its Battle of Midway—its last major defensive engagement, the turning point in a war. "After that, we shifted to the offensive," says James Carty of the National Association of Manufacturers. "Instead of trying to beat back the efforts to create new regulation, we began pushing to eliminate regulation already on the books." On his NAM office wall, Carty has a framed copy of the defeated CPA bill, autographed by his colleagues in the coalition and with the final House vote scrawled across the front. On the other side of the Washington Mall, at the National Federation of Independent Business, John Motley agrees that the CPA's defeat was a turning point. He says: "The CPA fight made the business community believe in itself again." Above all, the long struggle over the bill subjected the American public to a barrage of arguments warning of regulation's dangers. This was a potent educational process. In the months following, the public was to hear more of these arguments and witness continued defeats of the Leviathan at the hands of the business community.

Business was not alone, obviously, in attacking regulation in the pre-Reagan years. Restricting regulatory excess has been championed since the mid-1970's by economists, public policy research organizations (the American Enterprise Institute, for example) and even, on certain issues, groups like Common Cause. Jimmy Carter early spotted regulation's potential as a political issue and successfully made it a whipping boy in his 1976 campaign. Though this did not get in the way of his strongly endorsing the Consumer Protection Act after becoming President, his administration took important swipes at regulation. Said Alfred Kahn, a Carter senior aide: [It is important to] "do our best to keep the hand of government as invisible as possible."[6] Even Senator Edward Kennedy, the quintessential apostle of government meddling, advocated selected deregulation.

The courts, meanwhile, began showing greater sympathy for businesses seeking relief from regulators. In the 1978 Barlow case, for instance, the Supreme Court ruled that F. G. Barlow had the right to eject OSHA inspectors from his Pocatello, Idaho, plumbing and heating shop because they had not obtained a search warrant. Though Americans long have taken for granted

their protection from unlawful searches, the regulators apparently had decided that they were immune from such constitutional
limitations.

Regulation's other setbacks of the pre-Reagan period are well
known. Thanks in large part to the determination of Alfred Kahn,
deregulation came first to the airlines—a development that some
of the major air carriers actually resisted at the start. Under the
Airline Deregulation Act of 1978, most of the marketing, pricing
and route controls that had been set and enforced by the Civil
Aeronautics Board for generations are being dismantled. The
CAB itself is scheduled to go out of business by 1985. The consequences of this deregulation were immediate: formation of new
airline companies, restructuring of routes, price wars on some
heavily traveled routes (in mid-1980, a daytime flight from New
York to Los Angeles on a scheduled airliner cost only $129) and
emergence of a thriving commuter airline industry serving the
towns and small cities abandoned by trunk carriers.

In relatively quick succession, deregulation came to trucking,
railways, banking and communications. Restrictions have been
eliminated, for example, on the kinds of programs that pay-televi-
sion stations may carry. Hundreds of new, low-power TV stations, meanwhile, are being licensed in order to intensify airwaves
competition. On the banking front, deregulation has abolished
the prohibitions on banks paying interest on checking account
balances and is enabling savings and loan institutions to expand
their services by issuing credit cards and managing trusts. Trucking deregulation is allowing truckers to change their interstate
routes, enter new routes and more easily interpret the restrictions
covering the goods they carry. Literally millions of commodity
categories, for example, have been reduced to a mere forty. Bil-
lions of dollars, meanwhile, no longer are being wasted because
of federal rules that once required more than one third of the
nation's trucks to return empty to their point of origin.

An assault on government controls and interference thus was
gathering on a broad front by the late 1970's. Deregulation's
advocates were to be found in both major parties and were of
many persuasions. Still, they were more likely to be Republican
than Democrat and much more likely to be conservative than
liberal. Those attacking regulation, after all, embrace a traditional vision of the American people's relationship with their government. It is a vision strongly biased against officialdom's

interference in both citizens' private lives and the economic marketplace.

This vision, to a great extent, is what inspired the fight against CPA. In this battle, the business community discovered the enormous synergistic payoff of cooperation. As a result, major business organizations and trade associations continue working together—sharing information, dividing tasks, mobilizing their members for grass-roots pressure on Capitol Hill. In this effort, the legacy of the CPA is frequently invoked. Says Jeffrey Joseph of the U.S. Chamber of Commerce: "Every step in the CPA fight was a case study of what works and what doesn't, what rallies public support and what doesn't, what holds a business coalition together and what threatens it." In other attacks on regulation, says Joseph, "I find myself saying, 'Why don't we do this and that, the way we did it on CPA.' I draw constantly from the CPA textbook. It's a formula and it works. And because it does, the business community is being reinforced by its victories and keeps coming back for more."

The ambitious dismantling of government rule-making and enforcement quite accurately is called deregulation. But elsewhere on the regulatory front, another movement of equal importance has been making significant advances. It is known as regulatory reform. Unlike deregulation, reform neither abolishes nor significantly strips an agency's authority. Instead, it concentrates on taming the agency by insisting that regulations be viewed in relation to other matters important to society. Regulatory reform does this by posing questions about a regulation's cost, effectiveness, reasonableness and impact. In short, regulatory reform attempts to introduce a measure of accountability in the regulatory process by emphasizing that for every one of regulation's achievements there almost certainly is some offsetting cost. Here, the message is that favorite free enterprise maxim: There is no free lunch, only trade-offs. Regulatory reform is the process which compels regulators to take these trade-offs into account when promulgating rules and enforcing controls.

Did it make sense, ask regulatory reformers, for OSHA to have tried to force industry (and ultimately consumers) to spend an estimated $500 million per year to meet super-stringent regulations governing the quantity of airborne benzene allowed in the workplace when, according to scientists, this might prevent just one death from leukemia every two or three years?[7]

Does it make sense to stick with the auto emission controls mandated for 1985 when the $11 billion annual cost will yield environmental benefits worth but $6 billion? This reverses the favorable ratio of early emission controls, which cost $4 billion and yielded $5 billion in benefits. Squeezing the last bit of pollution out of engine exhaust, it turns out, is astronomically more expensive than eliminating the first unit of pollution.

Does it make sense to reflexively assume that OSHA knows what it is doing in trying to make the workplace safer even though the $25 billion which business spent up to 1980 in complying with "safety" regulations failed to reduce accident rates? Indeed, surveys indicate that the rate of serious workplace injuries and illnesses actually has increased.[8]

Does it make sense to force businesses to incur considerable expense to prepare, print and mail to customers complicated notices about interest charges, credit rates and other matters, especially when it is doubtful that anyone reads the material? Northwestern National Bank in Minneapolis decided to check precisely this. Like other Federal Reserve member banks, it must distribute a pamphlet explaining its policies governing the automated teller machines that it has been installing. The bank spent $69,000 in 1980 to send such pamphlets to its 120,000 customers. In the text of 100 copies, Northwestern National added a special paragraph offering $10 to any customer who simply would write the word "regulation" on a postcard and return it to the bank. That Northwestern Mutual has not paid out a penny certainly demonstrates that no one bothers to read the inserts mandated by the federal regulators.

Why, then, has Washington been promulgating rules that make so little sense? The reason, according to analysts who study regulatory matters, is that regulation's advocates often are intent on achieving a riskless society, a society of no pollution, no dangers on the job, no accidents in autos and no unpleasant reactions to medication. Yet efforts to fashion a zero-risk society can create more ill side effects than do that last bit of pollution or that one-in-a-million hazard. As the nation has learned, mega-regulations fuel inflation and strangle the economy. Observes Paul Johnson, the British journalist and historian: "The only workplace totally free of hazards is one without workers—and if compliance with absolutist regulations leads to bankruptcy, that will indeed be the end result. Unemployed workers are . . . 100 percent hazard-free."9

Regulation's advocates counter that such arguments betray deplorable heartlessness. "You can't measure a human life in dollars," they indignantly assert, cloaking themselves in the garb of morality and humanitarianism. Yet society implicitly trades off lives and dollars all the time. A policeman on every one of New York City's blocks unquestionably would reduce significantly street crime, including murders (totalling 1,787 in 1980), just as a fire station on every block would cut deaths from fires. Yet New York is not at all unusual in setting its levels of law enforcement and fire-fighting manpower not solely according to need but also to budgetary constraints. New York and other cities routinely calculate the trade-offs between saving human lives and tax burdens on its citizens.

Forcing regulators to recognize society's unavoidable trade-offs is the message of regulatory reform. Technically all executive branch agencies have been doing just this since 1974, when a presidential order required them to start estimating the costs and benefits of their major regulatory proposals. This order lacked teeth, however, and the agencies have circumvented it easily. As a result of noncompliance, advocates of regulatory reform have little faith in the agencies' abilities to police themselves. The reformers now want laws requiring regulators, among other things, to justify their regulations, estimate their costs and investigate less expensive alternatives. Some steps in this direction were made before Reagan took office. The most notable was the Paper Work Reduction Act of 1980, giving the Office of Management and Budget authority to establish what amounts to a paperwork budget. In 1981, for instance, Americans spent more than 1.2 billion hours filling out 5,000 federal forms. The new law aims at reducing this by placing a ceiling on the number of hours of work that a regulator can impose on an industry and calls for an overall 25 percent reduction by late 1983 in the amount of information collected by the federal government.

Regulators also have been forced to recognize that small firms often cannot bear the burden of the government's rule-making. Such companies lack the manpower to keep up with the cascade of new regulations listed daily in the bulging *Federal Register* and cannot afford the attorneys needed to interpret fine print. To lighten this load, Congress in 1980 passed the Regulatory Flexibility Act, forcing agencies to analyze regulations' impact on small business. If the burden is too heavy, the agency must be flexible and modify the provisions affecting small firms. The Carter Administration opposed this measure, arguing that it would saddle government agencies with too much paper work. Though unintended, this plea was an eloquent admission of just how staggering is the paper-work load dumped on small businessmen by the regulatory process.

Small firms also are getting a break from the Equal Access to Justice Act of 1980. Previously a businessman who dared haul a regulatory agency into court bore all his legal costs even if the court ruled in his favor and against the agency. Under the Equal Access Act, Washington now must reimburse the businessman's attorney's fees if the court declares the government's regulatory actions substantially unjustified. This makes it much easier for small businesses to challenge unfair regulations in the courts. As in the case of the Flexibility Act, Equal Access was resisted by the White House and signed only reluctantly by Carter. His argument against the act was again an unintended confirmation of regulation's excruciating costs to business: He pleaded that reimbursing small businessmen would burden the Federal Treasury too much.

The most promising instrument for making government agencies view regulation in relation to other critical issues is also the most complicated (and controversial); it is an approach known as "comparative risk assessment." This attempts to set priorities based on evaluations of a potential regulation's costs, risks and benefits. Studies trying to devise a system or process for making such an evaluation are proliferating. Notes a 1980 report commissioned by the National Association of Manufacturers: "Risk-benefit-cost activities are on an exponential growth curve. Risk assessment, risk analysis, risk-benefit analysis and cost-benefit analysis have become 'buzz' words in Washington."[10] The National Academy of Sciences has a Committee on Risk and Decision Making surveying the entire field of risk analysis. The American Petroleum Institute and the Business Roundtable each sponsor studies of the regulatory risk-cost-benefit issue. And several congressional committees have been holding hearings on the subject. Yet the problems involved in measuring the risk-benefit trade-off are enormous. The NAM report cited dozens, among them: "How to update risk assessment without losing face as new scientific information becomes available. How should society account for risks which may be statistically remote, but the consequences—if the risk is realized—are huge. E.g., a major nuclear power plant disaster? How to preserve freedom of individual choice."[11]

The greatest problem may be selling the complicated risk-benefit argument to the press and public. Observes the NAM's James Carty: "As soon as you bring up the matter, people jump out of their seats, screaming that industry is trying to kill someone." Adds another expert: "There will be no way to deal with risk assessment in a nonemotional environment."

Yet there are signs of the public beginning to accept the risk-assessment formulation and the necessity of trade-offs. Cambridge Research Reports, for example, finds a growing share of the public supporting the proposition that "we must be prepared to sacrifice environmental quality for economic growth." While 21 percent of those surveyed agreed with this statement in 1976, the number climbed to 32 percent by mid-1979. Those willing to "sacrifice economic growth in order to protect the environment" remained almost static: 38 percent in 1976 and 37 percent in 1979. The group giving "don't know" as its answer, however, dropped sharply in this period from 41 percent to 32 percent. Support for economic expansion was even more pronounced when those surveyed were given a tough either/or choice between spending money to expand job opportunities or to clean up the environment; 62 percent backed job growth.[12]

Even with greater public awareness of trade-offs and a White House anxious to curb regulatory excess, the battle against regulation requires continued business community commitment. Demands for regulation will never completely abate. Some rules are always going to be imposed on the economic marketplace—zoning laws to keep steel plants out of residential neighborhoods, fire-safety codes and a host of other measures that make sense to the vast majority of Americans. The danger is that each perceived need for a rule offers the Leviathan renewed opportunity for aggrandizement. This can be checked only by procrustean determination to shape and trim proposed regulations until they fit risk assessment standards based on reasonable trade offs.

Curbing the Leviathan's insatiable appetite for tax revenues is as important as checking its propensity to meddle directly in economic activity. There are few Americans who were not shoved, by inflation's persistence, into ever-higher income tax brackets during the 1970's, even though their income (measured by purchasing power) dropped. According to an American Enterprise Institute study, the average American in 1980 paid a confiscatory 50 percent tax on the last dollar that he earned, combining all federal, state and local levies. And income from bank savings accounts or stock dividends often is being taxed more than 100 percent when taking inflation into account. Is it any wonder that New York Governor Hugh Carey told his legislature in 1981 that "in my travels around this state, the people spoke with one voice in their support of tax cuts and an end to government spending increases that diminish incomes already decimated by inflation."[13]

That high tax rates have been wounding the U.S. taxpayer is bad enough; what is worse are the injuries inflicted on the U.S. economy. They have slowed the rate of savings and investment, shrunk the pool of capital available for expanding and modernizing production and gnawed at productivity. Throughout the 1970's, even Britain's rates of savings and investment beat the American. Americans in 1979 saved a pathetically meager 4.5 percent of their disposable income—the lowest share since the exuberant spending-spree days following World War II. In 1980's final quarter, that rate dropped to 3.3 percent. So while the nation was being strangled by overregulation, it was being starved by high taxes levied to pay for proliferating government programs.

The Reagan tax cuts are a bold attempt to reverse this trend. But here too, the new administration has been able to draw on a business-led movement that has been picking up momentum since the late 1970's. In this battle, 1978 again was a landmark year. Not only did it witness the burial of the Consumer Protection Act, but also turned the tide of tax legislation. The year began with Jimmy Carter introducing what he labeled a tax reform bill. Under its provisions, the Treasury would have collected more, not less, from business and successful investors.

For years, tax legislation had followed this same, distressing pattern of redistributing the nation's wealth—transferring it from those producing and harvesting it to those doing so to a much lesser extent or, quite often, not even at all. This policy was more than bad economics. It was faulty altruism, ultimately hurting those whom it had sought to help. History's lessons clearly teach that the more government takes from wealth's producers, the less willing they are to work a bit harder or take an extra and often critical economic risk. It is a lesson which Americans have learned well. When surveyed by the Gallup Organization in August 1980, three times as many respondents said that people would work more rather than less if there is "a substantial cut in income taxes;" the numbers were a decisive 55 percent versus 18 percent.[14]

Carter's 1978 tax package ignored history's teachings. Rather than encourage investment, the Carter proposals sought to penalize it by raising the taxes paid on capital gains. This attempt mobilized the business community as had the Consumer Protection Act. Although "supply-side" was a term not yet in vogue, the goal of business was not only to stop Carter's hike, but to roll back capital gains taxes in order to provide the material incentives to spark the sluggish economy. Business lobbyists pounded away in Washington and salvos were called up from the grass roots. This was the issue, after all, that prompted W. R. Grace and Company to launch its effective advocacy advertising campaign.

Partly as a result of business pressure, of its own analyses of the economy and of the Republican gains in the November 1978 congressional elections, Congress ultimately rejected the Carter policy and instead enacted tax relief. It sent to the Oval Office a bill which had been turned around 180 degrees since Jimmy Carter originally had submitted it. Instead of boosting business and investor taxes, the congressional tax measure slashed the maximum capital gains rate from 49 percent to 28 percent and made more generous the credit allowed businesses for purchasing capital equipment. It was with undisguised distaste that Carter signed the legislation.

Key members of the business community regard their fight against Carter's 1978 proposal as their last defensive stand on taxes. Since then, they have been on the offensive. Though many trade associations and business groups, to say nothing of individual companies and economists, are waging this fight on a very broad front, the charge is being led, in many respects, by what is known as the Carlton Group, so named because of its regular breakfast strategy sessions at the Sheraton Carlton Hotel in downtown Washington. Its members represent the organizational muscle of the business community in Washington. It includes the principals in the fight against the CPA—the NAM, Chamber of Commerce, National Federation of Independent Business and the Business Roundtable—and about a dozen other groups such as American Council for Capital Formation and the Retail Tax Committee.

How frequently they gather depends on the tempo of tax activity in the capital. Sometimes they meet weekly, other times a month passes without a session. The breakfasts are almost always in the South Lounge of the Sheraton Carlton Hotel, where the menu never varies (scrambled eggs, bacon, sausage, potatoes, toast and coffee). Equally predictable is the agenda, an informal comparing of notes about their campaign for lower business taxes. One member reports on how he is coming along in drafting a bill to be introduced by a sympathetic senator. Another member brings the group up to date on the search for cosponsors for this measure. Others review tactics for mobilizing public support, especially at the grass roots. Both the Chamber of Commerce and the NFIB have become experts at this. They can alert their members and unleash a torrent of letters, telegrams and phone calls on Capitol Hill. Or, if more appropriate, they can call up a few carefully aimed thunderbolts. With their membership lists now on computers, the Chamber and NFIB can rally members, say, whose congressmen sit on the powerful Ways and Means Committee just when this panel is about to vote on an important business measure.

If the Carlton Group, through its vast network of associates and contacts, learns that a key senator or representative is wavering in his support of a pro-business matter, grass-roots pressure can be quickly focused on him. The NFIB's John Motley recounts a number of instances when a congressman was converted completely on a bill simply because he suddenly started hearing from a thousand or so small businessmen from back home. Explains John Thomas of the Chamber of Commerce: "When we go to what we term an *Action Call,* I can pull the names of all of our members in a specific district and tell them that next Tuesday their congressman is voting on such-and-such a bill of great concern to them. The computer can also give me a list of all newspaper editors in any congressional district, something very useful if we want to get information directly into their hands that could influence the congressman."

Though the Business Roundtable has only a couple hundred members, these firms have thousands of plants and offices scattered across the country. On major issues, managers of these local plants can be marshaled to pressure the congressman from the area. "An increasingly important part of a plant manager's job is his ability to contact elected officials and the congressman in the plant's area. Some companies actually write this into the manager's job description," explains Christine Vaughn, the Chamber of Commerce representative on the Carlton Group.

With these methods and the more classic lobbying techniques, like personally wooing congressmen and their staffs, the Carlton Group campaigned for what has been its top tax-cutting priority—a bill allowing businesses to more rapidly depreciate, for tax purposes, their plant and equipment. The 1981 Reagan tax cut gave the Carlton Group much of what it wants, a means of offsetting through tax allowances the damage inflicted by inflation on the nation's productive plant. With business able to depreciate its capital investments more quickly, it is more likely to have the resources to reinvest in new plant and equipment.

While business has been driving down taxes on the nation's productive plant, an enormously broad movement has been slashing levies paid by individuals. By the end of the 1970's, sparked by the phenomenal victory in California of Proposition 13, the chorus calling for cutting personal taxes had swelled to a near-deafening roar. Few movements in memory have erupted as suddenly or generated as much popular enthusiasm. Dozens of tax-cutting proposals were dropped into the congressional hoppers, scores more were debated publicly. Like the business tax measures, they are complicated. Yet again the underlying theme and philosophy are clear-cut and widely accepted. Material rewards for hard work, initiative and creativity have to be improved; to do this, Americans must be able to keep a larger share of what they earn. And if Congress and the state legislatures are not up to cutting taxes and government costs, then the voters are going to do it for them through initiatives, referendums and even the threat of a constitutional amendment.

Most of the popular ferment has been in the states. It is there and at local levels where Americans traditionally have had their most direct and dramatic impact on public policy. Iowans have formed the Yes For Less Committee, Arizonans have joined Citizens for Tax Relief and Missourians apparently do not seem to feel that they are exaggerating when they call their group Taxpayers Survival Association. These and the dozens of other tax-cut organizations cooperate and learn from each other. Their leaders gather to share experiences and discuss such critical matters as how to finance the tax-cutting movements, circulate petitions to get tax-relief questions on ballots and woo voters. Much of the talk at these gatherings is of their victories. By 1980, limits had been imposed on spending, taxes or both in twenty-five states. And this understates the gains because there has been little activity in the South, where taxes were already relatively low.

Midwiving the tax-cutting drive are a pair of national organizations. Both are based in Washington and regularly dispatch experts up Capitol Hill to testify on revenue issues and related matters. The older group is the National Taxpayers Union. For eight years after its 1969 founding, it languished, operating mostly as a Washington lobby fighting waste in government. It opposed federal funding for development of a supersonic transport airplane, for example, maintaining that the project was not an appropriate use of taxpayer money. (Opposition was not based, as was that of other groups, on environmental considerations.) In 1976, NTU's membership stood at 25,000; since then, its rolls have swelled to nearly 200,000, while its local affiliates boast an additional half-million. Attracting these new legions is NTU's aggressive campaign to check government spending.

Similar grass-roots activity characterizes the National Tax Limitation Committee. Though founded only in 1975, its membership topped 500,000 by 1981. Its sole aim is enactment of constitutional amendments limiting "spending and taxes at all levels of government." Among other things, it helps local groups organize and place initiatives on statewide ballots, sponsors conferences at which Milton Friedman and other widely respected experts speak and gathers signatures on a national petition calling for limiting federal spending.

California set the pace for the movement, starting in 1978 with its now-famous Proposition 13. Approved by a nearly two-to-one majority, it slashed property taxes by $7 billion in its first year. This was followed in 1979 by the approval of Proposition 4, freezing state and local government spending at their 1978–79 levels, allowing adjustments only for population growth and inflation. So doing, it achieves one of the primary aims of the broad anti-tax movement and one quickly adopted by the Reagan Administration: halting the seemingly inexorable growth of government spending. Although California voters soundly defeated another tax initiative in 1980, analysts do not interpret this as evidence of the tax revolt waning. For one thing, personality issues clouded the campaign for the 1980 measure. For another, voters were still digesting the $24 billion tax reduction that they had received in the closing years of the 1970's.

A parade of states has followed California's lead. Idaho and Nevada limited property taxes to 1 percent of market value. Minnesota trimmed taxes by nearly three-quarters of a billion dollars. In Virginia, Kentucky and New Mexico, a cap was placed on the amount that the state can collect through property taxes, while Wisconsin rolled back its income tax brackets and actually declared a two-month moratorium on payments.

Even Massachusetts joined the movement. Levies there had climbed so high that the state widely became known as "Taxachusetts" and found it increasingly difficult to attract the skilled and well-paid engineers needed to keep its high-technology industries thriving along famous Route 128. At last, Massachusetts voters said, "Enough!" In 1978, they elected as governor Edward King, a zealous tax-cutter who pushed through a 60 percent reduction in the state's capital gains tax and a ceiling on local government spending. Two years later, voters enthusiastically approved what is popularly known as Proposition 2 1/2; the measure prohibits communities from levying a property tax exceeding 2.5 percent of full market value. Half the state's localities are cutting their taxes in order to comply with the measure. The sharpest cutbacks are required by Boston, whose megatax rate was over 10 percent of property value.

Opposition to tax-cutting invariably comes from those grown fat at the public trough. Bloated battalions of bureaucrats usually lead the fight defending high taxes and state spending. Their favorite tactic is to bombard the public with jeremiads painting grim scenes of financially starved governments massively eliminating police protection, public works, health services, libraries and schools. But unlike their biblical forefather, these gloom-and-doom prophets do not rejoice in their warnings' fulfillment. Though California communities have had to take a healthy look at the cost of many services and subsequently have pared some, the sweeping tax-cutting has improved significantly the state's economic health by almost every accepted measure. This too is Wisconsin's happy experience following its tax rollback. Though Massachusetts' adjustment to the end of the big-spending, big-taxing epoch has been painful, communities are being forced to look hard at programs and determine priorities. And just about nowhere have the doomsday predictions come even close to coming true.

The best measure of the tax revolt's impact is its effect on the American pocketbook. Its purpose, after all, is to allow workers and investors to keep more of what they earn. Here, the evidence is very encouraging. A study for the National Governors Association reveals that after decades of climbing, the share of national income devoured by state and local treasuries has begun decreasing. And this decline dates precisely from the anti-tax movement. In 1977, state and local taxes took a record-breaking 12.7 percent of national income. Then the trend mercifully reversed, falling in 1979 to 11.9 percent and to 10.1 percent in 1980.

One of the clearest messages broadcast by the nationwide tax revolt is that since legislators seem incapable of disciplining themselves on tax and spending matters, the public will do it for them through direct action at the ballot box. Washington is being sent a similar message. The National Taxpayers Union, for example, is calling for a constitutional amendment mandating a balanced federal budget, and scores of resolutions demanding this have been introduced in the Congress. More important is the call to convoke a constitutional convention for the express purpose of drafting and adopting such an amendment. This would be an extraordinary step; the last time a constitutional convention met was at Philadelphia in 1787, when delegates from twelve states crafted the fundamental charter under which the nation since has lived. Understandably, therefore, the move for a new conclave stirs considerable controversy. Though some thirty-two states, of the thirty-four required, have passed legislation calling for a convention, the validity of a number of these state resolutions is in question. Critics argue, moreover, that once assembled, the delegates will be irresistibly tempted to rewrite other parts of the Constitution.

A somewhat different approach to taming the federal budget is urged by the National Tax Limitation Committee; it supports an amendment to limit government spending. Drafted by Milton Friedman and other leading conservative economists, it would in effect freeze expenditures and, through a number of intricate steps, gradually reduce the national debt and the share of national income now consumed by Washington. This measure already has been introduced in Congress and, in mid-1981, had the backing of eight states. The amendment's purpose, stated in its Senate version, is "to protect the people of the United States against excessive government burdens and unsound fiscal and monetary policies by limiting total outlays of the government." The National Tax Limitation Committee is dispatching squads around the country to drum up support for this measure. Milton Friedman, for instance, has been stumping extensively. "This amendment is the first step in bringing discipline into government policy," he says. "What causes inflation is that Congress, instead of limiting spending, just adds more money to the bill without any guidelines."[15]

Whether efforts to change the Constitution succeed is problematical. The founding fathers deliberately placed great hurdles along the amending course—so many, in fact, that only rarely have they been vaulted, a lesson painfully being learned by Equal Rights Amendment advocates. Still, campaigns for the budget-balancing and spending-limitation amendments pay dividends by giving focus to the public's mounting rage at the spectacle of the federal government out of control. With more than half of the states calling for rewriting the Constitution, the rage cannot be ignored. That Ronald Reagan understands this surely contributed to his surprisingly large margin of victory. How well he delivers the goods on this issue may determine in great part how the nation judges his administration. His advantage is that he arrived in a Washington seemingly ripe for rhetoric and action designed to shrink the role of the federal government.

Reagan's famous, applause-prompting punchline, "The government is not the answer, the government is the problem," articulates a conclusion that Washington and much of the country were already drawing on their own. Observed Kaiser Aluminum's Cornell Maier with some astonishment just before the 1980 election: "All of a sudden, good economics has become good politics in Washington. A lot of people who are very liberal are suddenly supporting things that business supports. It is not that they love business. It is just that there is a general recognition that if we don't get our act together, we are going to have fewer jobs, higher inflation and more unemployment." Even before the November

1980 conservative sweep, liberals started sounding uncharacteristically defeatist. Representative Stephen Solarz, an ultraliberal from Brooklyn, told *The New York Times* in spring 1980: "It's not our moment. We may have to hunker down and wait for these storms to pass over. Instead of fighting to expand programs, now we are just fighting to hang on and to avoid cutbacks."[16]

The election of Ronald Reagan, a Republican Senate and several dozen conservative Democratic congressmen will keep Solarz and his big-spending colleagues waiting a long time for the "storms" to blow over. What Solarz thought was just a "storm," in fact, actually might have been early signs of a major change of climate. Prevailing economic winds were shifting on Capitol Hill, blowing in renewed respect for capitalism, the marketplace, the free enterprise system. Blossoming in this new climate is a doctrine known as "supply-side" economics. It is so called because it concentrates on expanding the supply of goods rather than demand for them and on rewarding the producer rather than on artificially stimulating the consumer. Most important, its commitment is to dynamic expansion of wealth rather than to redistribution. Economists Arthur Laffer, Jude Wanniski, Paul Craig Roberts and Norman Ture have developed and popularized these arguments. The theory itself, however, boasts a much older lineage, tracing its pedigree back to Jean Baptiste Say, the early nineteenth-century French economist who proclaimed, as Say's Law, "Supply creates its own demand."

A host of congressional proposals at the end of the decade incorporated supply-side economics. None has had more impact or stirred more controversy than the sweeping tax cut proposed by two Republicans, Representative Jack Kemp and Senator William Roth. Their Kemp-Roth Bill called for slashing individual taxes 11 percent annually for three consecutive years. This measure and the commitment to economic growth it represents were endorsed by the G.O.P. both in the 1978 and 1980 elections. In slightly modified form, the Kemp-Roth Bill is the core of Reagan's tax cuts and a key ingredient of his prescription for national economic recovery.

The climate that has been so friendly to supply-side economics has been cruel to the theories of British economist John Maynard Keynes, a development of extraordinary long-range importance. For decades, Keynesianism was taught as the revealed word in classrooms, advocated by almost all professional economists and widely embraced by officials and the public. So universally accepted had this doctrine become that even a Republican President, Richard Nixon, could proclaim grandly in 1971, "I am a Keynesian now."[17] According to Keynesian dogma, it is anachronistic to trust the marketplace to play the dominant role in allocating resources and making economic decisions. Far better, said Keynesians and the armies of liberals whom they influenced, is to rely on government experts to fine-tune the economy—to provide stimulation when needed, to direct the flow of investment and to divide up (and redistribute) the economic output.

Whatever else it did or did not, Keynesian economics sanctified big government and crowned it with a theory of divine right. Whether or not true to their founder in every respect, the Keynesians provided the intellectual and theoretical underpinnings for government's initiation of vast programs and creation of bureaucratic hordes. Keynesian economics, in sum, has been the conceptual justification for the Leviathan, wrapping it in intellectual respectability and legitimacy. Today the concept is discredited and is almost certain to remain so. It is not simply that Ronald Reagan is President and that the non-Keynesians man every key economic post in the executive branch. Rather, the Keynesian forces have been so thoroughly routed that they have scant chance of regrouping. There is no Keynesian cavalry on the horizon, no one is charging up to rescue the besieged ideology. The simple fact is that the supply of Keynesian reserves is being cut off at the source: the university.

In economics departments from one campus to another, the ideological center of gravity has been shifting dramatically. For nearly two generations, with few exceptions, these departments had been votaries of Keynes in matters of macroeconomic theory and economic policy. They produced wave after wave of Keynesian graduate students, filled journals with Keynesian arguments and provided government officials with Keynesian guidance. No longer. Slowly, gradually, with the deliberate motion befitting academia's stately towers, these departments have been shedding Keynesian garb.

So complete is the disrobing that it now is nearly impossible to find a first-rank economist under age forty who is a Keynesian. Writes Robert Lucas, the University of Chicago economist who is one of the most prominent and creative of the new breed: "Keynesian economics is dead (maybe 'disappeared' is a better term). I don't know exactly when this happened, but it is true today and it wasn't true ten years ago." With some pleasure, he notes, "People even take offense if referred to as 'Keynesians.' Leading journals are getting fewer and fewer Keynesian papers submitted." While there are still some influential Keynesians in universities, he observes, they are aging and "there is no fresh source of supply."[18]

In a sense, Keynes prophesied his own demise when, long ago as he was battling the theories of an earlier day, he complained that "practical men, who believe themselves to be quite exempt from any intellectual influences, are usually the slaves of some defunct economist."[19] Young economists seem to be taking this warning to heart and are refusing to be slaves to defunct Keynesianism.

Examples abound of the changing intellectual climate. Suddenly Milton Friedman finds himself a campus celebrity. More astounding is the resurgent interest in Austrian economist Friedrich Hayek, a champion of Adam Smith and a foe of government economic meddling. In writings spanning nearly four decades, Hayek argues that the marketplace, by disseminating countless and uncountable bits of economic information and by coordinating the economic activities of millions of individuals, is infinitely more capable of making economic decisions than any government regulator. What is just as important, adds Hayek, is that history teaches that the free market is the surest guarantor of liberty. That these views have an audience is obvious from the surging sales in college bookstores since the mid-1970's of Hayek's 1944 classic, *The Road to Serfdom*. His rediscovery by students bemuses him. In a 1979 *Forbes* interview, when he was eighty, Hayek observed: "When I was a young man, only the very old believed in the market. In my middle age, almost no one believed in it. Now, today, I find that most of my support is coming from the very young. It's almost a complete intellectual shift in relation to the generations."[20]

Economics textbooks confirm this shift. Paul Samuelson's classic, for instance, has changed considerably since it first appeared in 1948. Take the differences between his third edition, published in 1955, and the eleventh, released fifteen years later. In the earlier edition, Adam Smith gets barely a nod; he is mentioned only four times, blandly and without praise. By the eleventh, not only are there sixteen references to Smith and eight quotations from *The Wealth of Nations,* but several citations are downright effusive and a Smith quote even heads a chapter. The fortunes of John Locke, Jean Baptiste Say and Hayek similarly have soared; from nary a mention in the third edition's main text, they are credited in the eleventh with major contributions to economics.

When Samuelson's third talks about federal budgets, it is in a strictly Keynesian context; yet the eleventh acknowledges that some economists regard a balanced budget as essential for the economy's health and that others feel that chronic government deficits impede capital formation by crowding private borrowers out of the credit market. As for the minimum wage, it is ignored in the third edition while the eleventh acknowledges that it may be hurting those it is designed to help. Though Samuelson makes it very clear that his own Keynesian roots and commitments remain deep, he concedes that "there is very definitely a conservative trend within the profession." His eleventh edition is a barometer of this trend.

Barely a campus has been untouched by it. Even Harvard and M.I.T., bastions of liberal economics, seem to be entertaining second thoughts. Observes a Harvard economist who requests anonymity: "The old-guard economists in Boston and Cambridge are just not active anymore. They still have their offices in the departments, but they're not the moving and shaking forces they once were. And the young blood, those like Martin Feldstein and Dale Jorgensen, who set the tone for the Harvard department, have a much higher appreciation for the market economy than did the old guard." One measure of how much the atmosphere has altered, notes this economist, is the way national problems are viewed. "The answer for such problems offered around Harvard always used to be some government program," he says. "Now government no longer is the automatic alternative; it is recognized that government action too has a price."

Rethinking economics is proceeding at a different tempo and in different ways at each university. What is happening at the University of Minnesota, while not necessarily typical of the others, does highlight the changes in economic thinking and teaching taking place across the nation. Minnesota has a medium-sized economics department with a long, distinguished history. It is

nationally respected, among other things, for the highly demanding work of mathematical economists like Leonid Hurwicz. It also
has been home to Walter Heller who, after serving as John
Kennedy's key economic advisor, became America's best-known,
most visible Keynesian. When journalists have wanted to quote
a quintessential liberal economist, they have called Heller. When
newspaper op-ed pages have wanted a liberal economic viewpoint or when a widely recognized Keynesian was sought for a
panel, Walter Heller perfectly filled the bill. Because of his very
high visibility, he symbolized the University of Minnesota economics department. To much of the American public, Walter
Heller was Minnesota economics. While his colleagues in the
department caution that things never were quite that simple, they
agree that by and large they were rather comfortable with the
departmental image that he projected.

Walter Heller is still at Minnesota; this has not changed. Almost everything else has. Though he by no means is isolated, he
is out of step with most of the exciting work now going on in the
department. Its glittering lights are its youngsters—Edward Prescott, Thomas Sargent, Christopher Sims, Neil Wallace—and they
have turned their backs on Keynes. Explains John Kareken, a
Minnesota economist a half-generation ahead of the younger
group: "The change from Heller to Sargent is a very big change,
and it is symptomatic of the profession."

If anyone today symbolizes Minnesota's economics department it is indeed Tom Sargent, a slightly built, articulate and
enthusiastic advocate of the new "rational expectations" school
of economics. Like just about all his colleagues, Sargent began his
professional life as a Keynesian. "When I started teaching, I gave
my students the standard Keynesian stuff," he explains in his
cluttered office in the University's Business Administration
Tower in Minneapolis, overlooking the Mississippi River. "It was
the most careful presentation that I could make as a true believ-
er." Yet this belief gradually crumbled, and Sargent's account of
his loss of faith could be repeated by scores of economists all over
the country. He and they have had to confront the ineluctable
accumulation of data which punched holes in the Keynesian
system.

For Sargent, the moment of truth came while working with
Neil Wallace on a project at the Federal Reserve Bank in Minneapolis. "This study was the apotheosis of Keynesianism," re-

calls Sargent. "We were thrilled to be working on it. But about eighteen months into the project, Neil and I realized that it was flawed. It was a tragic realization—and painful. We scrapped the project and that hurt." What Sargent and Wallace finally discovered was a fundamental flaw in the Keynesian analytical method itself. Sargent's faith in the validity of the Keynesian analytical process began to dissolve. Eventually he concluded that Keynesian "economic models do not work well; they give bad predictions."

In place of Keynesian analysis, Sargent and his colleagues, along with Chicago's Lucas, have been developing rational expectations economics. This is an extraordinarily complex way of analyzing man's economic behavior and requires, among other things, mastery of microeconomics and skilled use of the computer. Rational expectationists argue that valid economic theory must take into account how individuals behave. One problem with the Keynesians, these young critics contend, is that too little attention is paid to the individual as a rational economic actor and to the consequences of his rational action. When individuals make economic choices, according to the rational expectionists, they weigh more than simply those factors present at the moment of the choice. They have memory, learn from experience and may even know something of history. These help shape an individual's expectations of the consequences—the rewards or penalties— that could flow from a specific economic decision in a specific economic situation.

The problem is that the number of factors shaping an individual's expectation are conceivably beyond measuring. This makes it extremely difficult to predict how individuals will react to, say, government economic policies. In fact, argue the rational expectationists, limitations of theory currently make it impossible to predict with much confidence individual reaction to policy. This means that accurately forecasting the results of government intervention in the economy is not possible. Without such predictions, policies of intervention are little more than guesswork and should not be tried. The moral: Government should stay out of the marketplace.

Drawing such a conclusion is not necessarily what rational expectationists intended. Yet their theory makes a powerful case against government schemes to manage or "fine-tune" the economy. As such, rational expectations economics strongly rein-

force the conservative argument. Leonid Hurwicz, who as a mathematical economist stands outside the rational expectations debate, observes that this theory "can legitimately be read as saying
that the government can do nothing; that it can have no effect.
Thus, we have gone from theories of government omnipotence
to theories of government impotence."

This shift, says Tom Sargent, is a "scientific revolution."
Thinking back on his first years at Minnesota when he was teaching courses based on Keynesian analysis, he says: "It makes me
sick to my stomach." Yet in some ways he is saddened by the
demise of Keynes. He explains that "I was going to college when
the Keynesian giants were producing their great works. I looked
up to them. I would not have believed that these men could have
been so wrong. It's been like discovering that your parents are
wrong." Though he still lectures on the Keynesian approach, he
does so briefly and treats it mostly as history.

Sargent and his colleagues at Minnesota, along with Robert
Lucas at Chicago, have attained national recognition through
their work on rational expectations economics. This theory, of
course, is not universally endorsed and remains controversial and
is rivaled by other theoretical refutations of Keynesianism.
Together, however, such theories contribute substantially to the
emerging non-Keynesian consensus. It is a consensus whose
confidence in the government as an economic manager is falling
as its faith in the marketplace is ascending. In this intellectual
environment, the Leviathan cannot thrive.

Final victory over the Leviathan, however, is far from assured.
Its legions of defenders are well entrenched. The federal government itself spends about $1 billion yearly on public relations to
burnish the image of its programs. And although Ronald Reagan
has swept into office determined to trim the government, even
Republicans appointed to head agencies have been known to
succomb to the common bureaucratic malady that turns them
into protectors—even expanders—of their turf. Bureaucrats at all
government levels, moreover, constitute a powerful and vocal
bloc which turns out at the polls in great numbers. Obviously
sensing mounting public scorn, AFSCME, the public employees
union, has been taking to radio and television with advertisements that melodiously depict happy and dedicated bureaucrats
eagerly serving a deserving public. Much of the classic New Deal

coalition, moreover, remains wedded to big government and big spending and routinely dismisses the warnings that deficits and regulation spell economic disaster. Though weaker at the polls, this coalition still wields formidable political clout.

Then there is the problem of betrayal by those who should be spearheading the fight against the Leviathan. Credibility certainly is strained when a businessman one day rails against Washington's interference in the marketplace and the next begs for special favors. The hypocrisy is glaring when a corporate executive pleads for government subsidies, protection from the imports of foreign autos, steel, textiles, television sets and a whole catalogue of other goods. Former Treasury Secretary William Simon admonishes business leaders not to be "hypocritical leeches upon the state, who mouth platitudes about the free enterprise system, then come hat in hand to Washington." At the least, this spectacle confuses the public and prompts it to treat with cynicism incantations about the virtues of a competitive, unfettered marketplace.

In this regard, probably no individual in recent years has done more to discredit the free enterprise argument than Chrysler Corporation Chairman Lee Iacocca, through his incessant whining for government handouts for his failing auto company. It is a heartening indication of the business community's new mood, however, that both the Business Roundtable and National Association of Manufacturers have opposed aid for Chrysler. In the NAM's case, this contrasts markedly with its position a decade earlier, when it remained "neutral" toward the government bailout of the Lockheed Corporation.

Perhaps the greatest obstacle in the battle against the Leviathan is the public's ambivalent view of the government's role. On the one hand, Americans are increasingly critical of excessive regulation and aware of the penalty that the economy pays for all the government activity. On the other hand, Americans seem very reluctant to give up many government services. Studies by polling organizations reveal, for instance, that a majority wants the government to regulate drugs, the sale of barbiturates, the accuracy of claims made in advertisements and a host of other matters.[21]

What the public seems to be saying, conclude sociologists Seymour Martin Lipset and William Schneider in a *Public Opinion* article, is that "regulation is bad when it means telling people how to run their business or when it forces business to raise

production costs or prices unreasonably. Regulation is good
when it means protecting the public interest from the 'bad behavior' of businessmen."[22]

These findings mean that the right kind of leadership can
build on the public's growing disenchantment with regulation
and demonstrate that ultimately even "good" regulation can turn
very bad through its adverse impact on the economy's vitality.
The means for accomplishing this already are at hand—in the
Reagan White House and, what may be more critical in the long
haul, in the free enterprise legions of the traditionalist resurgence
—those companies, coalitions, trade associations and organizations which have been waging the battles against expansive government. Important strategic ground has been gained; the forces
are in place; the numbers are growing; and they have been learning from past victories. Today they are stronger, better prepared
and more confident than ever to serve as shock troops in a continuing offensive against the Leviathan.

IV

BACK TO CLASSROOM BASICS

"WE MUST STOP CHEATING young people, pretending they have learned when they haven't." So declared Governor James Hunt to his fellow North Carolinians in early 1979. In an unusual, dramatic step, Hunt was appearing on statewide television delivering a major speech on a single topic: public education. He was seeking broad popular backing for his drive to reverse the alarming deterioration in North Carolina's public school systems. Said he: "You and I both know of high school graduates who can't read a newspaper or a driver's license test." He told viewers of an auto dealer who had hired a "high school graduate voted most likely to succeed who couldn't figure up the sales tax on a new car."

Following Hunt's lead, North Carolina has acted boldly to restore the vitality of its schools: It has gone back to classroom basics. Now high school diplomas are denied students who fail to demonstrate minimum competency in the long-ignored skills of reading and mathematics. In taking such action, North Carolina is far from alone. With prairie fire intensity and speed, minimum competency tests are being adopted across the nation and already are mandated in thirty-six states, almost all since 1977. Statutes have been roaring through legislatures in record times and have been passing by near-acclamatory majorities. By so acting, the solons merely are bowing to pressure from a public whose patience is clearly exhausted with the countless examples of educational failure similar to those recounted by Hunt. Though public elementary and secondary education cost the U.S. $93 billion in

99

1980 and counted 41.8 million students in 16,056 school systems, instructed by 2,184,000 teachers, the payoff from this astronomic investment has become increasingly disappointing.

In the eyes of millions of Americans, the only thing that has been losing value faster than the dollar has been the high school diploma. At graduation, Johnny frequently can't read, can't write, can't add, can't subtract and can't demonstrate most of those skills which once had been the universal mark of education. Too often, writes Professor of Education Kenneth Strike, the diploma now "signifies little more than twelve years of reasonably faithful and nonbelligerent attendance."[1] The problem, observed Maryland Superintendant of Education David Hornbeck in 1977, is that "we do not, in any formal sense, ask at the end of the process what students have actually learned. We tend to focus on what might be called 'seat time.' " Many school systems, complained Hornbeck, are measured against "input standards . . . pupil-teacher ratios, number of books in the library, square footage in the classrooms, number of chairs available, sizes of auditoriums and a host of other similar factors."[2]

Is it any mystery then that student achievement is being neglected? And is it any mystery that parents, becoming aware of this neglect, have started demanding better performance from the costly public school system? To press these demands, parents have been organizing in hundreds and hundreds of small groups that together probably constitute America's most broad-based grass-roots movement. Whatever their ideologies and politics in other matters, when it comes to educating their children, these legions by and large are new champions of traditionalism—a traditional curriculum taught in a traditional classroom by a traditional teacher. This is the formula which mounting numbers of angry and even desperate parents are convinced will restore the faded quality of their public school systems.

Public education's deterioration has been documented and analyzed in a blizzard of books, articles and speeches and dissected at scores of conferences, seminars and official hearings. Yet the most devastating evidence is found in just a handful of simple statistics. A 1979 federal study estimated that 13 percent of the nation's high school seventeen-year-olds are "functionally illiterate;" they cannot read newspapers, road maps or other material needed to function in contemporary society. In even worse shape, undoubtedly, are the seventeen-year-olds who have dropped out of school. Meanwhile, those who do graduate are not measuring up to previous years' graduates. Reversed now is the pattern of the 1950's and early 1960's, when average scores on the widely used Scholastic Aptitude Test administered by the College Entrance Examination Board rose slightly or at least remained level. In 1964, results on both the verbal and mathematical skills tests began dropping. At first, the slide was gradual and then, after 1970, accelerated. In the same period, other standardized test scores also have been dropping.[3] In college after college, including elite institutions, more than 30 percent of the entering freshmen now have "serious problems" in reading, writing and mathematics.[4]

Confirming these numbers is extensive anecdotal evidence— observations by teachers, businessmen and others who deal continually with high school graduates. At one manufacturing company, an employee who could not read a simple ruler mismeasured and wasted hundreds of dollars of material. At another firm, a worker was killed because he could not read a warning sign. Of 800 companies surveyed by the Conference Board, a business association, more than one third provide their employees with some remedial education in the 3 R's. A Continental Illinois Bank officer told *The Wall Street Journal* in 1981 that "more and more of the applicants whom we're seeing straight out of school can't write a complete sentence." And in one telling experiment designed to compare today's high school education with that of previous generations, freshmen entering the University of Minnesota in 1978 were given a reading exam that had been taken by freshmen a half-century earlier. The result: The 1978 grades were decidedly lower than 1928's; in fact, even the best contemporary students did not perform as well as the best of 1928. The Internal Revenue Service, meanwhile, is being forced to cope with eroding educational standards. When it changed the income tax forms in 1981, revisions were written at ninth-grade level, two full grades below the reading level of earlier IRS forms.

Who are the culprits ruining American education? Indicting fingers point in several directions. It certainly seems, for example, that schools suffer from task overload. Among many other things, schools have been providing driver training and sex education, fighting tooth decay, solving racial discrimination, serving hot meals and running a major busing system. All this not only devours much of the school day but also saps educators' energies and deadens their enthusiasm.

More deadening is the fear pervading public schools. A study commissioned by the National Institute of Education in the late 1970's finds that one of six high school students regularly avoids at least three places in school because they are too dangerous. Some 500,000 high schoolers said that they are afraid most of their time in school.[5] Many frightened students simply stay away from school and contribute to today's record absenteeism. With attendance irregular, it becomes extremely difficult for teachers to proceed through a course of study that has been designed to build each new lesson upon the previous day's learning.

Most shocking, perhaps, is that pupils are not the only victims of violence. Across the U.S., according to a 1979 study, half of all teachers report being verbally assaulted or the object of obscene gestures; 5,000 are attacked physically each month.[6] Writes Professor Jackson Toby of Rutgers University: "A generation ago . . . assaults on teachers were punished so swiftly that they were almost unthinkable. Even disrespectful language was unusual."[7] Today students are brazen and teachers are cowed; one of eight teachers, in fact, admits to being afraid to confront students. What is worse, the teacher no longer can count on backing from the principal when there is a showdown with a student.

Partly at fault here are court rulings decreeing that students cannot be suspended or expelled from school without due process of law. This often means formal hearings. At the prospect of lengthy, bitter proceedings, principals generally balk at taking stern action against troublesome students. Unpunished, they return to class to resume harassing the teacher and disrupting instruction. At fault too for the lax discipline are the fashionable pedagogical theorists of the 1960's and early 1970's. Best-selling books in these years by John Holt, Jonathan Kozol, James Herndon and Herbert Kohl, writes Jackson Toby, "portrayed teachers, especially white middle-class teachers, as the villains of education —insensitive, authoritarian and even racist." As these ideas percolated through American society, the teacher increasingly was seen as a cruel enemy and thus, notes Toby, "striking a teacher might almost appear to be a deserved punishment."[8]

The chic theories of the late 1960's delighted in denouncing schools for an authoritarianism which allegedly destroyed pupils' budding creativity. What was needed, counseled these theorists, is to replace the traditional teacher-dominated learning process with a "student-centered" classroom in which teachers treat students as peers. It is fallacious as well as unjust, they further argued, to suppose that teachers really know more than their students about educating. As for the curriculum, that too must be thoroughly revamped to stress "creative learning" opportunities in which expression came to replace thinking and knowing.

This classroom did not remain experimental, but has been widely adopted, making casualties of the 3 R's. Writing has been short-changed the most, but reading and mathematics also have suffered greatly. Current eleventh-grade textbooks, for example, generally are written at a ninth or tenth-grade level. A growing share of a textbook's page is consumed by pictures and wider margins, while words, paragraphs and sentences are becoming shorter. As for homework, this has been cut in half since the mid-1940s.[9] In mathematics, drill has been eliminated because the theorists complained that it "inhibits" spontaneous creativity. It counted for little apparently that generations of teachers have found drill essential in education's early stages. In his influential critique of American education, *The Literacy Hoax,* Paul Copperman writes: "Repetitive drill and memorization of basic facts result in the ability to gain immediate and automatic access to certain basic stored information, an ability which is the basis of any skill."[10]

Restructuring the very setting of instruction is the most destructive legacy of the theorists' assault on traditional education. In the name of unfettered creativity, the so-called "open classroom" has been introduced. Classes divided by grade levels have been abolished so that students can wander about the room and learn at their own pace. Report cards, meanwhile, have been replaced by parent-teacher conferences. "There was a terrible confusion in the late 1960's and through the 1970's about who young people are," Copperman told a 1980 conference of educators and parents in San Mateo, California. "We were told to recreate schools on the model of playgrounds. Work was replaced with play."

The theories have failed and American society is paying the price for allowing such pedagogical folly. It is now time, Copperman told the San Mateo gathering, "to recognize young people for who they are. You can't give fourteen-year-olds a wide choice of courses. A teacher has to define the curriculum and do it with confidence." The voices agreeing with Copperman are growing to a thundering national chorus. It is demanding change in the schools. To be sure, education in the U.S. has witnessed wide pendulum swings over the years. Concepts embraced with enthusiasm in one age embarrass the next; theories slide in and out of favor—and then sometimes back in again. Yet this time there is a special quality to the debate; the tugging and the pulling are not just between competing schools of education experts. This time, the public is deeply involved and is calling, over the experts' heads, for direct action.

North Carolina's James Hunt understood this. He made raising the state's educational standards a main plank in his successful 1976 gubernatorial campaign and found voters responding enthusiastically to the issue. Almost nothing he said in his inaugural address was interrupted so loudly or so long as his pledge to improve North Carolina's school systems. Soon after taking office, he sent the General Assembly a bill designed "to restore public confidence in the public schools." Within the year, he signed into law the tough measure that now requires high school graduates to pass the minimum competency examinations in reading and mathematics in order to receive their diplomas. Those failing are given only a school-leaving certificate.

As they drafted their minimum competency program, North Carolina officials faced a number of sticky problems. At what level, for example, should the pass/fail line be drawn? What precisely should the test measure? How difficult should questions be? What safeguards can prevent questions from being inherently biased against minorities? To deal with these and similar problems, North Carolina's Competency Test Commission ranged across the nation talking to educators, testing specialists, psychologists and officials experienced in administering test programs. The Commission also contacted nearly two dozen firms that already had developed standardized competency tests. Within North Carolina, the Commission solicited the views of businessmen, local officials, school board members and parents.

After the test had been designed and approved, reporters were invited to take a sample examination under exactly the same conditions as those in which eleventh graders were to be tested. This was to make the test less of a mystery and to calm the public's understandable nervousness. In the sample exam, the reporters had to read selections from job application forms, classified ads, dictionaries, newspapers, telephone directories and instructions for "do-it-yourself" projects. Then they faced questions based on what they had read. After that, they had to solve math problems dealing with checkbooks, hourly wage tables, credit card statements, tax forms, installment credit agreements and distances on road maps. Press accounts of this mock exam-taking received wide attention, as did almost every step in the process as the first real test approached.

It was to announce its results that Hunt made his television address. He looked grim when he revealed that 13,312 high school juniors, one out of six, had failed part of the exam. Those who did not pass, he said solemnly, have "some hard work ahead" to ready themselves for their three additional opportunities to take and pass the test. If they continue to fail, he warned, they would not receive diplomas. To his statewide audience, he said: "I want to challenge every one of you tonight to get involved in this effort . . . to help one of the students who has failed." He called on civic groups and PTAs, churches and Sunday school classes and state employees to aid students preparing for the tests. And to those students who already had passed, he said, "Help your friends and schoolmates who didn't."

North Carolinians responded enthusiastically. Church groups in Charlotte "adopted" a school and dispatched parishoners to assist in its remedial effort. Business executives in East Mecklenburg and retired teachers in Fayetteville coached high schoolers. Across the state, communities launched similar projects, while Hunt and his wife, Carolyn, tutored Raleigh students in reading. And with funds from the state, local school districts expanded remedial programs. These efforts to end deficiencies in the basics paid off, at least when measured by test scores. Each time those who had not passed the exam tried again, half succeeded. By graduation day, only 2 percent of the Class of 1980 were denied diplomas. To North Carolina officials, this is success. The program's aim, they emphasize, is not to reduce the number of high school graduates, but to ensure that they possess, as the statute mandating the test decrees, "those skills and that knowledge necessary to function independently and successfully in assuming the responsibilities of citizenship."

North Carolina is neither first nor unique in rediscovering classroom basics. Similar programs have been springing up across the country at a dazzling pace. For the Class of 1977, for instance, only in Arizona did high school graduates have to demonstrate proficiency—a ninth-grade competency in reading, writing and arithmetic. The other forty-nine states merely were requiring their youngsters to attend secondary school for a specific number of years and to complete certain courses. Various localities, of course, could and did impose tougher standards within their jurisdictions. By 1980, the picture had changed dramatically. A majority of the states—including California, Vermont, New York and Tennessee—were linking the diploma to a minimum competency exam, while a dozen others were using tests to evaluate their students' progress and to identify those needing remedial help.

As in North Carolina, it has been the legislatures which have imposed the tougher education standards in California, New Jersey, Florida, Virginia and a dozen or so other states. In Delaware, Massachusetts and New York, the action mandating testing was taken by the state boards of education or similar agencies. Just about everywhere, however, these actions have been prompted by mounting public pressure. The Tennessee board, for instance, acted primarily because of moves initiated by State Representative Stephen Cobb, a Democrat from Nashville. Explains Cobb: "I was meeting with small groups of constituents all across my district, staying up late, talking about issues. Almost everyone's Number 1 concern seemed to be education. This surprised me. But what shocked me most was seeing full-fledged, card-carrying, unabashed liberals pulling their kids out of public schools and sending them to private institutions. When I asked them why, they told me, 'The public system is not doing the job.' I decided that I had to do something." He introduced a tough minimum competency bill in the lower house and mobilized so much support for it that the Board of Education was spurred to preempt the legislators and act on its own—and quickly. In late 1977, the board decreed that Tennessee high school students, in order to graduate, must pass a minimum competency test in math, spelling, language and reading.

Though the exact contents of such examinations vary greatly throughout the nation, they usually cover at least reading and mathematics. A number also include writing, spelling and language arts, while a few test speaking, listening, consumer economics, science, government and history.[11] Exam guidelines often are very precisely drawn. Albany, Oregon, for example, measures writing competencies in a 100-word essay by permitting no more than five errors in spelling and three each in punctuation and capitalization. Oregon's counties and cities, in fact, probably take the prize for the quantity and detail of skill requirements. Lincoln County tests more than 200 competencies; Albany examines nearly 100. Albany's list had contained 165 items but parents protested that too much was being required, particularly nonessentials. They forced authorities to trim the list. Eliminated, among other things, was a "personal cleanliness" standard which students had to satisfy by showering after at least 80 percent of their physical education classes.

The minimum competency testing movement is meeting almost no popular opposition. New Yorkers did complain, however, that the original test introduced by the Board of Regents was too easy; it subsequently was toughened. In a few instances, tests have been challenged in court, usually on behalf of minority groups. Black organizations have argued that "cultural bias" in exam questions make them more difficult for a black than a white. The result, argue these critics, is that a disproportionate number of blacks will be denied diplomas and hence not considered for better jobs. This basically was the argument in a widely noted lawsuit brought against Florida's Educational Accountability Act. At the time of the court's mid-1979 ruling, 1,342 whites and 3,445 blacks had been denied diplomas for failing to pass the minimum competency exams on all three attempts, despite remedial tutoring. They represented 2 percent of whites and 20 percent of those blacks who had taken the test.

The plaintiffs in the Florida lawsuit wanted the exam declared unconstitutional. Their brief argued, among other things, that Florida had not given the students adequate lead time before imposing the tests, that the tests contained biased questions based on material untaught in the schools and that those who failed were unjustly stigmatized because they would always be branded as "failures." Federal District Judge George Carr agreed with some of these contentions. He ruled, for example, that Florida had been hasty and provided insufficient time for students to prepare for the exams. To remedy this, he ordered diplomas awarded to all who had satisfied the other graduation requirements, such as attendance and completion of specified courses. He also prohibited Florida from making the test a condition for

a diploma until the 1982–83 school year, by which time youngsters will have been in school long enough to ready themselves
for the test. On the most critical question, however, minimum
competency was vindicated. Carr upheld the constitutionality of
the testing and declared that the Florida examination should not
be "invalidated for racial or ethnic bias" reasons.[12]

In contrast to the public's support, the exams receive little
backing from teachers and other educational professionals. This
is to be expected. Implicit in the widespread demand for testing
is a fundamental criticism of the professionals' stewardship of the
public school system. The professionals counter, however, that
testing is no way to raise standards. All that it does, they say, is
force teachers to "teach to the test," short-changing other subjects in order to concentrate on areas covered by the exam. Explained Arthur Wise of the Rand Corporation: "What you do is
cause local school people to become obsessed with the test. The
desire to bring about a good performance on the test will drive
out the rest of the curriculum."[13] In practice, however, this seems
not to have happened, and schools in minimum competency
states continue offering a range of subjects.

Even were Wise's concern justified, it would prove that students indeed do need most of their classroom time for basics. If
anything deserves priority, it should be basic skills. Notes Fred
Burke, New Jersey's Commissioner of Education and a champion
of minimum competency standards: "[Teaching to the test]
doesn't worry me if the tests actually represent standards of mastery to be reached. You've got to teach toward something."[14]
Recent studies confirm what ought to be the commonsense observation that "children who spend more time struggling to
master basic skills outperform children who spend more time on
other pursuits."[15] Minimum competency advocates, moreover,
do not promise miracles. "I'm not so naive to think that our test
is a panacea," says Tennessee's Representative Cobb. "It's a
small first step. But at least with it we can demonstrate to the
public that we are concerned about ensuring quality in the
schools." Cobb here identifies the essence of the passion for
minimum competency. Parents want something done to improve
education and are not willing to trust the professionals to do it.
They thus are demanding laws or decrees to make the educational establishment accountable.

This accountability has been limited mainly to student performance—so far. It has been widening, however, to include the instructional competence of teachers. Says Russell Vlaanderen of the Denver-based Education Commission of the States, an organization established by the states to study education issues: "The movement has all the earmarks of an incipient bandwagon." It is being spurred by the proliferating horror stories of teachers, mostly in elementary schools, who seem to possess barely a nodding acquaintance with the basics. Too often, parents receive a note from their child's teacher that is written in ungrammatical English. And too often are incomplete sentences scrawled by teachers on classroom blackboards.

By mid-1981, a dozen states had begun tightening teacher certification standards; three already were requiring applicants to pass a competency test. A pacesetter in this movement is Florida, which has enacted a teacher competency law over vigorous opposition from the state's chapter of the National Education Association, the nation's largest teacher union. Under a 1978 statute, Florida teachers must demonstrate what ought to be taken for granted: that they can write in a logical and understandable style with appropriate grammar and sentence structure and can comprehend and work with fundamental mathematical concepts. Prospective teachers also must demonstrate that they can comprehend and interpret an oral message.[16] Iowa has adopted the Florida law and intends to get even tougher by requiring that already-certified teachers pass a competency examination.

Rediscovery of basic skills has lead to a rediscovery of the Council on Basic Education. For the past quarter-century, this Washington-based organization, funded mainly by corporations and foundations, has been trying to promote the study in elementary and secondary schools of English, mathematics, science, history, foreign languages and the arts. These are what the Council calls the "generative subjects" that enable a student to master life's other subjects. The Council published some papers, commissioned some studies and generally served as a dependable, persevering advocate of the basics. Its impact, however, was limited. "For a long time here at the Council, we were lonely," admits Associate Director Dennis Gray. No longer. "Now we're overwhelmed with demands," he says, smiling. "We're called on to make speeches, write articles, serve as consultants. The press keeps calling us for information and interpretations. Local school districts are asking us to set up workshops to explain basics for school board members, principals and teachers. It's quite wonderful."

For some parents and educators, though, it is not wonderful enough. They want more than just the bigger dose of basics being injected into the curriculum under pressure from minimum competency exams. They want a curriculum built solidly around the basics. Theirs is a faith that the public school system can be revitalized only by fully embracing the old-time education. These are the purists of the back to basics movement, the most avid advocates of traditional education. It is they who are transforming educational issues into political movements. They represent a phenomenon so new that their numbers have not yet been accurately counted. Yet their enthusiasm and determination are sending ripples across the nation. In Charlotte (North Carolina), Mesa (Arizona), Pasadena (California) and scores of other communities, they have taken over and completely transformed public schools into what are variously called Basic Skills Schools, Structured Classrooms, Fundamental Schools, Academics Plus Schools and by other names conveying deep commitment to basics education.

It was just such a commitment that brought a couple hundred parents, teachers, principals and school board members to San Mateo, California, in late 1980. Their two-day conference was part tent revival meeting—with its witness to the healing powers of basics education. It was part pep rally—with its rousing speakers. It was, however, mostly a how-to-do-it training session—full of practical advice for those fed up with the instruction and discipline in their local schools. The workshop titles themselves could provide a basics education blueprint: "How to Start a Basic School," "School Board Involvement," "Discipline and Classroom Management" and "What do Parents Expect."

This is what Denise Burian had come to San Mateo to learn. Though her two children were still of preschool age, she had been growing increasingly alarmed over what she was hearing from her Pittsburg, California, neighbors. "They told me that their kids have come home from school in the middle of the day and that their teachers didn't even know that they had left the classroom," she says angrily. "Other parents have been shocked when they transferred their children to private schools and were told that the kids would be put back one or even two years in grade because the public school had not been doing a very good job of teaching."

Determined to do something to improve her children's chances of getting a solid education, Burian invited other worried parents to a kaffeeklatsch. Her house was packed. It soon became clear that many residents of industrial, blue-collar Pittsburg saw the public schools as their only educational option. Explains Burian: "I'm committed to public education; I have to be. Many people just can't afford paying for private schools." At the kaffeeklatsch, she and her neighbors decided to ask their school board what could be done to improve instruction. "We went to the board," she says, "and we asked, 'What can we do as parents?' Do you know what they told us? They said that there's nothing we can do, that changes are already underway and that it is a very slow process."

Dissatisfied and angry by what they felt was a patronizing dismissal of their complaints, Burian and her neighbors concluded that they might have to act on their own. While exploring their options, they discovered the basics education movement. "We began learning about basics education and had meeting after meeting; sometimes we met twice a week," she recalls. "To contact others, we sent out newsletters and held bake sales to pay for them." Eventually the school board agreed to conduct a survey to gauge parent interest in a basics school. The board was shocked to learn that more than 30 percent of the respondents wanted such a school. "This would be enough to fill two elementary school buildings," notes Burian triumphantly.

At this point, she heard about the Second Annual Basic Education Leadership Conference in San Mateo and decided to attend along with another Pittsburg parent. Their goal, she says, was "to learn the tactics of establishing a basics school. I wanted to learn how to set up a curriculum, a dress code and a discipline system." She found a couple of surprises at the conference. For one thing, she was pleased to learn that what she and other Pittsburg parents already were doing had worked elsewhere. For another, she did not feel out of place politically. "I'm a McGovern Democrat," explains Burian. "Pittsburg is solidly Democratic and Carter beat Reagan there by a landslide. So I was afraid that getting into a basics education movement meant getting mixed up with a bunch of right-wingers. Was I wrong! They're certainly not that and they're certainly not segregationists. All they are is concerned about their children's education."

They are also convinced that they are riding the crest of a powerful education wave. Enthusiasm rippled through the conference. The hospitality suite, for instance, was cluttered with displays from basics public schools around the country. There were samples of the certificates which schools almost everywhere at one time awarded students to encourage hard work but have become unfashionable—except mainly in traditional schools: "Outstanding Citizen Award," "Academic Excellence Award," "Bursting with Pride" certificate. Piled on a table were the handbooks used by the basics schools, such as the thick Instructors' Manual and Student-Parent Handbook from John Marshall Fundamental Secondary School of Pasadena, California. On another table were copies of the newsletter sent to parents by Sierra View School of Chico, California; one issue announced something that, in an earlier day, would have been a common occurrence in public schools but now would be remarkable—the winner of a handwriting contest. Scattered about were basics schools' scrapbooks stuffed with newspaper clippings, excerpts from student handbooks and copies of the agreements that parents sign when enrolling their children in basics public schools.

The collective portrait emerging from these displays is the antithesis of the student-centered, open classroom that, in varying degrees, typifies the American public school system as it developed during the past two decades. Take, for example, the handbook from Myers Park Traditional Elementary School of Charlotte, North Carolina. It explicitly declares: "The teacher is the central part of the school. She must provide good order, discipline and motivation . . . All classes will be self-contained . . . Reading and mathematics are the most important areas of the curriculum." To the argument that objective grading can injure a child psychologically, the handbook counters: "It is not enough for a child to compete with himself . . . He should also be aware of the accomplishments of others in the class and grade level . . . An honor list will be posted each reporting period." As at other basics schools, Myers Park is old-fashioned in insisting that pupils behave. "Discipline teaches obedience to authority as well as independence," states this public school's handbook. "A child should understand why certain people have authority . . . Corporal punishment is used as the final alternative." Patriotism does not embarrass basics schools. Myers Park is typical in declaring that "every child should know about his country and take pride in it. He must know our great leaders and revere our Flag . . . The Pledge of Allegiance to our Flag is incorporated into the classroom procedure . . . Patriotic songs are encouraged."

At Myers Park and other basics public schools, reading, mathematics, spelling, grammar, composition and other language skills are the curriculum's heart. Though such subjects as science, physical education, social sciences and health also are taught, they are regarded as secondary disciplines.

Classrooms at these schools probably would look familiar to every American over age thirty-five. There is only one teacher in a room, students sit together (usually in rows) and everyone follows the same lesson. Missing are such open-classroom hallmarks as teaching teams, parent aides and the dials, screens, lenses, spools and other hardware of modern pedagogy's mechanical arsenal. Absent too are clusters of youngsters working at a pace and on a topic of their own choosing. In basics classrooms, lines of responsibility are very clear; everyone knows his or her task and recognizes who is in charge. Says Joan Ranney, principal of the Greenville Fundamental School in Santa Ana, California: "I expect the students to learn—and they do; I expect the teachers to teach—and they do; and the superintendent expects me to run the school—and I do."

Equally familiar to the older American would be the demands made by the basics public school. Homework is assigned on at least four nights every week. San Anselmo school in San José, California, expects students to devote Monday and Wednesday evenings to reading and language skills, Tuesday and Thursday evenings to mathematics and Friday evening to long-term reports. Tests are given regularly; almost without exception they require computing math problems and writing sentence or paragraph answers to questions in other subjects. Gone are the undemanding multiple choice, fill-in-the-box answers. Report cards accurately mirror test scores. The grading is almost quaint—running from *A* through *F*—and frequently include marks in citizenship, courtesy and other aspects of behavior. Predictably, promotion from grade to grade is based entirely upon a student's demonstrated mastery of skills.

Though parents are kept out of the classroom, they are expected to be deeply involved in the educational process and usually sign contracts detailing their responsibilities. Typical is the "Agreement of Support for the Fundamental School Program" of the Rolando Park Fundamental School in San Diego. In it, parents must sign a statement that they "have read and understand the goals and philosophy of the school." Then they pledge, among other things, to provide "a time, place and appropriate atmosphere" for homework and to "remove our child from this program if the rules and policies of the school are consistently broken." At another basics school, parents are pointedly reminded that "teachers reinforce moral values, but moral training and religious training are the responsibility of parents." To keep parents abreast of their children's progress, the Hoover Structured School of Palo Alto, California, weekly sends home reports which the parents must sign and return.

Discipline and order are critical elements of the basics public school, and there is little doubt about what constitutes good behavior. Rolando Park requires its students to sign a ninety-point code of conduct, pledging, among other things, to use self-control at all times, to "respect and obey our parents, teachers and other elders," to be "clean in all we think, say and do," to "respect the flag," to "never accept rides from strangers," to stay in line and not push at drinking fountains and to keep "hands off the walls, bulletin boards and windows."

Because basics advocates believe that proper attire contributes substantially to a respectful atmosphere, their schools impose detailed dress codes. At San Anselmo, proscribed clothing includes blouses that do not cover the midriff, high-heeled platform shoes and any clothing bearing slogans in "poor taste," such as T-shirts with "suggestive patches" or ads for alcoholic beverages. Teachers too are sartorially restricted. For San Anselmo's faculty, this means no tank tops, T-shirts with "questionable and inappropriate sayings" or blue jeans. Most basics school have a weekly dress-up day; on it, girls and female teachers wear dresses, male teachers wear ties.

"We have a rigorous code and I sometimes wonder if it really is *that* important, if it really makes *that* much difference if kids wear tight jeans," muses a basics school principal. "But I feel that such things contribute to the mood and atmosphere of the school." If her pupils disobey the code, she calls their parents and sends them home to change clothes. If the parents are not home, she has devised a very effective way of dealing with code violators.

She clads them in acceptable garments that have been donated to the school. "We have a lot of white shirts for boys," she explains. "Well, wearing a white shirt is such an outrageous violation of their fashions that they seldom, if ever, again risk coming to school improperly dressed."

Basics schools, of course, are not always as orderly as advertised. Discipline at times relaxes and not all troublemakers are booted out—despite the tough talk. But here, as with the other main precepts of the basics movement, compromising occurs but rarely. This is especially true of the curriculum. "The children are in school for education and not for all sorts of other things, even if they are worthwhile things," Wallace (Bud) Clark told the San Mateo conference. Founder and principal of Palo Alto's Hoover Structured School, Clark is a widely respected pioneer and zealous advocate of the basics public school movement. He stresses that he will not "take away precious time from teaching the kids what they have to know." Absent from Hoover, therefore, are many social activities which elsewhere are integral parts of the public school year. There are assemblies, but they are not held often; when they do take place, they are only during the lunch period so that students lose no instruction time. Students eat while listening to the program. Equally strict are Hoover's rules on parties. Says Clark: "We permit only four parties per year and each lasts only thirty minutes. And we do not waste a lot of time building up to the parties through elaborate preparations." Parents strongly approve of this. Says Clark: "They tell me, 'You do the educating and leave the socializing to us.'"

Frills similarly are not tolerated at Benjamin Franklin Elementary School in Mesa, Arizona. Principal H. Marc Mason told the San Mateo conference that Franklin does "not emphasize the decision-making skills and lifestyle skills that take up so much time at other schools." When teaching a subject, Mason's faculty stresses fundamentals. "In social studies," he says, "we are much more concerned about teaching where Miami is than about Miami's problems with Cubans."

Mesa parents apparently like what has been happening at Benjamin Franklin. Says Mason: "There is such a great demand to get into our school that parents camp outside our office on the night before registration to be sure to get their kids registered." Other basics principals tell similar stories, and so do many parents. Mrs. Stephen Scable, in an interview with the *California*

Monitor of Education, says that she arrived at the Sequoia Academics Plus School at "3:30 P.M. on the day before registration in order to secure my children a place."[17] In Pasadena, demand had become so insistent after the first basics public school opened in 1973 that the school board was forced to bow to pressure and allow three additional schools to reorganize with a basics curriculum. Attracting parents to Pasadena's basics schools, in part, is the fact that their students have begun scoring higher than other public school students on statewide achievement tests.

Only a small fraction of the nation's public schools have been transformed into basics institutions—so far. A decade ago, however, there were none. What seems to assure their continued growth are mounting parent dissatisfaction with what has been happening to the public schools and the determination of basics' pioneers to spread the word. In this, they are becoming increasingly adept and are organizing to help other parents who want to establish basic schools. One of the first of these groups is the Basic Education Corporation of Sunnyvale, California, cofounded by Bud Clark.

Many communities, meanwhile, have first heard of basics education from Henry Myers, Jr., a member of the Pasadena school board and a one-man organization dedicated to spreading the basics gospel. He travels the country, boosting basics education and conducting nuts-and-bolts workshops on how to convince school boards to establish a basics school. If the board balks, as it often will, says Myers in one of his frequent speeches, "remind the members in a nice way that they are not being responsive to their constituents." Then, he advises, "start a letter-writing campaign; visit the editors of your local newspapers; ring doorbells; and spread a few rumors about the possibility of a recall election for the board." And if it comes to the ballot box, Myers is especially well-prepared—with his forty-three-page manual, *How to Win a School Board Election,* based on his own successful race in Pasadena. The manual offers an overall strategic plan, tactics for organizing precinct committees and samples of electioneering material. As the founders of a number of basics schools attest, voting a sympathetic majority onto the school board is the surest way of getting a green light for a basics school.

Even with these strategies, the vast majority of America's public schools are not going to convert formally to a full basics curriculum. As the pure distillate of the traditionalist movement in education, the basics school and its tenets may be too rigid for most communities. Yet the phenomenon's overall impact cannot be measured only by its numbers, because it influences many of the schools that it does not convert. Apparently because of the example set by the Benjamin Franklin School, other schools in the Mesa, Arizona, area have tightened discipline, adopted a dress code and greatly increased the homework load. Similarly, after a basics school opened in the Chico, California, school district, the "regular" schools restored letter grades on report cards, instituted weekly reports to parents and are limiting the use of parent aides in classrooms. Stories like these are repeated often where basics schools have been established. Though parents may not be demanding a pedagogical swing to the extreme represented by the San Mateo conference, they clearly want more basics in the classrooms. In short, they want a traditional education for their children.

Nowhere perhaps is basics being tested more rigorously than in inner-city St. Louis, one of those bleak, despairing urban deserts where little blossoms, particularly education. On the north side of the city, in an area almost 90 percent black, the basics approach is taking hold of what was a fast-deteriorating school and is transforming and revitalizing it. So dramatic is the change that the school's recruiting poster in truth can proclaim: "Discover the potential in you. Choose Cardinal Ritter Prep High School."

As a private Roman Catholic school, administered by the St. Louis Archdiocese, Ritter is not quite the kind of institution on which the basics movement has been focusing. The main target, after all, is the public school system. Yet Catholic schools have been spared few of the problems that have plagued public educational institutions in recent decades. In addition, Catholic school enrollment is down dramatically and hundreds of schools have closed. This certainly has been the case in St. Louis, where four Catholic high schools have been shuttered since the mid-1960's. And a fifth, Labouré High School, was on the ropes. An all-girls institution, it was located in a neighborhood that had shifted rapidly from nearly all white to nearly all black. Following the depressingly familiar pattern of many other once-vigorous urban schools, Labouré's vital signs started weakening and, most alarming, its enrollment plummeted from 400 to 188.

In an attempt to save the school, the archdiocese called in Stephen Wesley as a consultant in 1978. Though still in his early thirties, Wesley already had earned impressive credentials within the Catholic educational system. Born in Philadelphia and educated in its Catholic elementary and secondary schools, he had studied for the priesthood on scholarship at St. Mary's University in San Antonio and picked up a couple of masters degrees in education, with a speciality in curriculum. After teaching for a few years, he became principal of a Chicago Catholic elementary school and subsequently one of that archdiocese's most dynamic and ambitious young black educators. He soon was lured to Cincinnati and the post of assistant superintendent for that archdiocese's urban schools.

Wesley's work with inner-city schools in Ohio brought him to the attention of the St. Louis hierarchy as it was searching for a way to save faltering Labouré High School. At the request of the hierarchy, Wesley agreed to come to St. Louis to take a look at the school. "When I entered Labouré for the first time, I knew that it was in its death throes," recalls Wesley. "It matched the pattern typical of the dying urban school—like Philadelphia, like Dayton, like so many others. Technically the school was open; in fact, it was almost closed. The staff was confused, the leadership was shaky, the building was filthy and no demands were being made of the parents. These were the same kinds of things that had killed hundreds of once-thriving urban schools."

For hours, Wesley walked through Labouré, looking into classrooms, checking the lunchroom and the gymnasium and chatting with teachers. Remembering this first inspection makes him grimace. "Behavior was a disgrace," he remembers with distaste. "The bell rang and the girls ignored it. They wore hats and earrings in the classroom and they called teachers by their first names. Teacher behavior also was atrocious; some even were wearing blue jeans." The scene for Wesley was *déjà vu.* He explains: "What happened to Labouré is what usually happens when a school goes from mostly white to mostly black. The white faculty just lets go of those things which are traditional to Catholic education. They were told by someone, and they accepted it, that blacks come from a different culture and thus should not be held accountable to the same standards as whites."

After further inspecting the school, Wesley knew what had to be done. He told archdiocesan officials that any attempt to rescue and restore Labouré to what it once had been would be futile. Instead, the school had to be fundamentally transformed into a college preparatory institution with high academic standards. "At first, they thought that I was nuts," says Wesley. "Some of them said that an all-black prep school just couldn't work." What the archdiocese wanted, in fact, was a so-called "comprehensive school" which, in Wesley's words, "would take in everyone and be everything." Stephen Wesley is a first-rate salesman, however, and got his way (those who know him say that he usually does). He was authorized to restructure the school completely and hire the staff he needed. Scouting the country and recruiting Catholic teachers eager to accept the challenge of bringing quality education to the inner city, Wesley eventually replaced half of Labouré's staff; today the faculty is divided about equally between black and white and lay and clerical. The once all-girls institution was made coeducational and, in 1979, to symbolize the new start, it was renamed after the late Joseph Cardinal Ritter of St. Louis.

Curriculum and discipline have been Wesley's most important reforms. Although he protests that he is not part "of any back to basics movement" and insists that Ritter is a "very futuristic school," he in fact is creating an institution that would satisfy almost anyone at the San Mateo conference. At Ritter Prep, education is just about synonymous with the basic skills. Explains Wesley: "Our approach to curriculum is to tell the kids exactly what they will study for the first two years. I'm not impressed by high schools offering a long, fancy list of electives." Reading, writing and mathematics, for example, are drilled into Ritter students over and over. This seems to be paying dividends. Sister Jacqueline Toben, who teaches English and is the school's director of admissions, was at Labouré when Wesley came aboard. "Five years ago," she observes, "the students didn't know enough grammar to write a complete paragraph. Today all we do is write *at least* paragraphs. And in the junior and senior years, everyone now must study American and English literature; there are no electives—no cinema, science fiction or whatever."

Ritter assigns a great deal of work. Wesley boasts that "we keep them at it all the time." This is confirmed by the students, all of whom come from the surrounding ghetto neighborhood. Says Brian Allen, who sports a moderate Afro haircut and wears Ritter-regulation white shirt, tie and gray slacks: "Here, on the first day of school, there is homework to take home. And you never know when they are going to pop a surprise test on you. You've always got to be prepared." Adds Jeri Mitchell, whose white blouse and maroon skirt are mandated by the dress code: "I'd like to go to parties every weekend. But sometimes my mother won't let me. She knows how much work I bring home from school and that it has to get done."

Classrooms at Ritter are self-contained, with one teacher instructing the entire class. Wesley regards the concept of the open classroom with open contempt. "The best way to close down an urban school," he maintains, "is to go to the modular classrooms." His reasons: "The most important thing that we can offer these urban kids is a system that is structured and in which they are held accountable." Predictably, discipline at Ritter is very strict. "Rowdy behavior" is unacceptable, as is "any unladylike or ungentlemanly conduct in word, attitude or action." Cutting classes is a major offense. The school's student-parent handbook states that "if a student decides to cut a class or day of school, the administration will interpret this action as the student making the decision to disenroll him/herself." To return to class, the student must technically re-enroll and pay a fifteen-dollar readmission fee. Fighting leads to automatic probation, so does showing disrespect to teachers or possessing or being under the influence of alcohol or "nonmedical" drugs. These rules are strictly enforced. "We mean what we say," stresses Wesley. "A high school has got to make good on its threats; it cannot afford to bluff. You have to train kids for responsibility."

Though Ritter Prep has not been operating long enough for its performance to be measured—by the number of its students continuing their education at colleges, for example—a visit to the school provides striking evidence of Wesley doing something very right. No policemen are stationed at the school's entrances, nor are hall monitors on patrol. Yet students do not cluster on stairways or in vestibules, transistor radios do not blare and wafts of smoldering marijuana do not lace the air. So quiet are the hallways that classroom doors are kept open and the only sounds filtering out are the voices of teachers teaching, chalk striking blackboards and students responding to questions.

Ritter Prep students are neatly dressed, well-mannered and pay attention to the lesson. As elsewhere in the school, classroom walls and desks are free of graffiti, that infuriatingly ubiquitous signature of fading standards. The school appears very safe. Stu-

dents are not afraid to go into the lavatories, as are their counterparts in other St. Louis schools. Many students appreciate that
they are at a very special place. Says one freshman, alluding to the
heavy homework load: "If my mother can spend the hundreds of
dollars to send me here, I can spend the time to get an education." In sum, to visit Ritter Prep is to journey eerily back through
a decade. Yet the school exists in the present and in, of all places,
north St. Louis. Surveying the quiet, clean corridors and the
polite, industrious pupils, Wesley muses: "And we get the same
kind of kids who go to the other schools in this area."

What Wesley is doing with Cardinal Ritter Prep offers hope
to inner-city schools. If basics can take root in north St. Louis, it
surely can flower anywhere. Basics costs no more (perhaps even
less) than other teaching strategies and requires neither specially
designed buildings nor fancy pedagogical gadgets. But for great
and increasing numbers of parents, the improvements in public
education promised by the basics movement and by minimum
and teacher competency testing are coming too late. They already have given up on the public school system and are fleeing
into private schools at a pace that is creating a boom unprecedented in the history of modern American education.

At a time when the nation's school age population is declining, private school enrollment keeps climbing. New private
schools are popping up nonstop. Growth rates range from the
steady one new school every ten days for those institutions affiliated with the old-line National Association of Independent
Schools to the dizzying two to three new schools per day established by Christian Fundamentalists. Even boarding schools,
after a decade out of favor, have seen their applications jump 25
percent yearly since 1977. In all, some 5.1 million students were
attending private schools as the 1980's opened.

Paradoxically, the private school boom is not reflected in
overall enrollment totals. They actually dropped from 6.3 million
in 1965 to 4.9 million in 1973, before starting to inch up. Yet the
entire drop is accounted for by a single school system, the Roman
Catholic. Primarily because of dramatic population shifts in the
inner city, where the Catholic Church has operated many schools,
its elementary and secondary school population plummeted two
million from the mid-1960's through the end of the 1970's. Since
then, it has stabilized. By removing the Catholic component from

the overall figures, the true boom profile of the Baptist, Episcopal, Jewish and especially Christian Fundamentalist and nonsec-
tarian private schools is unveiled. Their combined enrollment
jumped from 823,000 in 1965 to 1.8 million in 1979, with their
most rapid growth in the late 1970's. In this same period, public
school population has remained constant at about 41 million.[18]

Parents are transferring their children to the country's approximately 20,000 private schools for a number of reasons. In
some instances, elitism is the main appeal. In other cases, it is the
availability of special facilities, such as those for the handicapped
or for military training. At many schools, primarily Christian Fundamentalist and Jewish, the special moral and religious tone is
particularly appealing. Throughout the nation, in fact, more and
more parents are displeased with the purely secular and, in their
eyes, anti-religious environment imposed on the public classroom by a series of court rulings.

Capping private school's appeal is, of course, high academic
standards, particularly the emphasis on basics. This consistently
appears near the top of the list when surveys ask parents why they
choose private education over public.[19] In a very real sense,
therefore, the surging interest in private schooling amounts to a
solid endorsement of basics education. It is a costly endorsement,
with annual tuition ranging from about $700 at some religious
institutions to more than several thousands of dollars at boarding
schools.

Basics even characterizes the deeply religious Protestant Fundamentalist schools. In his study of these institutions published
in *The Public Interest,* a respected and influential quarterly dealing
with social and economic issues, Peter Skerry explains that "the
salesmen, millworkers and auto mechanics who send their children to Christian schools are particularly incensed that the public
system does such a poor job teaching the basics, and they point
with pride to the impressive record of the Christian schools in
teaching reading and math skills."[20] Basics also is attracting an
unlikely (given the circumstances) group of parents to the Christian schools. According to Robert Reverski, the principal of Arlington Baptist School in Baltimore: "The largest single bloc of
parents by profession who send their kids to Christian schools is
composed of public school administrators and teachers. They tell
me that there is no way that their public schools can match our
discipline and academic environment." There is no more telling

indictment of the sorry state of public education than the spectacle of public school teachers and officials choosing private schools for their own children.

Arlington Baptist is a typical Christian school, although its enrollment of more than 1,000 makes it quite a bit larger than most. Its main mission is undeniably spiritual and is forthrightly declared by its parent-student handbook—to put "God and His Holy Word at the center of the educational program" and "to win your child to Jesus Christ as his personal Savior, and then to train him up for Christian service." But prominently listed as the school's second goal is training students "to calculate, read, write, speak, listen and communicate thoughts and ideas to effectively function in today's society." Arlington's curriculum focuses sharply on basics and the school stresses academic competition. Homework is assigned nightly, forty-five minutes for grades one through three, for example, and two hours for high schoolers. As in secular basics schools, discipline and dress codes are exacting and rigorously enforced. Arlington students are penalized for "disrespect to teacher, unclean life, disrespect to others and fighting." Dress regulations go on for four handbook pages and end with the warning that those failing to meet the standards "will not be allowed to attend class."

The swelling private school enrollment is changing the character of these institutions. Long passed is the day when they, with any precision, could be described as elitist or snobbish. Still, denunciations along these lines continue. In a 1978 speech, John Ryor, then president of the National Education Association, blasted private schools as "private enclaves" for the children of "upper-class folks."[21] Though it is understandable why a teacher's union fears expansion of nonpublic education, Ryor's remarks are particularly groundless. It is a fact that children from working-class households have been streaming into private schools in such enormous numbers that in 1980 some 60 percent of private school parents earned less than $20,000.[22] "Most private schools, including Catholic schools, primarily serve the poor —even the underclass," observes a lay consultant to the Catholic school system. "This turns on its head the commonplace assumption that private schools are the province of the wealthy." Working-class parents pinch their pocketbooks painfully to give their children a private education. Says Principal Reverski: "I know of two sets of parents who, in 1979, sold their homes to enable their kids to stay in our school." Adds young Brian Allen at Cardinal Ritter Prep: "I come from a very big family. I know there are pressures on my mother to get money for my tuition."

There is increasingly less basis, moreover, for the assertion that private education is some new form of racial segregation. While schools have been founded for exclusionary purposes, the great majority have not. Indeed, enrollment in private schools by minorities, especially the black middle class, is soaring. At the nearly 800 institutions affiliated with the National Association of Independent Schools, for instance, 12.8 percent of the seniors taking the College Board examinations in 1979 identified themselves as minority—40 percent more than the number who did so the previous year. In California, where busing has been an explosive issue, parents who have pulled their children out of public schools have been enrolling them in private school systems that actually are more racially integrated than the public systems. And not only are blacks, Hispanics, Asians and other minorities attending Christian Fundamentalist schools, some of these institutions have been founded by black ministers.[23] They are seeking exactly what white clerics have sought, a Christian environment and an emphasis on teaching the basics.

Resurgence of traditional education has reached America's campuses. A third of the nation's colleges and universities are now reevaluating curriculums and undergraduate requirements in order to strengthen their once-thriving but recently faltering general education programs. So great is the interest that when an ad appeared in a 1978 issue of *The Chronicle of Higher Education* seeking volunteers for a general education project, more than 300 colleges responded. Meanwhile, countless conferences, seminars and workshops and an avalanche of journal articles, monographs and histories are debating, assessing and promoting general education. "There is a gnawing feeling across the land that we now need what general education has to offer," concludes a 1981 report of the Carnegie Foundation for the Advancement of Teaching.

What general education in fact offers is the antidote to the counterculture's legacy on American campuses. For the half-decade starting with the late 1960's, long-established academic standards were abolished wholesale in a spasm reminiscent of the Red Guards' destructive rampage through China's classical cultural institutions. Course requirements were so diluted that they effectively disappeared; the calibrated range of grades which once reflected academic achievement was squashed into a nearly meaningless two-mark scale of pass or fail; and where the old grading system was allowed to remain, it lost most meaning as a rampant inflation of sorts awarded B's and A's for a performance worth, on the old standard, C's and B's.

This counterculture pandemic afflicted every kind of college —humble and mighty alike. Northeastern Illinois University, a largely commuter campus on Chicago's north side, reduced by half the number of courses which it specifically required for a degree and established what one of its senior administrators calls a "do-your-own-thing curriculum." Elitist Stanford fared no better. For all practical purposes, it eliminated specific graduation requirements, allowing its students to earn degrees by shopping almost randomly among 2,000 electives. As a result, general education on most campuses by the mid-and-late 1970's had become what a Carnegie Foundation report calls "a disaster area." Observes Henry Rosovsky, dean of Harvard's Faculty of Arts and Sciences: "At the moment, to be an educated man or woman doesn't mean anything. It may mean that you've designed your own curriculum; it may mean that you know all about urban this or rural that. But there is no common denominator."[24]

It is to reestablish a denominator and restore standards that colleges across the country are looking at old-time basics with new appreciation. They are undertaking the long, complex and often acrimonious task of rewriting curriculums. Special faculty committees have been appointed and convene in a seemingly endless series of meetings; in some instances, they head off campus for weekend retreats. Through surveys, questionnaires and straw polls, the views of faculty, students and even alumni are collected, collated and weighed. At the heart of the process are the two key questions posed, in one form or another, wherever colleges and universities are restoring standards: "What are the areas in which students should show competence in order to graduate? What are threshold levels below which no student should be permitted to receive a bachelor's degree?"

From a distillation of the collected views and data, proposed curriculum revisions gradually take shape and then are submitted to the faculty for excruciating scrutiny. It was only with tongue slightly in cheek that Jerry Gaff has written a manual entitled *Avoid the Potholes: 43 Strategies for Reforming General Education.* This guide-book for curriculum reform is filled with helpful hints culled from experiences on a dozen campuses. Gaff knows only too well the gutted road of curriculum revision. He is director of the Project on General Education Models (known as Project GEM), a program involving fourteen institutions which are reviewing their general education requirements. The chronicles of Project GEM participants are monuments to the perception of Woodrow Wilson when, as president of Princeton, he observed that changing a college curriculum is more difficult than moving a cemetery.

Difficult it is, but not impossible. The changes are under way and are transforming the academic character of scores of American campuses. Some institutions, like Eckerd College in Florida and St. Andrews Presbyterian College in North Carolina, are adopting rigorous core curriculums which mandate a specific set of courses required of all students. Though most colleges are not going quite this far, they are narrowing considerably the field from which students can select courses to satisfy degree requirements. A few subjects, moreover, are becoming mandatory for all students in order to create something approaching the common denominator of which Dean Rosovsky spoke. All Stanford freshman, for example, now must complete one of several prescribed courses in Western culture. This had been a venerable Stanford requirement until it was abandoned in the frenzy of 1969. Says Carolyn Lougee, a historian who chaired the committee developing Stanford's new curriculum: "The Western civilization requirement was swept away a decade ago because it was denounced for not being 'relevant,' because it was a requirement and students then didn't want requirements, and because they were challenging the right of the institution to tell them what they should be studying." Today's attitudes are quite different. "Now we hear students saying, 'We need more structure; we need advice; we need guidance,'" notes Lougee.

Most curriculum revisions demand increased competencies in writing and quantitative skills; some restore foreign language requirements. Grading procedures also are being tightened. In a study for Michigan State University's Learning and Evaluation Service, Arvo Juola finds that "the decade and a half of grade inflation is finally over." Colleges not only are moving away from pass/fail and back to the traditional *A* through *F* scale, but many are again formally awarding a plus or minus to provide even more precision in measuring student achievement.[25] In sum, colleges and universities are repealing much of the late 1960's and early 1970's.

Repealed too are some of those theories which endowed the radical anti-traditionalist educational experimenters with a kind of intellectual legitimacy. To be sure, most of these theorists are now pretty silent. John Holt, for example, has just about abandoned the schools altogether, becoming a champion of schooling at home. Ivan Illych, whose ideas of "deschooling"—abolishing schools, teachers and texts to allow youngsters to learn by experiencing life—had great impact, has written little about schools in recent years. A notable exception is Neil Postman, the New York University professor who gained considerable notoriety with his 1969 book *Teaching as a Subversive Activity.* The title easily gives away Postman's fundamental message. Along with many other fashionable theorists of that era, he branded the schools authoritarian. Did they not, he argued, subject youngsters to "years of servitude in a totalitarian environment?" As a remedy, he called for a "new education." This meant, among other things, teachers who would deal with relevant topics "that matter" and not with canned, predigested subjects. In Postman's ideal classroom, there would be no tests, textbooks, grades, courses or requirements. In one striking suggestion, reflecting both the tone of his book and the tenor of the times, he proposed that the graffiti from school lavatories be reproduced on large posters and hung in the hallways. They would be, he insisted, more relevant than those posters usually adorning school corridors.

More than a decade has passed since Postman wrote this book, and time has greatly changed his mind. These years, he says, have transformed the role of the school so dramatically that teaching no longer should be subversive. Rather, as the title of his 1980 book proclaims, now there is need for *Teaching as a Conserving Activity.*

Is Neil Postman a reborn traditionalist? Almost. Through his studies of electronic media, he has grown alarmed at television's powerful and persistent assault on the structure of American society. He explains: "I was writing a lot about this and then it hit me: My God, countering the disintegrative effect of TV must become the task of the schools. It must provide the ballast for society to withstand the media's hurricane gales." Repeatedly he denies having joined the back to basics legions. "Crass technocrats who would reduce the schools' objectives to the most simplistic, mechanistic and trivial goals," he says of them. "A sociology of revenge," he calls the movement. For all this huffing and puffing, however, Postman has planted his feet not very far from the basics' mainstream. What his new teacher is to conserve turn out to be some of schooling's most traditional elements. To the delight of basics advocates, for example, he asserts that teachers are in school to teach and pupils are there to learn. And what is to be taught is not "relevance," that shibboleth of yesterday's radical theorists, but standard English, history, the works of Shakespeare, Milton and Melville and other unassailably traditional subjects.

As for the classroom, it must be disciplined, orderly and—traditional. Postman even recommends a dress code for students because it "signifies that school is a special place in which special kinds of behaviors are required [and] in which the uses of the intellect are given prominence in a setting of elevated language, civilized manners and respect for social symbols." If Postman has not quite joined the basics movement, at least he is repudiating forcefully (and, given his earlier writings, courageously) counterculture pedagogy. His new book states: "I suspect you will think in reading [this] that I have turned my back on twentieth-century 'liberalism,' which would be entirely correct."

Here, Neil Postman is by no means alone. Throughout American education, backs are being turned on the kind of liberal excesses that have ruled the nation's schools for nearly two decades. A powerful movement—in truth, many movements—is rediscovering traditional subjects, traditional roles of teacher and student, the traditional environment for the classroom and traditional standards. This return to classroom basics is broadly democratic. It has not been triggered by a handful of theorists, nor is it being led by a corps of elite educators. Rather, the cry for traditional education comes from the nation's grass roots, in calls for competency testing or basics schools, in the flight from the public educational system and in the tightening of college degree requirements.

Obstacles, of course, remain. The leaders of teacher trade unions are generally hostile, in practice, to attempts to raise educational standards. There also is the danger, warns Dennis Gray of the Council on Basic Education, that "everyone will try to ride the back to basics bandwagon. They will call everything 'basic' and you will discover such new 'basics' as physical education, sex education and consumer skills." Clifton Wharton, chancellor of the State University of New York, raises another problem, that "back to basics can mean educational nostalgia . . . the dream of the one-room schoolhouse where an overworked, gray-haired spinster regularly managed to inspire future Rhodes scholars."

And even if these potholes are avoided, can the basics movement successfully counter the unprecedented (and very likely destructive) impact of television on the structure of education? By the night of his or her high school graduation, for example, the average American has spent more hours in front of a TV screen than in the classroom. Can any system of instruction satisfy the appetites, nurtured by TV, for entertainment, constantly changing stimuli, instant gratification and information dished out only in small doses?

On these points, the jury is still out. Until it comes in, there can be no definitive answer to the question of whether returning to basics will better educate America. At least, though, the basics movement is advocating a pedagogy that succeeded in educating earlier generations of Americans. Where the verdict already has been rendered, moreover, is on the movement's impact on policy (and even politics); its momentum and enthusiasm, if little else, attest to a massive reaffirmation of educational traditionalism and the repudiation of the counterculture legacy in the nation's schools and, as such, reinforce the broader resurgence of traditional values.

V

RALLYING
AROUND
THE
FAMILY

IT WAS A TYPICAL WEEK in 1981 in the battle to save the American family. Across the nation, some 8,000 therapists and 1,600 specially trained clergymen were counseling married couples and their families. More than 4,000 university students were taking intensive advanced training in marriage and family therapy, while an additional 22,000 were learning general therapy skills for treating marital and family problems. Record numbers of medical students (twice that of a decade earlier) were studying family medicine. The federal government was administering 300 different family-related programs, some designed specifically for "preserving families." And as the end of this typical week was approaching, about 2,000 married couples were preparing to head off for a Marriage Encounter or Marriage Enrichment retreat.

Throughout the year, meanwhile, nearly 200 Ph.D. candidates were completing dissertations analyzing marital adjustment, happiness or satisfaction. Newsletters dealing almost exclusively with family matters were proliferating, new family-centered organizations were opening their doors (the National Institute for the Family in Washington, the National Jewish Family Center in New York and the Center for the Family in Transition in California, among others), national conferences on the family were being gaveled to order and momentum was picking up for the U.S. Roman Catholic Church's "Decade of the Family" program to develop "family ministry projects and theology."

Week after week saw similar activities and events. Though far from complete, this catalogue testifies to the mounting concern about the state of the American family. Nearly two centuries ago, British philosopher Edmund Burke described the family as "the little platoon we belong to in society." Today this platoon is more embattled than at any time in memory; some warn that the platoon is struggling for its very existence. Recalling what he had learned at 1980's White House Conference on Families, Conference Chairman Jim Guy Tucker said: "People are unwilling to put up with the continued neglect and harm to our families that come from thoughtless action and misdirected policies . . . Families are moving from apathy to anger to action."[1]

Family issues indeed are spurring legions of Americans into action. While political camps of nearly every hue now seem to proclaim deep dedication to the family, the most outspoken and active champions of family issues are the myriad of groups supporting what they regard as the traditional American family. To the howls and protests of their adversaries, they even have captured the politically powerful term "pro-family." Their campaign is a movement primarily of the political right and concentrates much of its mounting strength on the political arena, holding officials accountable on family questions. Many of these new activists campaigned vigorously for candidates who backed the proposed Family Protection Act, the ban on abortions and other key matters identified as "pro-family."

Swelling Ronald Reagan's victory margin and helping defeat more than a dozen prominent liberal senators and representatives, these legions of family traditionalists are emerging as perhaps the nation's most politically potent traditionalist constituency. Nonexistent just a few years ago, their network now spans the nation. Though composed of hundreds of individual, local movements, it is a real network—linked by conferences and newsletters that monitor and analyze whether or not executive, legislative and judicial actions strengthen the traditional family.

Forming this network's backbone are a number of increasingly powerful organizations—Moral Majority, Eagle Forum, Conservative Caucus—and countless local groups such as FLAG (Family Life America God) in Arkansas, which was founded by eighteen women in 1977 and boasted more than 800 members by late 1981. Many of the network's leaders have achieved national recognition: Phyllis Schlafly, Reverend Jerry Falwell and senators Paul Laxalt and Jesse Helms. Others may be less well known to the general public but are household names to "pro-family" activists. There are, for example, Connaught Marshner who edits the biweekly *Family Protection Report,* Betty Arras of the monthly *California Monitor of Education,* Jo Ann Gasper who founded *The Right Woman,* Howard Phillips of the Conservative Caucus, Onalee McGraw, who is education consultant to the Heritage Foundation, Edward McAteer of the Religious Roundtable and Paul Weyrich of the Committee for the Survival of a Free Congress.

Uniting these groups and their leaders is a determination to preserve the traditional nuclear family by defending it from what has been, in their eyes, more than a decade of attacks from anti-family forces on the left. Writing in *Harper's* in April 1976, Michael Novak, the theologian and resident scholar at the American Enterprise Institute, warned that increasing numbers of Americans were becoming impatient with the way the major political parties were treating the family. He warned: "Neglect of the politics of the family is the central issue. It is on this issue that 'a new majority' will—or will not—be built." Novak's words seem to have become prophecy fulfilled—if the surprising outpouring of family-issues activists and voters in the 1980 election is evidence of the movement's potential breadth and dynamism.

Is the urgent alarm over the family warranted? Though this question divides the experts, an all-too-familiar litany of statistics justifies distress about the health of the nation's families. Divorce appears pandemic, with only two thirds of the nation's couples remaining wed until death doth them part. Rarely is an American family encountered which has not had one of its members or close friends involved in divorce. Still-married couples find few exercises more depressing than listing friends who have not been divorced. Such catalogues are distressingly brief, particularly when compared to those that could have been compiled a generation earlier.

Since the start of this century, the divorce rate has soared 700 percent, almost matching the cost of living's acceleration. Except for a brief slowdown in 1977, the rate has increased each year since 1966. So have the absolute numbers. Since 1975, more than one million couples have been divorcing annually, with a record 1,182,000 splitting in 1980. This equals nearly half of that year's total of 2,413,000 marriages. Experts estimate that more than 1 million children annually are involved in divorce cases and that currently 13 million children under age eighteen are living in households with at least one parent absent. That such situations adversely affect children has long been a common sense observation. It is now verified in the 1980 study, commissioned by the National Association of Elementary School Principals, that finds children from one-parent homes have greater academic and disciplinary problems in school than those from intact nuclear families. In both elementary and secondary school, for example, 40 percent of those from one-parent homes earn *D* and *F* grades compared to 24 percent for children with two parents at home.

Even in families spared divorce, households are not quite the same well-tended nests which they were a generation earlier. Today mother most likely is on the job rather than in the kitchen. Over half of the nation's married women are now employed outside the home. It is partly for this reason that Americans are estimated to spend less time with their children than parents in almost any other country.[2] Other ills plague the traditional American family. Cases of illegitimacy and of child and spouse abuse are increasing. So is cohabitation, a phenomenon that weakens the image of the traditional family as a desirable norm. The number of unmarried couples living together jumped nearly 300 percent in a decade, climbing from some 523,000 couples in 1970 to 1,346,000 in 1979.

Professional journals reflect the family's mounting problems. Writing in the November 1980 *Journal of Marriage and the Family,* an issue reviewing the preceding decade's scholarly output, University of Florida sociologist Felix Berardo observes that "this issue contains a variety of topics which either were not included in the 1960's decade review [issue] or were given little attention: sex roles, teenage parenthood, family stress and coping, and violence in the family." In fact, notes Berardo, during the *Journal*'s first three decades, "there was not a single article on family violence . . . During the seventies, however, violence became a 'hot' topic."[3]

Alarming though these statistics are, other figures paint a somewhat rosier picture of the U.S. family. While divorce rates are high, for example, marriage itself remains extremely popular. Not only did the number of marriages in 1980 break all records, exceeding by about 130,000 the 1946 post-war stampede to the altar, but the vast majority of today's divorcees remarry, often very quickly. Within five months of divorce, 25 percent remarry;

another 25 percent do so within a year and still another 25 percent within three years. What this says to the experts is that while
Americans may be unhappy in specific marital situations, they are
not rejecting the institution of marriage. Even today's youngsters,
exposed as they are to the frequent divorces of their elders'
generation, remain exceedingly optimistic about their own
chances for a happy marriage. A 1979 survey by the University of
Michigan's Institute for Social Research discovered that almost
all high school seniors feel that they have a good chance of staying married to the same person for life. Writes University of
Minnesota sociologist Reuben Hill, one of the country's most
respected experts on family matters: "It does not appear that
family life has lost its attractiveness. Very few people in the U.S.
choose, or are forced by circumstances, to forego marriage. We
are still the most marrying of modernized societies."

The large number of one-parent homes unquestionably is a
problem. Yet it is not a recent one; only the circumstances have
changed by which a household loses a parent. In previous generations, desertion or death left vast numbers of children with only
one parent at home. In fact, not until 1970 did single-parent
households resulting from divorce exceed those resulting from a
death. As for the problem of working mothers, though they now
substantially outnumber those of a generation ago, only 23 percent of women with school-age children in 1980 were working full
time all year. And only 10 percent with children under age three
were doing so. Even the cohabitation figures do not necessarily
add up to doom the traditional family. A decade ago, when large
numbers of unmarried men and women began living together, it
was feared that this nontraditional arrangement would become a
popular alternative to marriage. This clearly has not happened;
cohabitation turns out to be a living and emotional arrangement
preceeding rather than replacing marriage. Less than 3 percent
of all American couple households consist of unmarried pairs
(and this includes the many elderly who live together for financial
reasons), compared to 15 percent for Sweden.[4] Communes,
meanwhile, have all but disappeared as a sustaining alternate
lifestyle. Reviewing the research on pluralism in marital and family forms, Eleanor Macklin of the University of Maryland's Department of Family and Community Development concludes that
for most people, the "complex relationship systems, such as mul-

tilateral marriage, sexually open marriage, and communal life [are] too stressful to allow for longterm participation."[5]

To the burgeoning traditionalist family movement, the factors tempering the dire predictions of the family's impending demise provide only minor solace. Threatening the traditional family not only are easy and frequent divorces, one-parent households and full-time working mothers. The greatest danger, and that transforming politically passive women and men into fully engaged activists under a "pro-family" banner, is the legacy of the counterculture's offensive against the validity and integrity of the traditional nuclear family. It is beside the point to "pro-family" advocates that this family model—a poppa breadwinner, a momma homemaker, two or three kids and a pet (typically a dog)—perhaps never quite existed in a majority of the nation's households or that its development is as recent as the nineteenth century. What matters critically, points out Allan Carlson of the Rockford Institute in Rockford, Illinois, is that this nuclear family has served as a healthy normative concept. Writing in *The Public Interest,* Carlson explains: "Cultural and social norms provide a civilization with its ordering principles, its measures of morality and deviance, and its legacy to subsequent generations. They define for individuals the nature of responsibility, the ultimate purposes of social life and the proper basis for human relationships."[6]

The norm of the nuclear family has been under assault for more than a decade, with almost all of the attacks coming from the left. Radical feminists have ridiculed the housewife and denounced the traditional family as an especially oppressive institution. Although she recently has recanted somewhat, Betty Friedan has called family and home a "comfortable concentration camp," while Kate Millett's *Sexual Politics* urges abolition of the family because it supposedly enslaves women.[7] Leftists have resurrected the dormant Marxist critique of the family as a despicable bourgeois institution rooted in male supression and exploitation of women. Beyond this, specifically anti-family leftists have insisted that all family forms are ethically, morally and socially equal and acceptable, including communes, unmarried couples and homosexual liaisons. Even established religious organizations have joined the anti-family offensive. By the early 1970's, explains Carlson, "liberal Protestant and Jewish groups had abandoned . . . normative support for the nuclear family" and just about applauded the emerging variety of family forms.8

These concepts eventually worked their way into legislation, judicial decisions, regulatory agency rulings, college textbooks and even the classrooms of elementary and secondary school pupils. It is this institutionalization of attitudes hostile to the family that has most outraged the traditionalist sectors of American society. "In days most of us still remember, to attack the family would be like attacking the flag," writes William Billings, the executive director of the National Christian Action Coalition, which published the "Family Issues Voting Index" during the 1980 election campaign. "It was not done by decent people. No one thought then of 'defining' the family. It was just there. The relationships were natural and unrehearsed. Everyone knew instinctively what a family was, how its members interacted in love, how each bore the others' burdens, and shared the others' joys. Times have changed."

So have official policies on critical social issues. Opposition to these new policies constitutes the main "pro-family" agenda. Item number one is abortion. Since the Supreme Court's 1973 decision, Roe *v.* Wade, permitting abortion on demand during the first trimester of pregnancy, abortions have become commonplace across the country, with clinics openly advertising for customers. Currently an estimated 1.2 million legal abortions are performed annually in the U.S., a number one-third that of live births. This horrifies traditionalists who argue that life begins with conception; as such, abortion becomes murder. To emphasize this point, abortion's foes use the term "preborn" rather than "unborn" in referring to a fetus. For them, the preborn are entitled to basic rights. Declares Michigan's Pro-Family Coalition in its "Statement of Principles:" "Children's rights must begin with the right to life from the moment of conception."

To turn around official policy on abortion, a very broad coalition has been forged into one of the nation's most powerful special interest groups. While pushing for a constitutional amendment to reverse the Supreme Court's ruling, it also has been fighting successfully to restrict public funding for the controversial operation. Because it concerns what many deeply believe is a matter of life and death, abortion is a *sui generis* issue, transcending the usual boundaries—liberal and conservative, left and right—between groups. Senator Thomas Eagleton, for example, generally earns high ratings from liberal organizations and is no friend of most traditionalist causes, but consistently opposes abortion and sponsored a bill in 1981 calling for an anti-abortion constitutional amendment. The anti-abortion coalition is thus much broader than any other single movement, although traditional family champions play a major role in it.

On a host of other social issues, however, the battle is being waged almost solely by traditionalists. Under the "pro-family" standard, for example, they are challenging the state's erosion of the traditional parent-child relationship. Parents have a right and obligation, maintain traditionalists, to nurture, educate and discipline their children. The health of today's family and of future generations depends on this unique parent-child bond. Yet court rulings and proposed legislation seem aimed at weakening the link and at transferring some of these responsibilities to the state.

This is precisely what the Domestic Violence Bill seemed designed to do and why traditionalists opposed and ultimately helped defeat it. Sponsored in the Senate by Massachusetts's Edward Kennedy and in the House by Maryland's Barbara Mikulski, both ultraliberal Democrats, the bill would have created a federal program to reduce what its backers insisted was an epidemic of spouse and child abuse and other forms of domestic violence. Leaders of the "pro-family" movement disagreed. For one thing, they said that there was scant evidence of any "epidemic." For another, and much more important, they argued that the measure would enable federal bureaucrats to meddle in some of the family's most private affairs.

When the bill came up for consideration in 1980, it enjoyed wide support and was expected to sail through Congress and be signed by President Carter. Like the Consumer Protection Act, the Domestic Violence Bill had an unassailable name. Who could be against a measure against domestic violence? Nonetheless, traditionalists mobilized to block the bill in the Senate. Spearheaded by the Moral Majority, they launched a telephone and telegram blitz urging senators to vote nay. Inside the Senate, the drive was led by Republicans Orrin Hatch and Gordon Humphrey. The campaign paid off; when the proposal came up for a vote, it passed with only a 46 to 41 margin, far from the landslide that originally had been anticipated. Those senators opposing it apparently did so, in part, because they accepted the traditionalist argument. Explained Senator David Boren, the Oklahoma Demo-

crat: "I voted against the bill because I do not believe that the
federal government should become involved in this area."9 The
close vote fatally slowed the measure's momentum. By the time
it was reported out of the House-Senate Conference Committee,
the November elections had given the Republicans control of the
incoming Senate. Though the old Senate could have tried to pass
the bill when it convened in lame duck session, G.O.P. filibuster
threats prevented it from coming up for a final vote. In effect, this
killed it.

The campaign against the Domestic Violence Bill was just a
skirmish. More critical is the battle raging in (and against) the
courts; it is there that the deepest wounds in the parent-child
relationship are being inflicted. Through a series of judicial decisions, parents are being deprived of the right of consent if their
minor, unmarried daughter wants an abortion; additionally, they
need not be notified if she obtains state-provided birth control
devices or is treated for venereal disease or drug and alcohol
dependency. The Washington State Supreme Court in 1975 even
granted a fifteen-year-old girl's request for what amounted to a
"divorce" from her parents. The grounds for such a drastic action: "incompatibility." Presumably accepting the child's argument that she was not getting along with her mother and father,
the court placed her in a foster home with guardians whose views
seemed more to her liking. Discussing the case in the *American Bar
Association Journal*, Bruce Hafen, a former law professor at Brig-
ham Young University and now president of Ricks College in
Idaho, observes that the heart of the matter is that the girl simply
decided "that she preferred not to be subject to the authority of
her parents, although the exercise of that parental authority had
been legally evaluated and declared nonabusive and nonneglect-
ful."10

Decisions like these, which undermine many of the most essential aspects of parents' control over their children, rest on a
relatively new juridical concept called children's rights of privacy.
In theory, the proposition scarcely sounds objectionable; in practice, so-called children's rights collide with the traditional right
and obligation of parents to head the household and raise their
minor children. Affirmation of this right is a central pro-family
plank in the traditionalist platform. In its statement of principles,
for example, the Arkansas FLAG organization proclaims: "The
most important function performed by the family is the rearing

and character formation of children, a function it was uniquely created to perform and for which no remotely adequate substitute has been found. The family is the best and most efficient 'department of health, education and welfare.' " FLAG rejects "children's liberation philosophy" and policies or court decisions based on the concept "that [minor] children have rights separate from those of their family and/or parents." Throughout history, argue traditionalists, children have had their rights restricted for their own good. Such limitations, explains Bruce Hafen, are "a form of protection against a minor's own immaturity and his vulnerability to exploitation by those having no responsibility for his welfare."[11]

A major area in which parents must retain supervision of their children, maintain family issue activists, is sexual education. Yet sex educators, social science professionals and, at times, federal agencies have been devising sex education programs and introducing them into school systems without adequately informing parents. This alone alarms traditionalists. Making matters much worse and transforming sex education into an explosive grassroots issue is the anti-traditionalist tilt of many sex education courses.

Traditionalists, including Moral Majority preachers and other Christian right activists, almost all favor sex education; it simply makes sense that they do so, given their fervent opposition to abortion. But they do not endorse every kind of sex course. Says Reverend H. Lamarr Mooneyham, the Moral Majority's North Carolina chairman: "If values are not taught along with sex education, then sex education should be confined to biology and hygiene." What troubles traditionalists is that sex education curriculums often are value-free. In the guide for a course proposed by California's State Department of Education but eventually blocked by family-issues activists, teachers are advised to discuss with twelve-year-olds whether there is "such a thing as normal." The guide suggests encouraging preteens to talk about the "advantages and disadvantages of the extended family, communes, group marriages, couples living together without marriage, single parenthood."[12]

An Arkansas curriculum favored by professional sex educators calls for junior high schoolers to play a "values clarification" game in which they draw one card from a deck and then discuss the topic on the card. Among the subjects: masturbation, group sex, virginity, abortion, homosexuality and oral-genital sex. Graffiti is another pedagogical method suggested in this curriculum. Apparently to desensitize them, youngsters are instructed to list on the blackboard all the dirty words they know and then discuss them. Too often, complain angry parents, these topics are presented without any reference to moral standards or notions of right and wrong or of preferred and discouraged behavior.

Not only are values absent, but the curriculum often includes material having nothing to do with the underlying reason for offering sex education in public schools—to convey information about conception and contraception. Many of the programs implicitly contain the hidden agenda of sexual consciousness-raising, especially about nontraditional sexual lifestyles. "There is no doubt that the new sex education movement accepts homosexuality, masturbation, bisexuality, group sex and other practices as merely varying aspects of the wide spectrum of 'human differences,'" observes Jacqueline Kasun, professor of economics at California's Humboldt State University and an expert on sex education programs.[13] Teaching understanding and tolerance of homosexual couples may be a commendable exercise in pluralistic America. But what this has to do with sex education strictly defined—the body's biological sexual development, pregnancy, childbirth and birth control—is far from clear. To legions of parents protesting new sex education programs across the country, such consciousness-raising does not belong in courses described as "sex education." Addressing a group of newly elected congressmen in late 1980, Connaught Marshner said: "People are upset that federal funding for family-planning programs has become a subsidy for promiscuity, pornography and endorsements for homosexuality."

This is only slightly hyperbolic, given some of the courses proposed by sex education professionals. Take the case of Arcata, California. There, a curriculum guide for a program intended for seventh and eighth graders includes a section on masturbation in which, says the guide, "the student will develop an understanding of masturbation and become aware of the attitudes related to it; learn the vocabulary and statistics of masturbation . . . [and] learn the four philosophies of masturbation—traditional, religious, neutral, radical, by participating in a class debate." Under the heading "homosexuality," the guide calls for the seventh and eighth graders to "develop an understanding of homosexuality and become aware of the attitudes related to it." Among the exercises designed to foster such understanding is learning homosexuality's "vocabulary and social fads."[14]

In the "Education and Human Sexuality" course at one time proposed by the State Department of Education in California, "learning activities" for nine-year-olds were to include "identifying all the contraceptive methods, services and products available." Then the youngsters were to draw a chart describing each method and "how it is used; how it is obtained; how expensive it is; the risks involved; and how effective it is." Twelve-year-olds, meanwhile, were to take a field trip to "a local drug store to check on the availability of contraceptive products." A passage in a suggested manual for use in an Arkansas sex education course for seventh and eighth graders declares: "Other boys, about one in ten, are interested sometime before puberty in the idea of putting another boy's penis in their mouths." Later the manual advises: "At some time or other, it occurs to most boys to try to put their own penises into their mouths."

Is it any mystery why, after discovering the contents of such courses, parents grow furious and swell pro-family ranks? In the case of California's "Education and Human Sexuality" curriculum, the tocsin was sounded, as it often is on such issues, by Betty Arras in the pages of her monthly, mimeographed newsletter, the *California Monitor of Education.* In the February 1980 issue, she writes: "For the physical, emotional, spiritual and moral wellbeing of our youngsters, this program must be stopped dead. Alert other parents and school officials and express your opposition." At the same time, local groups such as "Citizens for Responsible Education" and "Citizens in Defense of Decency" were mobilizing hundreds of angry parents to attend public meetings with officials to protest the sex curriculum. As a result of this pressure, the proposed "Education for Human Sexuality" course was shelved in favor of another course, which officials promised would not be objectionable to traditionalist groups. Similar victories are being won all over the U.S. when parents learn what really is being taught in the "new" sex education courses being introduced into their children's classrooms.

To test whether such programs meet "pro-family" standards, Phyllis Schlafly, founder of the Eagle Forum, offers parents a twenty-three-point "Sex Education Checklist." Among the questions it poses:

¶ Does the course omit mentioning chastity as a method (the only absolute method) of preventing teenage pregnancies?

¶ Does it assume that all boys and girls are engaging in immoral sex, thereby encouraging them to accept promiscuous sexual acts as normal?

¶ Does it fail to stress marriage as the most moral, most fulfilling and/or most socially acceptable method of enjoying sexual activity?

¶ Does it present abortion as an acceptable method of birth control?

¶ Does it require boys and girls to draw or trace on paper intimate parts of the male and female bodies?

¶ Does it present homosexual behavior as normal and acceptable?

¶ Does it ask unnecessary questions which cause boys and girls to doubt their parents' religious and social values?

Fighting the "new" sex curriculums, judicial erosion of parent-child relations, value-neutral education, readily accessible abortion, publicly assertive homosexuality and denigration of the nuclear family norm constitutes what many groups see as the "pro-family" agenda. It is a traditionalist battle plan for which traditionalist forces are increasingly ready to do battle. Nowhere was this more evident than at the 1980 White House Conference on Families and in the nearly year-long process leading up to it. For the first time, traditionalists challenged the radicals and their counterculture program at a national forum. For the first time, family traditionalists prevented their enemies from monopolizing the discussion of family issues. At the White House Conference on Families, what long had been a monologue was at last transformed into a debate.

The White House Conference on Families (WHCF) was the payoff for one of Jimmy Carter's election promises. During the 1976 presidential campaign, the onetime Georgia governor discovered audiences responding enthusiastically whenever he decried the state of the American family. To dramatize his commitment to family issues, he vowed that, if elected, he would convene a White House-level conference to assess and suggest what could be done to improve the health of the family.

As the WHCF began taking shape during the Carter presidency, traditionalists grew increasingly uneasy. Previous White House conferences, such as the 1970 Year of the Child, had turned into costly extravaganzas that did little more than provide a national platform from which social service professionals and bureaucrats pumped for expanded and new government programs. Particularly unpleasant was 1977's International Women's Year Conference in Houston. Radical feminists dominated this highly publicized forum, using it to savage the traditional family and homemaker.

For many traditionalists, the WHCF promised to become a carbon copy of its predecessors, an exercise that would have only the façade of an open forum. After the numerous hearings and speeches and ballotings, complained "pro-family" spokesmen, the WHCF would arrive at a predetermined conclusion: The family is in trouble and it needs government, especially federal, help. Typically suspicious was Samuel Skousen, a stockbroker in Warren, Michigan, who has served as a Mormon bishop, has considerable experience in family counseling and is very active in his state's burgeoning traditional family movement. "The whole White House Conference was a political gimmick," he says. "It was intended to portray the image of being a grass-roots process, of the nation having been consulted and of delegates having been freely elected. From all of this, it would have claimed that the people had spoken and what they said favored more government programs for the family."

What worried the traditionalists too was that advocates of expanded social programs would control the conference machinery. These fears seemed justified by the WHCF's top appointments. The chairmanship went to Jim Guy Tucker, a very liberal Democrat from Arkansas, while the critically important post of executive director went to John Carr, who had been on the board of the ultraliberal Americans for Democratic Action. Most alarming to traditionalists was the conference's change in name. Originally it was to have been a conclave on *the* family; under pressure from leftist groups, however, the Carter White House made an alteration which, though slight, revealed the hidden aims of the conference planners; instead of a conference on *the* family, it became one on *families*. Substituting plural for singular was an alchemic procedure that fundamentally transformed the conceptual framework of the conference; the traditional American family had been abandoned as a norm.

Family traditionalists were not about to allow these moves to go unchallenged. Just a couple years earlier, they had been caught off-guard by the International Women's Year gathering in Houston. Then they managed to respond only at the last minute by staging a counter-conference while IWY was meeting. This time, however, traditionalists were determined to get deep inside the conference process itself. To coordinate these efforts, a National Pro-Family Coalition was formed, headed by Connaught Marshner. Its twenty-six-member advisory board comprised a pro-family *Who's Who* and included, among others, Robert Billings of the Moral Majority, Onalee McGraw of the Coalition for Children, Charles Rice of Notre Dame Law School and Lottie Beth Hobbs of the Texas Pro-Family Forum. In part, this coalition had been created as a defensive action, after a number of traditionalist organizations had been denied membership in the broad, White House-endorsed ad hoc committee formed to support the WHCF. Called the National Coalition for WHCF, it not only included such established community groups as the Red Cross and the National P.T.A., but also outspoken advocates of the nontraditional family and alternative lifestyles like the National Gay Task Force, Zero Population Growth and the American Association of Sex Educators, Counselors and Therapists. "Pro-family" groups, however, were not allowed to join.

The WHCF process went on for well over a year. It began in September 1979 with hearings at the YWCA in Kansas City, Missouri, and at Bethel College in Lindsborg, Kansas, and continued through March 1981 when the conference staff submitted its final report and recommendations to a less-than-sympathetic Reagan Administration. In the meantime, there were fourteen days of national hearings, like those at the Kansas City YWCA, plus 500 forums and conventions at state and local levels and three grand finale gigantic regional conferences in Baltimore, Minneapolis and Los Angeles. An estimated 2,000 Americans testified (with testimony limited to five minutes in some cases and three minutes in others), 125,000 participated in the delegate selection process and 2,000 attended the three regional sessions as official delegates. At almost every level and in almost every forum, the "pro-family" movement emerged as the single most visible and best-organized participant, fighting relentlessly for adoption of positions reaffirming the traditional family.

In this struggle, merely defining the family turned into one of the conference's most embattled issues. Traditionalists wanted the WHCF to declare that the family is what long has been meant by "family"—a group consisting of persons related by blood, heterosexual marriage or adoption. Opposing this was a definition drafted by the American Home Economics Association and endorsed by many radical groups, including the National Organization of Women. Their definition of a family: "Two or more persons who share resources, share responsibility for decisions, share values and goals and have a commitment to one another over time . . . regardless of blood, legal ties, adoption or marriage." By this, of course, almost any grouping of men, women and children, in just about any configuration, would constitute a family.

It comes as no surprise that at WHCF sessions everywhere, traditionalists fought the radical definition. They enjoyed their greatest success in Minneapolis, where the conference adopted their definition. Elsewhere, at the urging of the WHCF staff, no definition was endorsed officially. Such "even-handedness" angered "pro-family" delegates, who questioned how the conference could address and analyze the impact of policies and programs on the family without a common understanding of what a family is. Complained the FLAG newsletter: "If one cannot agree on a basic meaning of family, it is impossible to have a dialogue" on the issues at the WHCF.

The most critical WHCF battle raged over selection of delegates to the three regional conferences. Just how far traditionalist forces had come since the debacle of the International Women's Year was dramatically evident as the first state-level gathering was called to order in Fredericksburg, Virginia, on a November 1979 weekend. Alerted through Bible study groups, sewing circles, churches, parents organizations and other segments of the "pro-family" network, hundreds of defenders of the traditional family poured into Fredericksburg. The plenary sessions and workshops there were awash in the sea of blue dots which traditionalist forces affixed to their convention identification badges. They dominated the proceedings, and when the votes were counted, they won all but two of the twenty-four delegates elected (an additional twelve delegates were appointed by the governor).

This sweep sent almost palpable shock waves reverberating across the U.S. Obviously terrified that similar forces in other states could organize equally well, the WHCF staff, liberal groups and state officials began changing delegate-selection rules to limit traditionalist influence. Their method was to reduce the number of elected delegates. Thus, while Virginia elected two-thirds of its delegates, the share was slashed dramatically in other states and the portion named by the governor and official agencies was increased. Some states, like Texas and California, did not even elect any delegates; there, purportedly grass-roots representatives were chosen by lottery.

Still, the traditional family bandwagon kept advancing, picking up momentum and delegates all across the country. At the Michigan conference, for example, it captured twenty-five of the thirty-two elected delegates (an additional thirty-one were appointed by the governor). Credited for this victory are Sam Skousen and his wife Beth, head of Michigan's Pro-Family Coalition. Their participation in the WHCF process illustrates how intricately interconnected and extensive the traditionalist network had become. As cochairman of the Anti-Equal Rights Amendment movement in Michigan, Beth had worked with Phyllis Schlafly, the national Stop-ERA chairman. Thus, when Connaught Marshner began forming the National Pro-Family Coalition in Washington and telephoned Phyllis Schlafly in Illinois to ask for contacts in Michigan, Beth Skousen's name naturally came up.

She and Sam relish recounting their campaign to mobilize a large traditional family contingent at the Michigan Conference on Families. "We beat them at their own game," she says. "We organized our people and the opposition didn't even realize what was happening." As they rallied supporters around the state, the Skousens carefully kept very low profiles, issuing no press releases and seeking no publicity. They did not want to alert the conference planners who, they feared, probably would have warned nontraditionalist groups. Sam and Beth Skousen, in short, were planning an ambush—a tactic that would have been completely alien to traditionalists just a few years earlier. To insure that officials remained unaware of just how many pro-family backers might show up at the conference, the Skousens did not request a large number of attendance application forms from the conference secretariat. Instead, hundreds of similar (and legal) forms were run off at a small printshop and distributed through the pipeline forged by the Skousens with the help of church groups, the Ronald Reagan campaign organization and Phyllis Schlafly's Michigan cohorts.

Among the several dozen traditional organizations mobilizing for the conference were M.O.M.S. (Mothers On the March), Christian Schools of Michigan, Concerned Women for America, Happiness of Womanhood, Michigan Alliance of Families, Stop ERA, Right to Life, Eagle Forum and the League of Catholic Women. Like successful chain letter operators, the Skousens sent out material to key contacts in these groups who, in turn, duplicated and forwarded it to members. Telephone chains worked the same way, although Sam admits that he added more than $300 to his phone bill. By the time that the Michigan conference convened in Lansing in mid-April, hundreds of pro-family participants were ready to show up, push their agenda and vote as a bloc for the candidate slate put together by the Skousens.

Most of them caucused an hour before the conference officially convened. Says Beth: "We told everyone that we wanted them there at seven A.M. For some, this was quite a hardship because they were already planning to get up in the dark and drive three or four hours to Lansing. But I just said to them that 'if it's worth your time to even come, it's worth getting there an hour earlier.'" The Skousens had no idea how many would turn up at the elementary school where they secretly had rented a room for the caucus. Though volunteers from Lansing had prepared orange juice, rolls and coffee for several hundred, food soon ran out as nearly 400 men and women crowded into the classroom. They were briefed by Sam. "I told them not to let themselves be manipulated in the workshops," he recalls. "I stressed that they will be pressured to compromise by the liberals and social service types who will be running the workshops in order to obtain a 'consensus' view which then would be reported—as if everyone was in accord. Well, we wouldn't be in accord and shouldn't let ourselves get tricked into making it appear as if we are."

At the caucus, Sam distributed a ten-point "Statement of Principles" and stressed, "Don't sway from this! Don't let anyone talk you out of it!" The statement contained the traditionalist definition of the family and such key "pro-family" precepts as parents' right to educate and nurture their children, the right of the unborn to be protected from abortion and the rejection of government programs as "solutions to family problems." So that they could recognize each other at the conference, Pro-Family Coalition members wore orange identification tags. "It was only when the conference planners and others saw all of us arrive with our bright tags did they finally know that something was up," Beth says gleefully. By then, however, it was too late; traditionalist momentum was unstoppable. As in Virginia, the coalition's members dominated workshops and elected almost their entire slate of delegates.

They did even better in Arkansas, winning all twelve of the elected delegate slots (seven others were appointed). There, the traditionalist movement was organized by Mary and George Schroeder of Little Rock, who belong to the increasingly influential FLAG group. Like the Skousens in Michigan, the Schroeders found themselves in the midst of the WHCF process because they earlier had worked with Schlafly's organization opposing Equal Rights Amendment ratification. The Schroeders' tactics closely mirrored those of Michigan's Pro-Family Coalition. Both groups, like others across the country, were learning from each other by observing proceedings at the conferences in neighboring states, and all were receiving advice and position papers from Marshner in Washington.

Spontaneity as well as organization was a hallmark of the traditionalists' operations. FLAG's case is typical. George Schroeder, an eye surgeon by profession, spent a great deal of time contacting sympathetic groups, planning for the state conference and traveling about Arkansas making speeches. A Sunday evening shortly before the conference was to convene in Pine Bluff, George spoke to a meeting at a Little Rock church. The talk was videotaped by a central Arkansas man who had been dispatched to Little Rock by his pastor, who had just heard about the upcoming conference. He wanted information about it and felt that George's speech would provide it. After viewing the videotape, the pastor invited about two dozen other clergymen, most affiliated with the Arkansas Christian Schools Association, to a Wednesday morning screening. There, they watched George on the tape describe the fast-approaching Pine Bluff conference and warn that it would be dominated by enemies of the traditional family unless defenders of the family attended in great numbers.

Convinced, the preachers went back home to their towns and that night, at regular Wednesday prayer meeting, told their congregations what they had learned. Two days later, these people by the scores began heading for the Arkansas family conference, arriving in Pine Bluff by the busload and swelling the "pro-family" bloc. At the conference, they received copies of a ten-page "information packet" laboriously compiled by George Schroeder. In it, he explained the session's procedures and candidly stated that one of the coalition's main goals is "to make it clear to the American Public through the media, and to demonstrate to our elected representatives, that the grass roots of American citizens reject the social engineering of the feminists and the Kiddie-libbers."

FLAG did precisely that at Pine Bluff, just as the Michigan Pro-Family Coalition had at Lansing and as similar groups were doing or were about to do in dozens of other states. Cumulatively, hundreds of traditionalist delegates were elected to the important regional conferences in Baltimore, Minneapolis and Los Angeles. To be sure, they fell far short of a majority and the recommendations adopted there do not, by any means, mirror a "pro-family" agenda; far from it. Yet the bloc was large and skillful enough to prevent the official recommendations, as had happened at previous national conferences, from being a wish list of the radical feminists, social service professionals, federal bureaucrats and an assortment of leftist and anti-traditionalist groups. Of the thirty-four recommendations endorsed at all three conferences, for example, support for the Equal Rights Amendment ranks a lowly thirty-two. Heading the list were such nonideological issues as calls for employers to adopt family-oriented policies (like flexible work times), new efforts to combat alcohol and drug abuse, an end to tax laws that financially penalize married couples when both husband and wife work and tax breaks to encourage home care for the elderly and handicapped

The White House Conference on Families did not become another Houston—another International Women's Year. "We pro-family people created sufficient opposition," says George Schroeder. "The liberals wanted to stage this thing, but we made it very clear to anyone reading newspapers or watching TV news that there is a very strong traditional stand opposing what the liberals want to do. It demonstrated to our elected officials that there is no consensus." And the WHCF demonstrated something else. It proved to "pro-family" activists and to those opposing them that the traditionalist movement on family issues is becoming a significant political force.

Even before the WHCF, there were early signs of "pro-family" political clout. In the 1978 congressional elections, anti-abortion groups and other segments of the "pro-family" coalition emerged as perhaps the most important grass-roots legions of the New Right. They campaigned against and helped defeat such prominent liberal senators as Iowa's Dick Clark and New Hampshire's Thomas McIntyre. That was only the start. By 1980, they were widely recognized as a powerful factor in national and local elections, registering voters and raising money and campaigning for candidates who opposed abortion and championed the traditional family.

That traditionalist opposition is extremely dangerous is something politicians now widely recognize. Many privately confide that they are becoming more careful when voting on family issues, realizing that an adverse rating by traditionalist groups could be very costly in the next election. Just how solicitous officials now are to pro-family groups is obvious from the booming popularity of FLAG's annual breakfast for Arkansas officials. Only a dozen of the guests invited in 1979 bothered to show up for the morning meal and briefing on family issues. Two years later, it was standing room only, with nearly three quarters of the 135 members of the General Assembly plus Republican Governor Frank White and Democratic Lieutenant Governor Winston Bryant turning up to hear Connaught Marshner plug the traditionalist agenda. Arkansas officials have come to know FLAG well. Its members actively campaign for candidates and frequently testify before legislative committees on the broad range of family issues. When a new sex education course was being considered, it was FLAG, after all, which alerted parents and mobilized opposition.

FLAG's success is mirrored, to a varying extent, by scores of similar groups across the country. They pop up to combat or support a specific issue and then, after it is resolved, often stay in business to deal with other family-related matters. Though their concerns center mainly on local policies, most are deeply committed to passing a constitutional amendment banning abortions. They also closely follow the progress of the Family Protection Act. Originally introduced in the Senate in 1979 by Paul Laxalt and then reintroduced two years later by Iowa's Roger

Jepsen, the thirty-one-section proposal manages to include almost every major item on the "pro-family" shopping list. A half-dozen sections, for example, strongly reaffirm the traditional child-parent relationship and would withhold federal funds from states failing to respect it. States would lose federal funds, for example, if they provide pills or other means of contraception or abortion services to minors without notifying the parents. The bill also would grant parents a "cause for action" in the courts if a school receiving federal funds does not permit parents to visit it or to review textbooks before they are introduced. And if sex education is offered at school, the Family Protection Act would permit parents to arrange for their children to be instructed on such matters by a clergyman or at home.

To bolster traditional family households, the bill would provide tax breaks for those caring for elderly parents, who have children or adopt them and who contribute to savings accounts earmarked specially for their children's education. Divorce would be discouraged by denying federal funds to agencies providing free or low-cost legal divorce services, while the image of the traditional woman would be burnished by cutting off federal support for purchases of textbooks and other educational material denigrating the homemaker's role. Reflecting the traditionalist view that homosexuals, unlike blacks, are not a legal minority, the bill would bar federal agencies from advocating or litigating on behalf of homosexual rights.

During the 1980 election, the pending Family Protection Act served as an important litmus of candidates' stands on family issues. "Everyone always says that they're for the family," explains Connaught Marshner. "But with the Family Protection Act, we've had a test against which self-proclaimed champions of the family could be measured. Candidates could be asked specifically if they were backing the Act and if they would cosponsor it." For traditionalists, this quickly identified their allies and, in a number of cases, helped them get elected. Now that they are in office, their positions and those of other legislators on family questions are going to be closely watched by "pro-family" groups ready to apply political heat to those judged as enemies of the traditional family.

Concern about the current state of the American family is not, of course, the monopoly of the "pro-family" movement. Other groups also are actively involved in family-related programs. Though few embrace the entire traditionalist platform on family matters, much of what they do and the assumptions on which they act in effect enhance the legitimacy of the "pro-family" cause. This is particularly true of therapy and counseling. Professionals in these areas would indeed protest angrily at being bracketed with the Schroeders, Skousens and other family-issues activists. Psychiatrists, psychologists and counselors share few of the traditionalist movement's specific policy goals and certainly almost none of its new enthusiasm for political battle. The direction taken in the past decade by much of therapy and counseling, however, reinforces the concept that the nuclear family is uniquely important.

Underlying recent therapeutic techniques is an implicit assumption that the preferred treatment goal is preserving and strengthening the nuclear family. Observes Peter Steinglass of George Washington University's School of Medicine: "Most family therapists believe in families and family life. They feel that the emphasis on individuals and the whole self-actualization movement, as it has been called, has tended to erode both skills and interests for working in groups. Family therapists, by and large, see themselves as advocates for the family." And in a 1978 interview with *Newsweek,* Salvador Minuchin of Philadelphia's nationally respected Child Guidance Clinic said that "the family approach is the future. I cannot conceive of seeing a child without the mother, a wife without the husband."[15] By placing the family at the center of their concerns, these therapists thus contribute to the public's growing sensitivity to family issues.

Statistics confirm the dramatic growth of family-centered therapy and counseling. In 1940, the country's sole family therapy institute was Philadelphia's Marriage Council. By 1970, according to a survey commissioned by New York's Ackerman Institute, this number had grown to fifty. And then it more than doubled as the family was being most ravaged by the counterculture, adding another seventy-seven institutes by 1980. Membership in the American Association for Marriage and Family Therapy, meanwhile, is soaring; its rolls jumped from 1,000 to 8,000 in the past decade. Scholarly literature is proliferating rapidly. The 1970's saw publication of over 1,500 articles and 200 books on marital and family therapy, along with the appearance of eight new journals in the field. Notes the *Journal of Marriage and the Family* in its November 1980 issue: "Marital and family therapy has emerged from its infancy in the 1950's, achieved childhood in the early 1960's, adolescence in the late 1960's and has reached young adulthood in the 1970's."[16]

Booming too are nonprofessional efforts to keep the family intact. Marriage Encounter sessions, having begun among Roman Catholics, are now sponsored by other Christian denominations and by Jewish organizations. Marriage Enrichment groups, meanwhile, are meeting all across the country. Some 2,000 couples weekly head off for the weekend retreats which typify the Encounter and Enrichment programs. At these retreats, a half-dozen couples (though the number, on occasion, has been several times this) listen to lectures, participate in group discussions and spend hours alone. On the retreat agenda are such topics as husband and wife conflict, sexuality, communication, arguing and even how to play and have fun together.

These themes are approached almost exclusively along traditionalist lines. Neither Encounter nor Enrichment welcome unmarried couples, members of communes, homosexual pairs or those trying to pursue what once was called "open" marriage. Traditional religion, in fact, shapes much of what is said and done during the retreat weekends. The program developed by Ralph Detrick and his wife, Mary, for the Church of the Brethren's Marriage Enrichment sessions, for instance, emphasizes that it relates "biblical faith to a couple's experiences" and interprets the "biblical basis of male-female relationships." Clergymen increasingly see Marriage Enrichment and Encounter as a means of strengthening the family and thus encourage parishioners to participate in the programs. "They are the 'in' thing among the denominations," says Ralph Detrick. "They are on the front burner, part of the landscape that we all assume."

For the couples on the Encounter and Enrichment weekends, as well as those seeking help from professional therapists, what almost always is meant by "family" is the traditional definition. Though these groups certainly are not comrades in arms with the "pro-family" activists, they are allies of a sort, despite how much they squirm at this implication. It is an alliance on an issue enjoying broad popular support. In preparation for the White House Conference on Families, the Gallup Organization conducted history's most extensive survey of American families and found 89 percent saying that the family is an important element in their lives. To 61 percent, it is the *most* important element; to 19 percent, it is one of the most important; and to 9 percent, it is fairly important. Only 7 percent said that family is unimportant.[17] Reviewing the poll results, George Gallup, Jr., says: "Any belief that Americans do not place top priority on the family and family life is completely refuted."[18]

What bothers many Americans, other responses in the poll reveal, is just what bothers the traditionalists. For one thing, nearly half the respondents feel that government has an unfavorable influence on family life. For another thing, and more important, respondents cite declining moral and religious values as major factors harming American families. Of all harmful factors cited, this trailed in importance only alcoholism and drug abuse.

The Gallup findings and the other developments on the family front surely confirm the 1978 observation of sociologist Nathan Glazer. "A funny thing happened on the way to developing a radical critique of the American family," he wrote. "It has turned out that the old model was not so bad after all."[19] It is the almost sacred reaffirmation of this old traditional model that the traditionalist legions have inscribed on their banners. That they are capable of carrying them successfully into political battle they proved in 1978 and 1980. If their numbers keep growing—as they seem to be—they are certain to become one of the most potent social and political forces of the new decade.

VI

LEGIONS
OF
HOMEMAKERS

THE JEAN STAPLETON COMMERCIAL caught Jo Ann Gasper's attention. The actress who had gained national fame by playing Archie Bunker's Edith was appearing on local Virginia television in late 1976 urging women to attend a Richmond meeting which was part of the International Women's Year process. It sounded interesting, and thus when a neighbor later mentioned that she was driving down to Richmond for the weekend gathering, Gasper decided to go along. Up to that time, she had given little thought to the feminist movement or to the Equal Rights Amendment. If pressed, she would have said that she generally supported feminism and the amendment—after all, who was against equal rights? Was she not, moreover, something of a modern, perhaps even "liberated," woman herself? She was the mother of three children, a business consultant and the first female to have earned a master's degree in business administration at the University of Dallas (and, later, she became a high official in the Reagan Administration). How could she not sympathize with what she perceived as the women's movement?

All this changed at the Richmond conference. There, Gasper says, she merely "snooped around trying to discover what the various issues and arguments were." Some discoveries shocked her, particularly the prominent role lesbians were playing in the official feminist movement. She was also shaken by the uncompromising attitude toward abortion and the bad-mannered hostility toward traditional women. Recalls Gasper: "Whenever resolutions came up that contained the word 'mother,' that word

was replaced with 'women.' I asked why this was being done and
was sharply told that 'mothers have babies' and thus the word
'mother' implies support for having babies and opposition to
abortion."

Jo Ann Gasper returned from the conference numbed but
politicized. The first evening home, she told her husband: "If the
women in this country knew what was happening, they would put
down their brooms, get out of their kitchens and start opposing
the feminists." And this is just what she began doing. She joined
the tens and possibly hundreds of thousands of women who have
been similarly shocked, horrified, disgusted and even traumatized by encounters with radicalized feminism.

With God, country and motherhood almost literally inscribed
on their banners, legions of traditional homemakers are mobilizing throughout the U.S. to challenge what at one time seemed the
unstoppable juggernaut of Women's Liberation. They comprise,
in Nathan Glazer's words, a "second women's movement." Its
growing strength and momentum has sent the women's liberationists reeling, forcing them to regroup, reevaluate their positions and tactics and, ultimately, genuflect before traditionalist
principles. By mid-1981, in the wake of the Reagan election victory and the rising tide of traditionalism, Betty Friedan, a women's
liberation founding mother and author of the influential *The Feminine Mystique*, issued a panicked *mea culpa* and plea for feminists
to change their course. Admitting to a "weariness of battle," she
confessed in a *New York Times Magazine* article that the movement
has rolled off track. It has been a mistaken "sexual politics," she
writes, "that cast man as enemy and seemed to repudiate the
traditional values of family."[1]

Friedan's article stops just short of capitulation to the forces
of traditionalism which she and her feminist colleagues so long
had dismissed and ridiculed. Yet she acknowledges reality. Led
by Jo Ann Gasper, Rosemary Thomson of Illinois, Lottie Beth
Hobbs of Texas, Jane Bowes of Florida, Beverly LaHaye of California and scores of other lieutenants—and under the general-
ship of Phyllis Schlafly—traditionalist legions have been winning
one critical battle after another. They played a major role in
preventing the White House Conference on Families from rub-
ber-stamping the feminist agenda; they have rallied opposition to
the Equal Rights Amendment (ERA); and they are emerging as

the most cohesive and numerous force in the campaign to ban legal abortions.

No longer does the feminist movement by itself set the agenda for debate on women's issues. No longer is this movement the voice which policy-makers hear speaking for all American women. Shattering this onetime feminist monopoly are women who previously were content to remain in their kitchens and care for their families and who defined "activism" as attending PTA meetings and baking for church bazaars.

Women's liberation, so fresh and full of hope at the start of the 1970's, has become embattled and intensely hated by the American homemaker. How this happened is a tale familiar to other recent social movements. Fundamentally sound concepts, rooted in valid grievances, have been distorted by extremists who have gained extraordinary power within the feminist camp, primarily by intimidating a moderate majority. As a result, the feminist movement has shifted its sights from what was its original main goal, redressing the most odious wrongs suffered by American women—lower pay than men for identical work, discrimination in job advancement, stereotyping in career choices and denial of essential credit and banking privileges.

A platform with these as planks would enjoy broad support. Public opinion surveys consistently find a vast majority of Americans backing equality for women in the marketplace and workplace. Traditionalist women, moreover, explicitly endorse demands for equal pay for equal work. As much as a decade ago, Phyllis Schlafly wrote: "Are women discriminated against in employment? They certainly have been." From her own experiences, she recalled that "when I started to work at the age of eighteen, I discovered within a few days that I was doing exactly the same work for $105 per month for which men were being paid $125 per month." It is for this reason that she tells feminists: "We support you in your efforts to eliminate all injustices."[2]

During the 1970's, however, injustices in the marketplace and workplace ceased being the main concern of the feminist movement, or at least of a very vocal and often decisive part of it. Less and less had the movement to do with specific and concrete women's issues. Instead, feminism swallowed the counterculture agenda and turned its guns on American society in general. What Jo Ann Gasper confronted in Richmond is what has become, regrettably, the increasingly common face of women's liberation.

Betty Friedan, for example, despite her recent discovery of family issues, has demanded on many occasions the complete restructuring of the nation's institutions. Several of Friedan's feminist colleagues go much further, calling explicitly for the overthrow of capitalism. As for religion, when prominent feminists publicly talk about it, they seldom do so sympathetically. Few statements seem better designed to enrage church-going Americans than the boast by Gloria Steinem, founder of *Ms.* magazine, a leading feminist monthly, that "by the year 2000, we will, I hope, raise our children to believe in human potential, not God."[3]

Feminist statements routinely excoriate males, seeing them as little more than constant oppressors of females. Men have been likened to "cannibals" and to a blood-sucking "Dracula." Some extremists actually assert that men simply are incapable of treating women humanely and that "rape exists any time sexual intercourse occurs when it has not been initiated by the woman."[4] Marriage itself, in the eyes of many feminists, is simply a cost-effective means instituted by men to suppress women, forcing them into an indentured servitude designed to provide husbands with free labor and free sex. Should sex lead to pregnancy, so much the worse. This unique womanly condition, exalted through the ages by the literature, art and religion of all lands, is deliberately maligned by some feminists as "the temporary deformation of the body for the sake of the species." The fetus, meanwhile, sneeringly is called a "tenant," "parasite" and an "uninvited guest."[5] Such remarks surely are what Friedan had in mind when, in her *New York Times Magazine* article, she deplored feminism's "lack of reverence for childbearing."[6]

Understandably, women who devote most of their energies to being wives and mothers are not going to be viewed kindly by the liberationists. The homemaker routinely has been ridiculed and denounced by feminists. Addressing students at the University of Illinois in April 1981, feminist writer Vivian Gornick called the housewife "an illegitimate profession" and then proclaimed that the choice of "being a family-maker is a choice that shouldn't be. The heart of radical feminism is to change that."[7]

While Gornick's statement seems calculated to be especially outrageous, even Betty Friedan has branded suburban housewifery a "comfortable concentration camp."[8] Such disdain for the homemaker deeply distresses women who regard themselves, or once did, as feminists. One of them, Jean Bethke Elshtain, a professor of political science at the University of Massachusetts (Amherst), tells of a feminist meeting which she and a friend attended in the late 1960's when they were graduate students at Brandeis University. "We were struggling with the whole thing of being graduate students and mothers," recounts Elshtain. "Yet when my friend said that this was the dilemma which brought her to the meeting, she was sharply cut off by the woman leading the session who reprimanded, 'We will have no diaper talk in this group.' " Elshtain feels that "this was a very pervasive mood in the movement. It filtered down to ordinary people, not wholly inaccurately, as an expression of contempt for them."

Mere wives and mothers suddenly began feeling strangely defensive. An implicit reproach is now almost universally expected when a woman, responding to a inquiry about what she "does," says, "I'm a housewife." In fact, she often feels so apologetic that she answers, "I'm *just* a housewife." Writes Queens College politcal scientist Andrew Hacker: "Some [of us] are old enough to recall when on radio or television a woman was asked her occupation, if she answered 'housewife' the rafters rang with applause."[9] In their book *The Assault on the Sexes,* Jim and Andrea Fordham tell of a fifty-nine-year-old woman who complains: "All of this women's lib business makes me feel . . . as though I'm nothing. Yet, before, I always felt as though I was doing so much good for my husband and children."

What much of the American feminist movement has become, in short, is a rejection of and an attack on the traditional family. Part of this unquestionably is prompted by lesbians, a small but powerful bloc within the movement. The greatest part, however, appears to stem from a deep-seated general hostility to traditional values. Writing in *The Nation,* Elshtain explains that, after comprehensively surveying feminist works, she has to conclude that "the insistence that the family must be destroyed or smashed (rather than reformed or reconstructed) is a theme running through much radical feminist literature."[10]

At no time has this anti-family, anti-traditionalist face of the feminist movement been more on public view than during the long process culminating with the November 1977 conference in Houston which was the official U.S. observance of the International Women's Year (IWY). Congress appropriated $5 million for the event and Bella Abzug, the ultraliberal New York politician, was appointed chairwoman by Jimmy Carter. No other event so politicized traditional homemakers. In case after case, when asked what first transformed them into activists fighting women's liberation, traditional women answer: IWY. "A lot of church women who had never been involved in public issues had no idea what the feminist movement was all about," says Eva Scott, the first woman to be elected state senator in Virginia. "Well, they learned during the Virginia conference for IWY. They heard the family being attacked; they saw the lesbian workshops and paraphernalia; and they were ill-treated by the feminists."

Almost a year before the Houston gathering, the states began holding their own conferences to adopt resolutions and select delegates. During this process, reports reached Senator Jesse Helms, the North Carolina Republican, that radical feminists were dominating the meetings and refusing to give fair hearing and representation to traditionalists. If true, this would violate the congressional directive that all sides be allowed to participate. To investigate the charges of foul play, Helms convened two days of hearings.

From the testimony of some seventy witnesses, a portrait emerged which substantially confirmed the charges. As a result, Helms submitted to the Senate a report highly critical of the IWY process. The state sessions, stated this report, showed "hostility and discrimination against nonradical groups," contained "lesbian workshops, pornographic entertainment and anti-religious activity" and permitted illegal lobbying for the Equal Rights Amendment and for federally funded abortions. In addition, continued the report, there were frequent "parliamentary violations, railroaded resolutions and rigged elections."[11] Witnesses told of display tables at various state IWY conferences loaded with "militant Marxist literature" and of workshops "on revolution and sex, including an explicit 'how to' course in oral sodomy."

At the California conference, according to one testimony, abortion advocates were offering to teach pregnant women how to abort themselves. In Hawaii, a woman who had wandered into a workshop entitled "Coming Together," which she had thought probably was a panel addressing the reconciliation of differing viewpoints, found herself watching a lesbian skit. It included, among other things, "two lesbians making love together on the stage." Asked Helen Priester of Honolulu, at the Helms hearings: "Why did my tax money go toward [the] showing of a porno stage show?" In Wisconsin, meanwhile, the session was so one-sided that a Chicago newspaper reporter thought that the meeting was being sponsored by the National Organization for Women, the country's leading radical feminist group.[12] And in a testimony before another congressional panel, Rosemary Thomson, an Illinois homemaker and prominent leader of the stop-ERA drive, reported that feminist-controlled steering committees banned invocations at many of the state conferences. Some even refused to permit the display of an American flag "although the United Nations International Women's Year symbol prevailed everywhere." Thomson chronicles the entire IWY saga in her book, *The Price of Liberty.*

The situation was no better at the Houston finale. With only a few hundred of the 2,000 delegates identifying themselves as traditionalists, the radical feminist proposals were overwhelmingly ratified, including pro-abortion and lesbian rights planks. This made them part of the official U.S. statement on IWY. Though feminists triumphed at Houston, the extensive press coverage of the event gave many Americans their first peek at the extremists' powerful presence within the feminist movement. Millions of American women, watching the evening TV news, could only conclude: Those women do not represent me. Cameras caught the near-pandemonium, for example, after a lesbian rights plank was adopted. Women embraced each other or waved clenched fists; one poster obscenely proclaimed, "The Pope Has Clitoris Envy—He Wears Skirts, Doesn't He?" And the balcony was nearly obscured by countless helium balloons emblazoned with the lesbian boast: "We Are Everywhere." Recalls South Carolina State Senator Norma Russell, a delegate at IWY: "I really thought that nothing could shock me. But what I saw in Houston truly left me shaken. It was the closest thing to Hell that I can imagine."

Press coverage from Houston also provided many Americans their first glimpse of the incipient traditionalist movement. Reporters and cameras captured the excitement of the National Pro-Family Rally, hastily arranged to counter the feminist-dominated IWY. In the Astro-Arena, across town from the IWY, some 15,000 women and men gathered from all over the U.S., though no government money paid their way. They endorsed a constitutional amendment banning abortions, opposed the ERA and the "glorifying" of homosexuality in the schools and backed the right of parents to raise their children.

The November weekend in Houston was a turning point in

the contemporary American women's movement. The IWY conference, as it has turned out, was radical feminism's high-water mark. At the same time, the Astro-Arena counter-conference was a launching pad for a mass grass-roots traditionalist campaign. Catalyzed by what they saw as the horrors at IWY and inspired by the numbers, enthusiasm and national coverage of their own rally, traditionalists around the country started fighting back. In so doing, they discovered that the leadership of a number of established women's organizations had fallen into the hands of leftists. Shut out of these groups, traditionalist women have established their own, new structures and their early platoons have grown to legions.

Just how numerous are the traditionalist women's groups now addressing public policy issues is uncertain. They have neither a central secretariat nor a clearinghouse. Some span the nation, such as Eagle Forum and Happiness of Women (HOW); some, like Florida's Women for Responsible Legislation and Arkansas' FLAG, confine their activities to a single state. Others work solely within their congressional or school district. In all, these organizations total in the very high hundreds. Much of their business is conducted over kitchen tables or at coffee shop lunches and many of their volunteers are recruited by telephone or after church services.

Like their close allies in the traditional family movement, these organizations are loosely tied to each other by frequent workshops and conferences at which their leaders share information and compare tactics. Widely read newsletters and magazines closely monitor government action on key issues, provide background material useful for countering feminist arguments and report on the projects of the traditionalist groups. The *Phyllis Schlafly Report, Pro-Family Forum* and *Family Protection Report,* for example, are read by women all over the country.

The most specialized newsletter probably is Jo Ann Gasper's *The Right Woman.* After her numbing encounter with radical feminism at the Virginia IWY conference, she began investigating the IWY process and reported on what she was uncovering in a bulletin she wrote and duplicated herself and then distributed through the growing traditionalist network. Gradually sharpening the newsletter's focus, she began concentrating on congressional activity. Published monthly, *The Right Woman* runs about a dozen pages and lists hundreds of bills of potential interest to traditionalist groups. The newsletter monitors not only the anti-abortion Right to Life legislation and tax measures affecting married couples, but also bills dealing with forced school busing, Social Security benefits and similar matters.

Because *The Right Woman* provides the name of each bill's sponsor and the committee to which it is assigned, organizations know whom to lobby. Once tagged, a bill is tracked as it moves through the legislative process and its status is reported in *The Right Woman.* For up-to-the-minute information, a telephone hotline provides a three-minute tape-recorded bulletin about fast-breaking developments on Capitol Hill.

Unlike a number of feminist organizations, such as the NOW Legal Defense Fund, which received $160,000 in 1980, and "9 to 5," which received $15,000, traditionalist groups get no funds from the federal treasury and thus cannot afford costly commercial offices. They typically are run out of their members' homes. Rosemary Thomson, for instance, has headed a group which monitored IWY, organized the massive anti-ERA campaign in Illinois and has written two books (the IWY volume and one on the White House Conference on Families)—all from her home near Peoria. The dining room table often is her desk; the kitchen counter doubles as filing space; and the basement, with its venerable hand-cranked mimeograph machine, is the printshop for her newsletters, bulletins and alerts. "I operate on almost nothing," says Thomson. "Feminists probably do not believe that there are people so committed to the American way that they work without government money and sacrifice getting new shoes or new carpets and give their resources and time to a cause."

Traditionalist women agree broadly on what this cause is: opposition to legalized abortions on demand, opposition to expanding government (especially federal) authority, opposition to policies that interfere with parents' rights to raise their children, opposition to sex education classes not requiring parental consent and opposition to state-run child-care centers. They ringingly endorse the free enterprise system, patriotism and policies that take account of the differences between men and women. Law must recognize, they argue, a man's obligation to be the primary financial supporter of his family and primary defender of his community. An Eagle Forum brochure insists, for example, that society has a right "to protect itself by designating different roles for men and women in the armed forces and police and fire departments." In contrast to many feminist groups, therefore, traditionalists strongly object to drafting women or sending them into combat. And while traditionalists support equal employment opportunities for all, they reject discriminating against men through affirmative action and quota programs tilted toward women.

Equal opportunity, moreover, particularly includes the option of becoming a homemaker. A minority report on IWY prepared by traditionalists declares: "We recommend that young women be encouraged to train in the career of their choice, and that if they choose the career of wife and mother they understand the value of that career to the strength of the nation."

Many Americans agree with these traditionalist propositions. When asked in surveys if "women's place is in the home," nearly half of the respondents say "yes," while only 30 percent say "no;" these numbers have barely changed in a decade.[13] Women even feel more strongly about this than do men. In the Roper Organization's 1980 poll of American women for Virginia Slims, 51 percent said that they "prefer to stay home" rather than have a job; when this question was put to just married women, 55 percent said that they would like to stay at home.[14]

Being "merely" a homemaker, moreover, is gaining prestige as a career choice. A 1980 study for the President's Advisory Committee for Women reports "a growing appreciation and respect among the public for what homemakers do . . . Since the early 1970's, virtually all Americans have come to feel that bringing up children properly takes as much intelligence and drive as holding a top position in business or government."[15] No wonder that great numbers of women are offended by radical feminism's anti-homemaker rhetoric. In fact, the Committee for Women survey discovered that a large number of Americans are worried about the potentially adverse impact of the feminist movement on the family. Of those polled, 44 percent say that the "women's movement . . . has been a major cause of family breakdown;" 18 percent say that it created "a better family structure," while the remainder feel that it "hasn't made any difference."[16]

Clearly tens of millions of men and women are, to some degree, alarmed by radical feminism. They thus also represent potential recruits for the traditionalist movement. Bringing them into the ranks may require little more than making them aware, as Jo Ann Gasper and others became, of how incessantly their values are being assaulted by the radicals.

This is what happened to Lottie Beth Hobbs of Ft. Worth, Texas, a prolific writer and frequent public speaker who organized the 1977 anti-IWY rally in Houston. Until 1974, however, she had paid little attention to feminism or ERA. After speaking to a woman's group in north Texas that spring, Hobbs was handed a half-page tract attacking ERA. It shocked her. For days, she searched for and read everything that she could find written by prominent feminists. "The more I read, the more I realized that what these women were advocating was 180 degrees opposed to what most women in this country have always believed," she recalls. "I realized that they were out to change the traditional role of women. I just had to help stop them."

Hobbs went right to work, writing her now famous "pink sheet," a single-page flyer printed on pink paper because, she says, "the color is feminine." In it, she reminds the reader that "no women in history have ever enjoyed such privileges, luxuries and freedom as American women." All this is now endangered, the "pink sheet" warns, because "a tiny minority of dissatisfied, highly vocal, militant women are determined to 'liberate' you— whether you want it or not!"

The broadside was an instant success and remains in enormous demand. Its wide distribution has helped mobilize great numbers to oppose the ERA and other feminist measures. Hobbs then founded Women Who Want to Be Women, a group advocating traditionalist measures. Soon men started joining—so many, in fact, that the organization's name had to be changed. Now known as the Pro-Family Forum, it boasts members in all fifty states and in Washington, D.C., and is a major lobby for traditionalist policies.

The youngest traditionalist group probably is Christian Women's National Concerns, established in October 1980 as part of the James Robison Evangelistic Association. "Our purpose," explains Co-director Karen Cameron, "is to educate Bible-believing Christian women in how to apply their convictions in a practical manner." She and her colleagues do this through a series of day-long workshops that, surpassing expectations, have been attracting some 500 women each. Few of these women ever have been politically active. Though workshop speakers scripturally approach such topics as abortion, ERA, homosexuality and drug

abuse, emphasis unmistakably is on the nuts-and-bolts techniques of influencing public policy. Participants are coached, for
example, on how to write and lobby elected officials and how to
prepare for debates, talk shows, lectures and even testimony
before legislative committees.

Traditionalist consciousness too is raised as workshop speakers vividly paint an evil profile of the feminist enemy. Seldom
does Karen Cameron miss a chance to cite Gloria Steinem's boast
that America's children will not believe in God by the end of the
century. To emphasize feminist contempt for the homemaker,
Cameron tells of her own experience at the Texas IWY conference: "When it was my turn at the microphone, every time I
mentioned the words 'wife,' 'motherhood,' 'God' or 'country,' I
was booed and hissed at."

It was at this IWY session that she knowingly encountered
lesbians for the first time. "They were wearing T-shirts bearing
terribly filthy language," she recalls. "And in the bathrooms, they
put up posters inviting other women to experience their sexual
lifestyle. The language on the posters was so explicit and vulgar
that it was three days before I was able to talk to my husband
about it." Such stories invariably shock workshop audiences.
"What I have learned," observes Cameron, "is that the best way
to get a Christian woman committed to being an activist is to put
her in the company of feminists."

Cameron may be slightly wrong. Probably nothing ignites
traditionalist commitment more than exposure to Phyllis Schlafly.
The Alton, Illinois, housewife, mother of six, attorney, author,
political strategist and foreign policy and defense expert is the
traditionalist movement's mega-woman. That she is intelligent,
articulate and charismatic may be the only things on which her
many enemies and many admirers agree. The only other area of
agreement may be that it is thanks to Phyllis Schlafly that the
traditionalist women's movement today has a national identity.

Through her *Phyllis Schlafly Report* and Eagle Forum newsletter, she disseminates nationwide well-researched material and
persuasive arguments against feminist proposals, especially ERA.
At her leadership training conferences in St. Louis, she annually
coaches several hundred men and women who have come from
all over the U.S. to learn how to influence elected officials, raise
money, organize telephone campaigns and develop good press
relations. So numerous are her alumni that when activists in

traditionalist groups are asked where they have learned their techniques or how they have developed their ideas, frequently they reply: from Phyllis.

She also is a one-woman traveling traditionalist truth squad, testifying on Capitol Hill and before state legislatures, appearing on nationally televised and local talk shows, addressing rallies and banquets, debating feminists and fielding venomous questions at a seemingly endless series of press conferences. After founding Stop-ERA in 1972 and Eagle Forum three years later, her incessant opposition to the Equal Rights Amendment (but not to equal rights) has become a trademark. Yet she is accomplished in other areas. Barry Goldwater's surprising capture of the Republican Party's 1964 presidential nomination owed a great deal to her best-selling, self-published book *A Choice, Not an Echo*. In it, she powerfully argued for a conservative as G.O.P. standard-bearer. Eight books have followed, including one denouncing the SALT nuclear arms limitation process and another sharply criticizing Henry Kissinger's foreign policies.

Few Americans arouse such intense passions. Probably no one is reviled more by the feminists. They have burned Schlafly in effigy, insulted her with vulgarities and treated her more rudely than any other person in memory. In a biography of Schlafly, syndicated columnist Carol Felsenthal (who regards herself as a feminist) writes that "feminists seem positively obsessed with her. She is a symbol." They hate her, says Felsenthal, "with an intensity usually reserved for history's full-fledged villains."[17]

With equal intensity is she adored by her supporters. Called variously the "Sweetheart of the Silent Majority" (the title of Felsenthal's biography) and the "First Lady of Conservatism," she is consistently named by conservatives as one of their very most admired woman. Explains political scientist Jean Bethke Elshtain: "Phyllis Schlafly has been able to speak to the fears and concerns of traditional women, in their language, in the way that the feminists have not been able to do. And the fears that she has been raising—such as daughters being hauled into the military—are turning out to be legitimate." It is indeed perhaps because Phyllis Schlafly talks to the American homemaker in a voice and with a vocabulary foreign to the feminists that she so threatens them. Yet even some who hate her confess to a grudging admiration. Karen DeCrow, a former president of the National Organization for Women, told Felsenthal: "I just can't think of anyone who's so together and tough [as Schlafly]. I mean, everything you should raise your daughter to be."[18]

It is the sustained battle against the Equal Rights Amendment that has forged Phyllis Schlafly and her colleagues into a serious social and political force. Yet ERA very nearly slipped past them. When the amendment was approved by Congress on March 22, 1972, ratification by the required three fourths of the states seemed a mere formality. States just about tripped over each other in their haste to ratify. First-place honors went to Hawaii, whose lightning legislature gave its okay just hours after the bill had left Congress. Eight more states ratified it within a week, five more within a month and a staggering thirty within a year. Only eight additional states were needed to complete ratification. That this rush to ratify was long on enthusiasm and short on research and debate hardly seemed to matter. After all, who could object to a proposal which so simply proclaims what seems an obvious democratic maxim: "Equality of rights under the law shall not be denied or abridged by the United States or by any state on account of sex." Nothing appeared to stand in the way of ERA becoming the Twenty-Seventh Amendment to the U.S. Constitution.

Nothing, that is, but Phyllis Schlafly. She and a handful of other conservative women active in public affairs saw ERA as a particularly insidious attack on traditional values. It would elevate to constitutional level, they feared, some of the radical feminist agenda's most obnoxious aspects, deprive women of existing rights and expand federal authority at the expense of the states. It was not until ERA was almost through Congress, however, that Schlafly turned her attention to it, firing her first broadside in the February 1972 issue of *The Phyllis Schlafly Report.* This was the opening shot of a decade-long fusillade.

It began hitting bull's-eyes almost immediately. The fledgling anti-ERA drive slowed, probably fatally, ratification momentum. Only three states approved the proposed amendment in 1974, one in 1975, none in the following two years and one in 1977—bringing the total to thirty-five, still three shy of the magic number. In the meantime, Nebraska, Tennessee, Kentucky, Indiana and South Dakota changed their minds and voted to rescind their earlier approval, an action challenged in court.

ERA's faltering momentum stunned its backers, a sparkling

array of prominent Americans including Presidents Ford and Carter and their First Ladies, Establishment women's organizations like the YWCA and mainline liberal Christian churches. How could a handful of conservative ladies buck all this?

With massive lobbying is how. Schlafly was absolutely convinced that once legislators understood ERA's implications, they would balk at appending it to the Constitution. Over and over at legislative hearings and debates in states considering the amendment, anti-ERA forces have argued that the proposed measure barely addresses the matter of equal opportunity. From the very start of her campaign, Schlafly wrote: "Are women exploited by men? Yes, some women are, and we should wipe out such exploitation." But it is not, she has insisted repeatedly, going to be wiped out by ERA.[19] At one of the Christian Women's National Concerns workshops, Karen Cameron was asked by a puzzled woman: "Doesn't ERA simply mean equal pay for equal work?" Cameron replied, as does just about every traditionalist spokewoman: "No, it doesn't. Of course we're for equal pay. We're for equality, but not sameness. And that's what ERA would mandate. Equal rights are not identical with the Equal Rights Amendment." Equal job access and equal pay, argue Stop-ERA women, already are guaranteed by such statutes as the Civil Rights Act of 1964 and the Equal Employment Opportunity Act of 1972.

That ERA gives women no new rights, however, is the least of the amendment's faults in the eyes of traditionalist women. Their much more important objections are proclaimed by *Phyllis Schlafly Report* headlines of recent years: "How ERA Will Hurt Men," "How ERA Will Affect Churches and Private Schools," "How ERA Will Affect Our Local Police," "How ERA Will Affect Athletes," "How ERA Will Raise Insurance Rates," "ERA and Homosexual Marriages" and "What Sex Equality Means in the Military."

At the heart of traditionalist objections to ERA are four basic contentions:

¶ ERA is absolutist. Under it, laws could make absolutely no distinction between men and women in any matters. Insurance companies could not use sex as a criterion in setting premium rates, a practice that now results in cheaper life and auto insurance for women (because they live longer and drive more safely than men). Religions would be forced to

ordain women as ministers, priests and rabbis. Schools
would have to integrate sexually all sports, even wrestling
and football, and would not be allowed to hold father/son
banquets and mother/daughter teas. "Among the great dangers in the amendment," wrote Elder Boyd Packer of the
Mormon Church in 1977, "is the fact that it would deprive
lawmakers and government officials alike of the right by
legal means to honor the vital differences in the roles of men
and women." For example, argued Packer, a man needs "to
feel protective and, yes, dominant, if you will, in leading his
family." At the same time, "a woman needs to feel protected,
in the bearing of children and in the nurturing of them."[20]

¶ ERA would establish the unchallengeable right to
abortion. On this point, there is agreement by nearly all
those either backing or opposing the amendment. In pep
talks to their troops, pro-ERA leaders emphasize that the
amendment will grant women a constitutional right to abortion. According to a brief prepared by the very liberal American Civil Liberties Union, "abortion is a medical procedure
performed only for women." Because abortion obviously
could not be performed on men, a ban on the operation
"would be tantamount to a denial of equal rights on account
of sex." Just how central abortion is to the pro-ERA position
is evident from the hostility with which ERA advocates treat
deeply religious pro-ERA women who oppose abortion.
They have been insulted and ostracized. At a pro-ERA rally,
members of an organization called Feminists for Life even
have been been prevented from distributing literature proclaiming: "Pro-God, Pro-Life, Pro-ERA."[21]

¶ ERA would deprive women of traditional rights.
Among them: exemption from the military draft and from
assignment to combat units; the legal right, in many states,
to be supported by their husbands; labor laws that take into
account male-female physical differences. These and countless other rights, contend traditionalists, would be wiped out
by ERA. They cite court cases in states which have adopted
their own local equal rights measures. In one ruling, a court
declared that under the state ERA, a husband no longer has
to support his wife or even pay her medical bills. Voided in
various states have been measures that had limited the
weight loads which employers could ask women to lift, re-

stricted the overtime which women could be forced to work and granted women extra rest periods. A federal ERA, argue its opponents, would erase scores of similar statutes in states and cities long ago enacted to protect women. A widely distributed anti-ERA leaflet, "The Real World of the Working Woman," charges that the amendment "is promoted by a handful of women who sit at comfortable desks and never lift anything heavier than a stack of papers." Asks the leaflet angrily: "Why should we be forced to pay for their 'psychological lift' with our aching backs?"

¶ ERA is a federal power grab. The amendment's substantive provisions are not limited to the oft-cited Section I which makes the statement about "equality of rights." Though little discussed by the measure's backers, there is a second section to the amendment which grants to Congress "the power to enforce, by appropriate legislation, the provisions of this article." This wording departs dramatically from drafts of earlier ERA proposals; they would have given "Congress and the several states" enforcement power "within their respective jurisdictions." Now the states have been completely cut out. Should ERA become part of the Constitution, maintain the amendment's opponents, Section II would transfer to Washington the responsibilities which states traditionally have had for marriage, divorce, child custody and support, inherited estates, sex crimes and perhaps even prison administration. In the hands of an activist Supreme Court, this section could magnify Washington's power as tremendously as has the Fourteenth Amendment. Section II's wording, in fact, is identical with the language of the Fourteenth-Amendment. Warned North Carolina's Sam Ervin, Jr., during the 1972 Senate ERA debate, in a statement frequently repeated by ERA opponents: "[ERA will] come near to abolishing the states of the Union as viable governmental bodies . . . It will transfer virtually all the legislative power of government from the states to Congress."

The Equal Rights Amendment is being fought by a lengthening roll of organizations, ranging from local Republican Party groups and farm bureaus to religious and ethnic associations. The Union of Orthodox Jewish Congregations, for example, opposes the amendment as an effort "to legislate away the basic sex role differentiation fundamental" to Jewish law. To the Southern Baptist Convention, ERA ignores "the Biblical role which stresses the equal worth but not always the sameness of function of women." And the Lutheran Church-Missouri Synod balks at the amendment because, among other things, of its "assumption that a particular solicitude for women is inherently an insult to their humanity. Christians especially reject this insinuation."

Waging the main anti-ERA battle have been the groups spawned, in large measure, by Phyllis Schlafly. They have concentrated almost exclusively on states which have not ratified the amendment or where local ERA-type proposals have appeared on ballots for voter approval. To influence legislators, traditionalist women have organized letter-writing drives and phone campaigns, collected signatures on petitions at shopping centers and staged rallies. To win public backing, they have been speaking before any group willing to listen—Kiwanis and Rotary clubs, college student forums, Bible classes and church meetings. Even prayer has been marshaled, with statewide anti-ratification vigils in at least Florida and North Carolina.

Illinois probably has witnessed the most ferocious battle. By late 1981, its legislature had taken more than a dozen votes on the measure without mustering sufficient support for ratification. This particularly humiliated pro-ERA forces because it made Illinois the sole northern industrial state not to approve the amendment.

It is not that ERA backers have not been trying. Illinois legislators have been wooed and pressured on behalf of the amendment by some of the nation's most powerful leaders (Jimmy Carter, George Meany) and famous entertainers (Alan Alda, Jean Stapleton). Carter even flew in to address a joint session of the General Assembly, while Illinois Governor James Thompson suggested that there would be "jobs, roads and bridges" for legislators who came over to the pro-ERA side. Enormous resources, moreover, were committed in Illinois by such national pro-ERA groups as ERAmerica and the National Organization for Women. To orchestrate the ratification drive, NOW President Eleanor Smeal regularly commuted to the state. Her most spectacular effort was the May 1980 mammoth rally in Chicago's Grant Park which attracted at least 20,000 (estimates range up to 50,000) backers from across the U.S. and included 100 organizations, among them socialist, pro-abortion and homosexual rights groups.

What the Illinois pro-ERA movement has been bucking, however, is Phyllis Schlafly on her home turf. No more than a phone call away have been 20,000 Eagle Forum members and other zealous Stop-ERA volunteers. In each of the state's fifty-nine legislative districts, Schlafly has appointed a chairwoman who, in turn, has recruited and organized local (in some cases, even block) groups. This grass-roots network, on signal, has inundated the legislature with phone calls, letters and telegrams, has trooped into Springfield to visit and badger the lawmakers and has presented them with truckloads of homemade cakes, jam and apple pies to underscore the argument that ERA endangers the traditional homemaker. So thorough has been the Illinois Stop-ERA drive that it contacted local radio and television stations to remind broadcasters that the federal "Fairness Doctrine" requires balanced coverage of public policy issues.

A spark plug of Illinois anti-ERA activity is Elizabeth Clarke, whose spacious Lake Forest home is a hive of volunteers. There they prepare packets of anti-ERA literature mailed throughout the state and U.S. (cost: $2 to $3 per packet), organize phone campaigns and shopping center blitzes and arrange rides to Springfield for groups wanting to call on their state representatives. Others also drop by the Clarke household to search through her several dozen bulging ERA files for information needed for debates, speeches, talk show appearances, letters to the editor and fact sheets.

Clarke herself routinely has delivered a half-dozen anti-ERA speeches a week, a pace accelerating to several speeches daily during the peak periods of interest when ERA has neared yet another vote in the legislature. Wherever she goes, she lugs a folder heavy with data and anecdotes to buttress her case against the amendment. "I carry around enough information to relate ERA to any group," she says. "When I speak to businessmen, for instance, I outline how ERA will adversely affect their business. When I speak to church groups, I talk about how ERA can force ordination of women."

Clarke relishes most encounters with new converts to the anti-ERA cause. A favorite Clarke story involves a woman who came up after a speech and said that she now was against ERA because she has seen what absolutist, inflexible government regulations can do. This woman, it turned out, owned a maternity shop at which a young man had applied for a job. Explaining that most pregnant women probably would not want to be helped into maternity outfits by a man, she said that she would not hire him. As a result, she has had to defend herself against charges of job discrimination. Another convert was a music teacher. Recalls Clarke: "She told me that she never thought that she would agree with me but now does. What turned her around was an official notice that because of existing federal anti-discrimination laws regarding sex, her school had to abolish its boys' and girls' glee clubs (they discriminate by sex, after all), and merge them into a single chorus. She said to me, 'That is just crazy. I now understand what you are saying and I support you.'"

Clarke's efforts and those of her coworkers have been paying off, admit her adversaries. "Pro-ERA grass roots simply are not as strong as the anti-ERA grass roots," says John Matijevich, a legislator from North Chicago and chief sponsor of the 1981 ERA ratification bill in the lower house. "The reason men in the legislature are voting against ERA is not that they, as men, are opposed to it. It is because Phyllis Schlafly and her folks are so actively opposed to it."

It is this intense and sustained opposition that has been defeating ERA almost wherever it has been contested. There is no better evidence than this for Phyllis Schlafly's contention that ERA sped swiftly through so many state legislatures only because it had not been carefully scrutinized or sufficiently debated. Once time was taken for both, ERA began running into trouble. Not only have the five legislatures voted to rescind ratification, but ERA-type measures have fared poorly at the ballot box in some of those states whose legislators had approved the federal amendment. Voters have rejected state ERAs, for instance, in normally liberal Wisconsin in 1973 and in liberal New York and New Jersey in 1975.

Iowans followed suit in 1980, defeating their state ERA by 55 percent to 45 percent, although the measure's opponents were outspent six to one. Explains Iowa Stop-ERA Co-director Jean Baldwin, in a *Des Moines Register* op-ed article: "Today motherhood is being met with ridicule and hostility. Women choosing to be homemakers are being scorned. Voting down the ERA was one way for the public to show their support for traditional moral values."[22]

Though ERA has been stymied by an opposition of unanticipated ferocity, the amendment ironically has continued scoring high in public opinion surveys. The pollsters apparently have not been picking up the anti-ERA campaign's full impact. With their nationwide sampling, they probe areas not only in the thick of an anti-ERA campaign, but those in which there has been very little organized opposition to ERA. Once a state ratified the amendment, after all, the battle there in effect was over; there was no point in committing resources for an anti-ERA drive. (Notable exceptions have been states in which local ERAs have been on the ballot.) The anti-ERA effort thus has concentrated mainly on the twenty states which did not quickly ratify the amendment. As a result, many areas have not been exposed to a systematic and prolonged refutation of ERA. Residents there know little about the amendment but its alluring name. When asked if they support equal rights for all, understandably they are prone to answer "yes."

Polling on the ERA, in fact, is mostly an exercise in asking loaded questions to which a negative response is almost unthinkable. A Harris poll, for example, asks, "Do you favor or oppose the Equal Rights Amendment?" Gallup questions: "Do you favor or oppose a constitutional amendment which would give women equal rights and equal responsibilities?"[23] To be against ERA in these samplings, the respondent would have to admit to being against equal rights for women. Yet this is not what the fight over ERA has been about. Survey questions, indeed, generally fail to touch the issues most alarming Americans about ERA. This is why ERA scores high on the polls but low in the legislatures and ballot boxes.

A few surveys have focused on the issues making ERA controversial, and these yield quite different results. When asked by Harris if women should be assigned to combat, 68 percent opposed and 29 percent favored it. When CBS News/*The New York Times* queried whether "women should be ministers, priests and rabbis," female respondents said "no" by 50 percent to 43 percent (though men favored it 52 percent to 39 percent). On abortion, the numbers also tend to support the anti-ERA, anti-abortion position. Only a minority of Americans approve of abortion as a means of discretionary birth control. A majority favors abortions solely for saving the life of the mother and for terminating pregnancies resulting from rape or incest. Though no sampling specifically has addressed ERA's Section II, it is extremely unlikely that much of the public, given its current mood, supports that section's wholesale transfer of power from the states to Washington.

Perhaps more reliable than opinion surveys as a barometer of feelings about ERA are the 1980 election results. Voters in Illinois, North Carolina, Oklahoma, Florida and South Carolina—states in which the amendment was still being contested—increased the anti-ERA bloc in their legislatures. The only woman to be elected U.S. senator that year, moreover, was Florida's Paula Hawkins, an ERA opponent. ERA backers Elizabeth Holtzman of New York and Mary Buchanan of Colorado both lost Senate bids. Further evidence of waning ERA fortunes was its dismal showing at the 1980 White House Conference on Families.

As 1982 opened, ERA was heading into the home stretch. Its doomsdate is June 30; on that date, unless ratified by thirty-eight states, the pending amendment expires. A last-minute ratification is possible, though unlikely. Yet this would not diminish by much the impact of the impressive battle mounted and waged by Stop-ERA forces. It has been dramatic testimony to the resurgent strength of the "second women's movement." From the very start, it has been women who have fought ERA, and if it dies, traditional women will have killed it.

With the anti-ERA battle winding down, traditionalist women's groups are turning to other issues. "We are teaching our members how to get involved in their local communities," says Karen Cameron of Christian Women's National Concerns. "They are learning how to influence their school boards, how to be sensitive to semantic tricks in laws and resolutions and how to avoid being duped."

High on their emerging agenda is the fight against legalized abortion, an issue with which many women long have been concerned. Increasing attention too is being focused on sex education in public schools and measures to bolster parents' rights to raise their children. An important dimension of parents' rights is control over the textbooks used by their children. "How long has it been since you have read one of your children's textbooks?" asks a 1981 Eagle Forum letter signed by Elizabeth Clarke. A Texas couple, Mel and Norma Gabler, have been reviewing textbooks for two decades, and their work is widely used by tradition-alist circles. Now they are being joined by dozens of women's groups which obtain and scrutinize elementary and secondary school texts for their implicit messages on religion, patriotism, morality and traditional values. They must do this, explain tradi-tionalists, because feminists and radical groups have been pres-suring publishers for more than a decade. As a result, today's texts suffer from an anti-God, anti-religion, anti-patriotism, anti-capitalism and anti-homemaker slant. Asks the February 1981 Eagle Forum newsletter: "Why are our children not taught (1) the terrible risks & penalties of promiscuity, (2) the greatness of America, (3) the proven superiority of private enterprise, or (4) the failure of socialism?"

Especially alarming, claim these groups, is the disappearance from school books of traditional images of men, women and families. Bowing to feminists, publishers and state education offi-cials, it is argued, have eliminated the homemaker from the books, substituting the "liberated" woman. Charges Kathleen Sullivan, a leader of Illinois Stop-ERA: "They have changed the whole concept in children's minds of the roles of home and homemaker." In a 1981 testimony before the Illinois Commis-sion on the Status of Women, she insisted that "there is no legitimate reason why women in the home should not be por-trayed in our textbooks. We, the career homemaker, should be encouraged, should be honored and recognized as the amazing professionals that we are." To achieve this, she urged educators, publishers and legislators to reemphasize "the positive values of motherhood." This message is being carried to the publishers and to school boards and state textbook commissions by commit-tees being formed across the country by Eagle Forum.

With its interests expanding, Eagle Forum opened a Wash-ington office in early 1981. Though headquarters remains the Schlafly household in downstate Illinois, a Washington presence allows closer monitoring of the national legislative process and more direct impact on it. During its first months of operation, for example, it coordinated appearances of a dozen witnesses before congressional committees on matters affecting women and on behalf of Ronald Reagan's budget cuts in education. The goal, says Noreen Barr, manager of Eagle Forum's Washington office, "is to be close enough to the process here so that we can alert

our local organizations when an issue needs grass-roots backing
—or opposition."

It is the existence of grass-roots legions, battle-tested in the
fight against ERA, that contrasts most dramatically with the past.
In the 1960's and 1970's, only one voice spoke in the name of
American women and it was a voice hostile to traditional values.
For all its claims to have been speaking for a broad constituency,
this voice represented a narrow segment of the national community—mostly urban, mostly upwardly mobile, mostly professional, mostly secular and mostly articulate women. "I just couldn't
understand where a lot of these feminists were coming from,"
reflects political scientist Jean Bethke Elshtain. "Their attacks on
the family were so alien to my own experience. Their attacks in
general were nothing more than the universalization of a particular and limited kind of experience."

That this tiny group for so many years set the discussion
agenda on women's issues reflected, in great part, its close and
often intimate ties with the communications media. Sharing with
the feminists, to a great degree, a similar educational, social and
professional background, many in the media were inclined to
believe feminist analyses and accept feminist conclusions. For an
urban-bred journalist, the worlds of the Rosemary Thomsons
and Karen Camerons were (and remain) distant and alien. Otherwise hardened editors, moreover, were intimidated by feminists.
As a result, pro-feminist women were assigned to controversial
stories, such as the Houston International Women's Year and the
fight over ERA. Is it any wonder that discourse on women's issues
was conducted in a feminist tongue?

No longer, of course. Traditional women successfully have
ended the feminist monopoly of the public platform. After long
dismissing Phyllis Schlafly, Lottie Beth Hobbs, Jo Ann Gasper
and their colleagues, feminists have been forced to take seriously
the traditionalist movement. Exhorts feminist leader Betty Friedan in her 1981 *New York Times Magazine* plea for the movement
to alter its course: "Feminists intent on mobilizing women's
political power are, in fact, defeating their own purpose by denying the importance of the family."[24]

To be sure, traditionalists neither dictate the agenda nor
dominate the proceedings on the public policy platform. Yet they
have shattered the feminist domination and have proven to themselves that they can make a difference and influence public policy.

Were traditionalists to withdraw from the field, feminists are certain to reoccupy their old ground. But withdrawal seems unlikely. Insists Jo Ann Gasper: "We never again will be able to be just wives and mothers. We will remain activists. We have learned painfully that our families are threatened and that, to defend them, we must remain politicized. In a sense we have been traumatized. And in this sense, conservative women have been raped by the radical feminists—something we will not let happen again."

2

A NEW
TRADITIONALIST
MOOD

VII

FAITH
OF OUR
FATHERS

ONLY A HUGE SHEET of canvas was needed to make it the biggest tent revival meeting in American history. From across the U.S., more than 200,000 deeply religious Christians streamed into the nation's capital to pray publicly for their country at a day-long "Washington for Jesus" rally. Gathering in front of the Smithsonian Institute and later in various auditoriums, the friendly, enthusiastic crowd sang hymns, held hands, prayed and, mostly, listened to dozens of preachers calling for general repentance and divine intervention in the nation's affairs.

Among those journeying to the capital on that bright day in April 1980, were Michael and Cheryl Truitt. This was not the first time that they had come to Washington to demonstrate. In May 1971, they were among the hostile and at times violent throngs who had stormed into the city protesting continuing American participation in the Vietnam war. In the years since, Michael has become a pastor. As he told a *Christianity Today* reporter at the "Washington for Jesus" Rally, "the Lord made himself felt to us. He changed our lives and so here we are, for a completely different cause."[1]

Changed too are the lives and cause of some of the most popular and influential entertainers of the protest era. Changing with them is their music. Arlo Guthrie has converted to Roman Catholicism and writes songs proclaiming his new faith. Bob Dylan, now a born-again Christian, no longer rails against authority but sings gently about Christ's Second Coming.

By no means have all the youthful radicals of the countercul-

ture era converted from protest to prayer. Yet the Truitts, Guthrie and Dylan are far from unique. They symbolize a transformation of form and substance that is sweeping nearly all of
America's religious communities—Protestant, Catholic and Jewish alike. In denominations and congregations across the country,
the faithful are rediscovering traditional expressions of their belief and are demanding traditional forms of worship. They are
returning to the faith of their fathers. Observes Joseph Fichter,
a Jesuit who teaches sociology at Loyola University in New Or-
leans: "God is popular again. Everyone is talking about Jesus."
Fichter sees "an awakening of dormant Christians." This is a
development, he writes in the Catholic weekly *Commonweal,* contradicting "the much advertised spread of secularism, material-
ism and scientism in the American society."[2] To Protestant
theologian Richard Lovelace, the nation may be at "the beginning stages of a major religious awakening."[3]

The U.S., of course, has always been a profoundly religious
land, something that especially has astounded foreign visitors.
Alexis de Tocqueville, everyone's favorite overseas observer of
the American scene, a century and a half ago noted that "the
religious atmosphere of the country was the first thing that struck
me on arrival in the United States. The longer I stayed in the
country, the more conscious I became of the important political
consequences resulting from this novel situation." Gallup Organization surveys confirm that this still remains "novel." While 94
percent of Americans today "believe in God or a universal spirit,"
only 72 percent of De Tocqueville's fellow Frenchmen now do;
believers in West Germany total 72 percent, in Scandinavia 65
percent and in Italy, host to the Vatican, 88 percent. The faith gap
between Old World and New is even more pronounced in the
responses to Gallup's question: Do you believe in life after death?
In the U.S., 71 percent answer "yes," compared to 33 percent in
West Germany, 35 percent in Scandinavia, 39 percent in France,
43 percent in Britain and 46 percent in Italy.[4]

Other signs also testify to America's religious vitality. In surveys conducted in 1978 and 1979, for example, Gallup found that
more than 80 percent of Americans believe that Christ is divine,
a like number believe in the Resurrection, more than one third
of the adult population has had a "life-changing religious experience" (a phenomenon broadly known as being "born again"),
two thirds believe that God "rewards and punishes," half believe

that God started the human race by creating Adam and Eve, 42 percent of parents say grace before meals with their children and nearly one third of parents pray or meditate with their children.[5]

What has been happening within U.S. religion, however, transcends quantification. It is not so much a matter of church membership or attendance (though both are climbing), but of the nature of faith itself. Americans of all ages, educational backgrounds and social groups are filling the pews or watching the television preachers of those churches offering a strong measure of the old-time religion—a heady dose of Scripture, an inspiring liturgy, an explicit hierarchy of values and a stern code of morals that makes a clear distinction between right and wrong. It is religion which defines its primary task as ministering to the spiritual needs of the flock rather than as mounting crusades to "reform" their flock's social, economic and political institutions.

This movement has many faces—born-again Christians, evangelicals, Fundamentalists, the millions who get their religion from radio and television's electronic pulpits, charismatic Catholics and increasingly observant Jews. They are rediscovering traditional religion after a long period of theological experimentation, liberalization and permissiveness. "There has been a tremendous turnaround," University of Massachusetts sociologist Wade Roof told *The New York Times.* "Early in this century, the Fundamentalists were made to look as if they were out of step while the world was moving toward a modern, scientific viewpoint. Now the opposite prevails. Those who are affirmative and walking with confidence are the conservatives."[6]

As a traditionalist resurgence, Americans' return to the faith of their fathers shares characteristics with the broad movements discussed earlier—back to basics in education, business battling the government Leviathan, the pro-family offensive and the homemakers countering radical feminism. Yet the differences are critical. The resurgence of religious traditionalism represents mainly a change of mood. It is an essentially private affair and not at all activist in the sense of mobilizing to change public policy. The evangelicals, for instance, do not try to achieve their spiritual goals by circulating petitions, manning telephone banks or forming political action committees. Movement for them is seen in the faithful switching churches, replacing ministers or, in some cases, initiating new programs within a church or denomination. As such, the traditionalist momentum in religion does not have the same direct and immediate public impact as do the more activist traditional forces concerned with other sectors of life.

Yet the changes in religion are at least as and perhaps more important than the others in assuring the long-term ascendancy of traditional values. Those religious beliefs and practices now being enthusiastically embraced create the spiritual, moral and even intellectual framework that complements and reinforces the other traditionalist movements. And the changes underway in the nation's religious communities give great numbers of traditionalists confidence, usually for the first time, to address specifically nontheological social issues. It is this which is prompting preachers (and some rabbis) to step down from their pulpits to politics.

The awakening of traditional religion, like the traditionalist renaissance in other areas, to a great extent specifically rejects the dominant values and practices of recent decades. Being repudiated is a style of Protestantism and Judaism that became ultraliberal in its theology and politics and ultra-activist in its application of the social gospel.

In religion, such repudiation moves more slowly than in the other sectors. Dissatisfaction only gradually percolates up from the pews or, on occasion, filters down from the pulpits. Though gradual, the trend nonetheless is now so undeniable that liberal Protestantism has been declared "an endangered species" by no less a spokesman of mainstream American Protestantism than the University of Chicago's Martin Marty.[7] He is particularly talking about what are known as the mainline churches, those both long established and well established on America's religious and social landscape. They include not only the patrician denominations that dominated colonial and early America—Congregationalists, Presbyterians and Episcopalians—but also the nineteenth-century revivalist sects that since have achieved respectability, such as Methodists, Disciples of Christ, Lutherans and even some Baptists.

Endangering the mainline species is the steady hemorrhaging of its membership rolls, severely depopulating the congregations and turning worship services into lonely gatherings. Simple statistics tell the story. Throughout U.S. history, mainline churches continually added members—until the mid-1960's. Then a slide, unexpected and shocking, began. Between 1965 and the end of the 1970's, though U.S. population grew, the United Methodist

Church plunged from more than 11 million members to 9.7 million; the United Presbyterian Church fell from 3 million to 2.5 million, the Episcopal Church from 3.4 million to 2.8 million, the American Lutheran Church from 2.5 million to 2.3 million and the Disciples of Christ from 1.9 million to 1.2 million.

To some extent, these drops were the result of attrition as elderly members died and were not replaced by younger people. Yet there also has been a good deal of denominational jumping. A study commissioned by the Southern Baptist Convention finds that 40 percent of American Protestants now belong to a different denomination from that in which they were raised. When they switch, they typically move away from liberal mainline to conservative churches.

Here again, statistics speak volumes. Between 1965 and 1978, Southern Baptist membership soared from 10.7 million to 13.2 million (it totalled less than 5 million in 1940), Seventh-Day Adventist from 364 thousand to 535 thousand, Mormon from 1.7 million to 2.6 million, Jehovah's Witnesses from 330 thousand to 519 thousand and Assemblies of God from 572 thousand to 932 thousand. In this same period, the Roman Catholic Church climbed from 46 million to 50 million. Reviewing these figures in their 1980 book *The Search for America's Faith,* George Gallup, Jr., and David Poling conclude that "the Presbyterian, Episcopalian and United Church of Christ communions cannot long exist as viable church organizations nationally if the declines of the seventies persist in the 1980's."[8]

The search for the causes of their chronic membership losses has become something of a minor industry for mainline churches and their associated academic communities. By the mid-1970's, the Presbyterians, Methodists and the United Church of Christ had separately ordered major studies of their shrinking rolls. In the meantime, "church growth" emerged as a new area of theological specialization. Its practioners, like Donald McGavran of Fuller Theological Seminary, are eagerly sought out by endangered denominations for advice on how to halt and reverse the alarming decline.

There are no quick fixes, caution the academic experts. Nor are there simple explanations for the losses in some denominations and gains in others. Catholic University sociologist Dean Hoge has analyzed the phenomenon extensively. In a 1981 study, he warns that "church commitments do not exist in individuals' personalities in isolation from other values and commitments. Rather, they are a part of a cluster of values and attitudes." As such, a denomination may not be able to do much to regain or even hold members if it finds itself essentially out of tune with the tenor of the times. And the current tenor is increasingly traditionalist. Examinations of the data and discussions with a broad sampling of experts support, once caveats are stripped away, the rather bluntly stated conclusion of Reverend Bailey Smith, the president of the Southern Baptist Convention. Says he: "Every denomination that has gone liberal has gone down. They have less faith in God."

This argument is put more elegantly by Dean Kelley, a prominent Methodist minister, in his extremely influential 1972 study *Why Conservative Churches Are Growing*. The original title would have been an even better clue to his central thesis. He had planned to call the book *Why Strict Churches Are Strong*. What this means, he recently wrote, is that "for most of humankind, what matters in religion is not so much its doctrines and tenets as how it gathers the lambs unto its bosom and protects and supports and strengthens them and keeps them there."[9] The growing churches are gathering and supporting their flocks by maintaining rigorous standards, imposing strict discipline on its members' lifestyle as well as beliefs, projecting certitude and confidence and providing "authoritative answers to their perplexities."

By contrast, explains Kelley, the churches losing members primarily are relativistic and individualistic on matters of belief and very lax and permissive in enforcing their canons. They lack, moreover, missionary zeal and sense of purpose. "A person with religious needs," concludes Kelley, "would tend to be attracted to a religious group that seemed to take itself seriously by insisting that it knew what it was doing and that its members practice what they preach."[10]

Kelley's description of weak churches clearly fits mainline Protestant behavior of the past few decades. Standards have been low. Just about anyone could join the neighborhood Methodist, Presbyterian or Episcopal Church. There have been few entrance requirements; almost never are new worshipers asked to testify to their faith and explain, verbally or in writing, how Christ has come into their lives and changed them. In the enthusiastic attempt to pursue ecumenism, differences between denominations have been deliberately blurred. Suddenly Methodists were stumped trying to explain just how they differed from Presbyterians or Congregationalists. Denied by exaggerated ecumenism of being a very special time in a unique place, the worship service and the church began losing a measure of their uplifting majesty.

Spiritual uplift, in fact, no longer appeared to be the mainline churchs' top priority. Pastors became more administrator than padre, less concerned with saving souls than planning church dinners and bazaars and organizing bowling and softball leagues. "Coffee and mimeograph ink began to take on the nature of sacraments," says John Shelby Spong, the Episcopal bishop of Newark. Writing in *Christian Century,* he recalls that in a newly constructed church in which he once served, the "costliest room per square foot was the kitchen. It was the envy of every restaurant in town. That the building had a gymnasium and an elaborate kitchen, surrounded by a few classrooms, said a great deal about our concept of what a church is."[11]

What this says, simply, is that their churches were spiritually starving mainline Protestants. It thus should not be surprising that United Methodist officials, in a recent study of their small churches, discovered that growing congregations are those served by ministers trained not at mainline but at evangelical seminaries, where the emphasis is on spirituality, preaching and witnessing.

The mainline's spiritual hunger results from more than the bowling leagues and gourmet kitchens. At fault too has been the minister's determined (at times, fanatic) attempt to make his church socially relevant and politically activist. Preaching a 2000-year-old gospel thus has paled beside the opportunity to fulminate against the U.S. commitment to South Vietnam or to Western Europe. Women's liberation, affirmative action, rent control, oil company profits and nuclear power all have seemed more appropriate sermon themes to mainline clergy than the Old and New Testaments. This certainly has sent many of the faithful fleeing. It did D. Keith Mano, a novelist and columnist for *The National Review.* Writing in that journal, he describes the anguishing experiences which drove him from the Episcopal to the Russian Orthodox Church. Among his most painful recollections was his constant anxiety as he entered Episcopal parish churches in New York City, wondering "what would it be this week? A woman —a media-consecrated lesbian?—administering the chalice; a vapid-chic modernization of the liturgy; a sermon on Marxist-Christian dialogue?"[12]

Such dismay about the state of their churches is shared by many mainline clergymen. Take the extreme, but illustrative, case of Reverend L. Ray Sells. In many respects, he was the quintessential young United Methodist minister in the 1960's and 1970's. Between 1965 and 1971, he worked in inner-city Indianapolis as a church pastor and community center director. For the next seven years, he headed an urban ministry for the Gary, Indiana, area. "I was involved in all kinds of things," recounts Sells, "neighborhood groups, day-care centers, health-care facilities, the civil rights and anti-war movements. Eventually I came to realize that my spiritual life had become like a bar of soap—it got down to a very thin, transluscent sliver."

Just how thin that sliver had worn struck Sells dramatically one night. He had been pressing Indianapolis officials to raze or board up some abandoned housing in a run-down neighborhood. These efforts were getting nowhere and his frustration mounted. Then a young girl was raped by a vagrant hanging around the abandoned buildings. Sells was enraged. "Because the city was not moving fast enough to take care of the matter," he says, "some colleagues and I simply decided that we would have to move, take affairs into our own hands. We planned to torch the whole block of derelict housing. We would get rid of those buildings ourselves, rather than stand by and watch girls raped."

Sells actually went to the site with all the materials required for the arson. "There we were, ready to do it. But we didn't," he recalls with a shudder. "It just was too wrong a thing to do." Afterward, he says, "it scared me and made me look deeply inward. I discovered that I had been left without anything on which to decide those kinds of issues." Sells began reconstructing the foundations of his faith and even went on periodic retreats at a Roman Catholic monastery in order to regain a sense of spirituality. Today he helps direct the United Methodist Church's growing evangelical effort.

Planning arson, of course, is typical neither of what has been happening to mainline clergy nor to mainline congregations. More than most others, Sells was very deeply (almost totally) immersed in civic, rather than religious, affairs. Yet his experience is an instructive albeit extreme lesson of the dangerous consequences of spiritual hollowness. And it is such a hollowness which has become increasingly characteristic of mainline Protestantism.

How different it is in the traditionalist churches. In contrast to the indulgent and permissive mainline attitudes, the conservative message is unambiguous. It proclaims that finding God is not easy. It requires extraordinary effort and commitment. By defining this efforts and commitment and by making great demands of the faithful, conservative churches simply allow no opportunity for hollowness to set in. The required belief in Christ is too intense, the profession of faith too public and too frequent, the lifestyle too morally rigorous and the missionary obligation to spread the Good News Gospel too serious.

At the core of conservative Protestantism are some twenty-seven million adult evangelicals, half of them Baptist, a tenth Methodist and only 1 percent Episcopalian. (Another four million evangelicals are Roman Catholic.) This enormous and growing body of believers is sometimes referred to as the Third Force in American Christianity, taking its place beside the two older "forces"—established Protestantism and Roman Catholicism. According to a Gallup survey commissioned by *Christianity Today*, America's leading evangelical magazine, 62 percent of the nation's evangelicals are women, 25 percent of the evangelicals have completed college, 10 percent are professionals and a mere 5 percent are divorced or separated. Though they are evenly divided between all income brackets, they are not evenly distributed about the country; 43 percent are in the South, 25 percent in the Midwest, 17 percent in the East and 15 percent in the West.[13]

With such great numbers and so wide a distribution across the nation geographically and within the population, evangelicals understandably differ from each other in many respects, forming a variegated mosaic. Yet they also share some very important beliefs. Like other Christians, they see Christ as savior and redeemer. To this they add a fervent faith in Christ's imminent Second Coming to earth and a belief in the unique and essential inspirational power of Scripture.

Joining a church for an evangelical is an extremely important personal event, far more momentous than merely signing up at a local congregation. Evangelicals have to experience a spiritual conversion in which they accept Jesus Christ as their personal savior. Commonly this is known as being "born again" or "twice born," terms that come from the New Testament story of Nicodemus. In it, Christ says, "Except a man be born again, he cannot see the kingdom of God." Later in the passage, Christ explains, "A man is born physically of human parents, but he is born spiritually of the Spirit." For some, such spiritual rebirth is a dramatic, almost explosive moment of divine revelation. For most, however, rebirth comes gradually, in stages of ever-intensifying belief.

Evangelicals share a fierce determination to "evangelize"—to carry the good news, share the faith and win souls for Christ. They launch crusades *a la* Billy Graham, hold tent revivals and preach on radio and television. An evangelism handbook prepared by the Southern Baptists in Oklahoma states quite explicitly: "We have an evangelism mandate given by our Lord. He met about 500 members of the early church on a mountain and commanded them to go out and preach the gospel to everyone. There is no way that we can sidestep that mandate and honestly claim to be followers of Jesus Christ." It is this mandate which prompts evangelicals to approach strangers and ask: "Do you know Jesus Christ as your personal savior?" And it is this mandate that is inspiring the Southern Baptist Convention's "Bold Mission Thrust" campaign of tent revivals, crusades, house-to-house proselytizing, a publicity blitz of radio and TV spots, bumper stickers and billboards and intensive workshops to train one million "soul winners." The Baptists' goal: To "tell every citizen of the U.S. about Christ by 1990" and "every human being on the planet" by 2000.

One of the most successful nonstop evangelical efforts is Bill Bright's Campus Crusade for Christ, now a $71-million-a-year operation which has grown far beyond the U.C.L.A. campus on which it was founded in 1951. At more than 150 American colleges and universities and at many overseas, Crusade staffers organize evangelical students into teams to visit sororities, fraternities and dormitories and there personally testify to the saving faith that they have found in Christ. These teams, according to the Crusade, contact about one million students yearly.

Off-campus, the Crusade carries the gospel to special target audiences through nearly two dozen separate ministries. Athletes in Action, for example, literally fields teams in basketball, wrestling, track, soccer and gymnastics. They compete with lay teams (often compiling an enviable record) and then use the athletic field as a platform from which to describe how they have come to Christ, how this has changed their lives and how others too can be saved. On military bases, meanwhile, GIs are being "witnessed" to by the Crusade's Military Ministry. And at the hub of national political power, congressmen, White House and Capitol Hill staffers, judges and even foreign diplomats are the targets of the Crusade's twenty-four-member Christian Embassy Mission in Washington.

With its executive ministries, the Crusade annually hosts seminars and "evangelistic dinners" for some 10,000 businessmen and claims that more than 3,000 of them "indicated decisions for Christ" in 1980. At these dinners, the guests listen to prominent corporate executives explain how Christ has come into their lives. Bright's most ambitious current project is raising the extraordinary sum of $1 billion by the mid-1980's to finance a vastly expanded worldwide evangelical campaign. Much of this is earmarked for training great numbers of lay Christians to share their faith with others.

It is not only in their enthusiastic evangelizing that evangelicals differ from other Protestants. They also take their religion decidedly more seriously than do all Protestants as a group. According to the *Christianity Today*-Gallup poll, 89 percent of evangelicals versus about 60 percent of all Protestants say that they derive much consolation from their faith in God and that the only hope of getting into heaven is through a personal faith in Christ; 67 percent of evangelicals compared to 40 percent of Protestants view the devil as a personal being; 45 percent of evangelicals but only 16 percent of Protestants read the Bible daily and 13 percent of Protestants (0 percent of evangelicals) do not read it at all; 81 percent of evangelicals versus 58 percent of Protestants believe that human life started when God created Adam and Eve; and 46 percent of evangelicals versus 22 percent of Protestants donate a tenth of their income to their church.[14]

Within the broad evangelical movement, the most prominent branch is the Fundamentalist. Because all Fundamentalists are evangelical, the two terms sometimes are used interchangeably. But this usage is very misleading, for not all evangelicals accept Fundamentalism's strict precepts. In this sense, Fundamentalists are a sub-group within the huge evangelical body.

Fundamentalists take their name from *The Fundamentals,* a

twelve-volume series of articles published between 1910 and 1915. These tracts were written to reaffirm some of Christianity's most basic tenets against the critical onslaught by liberal theologians and the so-called modernists. History probably best remembers this early Fundamentalism for one of its most articulate and flamboyant spokesmen, William Jennings Bryan, and for one of its most humiliating moments—its 1925 Scopes trial battle against the teaching of Darwinian evolution. Popular press coverage of the trial, in fact, made Fundamentalism look so foolish that it withdrew from national public view for decades.

During this period, Fundamentalism was a hazy concept to most Americans; it was a term employed mostly in derision, synonymous perhaps with holy roller and descriptive perhaps of some backwater region called the Bible Belt. But with the emergence of Jerry Falwell, Pat Robertson and other Fundamentalist television preachers and the growing Fundamentalist involvement in the secular world through, among other things, political movements like the Moral Majority, this sub-group of evangelism has been receiving increased attention.

What most distinguishes Fundamentalists from their fellow evangelicals is an unbending fidelity to the Bible. Scripture is "inerrant," Fundamentalists maintain; it is literally true and provides the only acceptable guidance for human behavior. Capturing the essence of this maxim was the Southern Baptists' Bailey Smith when he declared: "I believe that Jonah was a literal man who was eaten by a literal fish and vomited up out of a literal stomach. And he was in a literal mess."[15]

Because the Bible is so central to their belief, Fundamentalists are unyielding on the matter of scriptural purity. For example, the Southern Baptist Convention in 1980, reflecting the ascendancy of Fundamentalists like Smith, adopted a resolution urging its seminaries and other institutions to "preserve doctrinal integrity" and to hire as staff and faculty only those "who believe in the divine inspiration of the whole Bible, the infallibility of the original manuscripts, and that the Bible is truth without any error."[16]

What most Americans probably note first about Fundamentalists is their fear of the secular world's corrupting influence. To protect themselves from corrosive secularism, they neither dance nor listen to modern music; they do not use tobacco, alcohol or drugs; they neither gamble nor play cards; and many even do not go to movies or watch television.

When they do get involved in the world outside their church, Fundamentalists generally are socially and politically conservative. For them, as for most other evangelicals, the Bible leaves no doubt that abortion violates the sanctity of life, that promiscuity violates marriage and that homosexuality violates the human body. Though they recognize a scriptural basis for a social gospel teaching concern for the poor, Fundamentalists insist that the church's top priorities must be preaching the Bible and winning souls for Christ. Other goals are secondary. Frequently quoted is Bible Institute Founder Dwight Moody's epigram: "You don't polish brass on a sinking ship." It is this conservativism that most sharply sets off Fundamentalists from left-wing evangelicals, a relatively small group advocating active involvement in social issues and supporting liberal government programs.

Integrating faith with life is the evangelical Christian's ideal. Probably nothing comes closer to realizing this than the nation's eighty or so evangelical college campuses. For their students and faculty, they provide not only a calm oasis of spirituality amid the world's secular turmoil but also the chance to achieve a peculiarly evangelical lifestyle. That these institutions are now thriving (some say booming), at a time when a shrinking college-age population is making it increasingly difficult for secular schools to fill their classrooms, is yet another indication of the evangelical surge in the U.S.

Evangelical colleges vary greatly in size, composition and academic environment. They range across the U.S., from Seattle Pacific University in Washington and Bethel in Minnesota to Oral Roberts in Oklahoma. A few are little more than glorified Sunday schools at which Christianity is nearly palpable and where pious young women can be sure of meeting pious young men. Many of the colleges, however, impose intellectual standards nearly as rigorous as those at distinguished secular liberal arts institutions. Common to all evangelical schools is their determination to maintain a Christian environment on campus and to present the broad spectrum of arts and science courses from a Christian perspective.

This special religious atmosphere is a major factor in attracting record numbers of students. In a survey conducted for the

National Association of Evangelicals, 55 percent of these youngsters said that they were attending their Christian college either
because God had led them to it, because they want "to grow as
a Christian" or because of the Christian social atmosphere. A
majority of the students polled were pursuing "helping" vocations such as counseling, church work, education and the ministry. About a fourth planned a career in business, 8 percent in
medicine and 4 percent in fields related to agriculture.[17]

Widely regarded as the best of the evangelical schools and
frequently called the "Harvard of the Bible Belt" is Wheaton
College, located on a tidy seventy-acre campus about an hour's
drive west of downtown Chicago. Well into its second century,
the school boasts tough admission requirements (half its freshmen were in the top tenth of their high school graduating
classes), high standards of scholarship and a distinguished roster
of alumni that includes Billy Graham and Carl Henry, one of
America's most respected theologians. So many Wheaton students go on to higher degrees that graduates from only ten other
American colleges earned more doctorates than did those from
Wheaton between 1920 and 1976.

The hallmark of the college, however, is the religious and
moral demands made of its 2,000 undergraduate and 400 graduate students. Though the campus is by no means grimly populat-
ed by junior Cotton Mathers—to the contrary, students are
relaxed, witty and obviously possessed with easy senses of humor
—it is a properly serious place. There is no missing its air of piety.
Observes a Wheaton student with a laugh: "If you're not a committed Christian, you'd be miserable here."

Wheaton is unambiguous about what it stands for. As its
motto, it proclaims: "For Christ and His Kingdom." Each year,
every member of the faculty and administration must reaffirm the
college's "Statement of Faith." Among other things, it declares
fidelity to the "Old and New Testaments as verbally inspired by
God and inerrant in the original writing, and that they are of
supreme and final authority in faith and life." The "Statement"
also asserts "the personal, premillennial, and imminent return"
of Christ and that "all who receive by faith the Lord Jesus Christ
are born again of the Holy Spirit." By entering the college, the
students, who represent about thirty different Christian denominations, explicitly accept the "Statement."

Equally explicit is the code of conduct governing the behavior of students—and faculty. To develop Christian character, states the code, "practices which are known to be morally wrong by Biblical teaching are not acceptable." Enumerated specifically are "drunkenness, stealing, the use of slanderous or profane language, dishonesty, occult practices and sexual sins such as premarital sex, adultery and homosexual behavior." Also unacceptable are attitudes condemned by Scripture, such as "greed, jealousy, pride, lust, bitterness, needless anger, an unforgiving spirit and harmful discrimination and prejudice."

Students are barred from possessing or drinking alcoholic beverages, tobacco and nonmedicinal drugs and from social dancing. They also are expected to exercise extreme discretion in the kind of movies and TV programs they watch, music they listen to, material they read, card games they play and organizations they join. On Sundays, they are strongly advised "to give primary attention to worship, rest and Christian fellowship and service." In practice, violations of the specifically proscribed acts are very rare and there are relatively few observed excesses in those matters for which discretion is urged. Says one Wheaton coed: "I loved to dance in high school; I did it all the time. But here I've given it up for the greater goal of leading a Christian life. This amazes my friends from high school."

While the codes of faith and conduct go far to accomplish the evangelical integration of faith and life, Wheaton's special task is to integrate faith and learning. The college attempts to infuse each of its nearly 800 courses with a Christian content and teach them from a Christian perspective. In the case of mathematics, computer sciences and a handful of other courses, this admittedly poses problems. Biblical teachings, however, apparently can be related to most subjects. This seems clear from the titles of seminar papers prepared by Wheaton faculty members. They include: "Can Sociology be Christian?" "Archeology and the Christian Mind," "A Christian Approach to History," "Energy, Environment and Christian Concern," "A Clarification of a Christian View of Music," and even "The Christian Mathematician."

When a student studies chemistry, explains Hudson Armerding, Wheaton's president, "a primary purpose should be to recognize the greatness of God in creation." The social sciences and humanities, he adds, "offer opportunities for a distinctive application of biblical truth," especially the precept that "man is not the measure of all things."

Lee Pfund, a former Wheaton basketball coach and now executive director of the Alumni Association, says that faith is integrated into sports by teaching students "how to respond in a Christian way to a bad call by a referee or umpire. It is teaching respect for your opponent, asking yourself whether you are really playing by the rules of the game." Political science instructors, meanwhile, address the ethical considerations in dealing with conflicts and in making political decisions. And journalism students, according to Richard Becker, assistant editor of *The Record,* the campus paper, "ponder the dilemma of how to be a Christian in the competitive world of the American communications industry." Becker and his fellow budding journalists learn, he says, "not to exploit or deceive anyone in order to get a story. It is better to give up the story than to treat people in an unchristian way."

A small but growing number of evangelical graduate schools also try to integrate faith and learning. Wheaton offers advanced degrees, as does Oral Roberts University. The newest probably is CBN University in Virginia Beach, Virginia, which promises its students, "More than a masters program, a master plan for life." The university's initials stand for Christian Broadcasting Network, which is headed by evangelist M.G. "Pat" Robertson, probably most widely known as host of the popular "700 Club" daily TV program of Christian inspiration. Robertson says that he has established the university under divine guidance and emphasizes that students are selected for their promise of using "the skills and knowledge acquired at the university to glorify God and to serve their world."

Since opening its doors in 1978, CBN University's major academic emphasis has been its school of communications, which had about 100 students in 1981. While a number of them previously had attended evangelical colleges, most came from secular institutions like Wisconsin, Massachusetts, Pennsylvania, Rutgers and the U.S. Naval Academy. A CBN school of education is just getting started and there are plans for schools of fine arts, theology, business administration, biblical studies and public policy.

"We give our students a chance to integrate their faith with their profession," says David Clark, the dean of the communications school. "Here they learn journalism in an environment in which the name Jesus Christ is invoked as something besides swearing." To be sure, Clark's instructors teach subjects typically found at other communications graduate schools, such as marketing, advertising, audience analysis, news writing, broadcast station management and television studio operation. Yet the curriculum also contains uniquely Christian courses: Evangelism and Communication, Editing Church Publications, Creative Christian TV Programming and Marketing for the Christian Organization.

Alumni from these Christian colleges and graduate schools are found throughout the country, in probably every profession and social stratum. Though most are unable to sustain the full, rigorous integration of their faith and their lives after leaving campus, their Christian college experience is for them and the evangelical community a standard of the manner by which a devout Christian copes with the secular world. The vitality of these academic institutions mirrors the vitality of evangelical Christianity in the U.S.

A mirror too is the booming electronic church—those clergymen who take to the airwaves to reach the faithful. There is nothing new about electronic preaching. Radio station KDKA in Pittsburgh inaugurated the era long ago, when it broadcast an evening vespers service from Calvary Episcopal Church on January 2, 1921. By the middle of the 1930's, over 400 evangelical programs were being carried by 80 radio stations. Ten years later, as many as 20 million Americans weekly turned their dials to Charles Fuller's "Old-Fashioned Revival Hour" from Los Angeles, while leading clergymen, such as Harry Emerson Fosdick, Bishop Fulton Sheen and Rabbi Stephen Wise, were appearing frequently on CBS's "Church on the Air."[18]

Yesteryear's audiences, however, are dwarfed by today's. Religious broadcasting now weekly reaches an average of at least 115 million on radio and 15 million on television. Some 35 TV and 600 radio stations transmit religious programming exclusively, almost all of it evangelical, while another 500 radio stations carry substantial amounts of religious programming. *Adweek* magazine estimates that a new religious-format TV station is launched every month and a new religious radio station every week.[19]

Some of the electronic preachers not only have become regular guests in American living rooms but almost certainly are the country's best-known clergymen—Jimmy Swaggart, Robert

Schuller, Richard De Haan, Oral Roberts, James Robison and, of course, Billy Graham. Jerry Falwell's "Old-Time Gospel Hour," broadcast weekly from Thomas Road Baptist Church in Lynchburg, Virginia, is seen on nearly 400 TV stations, and more than 300 radio stations carry his daily program. Evangelists Rex Humbard and Jim Bakker each reach millions via more than 200 TV stations, while about 150 outlets carry Pat Robertson's talk-show format "700 Club."

Increasing controversy swirls about this burgeoning electronic church. Some accuse it of offering a "superficial, magical God," while others worry that it undermines the very important concept of Christians gathering in congregations to worship. What is beyond dispute, however, is that broadcast preaching is reaching millions of Christians who do not regularly go to church and thus otherwise would be getting little formal religion. The Princeton Religious Research Center, closely affiliated with George Gallup, Jr., estimates that 61 million Americans are "unchurched." That is, they have not attended a church or synagogue for at least six months. Yet unchurched Christians are believers. Write Gallup and Poling in *The Search for America's Faith:* "[They] pray. They believe in Jesus Christ. They think seriously about life after death. They trust the Resurrection story of Easter morning."[20]

That they do not go to church may amount to yet another indictment of America's mainline religions. Many of the "unchurched" apparently turn to the electronic pulpit for the same reasons that other millions abandon liberal Protestantism: They seek spiritual uplift. Evidence for this, significantly, comes from the mainline itself.

In mid-1980, William Fore, an editor of *The Christian Century* (the voice of mainline Protestantism) and an official at the ultraliberal National Council of Churches, sharply criticized the electronic preachers in a *TV Guide* article entitled "Why TV Evangelists Can't Be Pastors." The response shocked Fore. Writing about it in *Christian Century* in early 1981, he admits that he had "expected letters in rebuttal, but not the almost 500 that have come so far." What he especially was not anticipating, he confesses, "in its anger and intensity or in its pervasiveness, was the outpouring against the local churches and their preachers as dry, unfriendly, cold, not filled with the Spirit, unbiblical, works of Satan, dead or dying."

One letter, for instance, complained that "when I needed

Christ, I got social and community planning and programs and softball but no Jesus. People want truth and salvation and assurance." Concludes Fore: "The responses indicated that the local church simply is not meeting the needs of many, many people."[21] Echoing him is a study commissioned by the National Council of Churches in which it finds that "people have left the traditional denominations and their traditional services and *then* found satisfaction or identity with electronic church offerings."[22]

Deeply disturbed by the continuing exodus from their pews while evangelical and electronic churches are prospering, mainline denominations are beginning to look back with increasing respect at the faith of their fathers. As a result, mainline churches are introducing traditional forms of worship, shelving community action manuals and dusting off books of devotional readings. Though they are by no means stampeding toward the old-time religion, mainline congregations clearly are taking steps—hesitant, unsure and uncomfortable—in this direction. Groups known as evangelical caucuses, "renewalists" and by a half-dozen other names are emerging as conservative wings inside nearly every liberal denomination. As the liberal theological and social activist platforms of these denominations become increasingly discredited, the conservatives grow bolder. They convened their first national conference in 1977 and since have been receiving support from moderates and even liberals within their churches. In fact, moans *Christian Century* editor James Wall, when many liberal Protestants today describe themselves, they "insist on dropping" the now damning appellation "liberal."[23]

Churches which long choked on the word "evangelism" are launching evangelical programs. "I go to some places where people have a hard time using the term 'evangelism,' " says Reverend Sells of the United Methodist Church's growing evangelism section. "I always tell them that I know how they feel and that when I first started working with this program, I would stand in front of the mirror and practice saying the word. It was two weeks before I felt comfortable with it. I assure them that the mirror didn't crack." Adds Reverend Grady Allison, the United Presbyterian's evangelism director: "One almost got the idea that [evangelism] shouldn't be mentioned in polite society."

Polite or not, it is today high on the mainline agenda. "Evangelism is the Number one priority in the life of the church," declares United Methodist Bishop James Armstrong of Indianapolis. The Episcopal Church, meanwhile, recently established its first office for evangelism and the Reformed Church in America, the nation's oldest Protestant denomination, has turned to evangelism to fuel a major membership growth drive. Reformed members are being trained to "gossip the gospel"—to grab every opportunity to talk to others about faith.

Over at the United Presbyterian Church, which one of its official publications admitted "was running into trouble," the 1977 General Assembly adopted a strategy called "Affirm the Good News." This requires "a far deeper commitment to sharing the gospel," declared the Assembly, because the Church "has not been faithful to its evangelistic responsibilities." Each congregation now is being encouraged "to examine the possibility of other times and places for gatherings for worship, Bible study and prayer in addition to its current practices."[24] So far, more than 2,000 congregations are participating in this evangelism campaign. As part of this effort, the denomination has issued a forty-six-page "Evangelism Resource Catalog and Bibliography" listing, among other things, evangelism pamphlets and tracts, a handbook promising to explain "The Why, When and Where of Evangelism" and a twenty-minute tape sketching a Cincinnati-based training program called "HELPER Evangelism Clinics." (HELPER is the acronym for "How to Equip Lay People to Evangelize Regularly.") That evangelism inspires even United Presbyterians is confirmed by a 1980 study that concluded that the new campaign already had saved and revitalized congregations teetering on collapse.

This same year, the Lutheran Church-Missouri Synod convened the first national evangelical conference in its history. "We were overwhelmed when 6,000 turned up in St. Louis for this," exclaims Reverend Erwin Kolb, the denomination's executive secretary for evangelism. "In an earlier day, such a gathering would have been ridiculed as being too 'un-Lutheran.'" Synod congregations now hold seminars on prayer, weekend retreats and witness workshops. In these, explains Kolb, "people are encouraged to talk about their faith and are trained to witness— evangelize—others. There is a real hunger for this."

To guide its increasingly ambitious evangelical efforts, the Missouri Synod has issued a sixteen-volume *Evangelism Resource Book.* Urging Lutherans to use "all resources and opportunities"

to witness, one of the volumes encourages them to join professional organizations, service groups, chambers of commerce,
PTAs, garden clubs and even sewing circles because these "open
doors for personal testimonies concerning what Jesus means to
you." Businessmen, meanwhile, are advised to practice "desktop
evangelism." Keeping a Bible on their desk, they are told, sparks
the curiosity of colleagues and permits the conversation to be
swung toward Christ and salvation.

These also are themes beginning to be heard once again from
mainline pulpits. For years, liberal clergy were so deeply immersed in secular causes that their sermons often sounded as if
they had been inspired by newspaper editorial pages rather than
sacred writ. Observes an eminent professor of theology: "It got
to the point in New England's Presbyterian churches that, on
Easter mornings, you could just about expect the minister to
preach about lilies instead of Resurrection." The sole gospel that
seemed to count for many mainline clergy was the social gospel.
And they saw its message as endorsement of ultraliberal economic, political and social movements.

The social gospel, however, is waning as Scripture makes its
mainline comeback. On the rise too are prayer and spirituality,
while relevance is yielding to revelation. "I worship quite differ-
ently than I did five years ago," observes Reverend Ballard
Pritchett, a Lutheran minister in Houston. "I emphasize worship
and liturgy more and there is more reverence in what I do. I no
longer try to be amusing or experiment all the time with new
litanies. And no longer do I use guitars or balloons—balloons
were big for a while." To encourage United Methodist clergy to
become more spiritual, Indiana's Bishop Armstrong has appointed a specialist in spiritual formation.

Methodists, Presbyterians and other mainline churches increasingly are turning for their new ministers not to their own
denominational seminaries but to evangelical institutions. In
great demand are graduates from multi-denominational Fuller
Theological Seminary in Pasadena, California, and Gordon-Conwell Theological Seminary in South Hamilton, Massachusetts.
When asked why they study at Gordon-Conwell rather than at a
Methodist school, young Methodists typically respond: "Our
seminaries are too liberal." Says Timothy Smith of Johns Hopkins
University: "When Gordon-Conwell ministers step up to the pulpit, they preach Scripture and people in the congregation nod in

satisfaction and say, 'That sounds just like it did in my grand-
father's church.' "

At the seminaries themselves, there is new emphasis on religion's spiritual dimension. While Protestant seminaries have offered courses on biblical criticism, Old Testament archeology,
historical theology and preaching techniques, there were almost
none on prayer or religious devotion, even at evangelical institutions. Typical was Fuller, founded in 1947. "We never thought
that prayer had to be taught," says a Fuller official. But in the late
1970's, seminarians began asking Fuller faculty for formal guidance in spiritual matters.

As a result, the school has added to the curriculum a program
in spiritual formation. It resembles the spiritual training traditionally required at Roman Catholic seminaries. In designing the
course, in fact, Fuller staff consulted with Catholic priests and
monks. During the first year of Fuller's new program, students
study "Foundations of Spiritual Life," "Prayer" and "Spiritual
Gifts." The following year, in addition to course material, each
student works with a faculty "spiritual director;" in the third year,
seminarians are paired as "prayer partners" to enhance each
other spiritually. The interest is so strong at Fuller that the school
now plans to establish an Institute of Spirituality. Interest, in fact,
is strong everywhere. According to David Schuller, associate director of the Association of Theological Schools, enrollments
have been surpassing projections at seminaries which have instituted courses on spirituality.

Resurgent interest in traditional religious practices is not
limited to Protestantism—though there the development is most
pronounced and affects the most Americans. Within Roman Catholicism too, are signs of a growing preference for old-time
religion. The church's fundamentals, for example, have been
strongly reaffirmed by the papacy of John Paul II. Rome has been
speaking out uncompromisingly on such matters as priestly
celibacy, ordination of women and birth control. As yet, of
course, there has been no major attempt to undo the nearly two
decades of sweeping changes triggered by the Second Vatican
Council. Latin is not being reestablished as the Church's almost
exclusive liturgical language (though Latin services are increasingly popular) and the mass still is celebrated according to the
new order, with priest and altar facing the congregation. On

matters of sex, moreover, many Roman Catholic young adults systematically ignore their church's moral teachings, particularly concerning premarital relations.

At the same time, paradoxically, the traditionally strict John Paul II enjoys immense popularity within the American Catholic community. George Gallup, Jr., explains this seeming contradiction. "We find that Catholics sense that the church's injunctions are not practical in this world but nevertheless feel that the church should stand for ideals from which to deviate," he told *Publishers Weekly* in 1980. "The Pope reaffirmed a lot of things that people were looking for. They wanted him to say the things he said."[25]

The American Catholic clergy, moreover, is growing more conservative as young priests evince deep and unexpected reverence for tradition. This is the near-consensus view of a sampling of Catholic seminary rectors who make no attempt to conceal their amazement at what they see occurring at their institutions. Says Monsignor Edward Ciuba, rector of Immaculate Conception Seminary in Mahwah, New Jersey: "A generation ago, the seminarians seemed determined to try something, anything new. The young fellows today, in effect, are saying, 'Let's try something old.' " This also is the case at Saint Mary of the Lake Seminary in Mundelein, Illinois. "Five and ten years ago," recalls its rector, Father James Keleher, "we responded to demands for informality by having mass around a coffee table—an actual coffee table. But today, seminarians are much more conservative on matters of worship. They explicitly have told me that they don't want coffee table mass." What they want, says Keleher, "is mass in a chapel, at a regular altar with priests in regular vestments."

Seminarians at Mount Saint Alphonsus Seminary in Esopus, New York, "are much less wild liturgically than were their predecessors of the late 1960's and early 1970's," observes Father Edward Gilbert, the rector. "Today they are more into the traditional forms of worship that characterized the church of the 1950's and into the 1960's—such as benediction and veneration of the blessed sacrament. These forms are suddenly reappearing and they are not being imposed from above." Monsignor Ciuba agrees, noting today's "greater appreciation of traditional liturgical symbols like vestments and candles."

Dress codes were a sticky problem a decade ago as seminari-

ans demanded the right to garb themselves as casually and color-
fully as the laymen of that day were doing. This too has changed
dramatically, say the rectors. Shined shoes, crisply pressed trou-
sers and traditional clerical suits (with the clerical collar) are back.
Quips Father Gilbert: "In the 1960's, to keep peace here, I had
to fight the extreme liberal seminarians; now I guess I'm going
to have to fight the extreme conservatives because there is tension between them and the older, more liberal priests on my
faculty."

Also contrasting the contemporary seminary generation with
its predecessor is how its members see their calling. Many of the
earlier group became activist priests or what was known as the
"hyphenated" priest—a cleric who had recognized secular credentials or responsibilities, such as a priest-sociologist, priest-
teacher or priest-social worker. "Now they mainly want to be
'just' parish priests, without a hyphen," says Father Keleher, "and
they want a traditional big city parish—not the inner city, not the
suburbs, but one of those typical urban Catholic neighborhoods
where they expect that the emphasis will be on the sacramental
aspects of the ministry. In effect, they want to be a padre rather
than a social worker or parish administrator."

Within American Judaism, traditionalism also seems ascendant. "Synagogues have been moving from left to right," says
Bernard Reisman, professor of American Jewish communal studies at Brandeis University. "You see almost none becoming more
liberal." Confirming this is Brooklyn College sociologist Egon
Mayer, who visits Jewish communities all over the U.S. "I give
talks in many synagogues and I've yet to find one becoming less
conservative," he says. "All movement is in the opposite direction—to traditionalism."

Many synagogues which once conducted their services almost
entirely in English have been introducing ever larger doses of
Hebrew. Within Reform Judaism, the most theologically liberal
branch of the religion, many congregations have been adopting
a prayer book published in 1975, *The Gates of Prayer,* that is considerably more traditional than its predecessor, the *Union Prayer
Book.* The earlier book, explains Reisman, is "a much more hu-
manistic, Protestant-like document; it is almost Unitarian. Aside
from the occasional Hebrew, you could have almost used it at a
Unitarian service."

Services in liberal synagogues are becoming longer and include increased communal chanting of prayers. Like their Christian counterparts, rabbis are preaching less about social and political issues; the main exception, predictably, is the subject of Israel. Says Mayer: "They aren't making so many commentaries about the latest item on the editorial page. Instead, they are talking more about the word of God." A study by Mayer and fellow sociologist David Glanz finds that students at the Jewish Theological Seminary, which prepares Conservative rabbis (those standing theologically midway between Reform and Orthodox), are increasingly concerned "with the personal affirmation of 'being Jewish' in the modern world." Mayer and Glanz see this as a "radical departure from the concerns of earlier generations of seminarians with 'human relations' and relevance to 'social problems.' "[26] Inside the congregations, the rabbi's role also seems to be changing. "He is becoming more old-fashioned," notes Mayer. That is, he sees himself less as administrator and fund-raiser than as biblical teacher and spiritual leader.

In traditional forms of religion, Americans are finding the faith they want—spirituality, uplifting liturgy, Scripture-based preaching and theological structure. Not only are the liberal wings of Christianity witnessing a retreat from their pews, but the para-religions of the 1960's and 1970's are shrinking. By the late 1970's, according to a Gallup Poll, only 2 percent of Americans were involved in Transcendental Meditation, 1 percent in various Eastern religions and cults and 3 percent in all forms of yoga.[27] Though there is little evidence that the tens of millions of thoroughly secular and unbelieving Americans have found God and are heading to church, the scores of millions who are religious are heading back to the faith of their fathers.

They are doing so with a self-confidence and a self-consciousness—and in such numbers—that make them a powerful force. It is the traditionalists in Christianity and Judaism, after all, who form the core opposition to abortion. It is the evangelical legions who comprise the stalwarts challenging regnant liberal positions on such social issues as prayer in public schools, family policies, the Equal Rights Amendment, pornography and aggressive homosexuality. And it is the religious conservatives who have joined and supported the Moral Majority and Religious Roundtable, specifically political efforts to translate moral values into public policy.

It is not simply because they are religious traditionalists that these great numbers are now supporting conservative approaches to social and political matters. But the world outlook forged by a conscious decision to become more traditionally religious is an outlook very hospitable to and supportive of traditionalist arguments. At other times in U.S. history, the dynamic of religious enthusiasm helped alter the nation's course. The religious awakening of the mid-nineteenth century contributed significantly to the abolitionist movement to free the slaves. Whether the U.S. now stands at the threshold of an awakening of similar moment with similar consequences is uncertain. Yet the breadth, intensity and momentum of today's conservative tide in religion can only reinforce an already dynamic traditionalist constituency.

VIII

VENGEANCE
AND JUST
DESERTS

To ESTABLISH JUSTICE, INSURE DOMESTIC TRANQUILLITY.

These responsibilities, mandated nearly two centuries ago by
the U.S. Constitution, are among the most fundamental that can
be delegated to a state. They are, along with providing for the
common defense, the near-universal goals compelling individuals to join together and raise up governments over themselves.
In recent years, however, Americans have been justifiably concerned about their government's ability to perform these most
basic tasks. Tranquillity has been shattered increasingly by
violence, while justice has become ever more uncertain and
haphazard.

By almost any measure and according to every set of statistics,
violent crimes are occurring with ever-greater frequency and in
ever-newer areas. Murder, assault, rape and robbery are up—not
only in crowded, impoverished inner cities, but in suburbia, ex-
urbia and the rural hinterlands as well. At the same time, criminals increasingly avoid imprisonment. Of the 130,000 men and
women arrested for felonies in New York State in 1980, reports
Time magazine, only about 8,000 actually went to prison.[1]

It is this and similar examples which prompted U.S. Supreme
Court Chief Justice Warren Burger to tell the 1981 American Bar
Association meeting that the U.S. has fashioned "a system of
criminal justice that provides more protection, more safeguards,
more guarantees for those accused of crime than any other nation
in history." As a result, said Burger, "today safety is very, very
fragile."[2] So fragile, in fact, that sociologists calculate that if the

robbery rate in large cities continues to grow as it did between 1962 and 1974, "by the year 2024 each man, woman and child in a large city would be robbed by force or threat of force 2.3 times per year."[3]

In light of such data, it is no wonder that dissatisfaction with the criminal justice system has been mounting all across the country. James Bagley encountered this in the mid-1970's when, as chief counsel to the judiciary committee of the Illinois House of Representatives, he attended a series of statewide hearings. These sessions, writes Bagley, "rapidly uncovered a broad-based consensus that the criminal justice system was simply not performing its mission. Witness after witness testified to its failure to reduce crime, prevent recidivism or rehabilitate offenders."[4]

This conclusion was echoed throughout Pennsylvania in late 1980 at a criminal sentencing commission's hearings. Observed a Lehigh County judge testifying in Philadelphia: "We must recognize not only that crime exists, but that the public feels increasing futility regarding it. The answer is not to make it more difficult for judges to send people to jail." Added the Chester County district attorney: "I have yet to hear the public complain when the maximum sentence is imposed." The matter is perhaps most bluntly put by an Indiana citizens group called "Protect the Innocent." A membership recruiting leaflet asks: "Are you displeased with criminal laws? Do you feel insecure in your neighborhood, even in the daytime? Are you tired of criminal defendants who are out on bond committing further crime? Does it disturb you that the criminal may have more rights than you, a possible victim of crime?"

As Americans everywhere answer "yes" to these and similar questions, they are forcing legislators to carry out what amounts to a minor revolution within the criminal justice system. Suddenly in full retreat are the long-entrenched liberal theories of crime and punishment. Since 1977, nearly two-thirds of the states have drastically revamped the way they deal with criminals. In each instance, their intent has been the same: to curb leniency by limiting the discretion long-exercised by judges in imposing sentences. In place of the judges, legislatures are assuming primary responsibility for setting specific sentences for specific offenses and, almost without exception, are setting longer, tougher sentences.

Impetus for this is coming not from criminologists or other

experts. It is coming from the grass roots, just as it is in the back to basics movement in education, in the drive to strengthen the traditional family and in the return to tradition in religion. Americans have been losing faith in their courts and no longer trust judges to deal appropriately with those guilty of crime. More than 80 percent of the American public, in fact, now feel that courts are "not harsh enough;" less than half felt this way in 1965.[5]

To make their courts harsher, Americans are demanding a return to an earlier view of how society should deal with law-breakers, an approach anchored in the Judeo-Christian tradition. It teaches that the community is entitled to be enraged at criminal behavior and is entitled to vengeance. The community also has a right to punish the guilty, meting out what criminologists once again are calling—without apology—just deserts.

The origins of these tougher attitudes are found in ancient and biblical times. The Code of Hammurabi, written about 1700 B.C., decreed that a noble's bone be broken if he had broken the bone of another noble, that a slave's ear be severed if he had struck the cheek of a noble and that a son's hand be cut off if he had hit his father. In the Old Testament, justice is an eye for an eye and a tooth for a tooth. Two millennia later, even minor offenses in the American colonies drew what today would be considered unacceptably brutal punishment—ear-clipping, mutilation, blinding, dismemberment, branding and, of course, hanging. During those days, more than 20 percent of the sentences handed down by the New York Supreme Court imposed a penalty of death.[6] Even Thomas Jefferson, who ranks among the most venerated of liberalism's ancients, believed that punishment has its uses. Guidelines which he drafted in 1779 proclaimed that "whosoever shall be guilty of rape, polygamy, or sodomy with man or woman, shall be punished, if a man, by castration, if a woman, by cutting through the cartilage of her nose a hole of one-half inch in diameter at the least."[7]

Restoring such grisly penalties, of course, is not what Americans have been demanding. Yet they do want criminals treated less indulgently than they have been. This tougher attitude is reflected by mounting public support for the death penalty, reversing a three-decade trend. From 62 percent favoring capital punishment in 1936 for persons convicted of murder, the numbers slid to 42 percent in 1962. Then the public began having second thoughts, agreeing perhaps with political scientist Walter

Berns who writes in *For Capital Punishment* that death "is a terrible punishment, but there are terrible crimes." By 1973, support for the death penalty had climbed back to 60 percent and eight years later stood at 73 percent—with just 20 percent opposed.[8] Though murder is the only offense which a majority of Americans believe warrants execution, about a third actually favor it for rape, treason and airplane hijacking.[9]

Attitudes toward capital punishment are one barometer of the nation's feelings about crime. Another is the public's insistence that judicial leniency be curbed, particularly regarding sentencing. Americans simply want those found guilty of crimes to go to prison and stay there for a term bearing some relation to the severity of the offense. Among the variety of new measures that the states are adopting to insure this are flat time sentencing, mandatory sentencing, presumptive sentencing and determinate sentencing. What they have in common is drastic reduction of the courts' latitude in sentencing.

As such measures have been enacted in one state capital after another by sizable majorities, they have triggered controversy. A number of experts, for instance, question whether the sentencing changes actually will, as promised, deter potential lawbreakers from committing crimes. Others point out that statutes requiring tougher sentencing will increase the nation's prison population which, say some criminologists, already is unacceptably overcrowded. Is the public, they ask, willing to pay hundreds of millions of dollars for the thousands of new cells required to put more criminals behind bars?

Such criticisms are not without merit. Yet the public, desperate and impatient, is demanding that something be done. Americans obviously feel that common sense dictates that potential offenders will be deterred from breaking the law if they know that a criminal conviction definitely leads to imprisonment. Keeping criminals locked up, moreover, at least prevents them from committing new crimes. Observes Michael Kannensohn, who monitors changes in criminal justice systems for the Council of State Governments: "The feeling clearly now has become—'To hell with it, let's go back to basics. Let's base sentences not on someone's presumed ability to be rehabilitated but strictly on pure notions of retribution and deterrence.'"

This clearly was the feeling in Oregon in 1977 when two murders were committed by a pair of murderers who had just been released from prison. Inundated by demands that the courts do more to protect the public, the legislature quickly adopted a "just deserts" sentencing system. With its new policies, writes Elizabeth Taylor of the Oregon Board of Parole, "Oregon has announced that the commission of certain acts is wrong and demands punishment. Furthermore, the state has admitted that prisons actually punish."[10]

Such an admission represents a dramatic shift in the way society thinks about criminals and it parallels changing attitudes in other sectors of national life. It topples liberalism from its long dominance of the theory and practice of crime and punishment. For nearly a century, influenced enormously by liberal criminology, the criminal in America was generally regarded as being sick and capable of being cured. His illness, moreover, was believed to be caused largely by an uncaring, unsympathetic, unsupportive social environment. In other words, according to well-intentioned liberal penal reformers, the criminal is a victim—of poverty, of alcohol, of discrimination, of a broken home. As such, the community rather than the criminal is the true culprit. This argument, or variations of it, became almost universally accepted in the U.S. and has been carried on occasion to ludicrous extremes. The American Friends Service Committee, for example, has argued that most crimes are committed by "agencies of government."[11]

Once the criminal is made essentially innocent of the crime committed, punishing him becomes unfair. Justification thus evaporates for basing a criminal justice system on the concept of retribution. Over the years, in fact, liberal reformers managed to transform almost totally the purpose of society's court and prison apparatus: Instead of punishment, rehabilitation became the system's goal. This shift fits comfortably into liberalism's cosmic view. Curing rather than punishing, after all, appeals to higher humanitarian instincts. It also relies on that fundamental, deeply ingrained liberal tenent—an extreme faith in reason's ability to resolve man's ills. To the liberal, all that is required to cure an individual smitten with a criminal virus are heavy doses of the correct theory, proper resources and sincere efforts. Given these, it should only be a matter of time before the criminal justice system manages to eradicate the disease known as lawlessness.

The notion that American prisons should rehabilitate rather

than punish started coming into vogue about 1880. In the next half-century, more than two-thirds of the states redesigned their criminal justice systems according to the liberal blueprint; the remaining states followed suit by the 1970's.[12] What they produced was the "indeterminate" sentencing system in which legislatures gave judges great leeway in setting prison terms. The judges, in turn, left the precise sentence length undetermined, imposing only a minimum and maximum number of years to be served. How long the criminal actually spent behind bars ultimately had much less to do with the kind of crime committed than with his ability to demonstrate that he was responding positively to the "treatment" provided by the prison and that he was well on his way to being "cured."

It is the state parole board which typically has been responsible for deciding when a prisoner is sufficiently rehabilitated to warrant release. The vagueness of this "indeterminate" system yields those enormous discrepancies between potential maximum sentences and actual time spent in prison which astonish and horrify the public. It is this system, for example, which allows mass murderers to serve relatively brief terms. In Illinois, according to David Fogel, University of Illinois criminologist and former head of the state's Law Enforcement Commission, a convicted felon could draw a sentence ranging from 1,000 to 3,000 years and yet be out of prison in eleven years.

Many convicted criminals never go to prison at all, a fact that also, in part, reflects the criminal justice system's liberal tilt. During informal discussion after the hearings of the Pennsylvania sentencing commission, a Philadelphia judge recalled: "I became a judge in 1972. Then we were all taught to try anything as punishment except incarceration. It was the mood of the time. We were instructed to try Odyssey House, halfway house, this house and that house. We did it and now we see that it has not worked. We judges also are part of the public and we also are upset by the rising crime rate."

The sentencing policy changes now being enacted under grass-roots pressure aim at reducing indeterminacy, particularly regarding violent and repeated crimes, kidnapping, arson and drug-related offenses. With the new mandatory sentencing, for example, judges and parole boards retain little discretion; a specific crime carries a specific sentence that can be reduced only for good behavior calculated according to a strict formula. When judges make an exception, as they are allowed to do with narrow latitude, they must explain in writing why the sentence imposed by them is lower or higher than the typical or "presumptive" sentence set by the legislature.

Because the purpose of imprisonment no longer is rehabilitation, no longer is there need for an agency to determine when a lawbreaker is cured. As a result, states are abolishing their parole boards. Prisoners are released not when a board chooses but when the court-imposed sentence (less time for good behavior) is up. In sum, claim backers of the new policies, a prison sentence really becomes a sentence.

David Fogel is one of the most articulate advocates of these changes. Often called the father of the new sentencing movement, he has testified before almost two dozen state legislatures in the past decade. So accustomed are most lawmakers to the permissiveness of the old indeterminate system that at first they often fail to understand just what Fogel is telling them. "I would be talking about a life sentence," recalls Fogel, "and a legislator would say, 'Okay, but when can they get out?' I would respond that this is to be a 'true' life sentence. And he again would ask, 'Yes, but when can they get out?' I would have to repeat that a life sentence is going to mean serving for life. Exchanges like this show how common has been the notion that sentencing terms have meant little."

No longer. What sentencing terms now mean, continues Fogel, is that "when the convicted person goes to prison, we can tell him—'You want to go to the priest or to Alcoholics Anonymous or to group therapy or to school? That's fine. We have the responsibilities to provide you with opportunities for self-improvement. But we are telling you in advance that we don't care what the priest or psychiatrist writes on your behalf. This is not going to get you out of here any quicker. You're going to do the amount of time that the judge gave you, less only time off for lawful behavior."

Fogel's views are largely reflected in the 1978 revision of the Illinois criminal code in which determinate replaces indeterminate sentencing. Though every state's experience in changing its criminal justice system is in some respects unique, Illinois illustrates the broad outlines of what has been happening across the country. Responding to mounting grass-roots pressures in the mid-1970's, Illinois officials vowed to get tougher on crime. Stud-

ies were commissioned, experts' views were solicited from all
over the nation and hearings were held up and down the state,
even in some prisons. Crime and punishment became one of the
hottest items on the public agenda. Debates raged, for example,
over the very nature and goal of imprisonment. Should it be to
rehabilitate? Yes, said the organized bar, associations of former
convicts and several liberal groups. Or should it be to deter crime
and mete out punishment? Yes to this, said organizations of policemen, much of the public and, ultimately, nearly every newspaper editorial page in the state.

The debate, studies and hearings went on for three years.
What eventually emerged as law generally mirrors the nation's
current attitude. Among other things, the Illinois bill:

¶ Eliminates indeterminate sentencing by requiring
judges to set a precise prison term selected from within a
range established by the law. Previously the court handed
out a term ranging from a minimum to a maximum number
of years.

¶ Abolishes the parole board.

¶ Permits early release from prison only for good behavior (an incentive necessary to maintain prisoner discipline)
or by exercise of the governor's rarely used power to pardon
and commute.

¶ Lengthens sentences for nearly all crimes.

¶ Specifies especially tough sentences for those previously found guilty of similar or greater offences.

A special feature of the Illinois measure is a new category of
particularly obnoxious crimes that are only slightly less horrible
than murder. Comprising this so-called "Class X" category are
attempted murder, rape, armed violence with a firearm, aggravat-
ed arson and major drug crimes. Included too is a new offense
called heinous battery—deliberate use of a caustic substance that
causes severe or permanent disfigurement. Except for homicide,
Class X carries the most severe penalties.

The leading proponent of Class X was Illinois Governor
James Thompson, who personally led an energetic campaign to
win legislative and public backing. At one point, he even solicited
campaign funds which he promised to use solely on behalf of
legislators who supported his two top priorities: Class X and

trimmed budgets. Speaking to a Chicago business group in August 1977, Thompson stressed that Class X would signal that Illinois is coming down "hardest on the crimes of violence . . . the crimes which people fear the most." In a sense, he continued, Class X is a label chosen for its public relations impact. "If we want criminals to know we are serious about stopping violent crime, then we need to give them a message they can understand," said Thompson. "Class X is a message they can understand. In fact, I wouldn't mind seeing every gasoline station and grocery store in Illinois with a sign in the window: THIS STORE IS PROTECTED BY CLASS X. ARMED ROBBERY WILL GET YOU A MINIMUM SENTENCE OF SIX YEARS."

Thompson later outlined broader reasons for pushing anti-crime measures. Addressing the General Assembly, he acknowledged that "unfortunate social conditions" such as "poor education, unemployment and poverty" to some degree breed crime. Yet he emphasized that the time had come to "stop trying to rationalize away violations of the law. We must develop a system in which anyone who contemplates a crime will be aware that his or her conduct will be punished with swiftness and certainty." Legislatures in some three dozen states, including Illinois, have been trying to do exactly that.

The speed with which legislatures have been able to rewrite laws and turn penal philosophy on its head is due, in large part, to important earlier shifts in the field of criminological theory. The concept of rehabilitation was being discredited by the theorists throughout most of the past decade, pulling the intellectual supports from under officials still favoring it. Though many experts have doubts about the new sentencing systems, few any longer defend rehabilitation with much enthusiasm. The result: a revolution in criminal theory every bit as dramatic and important as the upheaval in the criminal justice system which is restricting judges on sentencing.

In its day, rehabilitation spawned a host of purported cures—counseling, behavior modification, individual psychotherapy, resocialization, vocational training, moral uplift and many others. The treatment of preference, like fads, changed over the years. At one time, offering criminals educational opportunities while in prison was hailed as the most promising treatment strategy. Then putting prison inmates to work at useful jobs, such as stamping automobile license plates, gained favor. Most recently, medical treatment—some highly controversial—has been touted as an alchemy for transforming lawbreakers into lawabiders. Though varying greatly, these strategies have shared the liberal article of faith that all problems are solvable.

By the mid-1970's, however, it was becoming very clear that faith was just about all that rehabilitation was resting on. Under the intense scrutiny of modern evaluative techniques, rehabilitation crumbled. An early skeptic was James Q. Wilson, professor of government at Harvard. "At first I believed in rehabilitation," he recalls. "It seemed that everyone did and you were regarded as mean-spirited if you didn't. I was going around the country lecturing confidently about the wonders of various rehabilitative methods, such as community correctional programs and intensive probation."

Wilson's doubts about rehabilitation started mounting in the late 1960's and his lectures began reflecting them. "I started to say such things as 'but on the other hand,' and so forth," he notes. The cause of this growing skepticism, he says, "was the accumulation of empirical evidence, the appearance of more and more studies which pointed out flaws in the basic rehabilitation argument. If you paid attention to the research and data, it became clear that rehabilitation was not working; it was not preventing recidivism among criminals."

The most telling blow against rehabilitation was delivered by Robert Martinson, who had been commissioned by New York State in the early 1970's to "take a comprehensive survey of what was known about rehabilitation." After reviewing nearly 250 studies in the U.S. and Britain, he concluded that "with few and isolated exceptions, the rehabilitative efforts that have been reported so far have had no appreciable effect on recidivism."[13] Subsequent studies by other scholars basically confirm his findings. These have led to the general conclusion: Rehabilitation, though prompted by laudable motives, is an experiment which has failed.[14]

Rehabilitative programs should not be abolished completely, advise critics of the system; they should remain available for prisoners who want them. But they must not be the reason for imprisonment nor the standard by which prison effectiveness is measured. One major difficulty with rehabilitation has been that no reliable means has been found for determining when a criminal is rehabilitated. Studies reveal, in fact, that prisoners easily master what has become the rehabilitation game. "In most instances," stated the summary report of the Illinois House Judiciary Committee in 1976, "[rehabilitation is] subject to manipulation by the prisoner himself . . . a prisoner is, in essence, 'play-acting' before prison officials and the parole board with the hope of convincing them that he is rehabilitated and thus eligible for release."[15]

The term "play-acting" is quite accurate. David Fogel tells of meeting a Roman Catholic priest who served as a drama coach at a prison. According to the cleric, prisoners would drop in to see him before going to the parole board room for their hearings. They would try out the performance that they had prepared for the board and he would evaluate it. Writes Fogel: "Prisoners discussed with the priest how to project respect, remorse, abjectness or whatever else might be indicated." Fogel adds that "with minor variations on the theme, clinicians help prisoners the same way, but perhaps with less frankness than the priest."[16]

To replace rehabilitation as the criminal justice system's guiding principle, theorists have been returning to traditional concepts. Some stress incapacitation—imprisoning criminals simply to remove them from society and prevent them from committing new crimes. Others favor vengeance or just deserts—meting out punishment to fit the crime because of society's right to revenge and the offender's right to be treated as a moral being responsible for his actions. Implicit in these concepts for imprisonment is a principle increasingly accepted by experts and widely endorsed by the public: deterrence. In his 1981 Bar Association speech, Chief Justice Burger argued that "deterrence is the primary core of any response to the reign of terror in American cities." As instruments of effective deterrence he listed "swift arrest, prompt trial, certain penalty and—at some point—finality of judgment."[17]

Deterrence theory is fairly uncomplicated, bordering almost on common sense. It holds that, with other factors remaining constant, the crime rate decreases as the penalty increases in severity and certainty. This occurs, according to the theory, because enough of the time a potential offender makes what amounts to a rational calculation weighing his potential gain from a crime against the price that would be imposed by the criminal justice system if he is caught and convicted. Though not without its critics, this argument is supported by the great majority of studies conducted during the past fifteen years.[18]

Some of the most influential scholarly works on deterrence are by econometricians. They employ the mathematical equations and models used in economic analyses to simulate and analyze the assumed calculations made by criminals committing crimes. Best known is the work of the University of Chicago's Isaac Ehrlich, who has focused on the deterrent effect of capital punishment. He argues that at least some murderers make a rational calculation which persuades them that they have more to gain from murdering than from not murdering. Whether or not the potential murderer must reckon with paying the price of his own execution for his murdering, says Ehrlich, greatly influences this calculation. A death penalty, he concludes, thus deters some murderers and saves some innocent lives. Running data through his econometric model, Ehrlich figures that from 1933 to 1967, eight potential lives could have been saved for each potential execution of a murderer.[19]

The studies by Ehrlich, his fellow economists and criminologists have stripped rehabilitation of its intellectual mantle. Without it, advocates of the concept have been increasingly hard-pressed to make a case for basing a criminal justice system on rehabilitation, especially when the public and its elected officials are demanding tougher treatment of criminals. Punishment rather than rehabilitation thus is becoming the principle on which the American system of justice rests. As a result, developing effective forms of punishment rather than seeking new formulas for therapeutic rehabilitation becomes a primary concern of criminal justice experts. Advises Walter Berns: "Punishment . . . must be rigorous enough to strike fear in the hearts of [the law-abiding] population but not so rigorous that that population sympathizes with the criminal. It must be rigorous enough to deter but not so rigorous that the people refuse to allow it to be imposed."[20] Striking this balance will be challenging, but at least promises to more effectively curb criminality than has rehabilitation.

Paralleling the public's tougher stance toward lawbreakers is its growing concern for innocent citizens who suffer because of criminal activity, particularly the witnesses and victims of crime. Often, they have had to endure shabby treatment from law enforcement institutions. A 1980 study for the Federal Law Enforcement and Assistance Administration reports that "police are not always sensitive, that victims and witnesses are not prepared for the criminal justice ordeal and that waiting times for court appearances are long."[21] Witnesses and victims who arrive at court to testify frequently have to wait for hours or all day in dingy corridors or rooms. If their case is not called, they are brusquely told to return at some future date. It is not unusual, moreover, for them to be intimidated and even threatened by the very suspects against whom they are to testify.

Mistreatment of witnesses and victims seriously impedes criminal prosecution. No matter how tough sentencing practices are, criminals cannot be sentenced until convicted and this requires the cooperation and testimony of crimes' witnesses and victims. Writes Wisconsin Attorney General Bronson LaFollette, whose state passed a Victim/Witness Rights Law in 1980: "When cooperation with the criminal justice system becomes too inconvenient, too dangerous and too expensive, citizens eventually refuse to cooperate. They do not call the police . . . they do not appear in court."[22]

Recognition of victims' and witnesses' rights is not entirely new. Justice Benjamin Cardozo wrote in 1934 that "justice, though due the accused, is due the accuser also."[23] The Supreme Court declared in 1953 that not only the criminal, but "the people of the state are also entitled to due process of law."[24] Until the 1970's, however, little was done to translate such pieties into practice. Since then, responding to growing community dismay with the treatment of witnesses and victims and with help from the Justice Department, hundreds of programs have been started across the country, from Portland to Brooklyn and Tucson to Peoria.

Witness programs typically concentrate on a single goal: Getting the witness into court. The eight-page manual issued by the Milwaukee County Victim/Witness Services informs the witness, in block letters: "Your presence and willingness to testify may be the deciding factor in determining the outcome of the case." To ensure that the witness appears, programs in Milwaukee, Peoria and elsewhere notify witnesses of court dates and postponements to spare them needless and infuriating trips to the courthouse. Without such a service, witnesses often become so frustrated by unnecessary trips that they stop responding to appearance notices, thus permitting the case to be dismissed and the criminal defendant freed. Employers are urged to cooperate with the program by granting time off with pay to employees who witness crimes. The Peoria Witness Information Service, among others, verifies to employers that their employees actually did appear in court. Posters at plants, shops and other workplaces inform employees that they will not be penalized if they take off time to testify.

Well aware that even routine judicial proceedings can be confusing to laymen, services try to prepare witnesses for their courtroom experience. Booklets explain how to get to court, where to find the assigned chamber and what to do after arriving. Volunteers stationed in the courthouse greet witnesses and answer their questions. The mere presence of these volunteers, according to reports, alleviates considerable witness anxiety and frustration. The services also try to alleviate fear—particularly intimidation by the criminal defendant. On occasion, for example, a witness waiting to be called to the stand has found himself or herself in the same room with friends or relatives of the accused criminal. Overt threats or menacing looks in such a situation have scared the witnesses into silence. To prevent this, witness services separate witnesses from the accused and his friends.

Witnesses also are being protected from intimidation outside the courthouse. Typical is the case of the Peoria woman who was to testify against the man whom she had discovered stealing her television set. He twice telephoned from jail, begging her not to testify. "He really scared me; he made me feel like I had done something wrong," she later told National Institute of Justice researchers studying the Peoria program. To make matters worse, one of the accused's friends who was not in prison also called to intimidate the woman. "I was terrified," she said, until the Peoria Witness Information Service intervened. Her telephone number was changed at no cost to her and the calls from the prison stopped; the other threats also ceased after the sheriff was notified of them.[25]

By all accounts, witness services contribute to the successful prosecution of criminals. Spared the frustration of long and often fruitless courthouse waits, witnesses have been appearing more frequently when they truly are needed. As a result, where witness programs operate, court dismissals of accused criminals for lack of witnesses have decreased. Police officers and district attorney staffers, meanwhile, find themselves concentrating more on tracking criminals and amassing evidence for trials because they no longer need to arrange the witnesses' court appearances. And because fewer trials are dismissed for lack of witnesses, police officers who testify make fewer unnecessary trips to court and waste fewer hours there.

In some respects, victims of crime, who after all are essential witnesses, have been treated especially poorly. "Twice victimized" is how experts often refer to them—victimized first by the criminal and then by the criminal justice system. Robert Reiff writes in *The Invisible Victim* that what most shocked him in researching the treatment of crime victims in the U.S. is "that the crime itself serves to launch the victim on a series of post-crime victimizations by the police, the courts, the human service agencies and the federal government."[26]

The rape victim justifiably receives most attention in this regard. Yet almost all crime victims seem to suffer doubly. At the hands of the criminal, there is physical pain and often financial loss. Emotional injury, moreover, is so serious at times that victims change lifestyles and jobs and withdraw from pleasurable activities which, in some manner, have become associated with the crime. Victims suffer extraordinary time losses in court proceedings and are often humiliated by insensitive questioning, curt bureaucratic procedures and a system geared mainly to the needs of judges, lawyers and the criminally accused. William McDonald observes that some police departments do not even give injured victims free rides to the hospital. And during trials, he writes, "the victim becomes very aware of his lowly status in the criminal justice system. The reserved parking lot is not for him . . . In many courthouses, there is no room where the victim can wait comfortably until his case is called."[27]

This situation too is now improving. Over half the states have passed legislation, mostly in the past decade, granting victims compensation for their losses. The 1973 Illinois Compensation Statute, for example, allows a victim (or his family, if the crime is a homicide) to claim up to $15,000 for expenses resulting from the crime. This reimbursement covers medical care, loss of earnings, living costs and funeral and burial expenses. Restitution by the criminal, moreover, is being imposed increasingly by courts as part of the sentence. This recalls the custom of pre-Revolutionary America, when defendants convicted of larceny paid treble damages to their victims. "If they could not pay," writes McDonald, "they were given to their victims in servitude for a length of time equal to the amount owed. If the victim preferred, he could sell the criminal."[28]

In addition to compensation, programs arrange for the return to victims of stolen property, offer crisis intervention counseling and information about the operation of the criminal justice system, provide modest financial aid if all the victim's available money has been stolen and install, at no cost, new locks and other security devices at the victim's residence after a burglary. New York City's Victim Services Agency has emergency food for victims and, in case of homicide, aids and counsels the victim's family. To acquaint potential victims of its services, the New York agency distributes literature in schools, community centers and churches, has posters in buses and subways and broadcasts spot radio announcements.

Along with witnesses and victims, law enforcement officers are enjoying increased citizen support. Police departments in the nation's biggest cities report a dramatic improvement during the past decade in the way that they are treated by the public. Thousands of New Yorkers voluntarily contributed to buy policemen bullet-proof vests. Police officials in Baltimore and Detroit find the public more cooperative in reporting crimes and helping with investigations. Los Angeles police say that they sense greater public respect. Law enforcement authorities everywhere have been getting help from U.S. Supreme Court rulings granting police somewhat broader latitude in questioning suspects and searching for evidence of criminal activity.

The legacy of earlier court rulings, however, remains a major barrier in the quest for vengeance and just deserts. Extremely permissive interpretations of the Constitution's due process guarantees still tilt the criminal justice system in favor of the suspected and convicted criminal at the expense of an innocent public. These rulings also have doubled the average criminal trial's length since 1960—and this does not include the time-consuming appeals process. Yet the courts cannot ignore shifts in the national mood and thus ultimately can be expected to respond by restoring a balance between community security and criminals' rights by expanding the former and contracting the latter.

Will mandatory sentencing, the discrediting of rehabilitation and the concern for the victims and witnesses of crime lead to more secure communities and safer neighborhoods? Will vengeance and just deserts deter criminal activity? Advocates of the recent changes answer affirmatively; yet it is too soon to tell. What is certain is that these developments are part of a broader national pattern. Though not an activist movement (or movements) like back to basics in education or the battle against the government Leviathan, the changes in the way American society views and treats criminals reflect a shift in mood. And as such, they are a critical part of the repudiation of liberalism and the reaffirmation of traditional values.

IX

TOMORROW'S TRADITIONALISTS

● At the University of California at Berkeley, a national symbol of the 1960's campus rebellion, *The Berkeley Barb,* one of the nation's most famous counterculture newspapers, folded in 1980 ·while the student cooperative store quietly decided to stop crusading for radical causes and start trying to make a profit.

● A Baptist clergyman who had ministered to students in the late 1960's and early 1970's was shocked when he returned in 1980 to a Texas campus ministry. "I haven't changed," he reported to his superiors, "the students have." Instead of looking to him mainly for help in organizing programs supporting leftist issues, they now wanted Bible study groups and evangelical revival meetings.

● At Brandeis University, another onetime radical hotbed, a professor who well remembers the previous decade's turmoil was on his way to class in spring 1981 when he was attracted by commotion from what he assumed was a protest against American involvement in El Salvador. Nearing the student cluster, he discovered that two demonstrations in fact were in progress. To his astonishment, the much larger, more animated group was actually a counter-demonstration, rallying to support U.S. government policies.

● A 1980 survey for *Seventeen* magazine finds that two thirds of high school boys hope that their future brides will be virgins. A decade earlier, a similar poll found that the

226

virginity of their brides was of no importance to three fourths of the boys.

THESE ARE BUT A FEW pieces of the vast, intricate mosaic of the behavior of American youth as the 1980's begin. What they indicate is that today's youngsters, like their elders, are embracing values contrasting sharply with those of the past decade. And like their elders, they are turning to traditional ways and beliefs, raising the prospect that today's youth are to be tomorrow's traditionalists. How certain is the prospect? Anecdotal evidence supporting it is plentiful and survey data fills volumes. But youth characteristically is fickle, impressionable and volatile in ideas and commitments, particularly from age eighteen to twenty-five. Perhaps the only safe assumption is that youth's collective personality changes from decade to decade. Quips Wheaton College philosophy professor Arthur Holmes: "Students come along in generations. First there was the generation without a cause, then the generation with too many causes, followed by the tired generation." The pace at which these succeed each other, moreover, has been accelerating. No sooner is a label firmly affixed than a new one seems compellingly more appropriate.

As much as youth is now changing, some imprints of the sixties are proving indelible. Faded are the long hair, torn jeans and contempt for basic hygiene, but not the easy attitudes toward drugs and sex. Gone too are the most grisly excesses of the sixties, such as widespread experimentation with LSD and other dangerous hallucinogens, yet marijuana use continues its climb, and sexual activity seems to start at ever earlier ages. Confirming this is venereal disease's alarming spread among the young.[1] Teenage drinking also is increasing and it, along with drug use, no longer appear confined to working-class families. According to a *Wall Street Journal* report, "recent studies indicate that better-off kids are catching up."[2] This would have scandalized the pre-counterculture generation of the 1950's and early 1960's, as would have contemporary youngsters' support for legal abortion and their easy tolerance of such unconventional lifestyles as homosexuality and cohabitation of unmarried heterosexuals.

At the same time, other important attitudes, drives, satisfactions and concerns of today's youth break sharply with the 1960's. It is here that the most striking evidence mounts of the return to traditional values. Ideological rebelliousness is over; so is the

wholesale assault on authority and the massive rejection of the
United States, its civilization and its history.

Unlike their parents' return to traditional values after rejecting liberalism, today's kids obviously are too young to "return"
to any set of values. Tradition therefore appeals to them not as
an alternative to a discredited value system but as a calm harbor
and sturdy moorings in a world which, during their short life-
times, has seemed unceasingly turbulent. "The current generation of students has grown up in a fractured community,"
observes Arthur Levine, who has extensively analyzed American
youth in his studies as a senior fellow at Washington's Carnegie
Foundation for the Advancement of Teaching. "The college
freshmen of 1980 were one year old when John Kennedy was
killed, six when Robert Kennedy and Martin Luther King, Jr.,
were assassinated and cities burned in riots, eleven when the U.S.
disengaged from Vietnam and twelve when a President resigned
from office in disgrace while other high officials were imprisoned
as criminals." With young people having witnessed so much societal dissolution during their very formative years, it is not surprising, as pollster George Gallup, Jr., told *Christianity Today,* that they
"are looking for more structure in their lives—be it from a priest,
a parent or a book."[3]

Exactly how youth is changing is documented by surveys. The
most widely used source comparing today's youth cohort with
that of the counterculture years is Alexander Astin's annual sampling of nearly 200,000 entering college freshmen. Sponsored by
the American Council on Education and conducted by U.C.L.A.'s
Laboratory for Research on Higher Education, the Astin study
has been asking freshmen about their backgrounds, activities and
attitudes for seventeen years.

Astin data reveal that by the mid-1970's, freshmen were becoming less hostile to authority and standards and more likely to
define their own success in material terms. To gauge attitudes
toward authority and standards, the freshmen are asked their
views of the grading systems used by the colleges and universities. A central aim of 1960's student protests was to force university administrators to adopt the permissive pass-or-fail marking
system in place of the more precise and judgmental traditional
scale of five or six letter grades augmented by pluses and
minuses. Of the 1970 freshman class, 44 percent wanted letter
grading abolished. By 1976, however, only 21 percent were call-

ing for an end to these standards, and in 1980 a mere 16 percent were.

Students again want grades which measure accomplishment, perhaps because they again respect and seek accomplishment. An Astin question asks freshmen, for example, if it is essential or very important for them to become an authority in their field. Those answering "yes" climbed from 60 percent to 73 percent between 1971 and 1980. Being an authority, moreover, is expected to yield material, tangible rewards. The share saying that "being well-off financially" is essential or very important has been rising steadily—from 39 percent in 1970 and 40 percent in 1971 to 53 percent in 1976 and 63 percent in 1980. For growing numbers of freshmen, this means choosing a business-related career. Business majors, in fact, composed nearly a quarter of the 1980 freshman class, up considerably from 16 percent in 1970. In the same period, engineering majors rose from 9 percent to 12 percent, while those in fine arts and social sciences each plunged from around 9 percent to about 2.5 percent.

Today's freshmen also seem much more willing than their predecessors to accept society's existing value structure. When Astin asked how much they want to develop a "philosophy of life," a decreasing share of the freshmen expressed their desire to devise their own philosophies. While this was essential or very important to 76 percent in 1970 (it had been 83 percent two years earlier), it slipped sharply to 61 percent in 1976 and then to 50 percent by 1980. Increasingly traditionalist attitudes toward social values and life's goals are mirrored, as could be expected, by an ideological shift rightward. In the decade following 1970, freshmen calling themselves "liberal" dropped from 34 percent to 20 percent of the class and those describing themselves as "far left" dropped from 3 percent to 2 percent. The left's entire loss is picked up by the "middle of the road"; its share of freshmen jumped from 45 percent to 60 percent. "Conservatives" and "far right," meanwhile, remained at 17 percent and 1 percent respectively during the period,

There even have been modest traditionalist gains on matters of personal behavior toward which youth remains generally indulgent. Legalizing marijuana, for example, is favored by 39 percent of 1980's freshmen; though this is up significantly from 19 percent in 1968, it is down ten points from 1976. Approval of cohabitation outside marriage also has been slipping slightly, dropping from 49 percent in 1976 to 43 percent in 1980.

Although based exclusively on samplings of freshmen, the Astin findings are supported by other surveys of the broader campus population. The Carnegie Council's Levine, for example, asked student personnel administrators at 586 colleges and universities in the late 1970's to choose from a list of 52 words those best describing student changes since the late 1960's. More than half responded that today's students are more career-oriented and concerned with material success, better groomed and less radical and activist; 40 percent reported that their students were less hostile.[4]

So concerned are today's students about their future vocations that Levine calls it "vocomania." Business courses are booming everywhere, with students prizing a business degree as the best passport to job security in a tight labor market. Just how dramatically attitudes on this have changed is apparent from Kenneth Keniston's observation, astonishing today, in a 1968 *American Scholar* article. He wrote: "No society in world history has ever provided its citizens with the automatic abundance that our society provides to a majority of Americans. In over ten years of interviewing students from middle-class and upper-middle-class backgrounds, I have yet to find one who was worried about finding a job, and have met relatively few who were worried about finding a *good* job."[5] It has been some time since very many students have been so enviably sanguine.

As business enrollments soar, history, political science and fine arts classes shrink. "In eclipse as well," notes Levine, "are many of the ballyhooed educational experiments of the 1960s. The philosophy which guided them—a studentcentered curriculum concerned with personal development and socially relevant studies—is out of vogue." Colleges which were most enthusiastically trendy, he says, now "are finding it more difficult to attract students, particularly those with top academic credentials."[6]

Catholic University sociologist Dean Hoge, a widely cited specialist on student trends, also finds startling movement away from activism and experimentation. Reviewing polling data, he observes in a 1980 study that "college students have become more conservative, less libertarian, more self-centered and more privatistic in the late 1970's. One finds little idealism or altruism in their viewpoints. At the same time . . . traditional religious beliefs and practices are strengthening." He foresees an era starting of "social and political conservatism [and] stronger traditional religious commitments" on college campuses.[7]

Specific trends noted by Hoge indicate increasing student support for the armed forces and mounting concern over Communist threats to U.S. security. Student backing also is increasing for the free enterprise system. Compared to the early and mid-1970's, a greater share of students today agrees with such statements as, "Democracy depends fundamentally on the existence of free business enterprise," and "Any man who is able and willing to work hard has a good chance of succeeding these days."[8] A survey at Barnard, Brown, Dartmouth, Princeton, Wellesley and the State University of New York at Stony Brook finds that during the late 1970's students grew more satisfied with their colleges and teachers. Says Joseph Katz, a Stony Brook administrator: "This is still a source of surprise to those of us who during the 1960's watched strong student dissatisfaction."[9]

More positive today than a decade earlier also are student feelings about the U.S.; very rare now is the counterculture's ritualistic vilification of the nation. Surveying a dozen campuses (including Sarah Lawrence College, Yale, Indiana University, Reed College, Stanford and the University of South Carolina), *The National Review* finds that 20 percent of the 1977–78 students regard the U.S. as a "sick" society, sharply down from twice the amount in 1969–70. During the same period, the portion condemning the U.S. for being "too repressive" has fallen from 41 percent to 22 percent, while those branding the nation "racist" has dropped from 46 percent to 26 percent.[10]

By international standards, young Americans are extremely patriotic, according to a 1979 Gallup survey of 18-to-24-year-olds in eleven nations. Among its findings: 68 percent of American youth are proud of their "history and cultural inheritance," compared to 16 percent of youth in Switzerland, 22 percent in West Germany, 54 percent in Japan and 68 percent in India; 45 percent of American youth are proud of their "culture and art," compared to 21 percent French, 27 percent West German, 8 percent Swiss, 30 percent Japanese and 56 percent Indian; 53 percent of American youth are proud of U.S. "potential for the future," compared to the 12 percent of both French and West German youth, 8 percent Japanese, 12 percent Indian and a robust 64 percent Australian; only 2 percent of young Americans feel that they have "nothing to be proud of," compared to 26 percent French, 18 percent West German, 14 percent Japanese, 9 percent Indian and 2 percent Filipinos.[11]

If the statistics leave any doubts about the nature of changing student attitudes, anecdotal evidence from campus does not. Take the death of *The Berkeley Barb* in 1980, when its circulation slid to an anemic 2,000. The paper's demise marked the passing of an epoch in the same way as does the death of the last aged veteran of some distant war. To America of the late sixties and early seventies, *The Barb* and Berkeley were synonymous with student rebellion—free speech for public obscenities, sit-ins, teach-ins, marches, mass protests, communities of hippies and dropouts and loose and fervent talk of impending revolution. For *The Barb,* police were "pigs" and easy drugs and sex were heralds of a golden future.

The Barb's performance echoed the rhythm of campus protest. Its circulation peaked at 90,000 in 1969, the height of student unrest. That school year, campuses were disrupted by nearly 1,800 demonstrations. In May 1970, following the start of U.S. ground operations in Cambodia, 57 percent of the campuses erupted in protest; some schools closed and administrators resigned. During 1969 and 1970, moreover, student unrest accounted for more than 8,000 incidents related to bombings, attempted bombings and bomb threats. Of the FBI's sixteen most wanted persons in 1970, ten were student activists. Among their crimes: murder, bombings and bank robbery.[12]

The nation had experienced rebellious students before—the 1920's coed challenge to conventional morality and the late 1930's mass pacifist demonstrations by the left—but nothing matched the near-uprising of the late sixties. As if emboldened by their unprecedented numbers, this student group pushed to an extreme the natural rebellion of adolescents against their elders' authority and institutions. Adolescent America, in a sense, overwhelmed a structure that had not been designed to cope with and tame such staggering numbers of youngsters—eighteen-year-olds reached a record high in 1970.

By the mid-1970's, the war in Vietnam, a main cause of student protest, had ended and, perhaps as important, the demographic bulge had begun graduating. The campuses calmed—Berkeley included. This was obvious to Arthur Levine, who visited Berkeley in 1980 while researching his book on contemporary college students. After observing a demonstration in Sproul Plaza, site of considerable 1960's turmoil, Levine reports: "The plaza was full of people—more than I had ever seen there before. On closer examination, however, there proved to be two groups. In one, a crowd of several hundred, many were applauding wildly, while a few were even jumping up and down. The other group, much more somber, consisted of perhaps fifty people, some sitting on the steps of the administration building, others marching in a small circle. It turned out that the large group was listening to a blue grass band, while the smaller assembly was the demonstration . . . This did not seem to be the radical Berkeley that I had heard and read about in the 1960s."[13] It indeed was not, as publishers of *The Barb* were discovering as they watched their readership plummet.

Like Berkeley, the University of Wisconsin at Madison is dramatically transformed. It symbolized, perhaps even more than Berkeley, protestors run amok. In 1967, students rioted violently against the campus visit of representatives from Dow Chemical Corporation, a major manufacturer of the napalm used by U.S. forces in Vietnam. Three years later, radicals detonated a bomb at the Army Mathematics Research Center in Sterling Hall, destroying millions of dollars in equipment and killing a thirty-three-year-old civilian scientist. Radicals routinely disrupted classes, smashed store windows and nearly besieged buildings in 1969 and 1970. Tension so mounted that officials considered closing the university in spring 1970 and canceling commencement exercises.

Few traces today remain of those embattled times. A visit to the Madison campus finds a scene and mood evoking the late 1950's. On busy Langdon Street, the central thoroughfare of a main housing area, radios blare as students sit casually on the porches and terraces of rooming houses, dormitories and sorority and fraternity houses. At one fraternity, a handmade sign welcomes guests to a parents' weekend. Crowding Lake Mendota's piers, students chat and sing. Their hair is short, attire neat and appearance crisp. While angry graffiti had blanketed whole walls in the late 1960's, buildings and fences are now clean. On bulletin boards, that unfailing barometer of institutional climate, notices mostly are for movies, room rentals and rides. Of the few political messages, a socialist announcement of a May Day rally competes with a conservative call for demonstrators to support U.S. policy in El Salvador. The most radical bulletin board, of sorts, stands outside the Campus Ministry; it simply lists organizations whose offices are inside, most of which are well-known, far-left, anti-capitalist groups.

Acknowledging Madison's return to traditional tranquillity are the editors of *The Cardinal,* a student paper and one of the few radical strongholds left on campus. They describe themselves as committed Marxists and political activists and complain that their junior staff colleagues are much less leftist than in past years. Says Mindy Blodgett, the paper's top editor: "Many of the journalism students on *The Cardinal* are more interested in their résumés than in issues and politics. We are less politicized." Grouses another leftist editor: "Now, if you talk to a freshman about getting active in a political organization, he or she asks, 'Will it look good on my résumé?' "

Conservative student organizations, while growing only modestly, no longer are harassed as they once were (violently at times) when they set up booths on campus to distribute literature and recruit members. The largest 1980–81 campus turnouts, moreover, were not political but toga and halloween parties. And one of the largest was the convocation welcoming 1980's entering coeds and encouraging them to rush sororities; 600 girls attended, paying ten dollars each. Since the late 1970's, in fact, the fraternity and sorority system has recovered sharply from the membership loss which had nearly obliterated it; one or two chapters a year now reopen their doors on the Madison campus. Welcome once again also are military and corporate recruiters. Student hostility and violence for several years had prevented on-campus interviews for seniors interested in jobs or enlistment. No longer.

To the 1981 visitor, the protest era thus seems to have left no legacy. When asked what remains of all those radical student demands and administration concessions, University of Wisconsin officials search long for examples. One administrator observes that many faculty members are still demoralized; another says that the Wisconsin Legislature remains suspicious of the campus; a third points to a few pock marks in buildings and dents in fences caused by student violence. There is not much more. Though Madison students fought tenaciously for a right to participate in governing the university, for example, few now bother to take their designated seats on administrative committees. And though Alumni Association rolls fell from 35,000 to 33,000 in 1969 and 1970 as student actions outraged old grads, membership gradually has revived and, by 1981, topped 40,000.

Scenes from other campuses mirror Berkeley and Madison:

¶ At Pennsylvania State University, Director of Religious Affairs J. Thomas Eakin tells of the campus service marking the first anniversary of the American hostages' Iranian captivity. "For the first time in my ten years at Penn State," he recalls, "we had a campus ceremony in which the ROTC band took part. Participating too were clergymen, the university president and several choirs and music groups. The ceremony, ending with the solemn lowering of the flag, was very moving, very patriotic. It typifies how things have changed in a decade."

¶ At Georgetown University, Father Lawrence Madden, the campus minister, marvels at the disappearance of the hostility to institutions. "I see it at campus receptions," he says. "For years after I arrived in 1971, I had to go up to students and introduce myself at these affairs. We faculty members had to do this to prove, in a sense, that we were not the enemy. Suddenly, a few years ago, students started lining up to introduce themselves to us. This symbolized that something was changing. Gone is the intense antipathy to the older generation and institutions."

¶ At colleges and universities throughout the U.S., students once again are turning to campus ministers for counsel on traditional matters. During the Vietnam war, large numbers of students asked clergymen for advice about avoiding the draft. Should the student profess to be a conscientious objector? Should he flee the draft board's jurisdiction by heading into Canada? Following the draft's end, there was a period when ministerial advice was hardly in demand. Now, say ministers, students again are seeking guidance about such traditional concerns as careers, emotional entanglements, sexual identification and behavior and relations with parents. Quipped one clergyman, perhaps not entirely in jest: "It had been so long since I was asked about sex that I forgot the correct answers."

Reflecting too the changed campus mood is ROTC's comeback. The target of rhetorical and violently physical attacks in the
late 1960's, the Reserve Officers Training Program was driven
from many schools. In just six years, Army ROTC's 1967 enrollment of 177,000 plunged to 33,000. The slide reversed in the late
seventies, with enrollment reaching 65,000 in 1980 as military
training programs started returning to campuses from which they
had been ejected.

Some issues, of course, continue to excite students. Demonstrations in recent years have been mounted against resumption
of the draft, American corporate investment in South Africa and
almost anything related to nuclear energy. According to Levine's
studies, however, today's hottest issues are "me-oriented internal
campus" matters, such as student fees, institutional facilities (like
student parking) and faculty hiring and firing.[14] And instead of
simply taking to the streets or quadrangle, students now are just
as likely to seek remedies for their grievances in courts or by
lobbying legislative bodies. Indeed, as student demonstrations
have waned, student use of lobbyists and lawyers has soared.

Nothing seems to excite today's students more than religion,
and in no area of student affairs is the traditional resurgence
more evident. Bible study groups bloom like dandelions in
spring; pairs of pious young Christians and Jews canvass dormitories and rooming houses to bring their fellow students the word
of God; and announcements for religious functions sprout on
campus bulletin boards in numbers not seen since the 1950's'
explosion of student religiosity.

By almost any measure, religion is booming on America's
campuses. Compared to a decade earlier, not only are more students religious, they also are more religious. Sociologist Dean
Hoge's data, for example, shows that while Dartmouth students'
belief "in a divine God, creator of the Universe" fell from 35
percent in 1952 to 25 percent in 1974, it climbed back to 30
percent by 1979; the pattern is repeated at the University of
Michigan.[15] At Williams College, Hoge and Philip Hastings of
Williams found that belief in Christ as "the human incarnation of
God" also has been bell-shaped, falling from 38 percent in 1948
to 19 percent in 1974 and then rising to 30 percent in 1979.
Frequency of prayer and "feelings of reverence" likewise decreased between 1948 and 1974 and then started climbing slightly. As for Williams students' faith in "personal immortality," this

slid from 38 percent in 1948 to 17 percent in 1967 and then rose to 29 percent in 1979. Since the mid-1970's, those believing that the "church is the one sure and infallible foundation of civilized life" have jumped from 30 percent to 41 percent. Conversely those regarding organized religion as "on the whole harmful" have dropped from 20 percent to 11 percent.[16]

In the broader twelve-campus sample for *The National Review,* 25 percent of the students in 1977–78 said that they substantially agreed with their religious tradition, up from 13 percent in 1969–70. For the same period, the share disagreeing totally with this tradition fell from 24 percent to 16 percent.[17] A Gallup Organization survey, meanwhile, reveals that as the 1980's began, 95 percent of all American teenagers believe in God, 87 percent pray, 52 percent say grace before meals and 27 percent belong to Bible study groups.[18]

Attendance at campus services has been climbing steadily, though not dramatically. What is remarkable, however, is the worshipers' religious intensity. One measure is the phenomenal growth of Inter-Varsity Christian Fellowship, from chapters at 450 colleges in 1970 to 700 in 1981. Inter-Varsity groups even meet to pray, sing and pursue other evangelistic activities on New York City and Brooklyn campuses, including Columbia University and the Julliard School of Music.

Unlike the Jesus movement of early 1970's, with its rock music and unchecked enthusiasm for sharing faith in Christ, today's youngsters want to worship in a traditional way. Like their elders, they are embracing the faith of their fathers. Absent from student services are the guitars, interpretive dancing, contemporary poetry readings and multimedia shows. In their place are pastors in robes, a traditional order of service, an uplifting liturgy and Scripture-based sermons. According to Charles Roselle, head of student ministries for the Southern Baptist Convention, students now constitute one of the most conservative elements in many Baptist congregations. "They are the ones carrying the big Bibles," he says.

A poll of Penn State students in fall 1980 asked why they attended chapel services. "What they told us," says Religious Affairs Director Eakin, "is that they are looking for traditional religious experiences, those to which they were exposed earlier in their lives. A few years ago, everyone was into contemporary liturgy. Today they are about as basic as they can get. They don't

want innovative stuff. They even have admonished me for para-
phrasing the Lord's Prayer and making a few other changes. They
hate it. They really hate it." Services now must be structured and
sacred. Observes Reverend Ballard Pritchett, the Lutheran pastor
at the University of Houston: "Students desire such things as the
procession of the cross and other historical parts of the liturgy.
The point is that these rituals set apart and make special the time
of worship."

To enhance student faith, revivals are back in vogue. There
are more of them and, according to Roselle, they are devoted
mainly to personal professions of faith in Christ; a decade ago,
revivals generally focused on Christian ethics or similarly "relevant" matters. Retreats too are growing in popularity. They
range from five days of near-total silence to a long weekend
designed to encourage considerable sharing of faith and internal
experiences. Says Georgetown's Father Madden: "Instead of
traveling during their spring break, some students make a five-
day silent retreat. This definitely was not happening in the mid-
1970's."

Rabbis on campuses also report changes in the past decade.
No longer is it extremely unusual to see young Jewish men wearing the traditional skullcap strolling through the quadrangle or
sitting in lecture halls. Nor is it exceptional for students from
liberal Reform households to turn pious upon reaching campus.
Across the country, the traditional rather than the Reform service
is now better attended at Hillel, the campus Jewish center. This
reverses the attendance patterns of the mid-1970's.

"There are fewer of what a decade ago we called 'creative
services,' " explains Rabbi Daniel Leifer, Hillel director at the
University of Chicago. He stresses that though observant Jews
still constitute a minority of Jews on campuses, they are "a growing minority and a more self-conscious, less inhibited minority.
They like the rituals—the service, preparing and sharing a sabbath dinner and celebrating the holy days."

Young Jews today, much more than their immediate predecessors, are likely to observe, with near proselytizing fervor,
the strict, *kosher* dietary laws and many other biblical and Talmu-
dic directives. "They want a religion telling them how to eat, how
to dress, how to be disciplined, what to do and what not to do,"
says Rabbi Harold White of Georgetown University's Hillel.
"They want order and hierarchy. I hear this from rabbis at Hillels

everywhere. Students no longer want a worldly sophisticate for their rabbi; they want a teacher of deep faith and piety."

Like their Christian counterparts, Jewish students in greater numbers are heading off on retreats. White organizes about eight of them a year and would schedule more, he says, were facilities available. He explains: "In the early 1970's, the occasional retreats we ran had themes—Vietnam or Israel or Soviet Jewry. Now the sabbath is the sole theme and prayer is the main activity." Participants read the Bible, discuss the meanings of particular prayers and share long moments of silence. White could be speaking for religion on campus generally as he adds: "Never, never did this happen a decade ago."

Though college students constitute only about half of the nation's 18-to-25-year-olds, broad generalizations about youth are drawn almost entirely from them. The rest frequently are overlooked. Opinion samplings, for example, concentrate heavily on students. For one thing, they are relatively easy to poll; they inhabit a small, discrete community. For another, students are nearly perfectly pure specimens of youth. The high school graduate who immediately enters the workforce, on the other hand, already has begun participating in the adult world and acquires many of its characteristics. He or she, in fact, often is more adult than young in attitudes, cares and responsibilities.

Youth of all sorts, however, reveal some basic outlooks by their attitudes toward one of the most important events in their lives: their weddings. Here too, the trend unmistakably is back to traditionalism. Disappearing rapidly is the barefoot-in-the-park nuptials or the ceremonies in which bride and groom, in T-shirts and blue jeans, exchange vows in an orange grove or on a hillside. An informal sampling of ministers, priests and rabbis in mid-1981 finds none who had officiated at a wedding in a park, field, hilltop or anywhere else out of doors in the past couple of years.

Such ceremonies have been recorded for posterity by *The Serial,* a spoof on life in California's ultra-trendy Marin County. In one scene in the movie version, a minister at a mountaintop marriage ceremony intones, "This is a wedding of two separatenesses under the Cosmos." And instead of pronouncing the couple "man and wife," he declares them "pair-bonded for as long as the relationship continues."

Though a caricature, this scene captures the outrageous tone of the counterculture wedding. No wonder the return to tradition is greeted with sighs of relief. Addressing a 1980 National Trade Association Conference, Milwaukee retailer Sam Pasch declared with enormous satisfaction that "the scruffy look and the cock-amamie idea of weddings being held *alfresco*" is finally at an end. As evidence, he noted that men once again are dressing formally for their weddings, an observation confirmed by Ron Sacino of St. Petersburg, Florida, the 1981 chairman of the American Formalwear Association.[19]

The same is true of women. *Bride's* magazine in 1981 identified what it calls "a new wave of tradition," stressing femininity and such old-time favorites as ribbons and "great laces." Barbara Tober, the magazine's editor-in-chief, told a trade group that she is seeing "a return to the formal wedding—at every price level . . . complete with wedding dresses and formal attire for men, double-ring ceremonies and longer, more thoughtful engagements." According to *Bride's* surveys, 98 percent of today's weddings have formal ceremonies, almost all of them in a church, chapel or synagogue; this is up from 90 percent in 1971.[20] Priscilla Kidder, of Priscilla of Boston, one of the nation's leading wedding gown manufacturers, observes that "even young brides of age twenty-two want to wear classic gowns." Indeed, bridal shops whose best sellers in the mid-1970's were peasant dresses are now selling mostly formal gowns, adorned with lace and even beads.[21]

The only nontraditional trend concerns financing the formal affair. With costs soaring, no longer is it universally assumed that the bride's family underwrites the celebration. Indeed, a Long Island caterer, cited by *Bride's* Tober, says that of the many receptions he prepares, the bride's family entirely pays for about one third; both families share costs for one third; and the bride and groom themselves pitch in for one third. Expenses probably could be pared by trudging back up to the hilltop or cutting back on the wedding's formality. This, however, would offend tradition and it is tradition which now is ascendant.

That it is ascendant among much of American youth in critical areas of their lives may be extremely significant for the broader traditionalist resurgence. Public opinion analyst Daniel Yankelovich, for instance, sees college students as an advance guard of societal innovation. Cultural change, he says, is transmitted from students to other youth and then to the entire population.

Hoge and Hastings, meanwhile, maintain that "of all population groups, none is more sensitive to shifts in the cultural climate than college students."[22] In this sense, the traditionalism emerging on the campus mirrors the shifts to traditional values within the much broader American society. As such, it confirms that the tide of traditionalism is running strong and deep—and it promises also to run long if today's youngsters become, as it appears they will, tomorrow's traditionalists.

3

A WAR OF IDEAS

X

ARSENAL
OF
IDEAS

THE MOST DRAMATIC EVIDENCE of resurgent traditionalism is at the grass roots—that point of contact between frustrated, determined activists and the institutions they want to change. They wage their battles with meetings, rallies, letter-writing campaigns and intense lobbying. Parents demand better teaching from their school boards. Christians demand a more spiritually centered worship from their churches. Citizens of all kinds demand tougher treatment of lawbreakers from their criminal justice system. Women demand greater respect for the traditional homemaker from their legislators. And businessmen demand a taming of the governmental Leviathan.

Traditionalist movements so far have scored impressive gains. Whether they manage, in the long run, to reshape the nation and fully recapture the ground long occupied by liberals depends to a great extent on how their activism is translated into political force directly affecting public policy. Turning the traditionalist agenda into public policy is the aim of the movement broadly known as the New Right. Long-range success of traditionalists also depends on how well their movement is reinforced and nourished—and challenged from within—by intellectual enterprise. Above all, it must be able to compete and prevail on the battlefield of ideas in that critical conflict which creates the conceptual climate within which policy options are evaluated and selected.

Not so many years ago, to talk about conservatives producing winning ideas might have invited ridicule. Ideas, as nearly everyone agreed, came from the left. To be sure, there long have been conservative intellectuals and philosophers of stature. George Nash profiles many of them in his 1976 book *The Conservative Intellectual Movement in America,* as did Clinton Rossiter a generation earlier in *Conservatism in America.* It was just after World War II, for instance, that the University of Chicago's Richard Weaver completed his extremely influential *Ideas Have Consequences.* Russell Kirk, moreover, has been writing and lecturing for three decades, while Robert Nisbet and Edward Banfield have been doing so nearly as long.

Prolific though they were, conservative intellectuals generally had but limited impact on the public policy process. Sprinkled about the nation, they were isolated from one another and, above all, lacked those special instruments that specifically are tuned to and address matters likely to turn up, sometimes rather suddenly, on legislative calendars. Said Kirk in a 1980 Heritage Foundation lecture: "We were sufficiently ignored by both Republican and Democratic Presidents . . . We had no central apparatus; few publishers approved our books; the great foundations rarely assisted us; in the Academy we were a forlorn remnant."[1]

How different has been the story for the left. Much of its intellectual output has been focused and generously supported by richly endowed institutes and foundations such as Brookings, Carnegie, Ford and Rockefeller, along with a number of smaller centers, like the Marxist-leaning Institute for Policy Studies in Washington. From them have come those lofty thoughts and concepts that ripple excitement through the crucially important communities of officials, academics, journalists and other public opinion makers. A more than quarter-century barrage of their ideas—economic strategies, welfare programs, foreign policy initiatives, weapons systems analyses, nuclear arms reduction proposals, educational theories, inner-city revitalization blueprints and a host of government solutions for other social ills— has profoundly influenced the subsequent actions of federal and state legislators and administrators.

Today the left no longer dominates the intellectual high ground. In the war of ideas, traditionalism is winning victories and framing the manner in which issues are considered. Solid scholarship is producing evidence and amassing data to bolster traditionalist arguments, and this output is being widely and skillfully disseminated—through journal articles, press briefings, seminars, essays for newspaper op-ed pages, television and radio panel discussions and workshops for congressional staffers and corporate executives. The very weight of this intellectual output is tilting the scale of opinion to the right and snapping the hold on the nation's minds long wielded by the conventional wisdom from the left.

Credit for this in large part belongs to traditionalism's arsenal of ideas, the several dozen conservative institutes which have emerged or achieved prominence since the mid-1970's. Washington's American Enterprise Institute (AEI) and Heritage Foundation and the Hoover Institution on War, Revolution and Peace at Stanford University are today full-fledged think tanks with multimillion-dollar budgets and platoons of resident scholars addressing a broad spectrum of issues. Other institutes are considerably smaller and concentrate on a few, selected topics. Though all the organizations boast rolls of individual donors, most of their funding comes from foundations and corporations normally found underwriting conservative efforts, such as the Scaife family trusts, Coors, Smith-Richardson, the Lilly Endowment, SmithKline, *Reader's Digest,* Pfizer, Dow Chemical and the John Olin Foundation.

Credit for shifting the climate of ideas rightward also belongs to one of the most exciting American intellectual developments in memory, the appearance of a group of first-rank scholars known generally as neoconservatives. Having abandoned assorted leftist beliefs, they have turned, at least in some critical sectors, to traditionalist concepts. Feisty, pugnacious and extremely articulate, neoconservatives are among the most powerful artillery in the battle of ideas. Together with the new institutes, these intellectuals have set bubbling cauldrons of traditionalist thinking, creating so much ferment and excitement that even liberals grudgingly concede that *the* ideas now are on the right. Some conservative thinkers seem incredulous at their new ascendancy. "Most of my life I've been in the minority," said Virginia Polytechnic Institute economist David Meiselman at a 1981 conservative gathering in Chicago. "Never in my wildest dreams did I think that I would find so many with whom I agreed—and who agreed with me."

Agreement is not total, of course, but there is a set of beliefs and assumptions shared by the conservative centers and intellectuals. Above all, they champion the free enterprise system as the essential guarantor of economic health and of individual liberty. Only with enormous skepticism (and usually distaste) do they view proposals for government solutions to economic and social problems. They look instead to the private sector, to individuals, communities and what AEI scholars define as "mediating structures"—family, neighborhood, church, voluntary associations and ethnic and racial subcultures.

Curbing government regulation of industry, therefore, is a top priority for conservative idea centers, as is reduction of government spending. Emphasizing repeatedly that there is no free lunch, they look for and expose the often hidden or ignored trade offs in programs. Forcing a manufacturing plant to meet extremely high environmental standards, for example, may result in cleaner air or water or a less noisy neighborhood. But does it not, ask the conservatives in volumes of carefully documented analyses, also result in curtailed production and hence fewer jobs for workers and higher prices for consumers? By refusing to view government programs in isolation, conservative studies persistently have been alerting the public to the collateral price of such activities. Says Irving Kristol, probably the most prominent neoconservative: "The unanticipated consequences of social action are always more important, and usually less agreeable, than the intended consequences."

Conservative institutes and scholars are firmly committed to political democracy and equality of social, economic and cultural opportunity. Just as firmly do they oppose attempts to guarantee equality of results. Like it or not, they say, inequality is inherent in the human condition. Not everyone toeing the mark at the starting line is going to hit the finish at the same moment; some may not reach it at all. Any attempt, they argue, to fix the race with quotas, guidelines, affirmative action, subsidies, special favors or other "equalizers" is doubly unfair. First, it penalizes the most talented and industrious participants and then, over the long course, penalizes the entire national community by poorly utilizing its best manpower resources.

Religion as an institution and a belief system subordinating the individual to a Supreme Being is very highly esteemed by conservative thinkers—though not all are devoutly religious. They believe that society requires the sense of morality and the sharply defined notions of right and wrong central to religions anchored in Judeo-Christian teachings. Along with religion, tradition and custom are required to define moral behavior and brake the impetuous actions of individuals and institutions. When this fails, conservative scholars do not hesitate advocating another brake: coercion. Individuals who violate society's laws are to be punished. And punishment too is to deter those countries which threaten American security and international peace. For this reason, studies by conservative institutions and scholars urge levels of military spending sufficient for an arsenal capable of deterring a wide range of hostile actions.

Battlefield action in the war of ideas is not easily monitored. Individual skirmishes are rarely ferocious, typically waged in the staid pages of a scholarly journal or as polite disagreements at a conference of experts. Seldom is there the fireworks of a debate's direct and heated confrontation or the unrelenting grilling of an especially well-informed legislative committee. Critical battles, in fact, can go almost unnoticed until the fighting stops when, in retrospect, the action's contours stand out in relief. Victory for an idea hence is a gradual process, percolating like a brew until by stages it grows strong and rich. Or it is akin, perhaps, to making rock candy—where crystals develop imperceptibly until suddenly they are formed and hardened.

Percolation or crystallization characterizes what has happened to the critique of government regulation. Today the anti-regulation idea is nearly regnant in the U.S. Just a decade ago, however, regulation's champions were legion. Whether it was for transportation, telecommunications, banking, worker safety or the content of breakfast cereals, government-imposed rules, guidelines or standards were seen as appropriate, effective and affordable instruments for balancing consumer rights against those of business.

A great many factors involving many experts and organizations have contributed to crystallizing the antiregulation mood. The liberal Brookings Institution, for example, commissioned early studies on regulation but then, as its president admits, "dropped the ball in 1975."[2] It was picked up by the American Enterprise Institute. No other organization has played such a critical role in reshaping the climate of opinion about regulation; none has been as persistent or thorough in addressing the issue.

"What concerned us," explains Thomas Johnson, AEI's director of economic policy studies, "was that so many of the stat-

utes creating regulations in the early 1970's were not based on
very much research or data. Legislators, in fact, admitted this."
Even so, there was scant official sympathy in those days for reviewing and rolling back regulations. Recalls Johnson: "During
the Nixon years, we held a conference on deregulating the airlines. One participant was a Civil Aeronautics Board official who,
at the sessions' conclusion, remarked with some disdain that
those of us who were suggesting deregulation were just a bunch
of dreamy academics out of touch with the real world. There was
absolutely no support for this, he assured us, on Capitol Hill or
in the administration."

He was right. Why, indeed, should there be support? The
nation's air transportation system was widely perceived to be
working well; thus, why fiddle with it? Not until these favorable
perceptions changed could deregulation proposals be taken seriously. Says AEI's Marvin Kosters: "There had to be a new climate.
Officials and even the public, to an extent, had to recognize that
although we had a good air transportation system, it still suffered
from inefficiencies and misuses of resources that could be remed-
ied. This perception gradually emerged. As it did, deregulation
proposals began appearing less farfetched when they hit legislators' desks."

What helped change the climate was the work of scholars at
AEI and elsewhere. Patiently, carefully, they constructed a base
of solid, respectable research, packed with hard evidence and
data that could not easily be dismissed or refuted. Armed with
this, countless experts trooped to conferences and legislative
hearings to argue forcefully that regulation-bred inefficiencies
were choking the economy. Referring to the AEI, strategy on this
and other matters, leftist economist Gar Alperovitz told *The New
York Times Magazine* in 1981: "They come at an issue with a lot of
firepower—statistics, studies, reports, each one of which can be
challenged, but it requires a lot of time and money."[3]

AEI started building its solid data base on regulation in the
early 1970's with a series of evaluative studies. Each examined a
specific government program—such as automotive safety, affirmative action, federal transportation subsidies—to determine its
cost and whether it was achieving its goals. This multivolume
project gave AEI scholars valuable experience in using political,
legal and microeconomic analytic tools to dissect government
operations, particularly those of the regulatory agencies. To

sharpen the focus of its regulation activities, AEI established in 1976 a Center for the Study of Government Regulations under the direction of Kosters, an economist who had served in the Ford Administration, and James Miller III, who later was named by Ronald Reagan to head the Federal Trade Commission.

The following year, AEI launched *Regulation,* a bimonthly journal concentrating exclusively on the topic's legal, procedural and judicial aspects. The approximately 10,000 copies of each issue go to an extremely influential readership—members of Congress and their aides, the staffs of public policy centers, professors and about 2,500 attorneys. A main goal of the journal's articles on regulations and their impact on a specific business or industry, explains Managing Editor Anne Brunsdale, "is to illustrate how the problems with the regulatory process are the same in every field. In a sense, we show that the problem is not a particular regulation but regulation itself."

An anti-regulation consciousness, meanwhile, was reinforced in 1975 with the publication, under AEI auspices, of a pioneering study which reached an unusually broad audience (for such a work) and convinced many conservative intellectuals that they ought to be paying more attention to regulation's threat to the free enterprise system. The book, *Government Mandated Price Increases: A Neglected Aspect of Inflation,* was written by Murray Weidenbaum, who was to become chairman of Reagan's Council of Economic Advisers. In it, he attacked the contention that regulation comes cheap because it costs the government (hence the taxpayer) relatively little to enforce. In fact, wrote Weidenbaum, regulation actually saddles the public with an enormous financial burden, a staggering, multibillion-dollar "hidden tax" as business passes on to the consumer the great expense of complying with government rules.

Weidenbaum's study fueled the developing debate on regulation, as did the activities of AEI's Center and *Regulation* magazine. Kosters and Miller, for example, were commissioning a torrent of studies on individual regulatory programs. "There were a great many meetings and marathon brainstorming sessions," explains Anne Brunsdale. "From these emerged a community of experts passionately concerned with regulation. It was marvelous sitting down with them at our sessions and seeing their anger rise as they discovered yet another economic sector in which regulation was wasting enormous resources and sums of money."

As the Center spots new areas of regulatory excess, it seeks scholars to analyze them. "This is Stage I," notes Kosters. "We find the researchers and suggest how they can give their work a public policy focus. We raise questions, indicate possible avenues of inquiry and so forth." At Stage II, these studies are presented at AEI-sponsored seminars and conferences. "These are publicizing events," Kosters says. "They bring the research to the attention of the press and the public. But they also change the perspectives of the participants. We try to assemble a diverse, yeasty group around the table—academics, government and regulatory agency officials, legislators, congressional staffers, lawyers and journalists. No one walks away from these sessions without at least having had some of his views challenged."

AEI publishes the proceedings of these conferences. It also produces panel discussions for radio and television and invites regulatory agency officials to come over for the "Meet the Regulator" program and be grilled by the AEI staff. They come. In monographs commissioned to analyze in detail a specific regulatory program or approach, AEI not only dissects those particular regulations but provides damning insight into regulation itself. One study on vehicle safety inspection, for instance, finds that despite an annual cost to consumers of about $1 billion, neither accident rates nor the number of injuries have been reduced substantially. Asks the study in conclusion: Is the safety regulation worth the cost? In this process, stress Kosters and his colleagues, no single conference, project or publication is *the* critical event which snaps on mental light bulbs and radically changes ideas. AEI has learned patience, confident that well-prepared conferences and studies over several years can transform significantly the intellectual climate.

There are occasions, however, when quick intellectual action yields immediate results—not effecting a fundamental mood shift but influencing a decision or event. It may well be that the policy-making mind, no less than nature, abhors a vacuum. Appreciation of this certainly seems to be what prompted the Heritage Foundation to release a 1,100-page political handbook, *Mandate for Leadership,* just weeks after Ronald Reagan's election victory. This detailed, articulate study was designed to fill a potential conceptual vacuum while the Reagan team was getting its bearings and settling into unfamiliar surroundings.

In prior changeovers from a Democratic to a Republican Administration, the newcomers usually had to rely heavily at first on holdovers. Said Heritage President Edwin Feulner, Jr., in an interview with *Human Events:* "Our strong feeling was that people who come in the Administration should have some sources of information and guidance other than what you get from the incumbents that you replace. In the Nixon transition, we were briefed by the Democrats, the very people whose jobs were at stake and who had a vested interest in maintaining the *status quo.*"[4]

It was specifically this *status quo* that *Mandate* attacks. Describing the project, a United Press International reporter called it "a blueprint for grabbing the government by its frayed New Deal lapels and shaking out forty-eight years of liberal policies." Nearly a year in the works and drawing on contributions from about 250 academics, government officials, attorneys, bureaucrats and Capitol Hill aides, *Mandate* analyzes the federal government's cabinet-level departments and every major agency. For each, it specifically recommends changes in policies and personnel (600 recommendations in all) to give the new administration a distinctly conservative personality.

Even before the full volume was ready for publication, sections still in draft or typescript were rushed to key Reagan appointees. Though they surely had general ideas about the policies they wanted to pursue and also were receiving advice and position papers from other sources, the Heritage studies provided them with a product unique for its breadth and detail. And it contained names, numbers and sums.

Precisely how many of Heritage's recommendations have been adopted by the administration because they appeared in *Mandate* is hard to say. A number of positions subsequently advocated by the administration were being urged by several powerful groups in addition to Heritage. This is the case in the call for cutting food stamps, rescinding the decree requiring bilingual education, cracking down on terrorism, permitting parents to take a partial tax credit offsetting the cost of private school tuition, curbing the Comprehensive Employment and Training Act (CETA) program and consolidating separately funded programs into a few block grants to be given to and disbursed by the states. Yet administration officials have acknowledged their debt to *Mandate,* saying that it eased transition into office. In addition, several of the experts contributing to the thick volume have joined the administration in positions responsible for areas which they addressed in *Mandate;* among them are Interior Secretary James Watt and senior Treasury aides Norman Ture and Paul Craig Roberts.

AEI and Heritage are the largest and most influential conservative research centers in Washington. The campaign to discredit regulation and the *Mandate for Leadership* project reflect their complementary differences. AEI concentrates primarily on the long (sometimes very long) range and fundamental transformation of the climate of opinion. Heritage, on the other hand, prizes its ability to move quickly to provide specific information to fill a gap, raise a doubt or change a mind on a matter under consideration. Both limit their agendas nearly exclusively to public policy matters. While research on the roots of the War Between the States or the linguistic patterns of Appalachia are legitimate scholarly endeavors, they have too little to do with contemporary public policy issues to warrant AEI or Heritage attention.

Because of the continent stretching between it and Washington, the Hoover Institution has less direct impact on policy formation than do AEI and Heritage. Yet with Seymour Martin Lipset, Edward Teller, Sidney Hook, Milton Friedman and other prominent scholars on its staff, and because of its close ties to Ronald Reagan, dating from his days as governor, California-based Hoover is seeing its influence on domestic and foreign policy matters grow significantly. Together, Hoover, AEI and Heritage can today deploy formidable armies on the battlefield of ideas—forces which traditionalist movements previously lacked.

A visit to the American Enterprise Institute's offices in downtown Washington reveals nothing particularly dramatic. AEI technically calls itself a public policy research institute. More commonly it is known as a "think tank"—a peculiar, relatively new term that captures the nature of organizations like AEI, Brookings, the Rand Corporation, Heritage, the Hudson Institute and Hoover. They gather thinkers of varying disciplines in one place, as one would fish in a tank. In this environment, brainpower is concentrated into a critical mass capable of setting off a cerebral chain reaction.

This is an especially apt description of AEI. On its premises are nearly fifty scholars, including some of the nation's most distinguished thinkers: economists Arthur Burns, Herbert Stein,

William Fellner and Gottfried Haberler; political scientists Austin Ranney, Walter Berns and Robert Goldwin; and public affairs analysts Michael Novak, Ben Wattenberg and Robert Nisbet. In addition, more than seventy-five adjunct scholars around the country are affiliated with AEI; among them are Irving Kristol, Robert Bork and James Q. Wilson.

This impressive lineup and the credibility that they bring to AEI contrasts dramatically with the organization's less than distinguished beginnings in 1943 as the American Enterprise Association. For years, it predictably echoed the views of the giant corporations funding it and thus, understandably, little influenced policy-makers or the public.

Modern AEI dates its origins to 1954 when William Baroody, Sr., a U.S. Chamber of Commerce executive, took over the floundering institute. Gradually he recruited major scholars to write AEI's analytical papers; Roscoe Pound and Milton Friedman were among the earliest. Growth was slow, but by 1970 the institute's budget was up to $300,000—four times its 1954 level —and Baroody was set to launch the rapid expansion that marked the following decade. A major spurt came in 1977, when nearly two dozen senior members of the outgoing Ford Administration joined AEI, including William Baroody, Jr., who became the institute's president the following year. By the start of the 1980's, the budget was topping $10 million, equaling Brookings, and AEI was raising a $60 million endowment fund.

Though AEI has a decidedly conservative and Republican cast, self-proclaimed and prominent Democrats like Wattenberg, Ranney and Novak direct important programs. Such ecumenism significantly enhances the institute's credibility, as does its careful political and ideological balancing of participants on its panels and at its conferences. No longer is it unusual to find such leading liberals as George McGovern, Ralph Nader, Gar Alperovitz and Gaylord Nelson on an AEI program. During these sessions, however, liberalism clearly is on the defensive, arguing against AEI's strong preference for free market, private sector, nongovernmental solutions to society's problems.

Activity within AEI's walls is not hectic; this would almost violate think tank decorum. There is a steady simmering, though, a buzz of the business of generating and propagating ideas. A conference on the ailing Social Security system may be under-way in the boardroom, a TV crew may be taping an interview with a

Middle East expert in his office, a group of theologians and clergymen may be arguing about Christian social thought with Michael Novak in one seminar room, next door journalists may be
attending a briefing on AEI's annual analysis of the Pentagon
budget and an AEI staffer or two may be hurrying out the door
to testify before congressional committees. Most of the institute's
staff, however, probably are in their offices or the library researching a topic for an upcoming report or conference.

Earlier in the day, Washington representatives of a couple
dozen corporations might have gathered in the dining room for
a breakfast discussion with AEI scholars on a pending legislative
matter. For lunch, the dining room may fill up, with the economists, as usual, preempting the largest table to continue what in
effect is a marathon symposium on current issues. At other tables,
staffers may be dining with each other or guests—academics visiting Washington, members of Congress, Capitol Hill aides, reporters, diplomats, administration officials, politicians.

Such activity is crucial to AEI's strategy for moving ideas from
academia's cloistered cells to the corridors of power. The process
can take several years and often starts at a lunch, a hallway conversation or a conference, when a topic arises which an AEI staffer
feels merits further study. The institute then searches for an
outside scholar to head the project. At the same time, AEI organizes an advisory board of experts to identify the ground to be
covered, the problems to be addressed and the questions to be
answered by the study.

Papers then are commissioned (paying honorariums of several thousand dollars) and a conference often is scheduled at which
the studies are presented. To it are invited other experts and
journalists. If the topic is "hot enough," as Tom Johnson puts it,
a "Public Policy Forum" panel discussion is produced, videotaped and distributed without cost to more than 600 television
and radio stations. In addition, some of the studies are condensed
into brief essays suitable for newspaper op-ed pages. Later, the
full reports and conference proceedings are published. In size,
they range from the 64-page *Reversing the Trend Toward Early
Retirement* to the 344-page *Drugs and Health: Economic Issues and
Policy Objectives* to the hefty 736-page *SALT Handbook: Key Docu-
ments and Issues—1972–1979.* In all, AEI released about 125 publications during 1980, including newsletters, analyses of pending
legislation and issues of its four journals.

AEI applies this formula for generating and marketing ideas to a wide variety of issues. When interest began mounting in a constitutional convention to adopt a budget-balancing amendment, for example, the institute invited four constitutional law experts to assess the idea's problems and risks. Their discussion later appeared as a forty-one-page booklet and is available in audio and video cassettes.

Impact of an AEI military manpower study is almost measurable. Prompted by growing concern about the quality of the nation's all-volunteer armed services, former Secretary of Defense Melvin Laird, head of AEI's Defense Advisory Council, prepared a brief, twenty-four-page report that was released by AEI with enormous fanfare. Widely read, it stimulated numerous news articles and at least one national magazine cover story. Maintaining, among other things, that armed services' compensation was too low, the study is partly responsible for congressional approval of a generous military pay hike. The study's discussion of problems within the forces, moreover, raises what have become widely asked questions about whether the Pentagon is relying on women volunteers for too large a share of the force structure.

AEI's operations generally are decentralized, with centers coordinating studies within broad policy areas. The Center for the Study of Government Regulation, of course, is among the most active. In mid-1980, it was about to launch an ambitious ten-study series on government regulation of social matters, such as water, air and noise pollution, mine safety, consumer product safety and the controversial Occupational Safety and Health Administration (OSHA). The project will conclude with a major AEI conference where draft reports will be discussed. Each is then to be published as a monograph.

Among the other key AEI Centers:

¶ Economic Policy Studies commissions a constant stream of papers dealing with the U.S. and international economies. One major effort examines the economic impact of the minimum wage; another probes the causes of the nation's declining productivity. Conferences organized by the center have analyzed the international monetary system, the new theories of rational expectations economics and the U.S. Social Security system. Contributions to the center's annual publication, *Contemporary Economic Problems,* are cited frequently by economic and other professional journals.

¶ Foreign Policy Studies covers the full range of U.S. overseas activities. One of its most influential projects has been to define the nation's Western Hemisphere priorities by analyzing U.S. ties, interests and vulnerabilities in Latin America. The main participants in this program—such as Jeane Kirkpatrick and Pedro Sanjuan—achieved such prominence that they were wooed by and joined the Reagan Administration. Among the matters studied by the hemisphere project have been the region's military security, investment opportunities and sources of energy.

¶ The Center for Health Policy Research focuses on such topics as the pros and cons of national health insurance, the operation of the Veterans' Administration, medical malpractice and the problems created by regulation of pharmaceutical research, development and marketing.

¶ Political and Social Processes analyzes campaign financing, special interest groups, the future of political parties and how the bureaucracy functions. An extremely ambitious project with a horizon distant even by AEI standards is the "Decade Study of the Constitution." Scheduled to be completed for 1987's bicentennial of the Constitution's ratification, the series of studies and conferences intends to spur analysis of the document's most basic characteristics. How democratic is the Constitution? asks one of the studies. How capitalistic? asks another.

Particularly innovative is AEI's democratic capitalism project. It explicitly is attempting to mobilize ideas for battle. The aim is to seize the high ground in the perpetual "capitalism versus socialism" debate by focusing on capitalism not only as an efficient economic process but also as a moral system. Explains Project Director Michael Novak, establishing the moral case would overcome capitalism's main disadvantage in the argument with socialism. Though many intellectuals have long acknowledged capitalism's merits—the ability to produce more wealth shared by more people than any other economic system in history—socialism consistently has been scoring debating points by appealing to idealism. It does this, explains Novak, by posing as a humanitarian concept and conjuring up visions of brotherhood, morality and equality. To counter socialism's moral appeal, Novak and his assistants at AEI have been churning out articles and booklets highlighting capitalism's historical record as society's best guarantor of individual liberties. One of Novak's works, whose very title conveys the flavor of his argument, is *Toward a Theology of the Corporation.* In addition, he is writing a full-length treatment of this subject.

About once a month, Novak hosts a seminar at AEI on Christian social thought and invites several dozen clergymen, economists, congressional staffers and theology graduate students. During the two-hour sessions, he and his guests debate his propositions about the moral basis of capitalism and the ethics of the corporation. Some participants, notedly the clerics, are unsympathetic (even hostile) to capitalism. For Novak, therefore, these sessions become valuable opportunities not only to hone his arguments on the embattled topic but to win new souls for capitalism.

That its output has established AEI as a major source of ideas and research is beyond question. The Institute's project directors now find it remarkably easier to recruit conference participants than they did a decade ago. AEI staffers have become familiar faces at congressional hearing tables. Reporters routinely call AEI for information and a free market viewpoint when stories break on a wide range of topics, from budget proposals and tax policy to initiatives in Latin America and defense spending to urban revitalization and Supreme Court rulings.

If further confirmation of AEI's influence is needed, it comes from Ronald Reagan. When this Republican, the first in twelve years to take over from a Democratic incumbent, sought talent for his administration, he looked to AEI—eventually luring away more than two dozen of the institute's members, half of them senior staffers. Signing on with the new Reagan team were AEI's Jeane Kirkpatrick as cabinet-ranking ambassador to the U.N., Murray Weidenbaum as chairman of the Council of Economic Advisers, Lawrence Korb as assistant secretary of Defense, James Miller III as chairman of the Federal Trade Commission, Arthur Burns as ambassador to West Germany, David Gergen as a key White House aide and Richard Erb as executive director of the International Monetary Fund.

The new administration did not raid the Heritage Foundation to fill top posts. No one, however, takes this as a sign of low White House esteem; Reagan insiders, in fact, have close links to the foundation. The absence of Heritage alumni from the White House merely reflects what Heritage officers argue is one of their main virtues: a youthful staff. Unlike AEI, Heritage neither boasts nor has tried to recruit the intellectual superstars who qualify for senior government positions. Such heavy guns simply are not needed, says Feulner, to accomplish his organization's central mission.

This mission was conceived by Feulner, Paul Weyrich (now head of a New Right activist group) and a few of their associates while serving on congressional Republican staffs. They discovered that, with Democrats in control of Congress, the House and Senate research groups by and large served liberal needs. The House Democratic Study Group, moreover, produced a steady stream of background papers providing data and arguments justifying ultraliberal programs. Conservative think tanks, on the other hand, were not paying much attention to the congressional process. When they were, they moved slowly, frequently delivering studies to Capitol Hill offices after a critical vote had been taken. Feulner and Weyrich concluded that conservative legislators sorely needed timely research prepared in a crisp, uncomplicated form that could be readily used for floor debates, questioning witnesses at hearings and changing colleagues' minds. "Having an idea in an ivory tower think tank or a college campus is not enough," says Feulner. "If they don't have impact on the public policy process, why go to the effort?"

With a quarter-million dollars from Colorado brewer Joseph Coors, Weyrich and Feulner in 1973 founded what has become the Heritage Foundation. Feulner took charge of it four years later. By 1981, Heritage's full-time staff had grown to about eighty working in four renovated buildings in a relatively low-rent neighborhood six blocks east of Capitol Hill. Its budget topped $7 million, a large share still coming from very conservative foundations and corporations (such as Coors, Noble and Scaife), but more than 40 percent raised from some 120,000 individual contributors.

Though Heritage won considerable attention with its massive *Mandate for Leadership,* its typical products are very much slimmer —twenty or thirty-page analyses of issues pending before Congress. Economics, defense and foreign affairs receive most attention, but Heritage studies also cover education, family policies, the environment and other social issues. Preparing several dozen of these papers every year are the foundation's two dozen policy analysts, many of whom have recently earned their doctorates and are, as Feulner likes to put it, "young, enthusiastic and hungry."

As do analysts at other research organizations, they stay atop developments in their specialties. At Heritage, however, they also must get to know the congressional and administration aides dealing within their area of specialization. At regular lunches and by frequent phone conversations, the policy analysts discover the issues which Heritage should be researching and what questions need answering. As important, through these contacts, Heritage staffers learn when bills are coming up for hearing, debate and vote. Heritage Executive Vice-President Phillip Truluck similarly meets with the directors of the House Republican Study Group and the Senate Republican Conference and other top G.O.P. congressional aides. Says Truluck: "From them, I get a feel of what's happening on the Hill and when. Timing is critically important."

When the administration changed into friendly hands, the Heritage staff also began touching base with government departments and agencies. Education and Health and Human Services were contacted in May 1981, for example, after Heritage decided to prepare an analysis of Reagan's proposal to give the states large block grants instead of specific funds for individual programs. "These are the departments most affected by the proposal and we asked them what kind of research is needed," explains Truluck. "They told us that a historical approach describing the background and constitutionality of the block grant concept would really be useful." Within two weeks, a thirty-seven-page Heritage *Backgrounder* on "Block Grants and Federalism" was in the hands of members of Congress, their appropriate aides and the press—in time for the hearings and debate.

Heritage can move even faster. When the Reagan three-year tax-cutting measure was proposed, opponents argued that it would fuel inflation. Republican congressional staffers called Truluck, asking whether there was any truth to these charges. Two days later, Heritage released a three-page *Backgrounder* entitled "Tax Cuts: A Remedy for Inflation." Though the study carefully avoided endorsing any legislative measure (to do so could jeopardize the foundation's tax-exempt status), it very briefly outlined an anti-inflationary case for a multi-year, across-the-board tax reduction. It was not the definitive statement on the subject, of course, but it got into congressional and press hands in time for the debate.

Heritage's timing has been just as good on other matters. A 1981 study on the Jamaican economy appeared only days before the state visit to the U.S. of Jamaica's new prime minister; a study linking international terrorism to the Soviet Union appeared a day after Secretary of State Alexander Haig indicated that combating terrorism was to be one of his top priorities; a study on American grain sales to the U.S.S.R. appeared in the middle of the Reagan Administration's deliberations on whether to continue an embargo. (The White House ultimately lifted the ban, though Heritage had urged maintaining it.)

Nearly all of Heritage's reports, bulletins and newsletters are produced by the organization's own electronic word-processing and fast-copying equipment. College students are hired to hand-deliver the reports to senators' and representatives' offices and to every congressional committee. Because congressional aides are computer-coded by their specialties, the reports can be addressed to the most appropriate person in a legislator's office. Of a senator's dozen staffers, therefore, it was the tax expert who received the tax-cut study. In all, Heritage in 1981 distributed 5,500 copies of domestic issues *Backgrounders* and 7,000 of those on foreign policy topics; 1,800 of each went to print and broadcast reporters and editors across the country. With increasing frequency, confirmed by Heritage's bulging press clippings file, these reports have been finding their ways into news stories, features and editorials.

Quick response with timely information also is the purpose of Heritage's Resource Bank. In it are the names of 900 scholars and 400 organizations identified by Heritage as taking conservative, traditional stands on issues. Stored both in a computer and large black binders, the entries are cross-filed by name, location and specialties. One binder, for example, lists experts in anti-terrorist measures, collective bargaining, urban finance, mass media of Uruguay, U.S. passport law, solid waste disposal, Korean affairs, naval strategy, British housing policy, politics of Mexico, bilingual education and labor law. Computer printouts can list all specialists in the U.S. on a particular subject or those in a single state or even a ZIP code.

Though other conservative research organizations also have compiled lists from which they recruit scholars for conferences or contributors to studies, none are as extensive or well organized as Heritage's Resource Bank. And none are in such demand. Each month, the Resource Bank handles about 400 queries. In early 1981, for instance, a Department of Health and Human Services official requested a list of conservative experts in adolescent development. The department was scheduling a series of seminars on the subject and did not want it dominated by liberal academics. The Resource Bank culled twenty-five names for the department. Calls come too from congressional committee staffers looking for conservative witnesses to appear at legislative hearings. Heritage in 1981 found scholars to testify on energy matters, against affirmative action, in favor of Reagan's tuition tax-credit proposal and even an engineer offering a free market approach to solar energy development.

The press also has learned to turn the Resource Bank for conservative sources. While preparing a major story on U.S. military needs, for example, a national magazine asked Heritage to recommend experts on the armed forces of the Soviet Union, West Germany and Iran. Heritage had a list ready within hours. The Resource Bank's most flattering requests, probably, have come from colleges; some have sought names of conservatives suitable for commencement addresses.

The Resource Bank concept grew out of the experience of Feulner and other Heritage colleagues who have worked on congressional staffs. "When academics testified," recalls Feulner, "almost always they were liberals. Seldom did you find professors arguing on the free market side of questions. The message conveyed was that there is a liberal consensus within the country's academic community."

More than any other program, the Resource Bank attempts to bring into the public policy process great numbers of academics based outside Washington. On occasion, Heritage even has paid travel and lodging costs of particularly persuasive conservatives so that they can come to the capital to testify on Capitol Hill. During their stay in Washington, Heritage arranges other opportunities for them to sell their ideas—press interviews, talk show appearances, luncheons or dinners with key members of Congress and even, given sufficient lead time, public lectures.

Heritage stays in touch with the scholars and organizations in its Resource Bank through a monthly *Insider Bulletin* whose twenty to thirty pages are an intriguing digest of conservative intellectual activity. It summarizes dozens of new studies and articles and notes where they are available. Typical is the May 1981 issue, listing, among many other things, a Hoover Institution study on South Africa, a Council for Inter-American Security report on Central America, the American Legislative Exchange Council's source book on state legislation, a National Tax Limitation Committee proposal for extensive federal budget cuts, a paper on welfare policy by professors at Harvard and Massachusetts Institute of Technology, a *Regulation* magazine article on new approaches to reducing highway congestion and *Reason* magazine's critique of Amtrak's subsidies.

The *Newsletter* also lists upcoming conferences. The thirty-two cited in the May issue include Emory University's session on controlling giant corporations, a Moral Majority political training workshop, the Foundation for Economic Education's summer seminars, an American Association of Christian Schools convention and CATO Institute's summer seminars on political economy. Other *Newsletter* sections review the status of at least several dozen cases being handled by conservative public interest legal groups and give the dates for twenty-one congressional hearings scheduled for that month.

Each spring, Heritage hosts a meeting in Chicago for Resource Bank academics and members of conservative organizations. The 1977 gathering convened in a hotel suite. Four years later, a full-size conference room was needed for the more than 100 organizations attending, a turnout clearly mirroring Heritage's prominence as a public policy idea broker. It also reflects America's shifting ideological mood that is breeding as well as being spurred by a proliferation of conservative groups. Their numbers probably would exceed the 400 in the Resource Bank. Through the studies they commission, the conferences they host and the intellectual battles they wage, these rightist groups are truly an arsenal of ideas, bringing formidable new units onto the battlefield of ideas.

No other conservative organizations are as large as Heritage and AEI. Most have existed only since the mid-1970's and focus on a relatively narrow range of ideas. In San Francisco is the Institute for Contemporary Studies, whose founders include presidential counselor Edwin Meese III. A miniature AEI or Hoover, ICS has commissioned and widely circulated studies on the Social Security system, tax policies and regulation and sponsored the important December 1980 conference of conservative blacks. Nearby in Menlo Park is the Institute for Humane Studies. It conducts workshops for law school faculty and students on law's relationship to liberty and economics. Its aim is to nudge these influential institutions toward a free market approach to jurisprudential, social and economic matters.

In Washington, D.C., the Ethics and Public Policy Center, founded by Ernest Lefever, underwrites studies analyzing the value systems within which business, schools and churches operate. Its criticism of the World Council of Churches' strong leftist policies has triggered hot debate, as has its critical study of the way recent U.S. foreign policy is portrayed in textbooks and taught in high schools. Controversial too is the Institute's argument that there are ethical justifications for a democracy to defend itself by establishing intelligence services like the CIA. Focusing on the state level is the American Legislative Exchange Council, which boasts more than 3,000 conservative state legislators as members. It is a clearinghouse of ideas and tactics and prepares model bills, incorporating conservative concepts, to be introduced in state assemblies. Its annual publication, *Suggested State Legislation,* contains sample bills to mandate minimum competency testing of high school graduates and teachers, tougher sentencing of convicted criminals and limits on state spending.

The content and liberal slant of network television broadcasting are what most concern Washington's Media Institute. It regularly monitors ABC, CBS and NBC newscasts and studies specific aspects of their programming. A 1980 analysis, for instance, discovered that 75 percent of the networks' 248 stories about inflation in 1978 and 1979 "tended to exonerate the government of inflation responsibility" even though the government-controlled money supply and budget deficits are being cited increasingly by economists as major causes of rising prices. The following year it commissioned the study which found that network dramas, comedies and other entertainment shows almost invariably negatively portray American business and businessmen.

Rough treatment of a different kind is what businessmen get from the Council for a Competitive Economy, another Washington-based group. "To win popular support for free enterprise," says Council President Richard Wilcke, "we have to show Americans that there can be a difference between big business and free enterprise." The small Council attempts to do this by exposing businessmen and groups who undermine the free marketplace by advocating government intervention. Primary targets of the Council are firms and associations seeking government favors. Each issue of *Competition,* the Council's monthly bulletin, spotlights firms and associations whose actions support or undermine "the free, competitive economy."

Among those rapped by the Council have been Union Carbide Chairman William Sneath for defending government regulation of business, Henry Ford II for endorsing import quotas on foreign cars and General Motors, Corning Glass and Bethlehem Steel for criticizing deregulation of the interstate trucking industry. When the Carter Administration announced rescue plans for the floundering Chrysler Corporation, the furious Council ran a full-page ad in *The Washington Post* proclaiming in block letters: "CHRYSLER MAY GO UNDER. THAT'S BAD. THE GOVERNMENT MAY BAIL THEM OUT. *THAT'S WORSE.*"

Several organizations concentrate mainly on defense and foreign policy matters. Along with AEI, Hoover and Heritage, they have been playing an important role in convincing Congress and the public that the Soviet Union remains a very serious threat to U.S. security and that the U.S. has legitimate interests in the Indian Ocean, Persian Gulf, Latin America and other critical regions. These groups have been equally persuasive in arguing that the American military arsenal must be rebuilt and expanded if the nation's strategic interests are to be defended and the Soviet threat countered.

The Georgetown University Center for Strategic and International Studies, founded in 1962, is widely regarded as Washington's most influential and creative source of analyses and ideas on foreign and military affairs. With a budget of nearly $5 million and a staff of forty specialists, including former Secretary of State Henry Kissinger and former Secretary of Defense James Schlesinger, the Center studies a wide range of security-related issues— from arms control and nuclear strategy to long-range energy policy and Third World politics.

Less academic in approach is the American Security Council. Most of its effort since its creation in 1955 has been to build public support for a "tougher" U.S. security posture, particularly toward Moscow. Its thirty-minute film, "The SALT Syndrome," sharply criticizes the proposed U.S.-Soviet Strategic Arms Limitation Treaty and has been telecast more than 2,000 times and shown to more than 10,000 groups. "Attack on the Americas," another Council made-for-TV film, warns of the Communist threat to Central America and the Caribbean. On the Council's membership rolls are more than 2,500 retired generals and admirals; dozens of them travel about the nation lecturing on defense matters, averaging about fifteen speeches a week.

Much narrower than the Council's audience is that targeted by the Committee on the Present Danger, whose founders in 1976 included former deputy Secretary of Defense Paul Nitze and former Undersecretary of State Eugene Rostow. This very small but very respected group of defense experts, in effect, lobbies Congress, the administration and the press, warning of SALT's pitfalls and the great danger in the continued expansion of Soviet military capabilities.

In the course of battles, victory is scented when enemy troops begin defecting. No different is it in the war of ideas. As such, no event has ignited as much excitement or comment as the defection of some of America's most prominent intellectuals from the left's front lines; few events are more significant. Their changing of sides has earned them the label "neoconservative," though not all easily wear it and not all see themselves as defectors. Indeed, they have crossed over only with great reluctance and regrets. Few, if any, feel completely comfortable marching in the right's ranks and all have some quarrels with the right's aims. Daniel Bell, in fact, calls himself "a socialist in economics, a liberal in politics and a conservative in culture."[5]

As defectors in any conflict, they are excoriated by those whom they have abandoned and regarded a bit suspiciously by those whom they have joined. Yet their switching sides is certain to influence the battle's outcome. In the intellectual arsenal, they are the heavy artillery and bring to the right an enormous tactical advantage—a firing position from within the camp of the East Coast intellectual Establishment. They are, in fact, among this Establishment's most glittering sociologists, political scientists, historians and public affairs analysts—Daniel Bell, Peter Berger, Midge Decter, Nathan Glazer, Jeane Kirkpatrick, Irving Kristol, Seymour Martin Lipset, Daniel Moynihan, Michael Novak, Norman Podhoretz, Ben Wattenberg and a dozen others.

All have been either active socialists, radical leftists or at least liberal Democrats at some stage of their lives. Many today continue to regard the Democratic party as their political home though they endorsed Ronald Reagan's presidential candidacy. Among the most articulate and prolific neoconservatives is Irving Kristol, editor of *The Public Interest,* a member of *The Wall Street Journal's* Board of Contributors and an AEI Senior Fellow. Describing himself as possibly "the only living and self-confessed 'neoconservative,' at large or in captivity" he explains that neoconservatism is not a movement. "It holds no meetings, has no organizational form, has no specific programmatic goals," he writes. "And when two neoconservatives meet, they are more likely to argue with one another than to confer and conspire."[6]

Nonetheless, these intellectuals have a strong common bond, having shared a searing experience: disillusion with and revulsion at what has happened to American liberalism since the late 1960's. They have been frightened and outraged by its excesses and galloping extremism—a welfare system being expanded into Big Brother paternalism; environmentalists crusading against economic growth; egalitarians using affirmative action and other directives to insure not merely equal opportunity but equality of results; unilateral disarmers slashing Pentagon budgets in the face of unprecedented Soviet military outlays and geopolitical expansion; radical feminists, students and homosexuals repudiating and assaulting traditional values; and academics, writers, intellectuals and other members of a burgeoning "knowledge elite" turning increasingly hostile to capitalism.

Michael Novak writes of being now repelled by even the milder ideals of socialism "and by feminism, gay liberation, the politics of some black leaders like Ben Hooks and Jesse Jackson . . . and 'liberation theology.' " He adds that he has "grown more critical of the welfare state, the interests it serves and the corruptions it is prone to."[7] Further evidence of the trouble with modern liberalism, asserts Kristol, is its bizarrely inverted priorities, prescribing "massive government intervention in the marketplace but an absolute laissez-faire attitude toward manners and morals."[8] In the U.S. today, he quips with characteristic wit, "the law insists that an eighteen-year-old girl has the right to public fornication in a pornographic movie—but only if she is paid the minimum wage."

Neoconservatives particularly are alarmed by what they call a "crisis of authority" that threatens to weaken those institutions and norms which created and bolster individual liberty. Bell is dismayed by a dominant tone in contemporary liberalism which, he writes, gives "issues such as equality, racism, imperialism and the like . . . precedence over other values like liberty and free enterprise."[9]

It is this brand of liberalism that, in effect, has been forcing the defection of this band of intellectuals. Their decision has not been painless. In *Breaking Ranks,* the moving account of his own ideological journey, *Commentary* magazine editor Norman Podhoretz writes that criticizing liberalism meant cutting himself "off from the most fashionable and in some ways the most influential circles in New York." So puzzling was the spectacle of an established intellectual breaking ranks, adds Podhoretz, that he was said to have lost his mind. There even was a rumor that his "new political turn had come about as the result of some kind of religious experience—and for certain people within the intellectual community that in itself was enough to establish a presumption of madness."[10]

In their books and lectures, through the pages of *Commentary* and *The Public Interest* and by occasional articles in *The Wall Street Journal, The New Republic* and a handful of other publications, the neoconservatives do battle. It is in *Commentary,* for instance, that Nathan Glazer writes about "American Values and American Foreign Policy" (July 1976), Daniel Moynihan addresses "The Politics of Human Rights" (August 1977), Michael Novak analyzes the Catholic Church's position on contemporary matters in "The Politics of John Paul II" (December 1979) and Midge Decter's "The Boys on the Beach" criticizes aggressive homosexuality (September 1980). It is *Commentary* too which solicits contributions from a score of intellectuals, spanning most of the ideological spectrum, for roundtables on culture, capitalism, socialism, liberalism and conservatism.

Though small, the audience reached by the neoconservatives is extraordinarily powerful, comprising much of the nation's opinion and policy-making cadres. Neoconservatives speak to them as insiders, in their own idiom and with their own code words and symbols. Much of the neoconservative barrage aims at defense, foreign affairs and broad economic issues. On these the message is clear: The Soviets, their proxies and communism in general are grave threats; economic growth is a requisite for social and political stability; a meritocracy rewarding individuals on the basis of merits rather than mandated quotas is an unalterable feature of a dynamic American social system; democratic capitalism is "the last, best hope" of humanity. In *Commentary*'s 1978 "Capitalism, Socialism and Democracy" roundtable, Kristol writes: "Never in human history has one seen a society of political liberty that was not based on a free economic system—i.e., a system based on private property, where normal economic activity consisted of commercial transactions between consenting adults. Never, never, never. No exceptions."[11]

Receiving special neoconservative attention is the "knowledge elite." Dubbed the New Class, it is seen as the enemy within. From key positions in government bureaucracies, communications media and universities, warn neoconservatives, this class wages earnest warfare against capitalism and traditional values. To blunt New Class influence, its network and goals are relentlessly being exposed by the neoconservatives and its nihilism is countered by a frequent, solemn reaffirmation of legitimacy, authority, self-discipline and the value of values.

As it turns out, these also are the cherished verities of the old, established conservativism, evidence that despite neoconservative disclaimers, the two camps may have quite a bit in common. Where they differ, in part, is on social issues and religion. Neoconservatives are somewhat less concerned about abortion, pedagogical theories, sex education, morality and similar matters than are established conservatives. And while neoconservatives enormously appreciate religion's importance, not many are personally devout. Then too, they are less enthusiastic capitalists than the venerable conservatives. Kristol's collected essays, published in 1978, are pointedly entitled *Two Cheers for Capitalism*. Established conservatives like *National Review* editor William Buckley, columnist M. Stanton Evans and *Human Events* editor Thomas Winter have no problem giving capitalism its third cheer.

The widest gap between the two groups is their differing view of the state's welfare role. Neoconservatives emphasize that they are attacking the excesses of the Great Society and are not rejecting wholesale the New Deal institutions. Writes Kristol: "A conservative welfare state—what once was called a 'social insurance' state—is perfectly consistent with the neoconservative perspective."[12] Established conservatism, on the other hand, is widely perceived to be implacably opposed not only to specific programs but to welfare in general.

Yet the breach on this matter may not be all that wide. It was veteran conservative Russell Kirk, after all, who told a Heritage Foundation audience in 1980 that "prudent change is the means of our preservation, and the great statesman is one who combines with a disposition to preserve an ability to improve."[13] Bridges already have been linking neoconservatism with other segments of the intellectual right. Symbolic of this was the much-publicized appearance by Norman Podhoretz and Midge Decter in late 1980 at the Heritage Foundation, which is much more closely tied to the New Right and Old Right than to the formerly leftist neoconservatives; Podhoretz lectured on "The Present Danger," Decter on "The New Odd Feminism." Of even greater symbolic import, Decter has joined Heritage's board. Similarly neoconservatives appear with great frequency and seem to feel ever more at home in AEI's conservative corridors.

The think tanks and neoconservatives together provide traditionalists with their mightiest intellectual arsenal in memory. They produce the data base and the rhetoric to confront and disarm liberalism's reigning conventional wisdom. To what effect? This is a query which few address comfortably. "The toughest question in public policy life is, 'Are you having an impact?' " says Heritage's Phil Truluck. "How do you measure it? By the number of times you are cited in newspaper stories or editorials? By the number of your people recruited by an administration? By the number of copies of your research that you distribute? By the number of times that you are mentioned on the House and Senate floors? I'm not certain that any of these are valid measures." But, concludes Truluck, "you have to take the long view. You have to rely on gut feeling of whether what you are producing is being picked up and influencing policy-makers."

So far, gut readings are that the conservative intellectual counteroffensive is making gains; long-standing assumptions are being questioned, perceptions are changing, traditionalist arguments are receiving a hearing. The opposing armies, to be sure, have not been routed, nor will they be. In the ranks of the left are the majority of America's academics, writers, editors, commentators, broadcasters and career senior government functionaries. Yet strong as they are, no longer do they command the entire battlefield. No longer do they monopolize the output and dissemination of public policy analyses and proposals. The war of ideas at last is a true contest between competing sides.

XI

THE NEW RIGHT

ONE BY ONE, moving down the rows in the Birmingham Hilton's Heritage conference room, they stood up and introduced themselves. There was a pastor from Mobile, next to him an engineer from Birmingham, then a very young preacher from Pensacola, several nurses from suburban Birmingham, an accountant from Selma, a judge from Birmingham, a physics professor from the University of Huntsville, a Florida food distributor, a dentist from Birmingham, the chairman of Auburn University's Young Republicans, a construction executive from rural Alabama.

In all, some fifty women and men, their ages distributed about evenly from the mid-twenties to the late-fifties, had paid thirty-five dollars and were attending the Alabama Moral Majority's June 1981 "Understanding Politics" training session. Asked to explain briefly why they came, they shyly volunteered—"I'm here to learn politics"; "I'm interested in getting moral people to run for office and get elected"; "I'm here to find out what people think of us"; and (emphatically) "I'm interested in strengthening the morals of the country."

At this day-and-a-half session and at similar gatherings in Michigan, Virginia, California and a dozen other locations during the year, an army was undergoing its basic training in politics. In nuts-and-bolts workshops, its recruits were taught such combat skills as "how to set realistic goals in order to win elections," "how to do survey research," "how to put coalitions together," "how and when to use direct mail to motivate voters" and "how to be an active lobbyist and stay out of legal trouble."

At one time, these would have been strange subjects for the Birmingham participants to be studying. Politics to them long had been an alien realm best left to politicians. Yet the participants also have been concerned long and deeply about their families, churches, schools, neighborhoods and nation. These are the people, in effect, who have been appearing across the pages of this study, folks who have grown puzzled, then irritated, then alarmed and then enraged by what they have seen happening to the social and community institutions which they most value. They believe and cite often Alexis de Tocqueville's observation that "America is great because she is good, and if America ceases to be good, America will cease to be great." Determined to help make America good "once again," they have become politicized and are swelling the ranks of what is called the New Right.

This increasingly powerful movement is translating the resurgence of traditional values into power at the precincts. So doing, the New Right has become the single most dynamic and feared force in American politics. Even its critics recognize the dynamo that it has harnessed. One reason for its success, says Rabbi Marc Tanenbaum of the American Jewish Committee, is that these groups "address themselves to a real problem, namely the moral malaise of the American people, and we discount that to our peril."[1] And William Raspberry, once the quintessential liberal commentator, wrote shortly after the 1980 elections that "you don't have to be a pro-Vietnam, anti-SALT, religio-political fanatic to agree that maybe [the New Right has] got a point." While he by no means endorses the movement, he concedes that "too many of the rest of us have opted for a tolerance that denies the very existence of a *societal* morality, that is willing to say: This is wrong."[2]

Not all liberals are as determined as Tanenbaum and Raspberry to understand the currents being harnessed by the New Right. For a good number of liberals, in fact, no term seems too harsh and no accusation too exaggerated to vilify New Right groups. The maliciousness is startling, even for American political discourse, which always has been flavored with heavy doses of hyperbole. Reverend Dean Kelley, a leading mainline Protestant theologian, brands the Moral Majority's Jerry Falwell a "political ayatollah." Rabbi Alexander Schindler, head of a major Reform Jewish confederation, talks loosely of "McCarthyism in clerical garb" and strongly implies that the New Right, somehow, is responsible for recent outbursts of anti-Semitism.—though he fails to cite any evidence. Even the usually reasoned, imperturbable David Broder, a nationally syndicated columnist, suggests that the New Right wants to have "the government dictate what [Americans] read, or think or say—or how and where their children pray."

For sheer thunder, however, few match the American Civil Liberties Union's exploitation of the New Right as a frightening specter in fund-raising campaigns. In newspaper ads and letters, the ACLU warns that the New Right in general and Moral Majority in particular intend to use the government "to establish a nightmare of religious and political orthodoxy" and that they violate "every principle of liberty that underlies the American system of government." A January 1981 fund-raising letter for the ACLU, signed by George McGovern, the ultraliberal South Dakotan, accuses the New Right of "posing an unprecedented threat to individual rights in America today." It seeks, he continues, "to destroy our basic rights and individual liberties" and "subvert the Constitution itself."

Charges almost always are leveled without supporting evidence. And when evidence is demanded, liberals have backed away from their accusations. Example: ACLU Executive Director Ira Glasser admits that his organization's ads and letters have been "engaging in hyperbole." He says: "I concede the use of rhetorical flourishes."

Though substantially groundless, the shrill denunciations confirm beyond dispute that the New Right, in its very brief history, has had enormous political impact. Debatable only is the extent. According to some New Right rhetoric, for instance, Ronald Reagan and just about every conservative member of Congress elected in 1980 owe their victories to the movement. These claims, however, are not well substantiated by data. Yet equally unconvincing are sweeping assertions by some of the New Right's detractors (including those within the G.O.P.'s moderate wing) that the movement has had only minor effect and possibly even has triggered a backlash damaging to conservative candidates.

What seems beyond dispute is that the New Right helped elect at least a half-dozen conservative U.S. senators—among them, Iowa's Charles Grassley, Oklahoma's Don Nickles, Alabama's Jeremiah Denton and Idaho's Steve Symms—and a good number of representatives. It also boosted Ronald Reagan's victory margin, particularly in the South. In this critical region, according to an ABC News-Lou Harris poll, Reagan beat Carter 56 percent to 34 percent among white Baptists, a principal New Right constituency; four years earlier, this important bloc had given Carter a 56 percent to 43 percent victory over Ford.[3]

The grandest claims for New Right clout actually come from its most bitter enemies, left and far-left politicians. George McGovern not only blames his own Senate reelection failure in 1980 on the New Right, but also credits it with defeating fellow liberal Democratic Senators John Culver of Iowa, Gaylord Nelson of Wisconsin, Frank Church of Idaho, Birch Bayh of Indiana, John Durkin of New Hampshire, Warren Magnuson of Washington and Robert Morgan of North Carolina.[4]

Echoing McGovern's pained assessment on the left is the Committee on Political Education, the AFL-CIO's political action arm. Its newsletter observes that New Right groups are "probably grabbing more credit than they deserve for the results of the 1980 election. What political group doesn't? But without them, there's a whole passel of persons sitting in the U.S. House and Senate today who probably wouldn't be there."

Nowhere is the New Right's new power more appreciated than on Capitol Hill. There office doors suddenly have begun swinging wide open to representatives of New Right organizations and the legislators often offer only token resistance to New Right pressures. Complained veteran McGovern aide George Cunningham in early 1981: "Liberals in Congress are absolutely intimidated by the New Right. All I hear on the Hill is defeatist talk."

The cause of all this are the approximately thirty secular and dozen religious groups of the New Right. Several of the most important participate in the "Understanding Politics" training sessions: Moral Majority, the Committee for the Survival of a Free Congress (CSFC) and the Conservative Caucus. Among others with nationwide membership are the National Conservative Political Action Committee, The Roundtable, American Legislative Exchange Council and Eagle Forum.

A great many of these organization's members (probably most) are new to politics, as are a number of its most prominent leaders—particularly Reverend Jerry Falwell and the other clergymen of the Moral Majority. "A sleeping giant beginning to wake itself," is how Reverend James Kennedy of Coral Ridge,

Florida, often describes the burgeoning Christian Fundamentalist involvement in political matters. New too are the New Right's
methods and tactics. What is not new are the passions driving
New Rightists—anger, discontent, frustration, despair. Some observers are alarmed, while others are exhilarated, for such intense
political feelings have led to both bruising and beneficial episodes
in the American past. Well aware of this, the New Right makes
great efforts to steer the passions which it mobilizes clear of
extremes. Even some of the movement's opponents appreciate
this. Addressing a 1981 American Jewish Committee conference,
Milton Ellerin, a political trends expert, carefully distinguished
between the New Right and the ultraright. "They are not para-
noid Birchers . . . not the anti-Semites of the Liberty Lobby," he
said. "The secular New Right has gone out of the way to be
respectable . . . to keep the hate groups at arm's length."[5]

At arm's length too are moderate Republicans and old-guard
conservatives. They simply are too timid, too middle-of-the-
road and too theoretical for the impatient, action-oriented New
Rightists. William Buckley and his *National Review,* for example,
are not of the New Right. At one time they were the twin suns of
the American right's solar system, but Buckley now has grown too
elitist, say New Rightists, and his magazine too removed from the
din of battle. "Not quite irrelevant, but also not very helpful,"
says a New Right leader. The old-guard American Conservative
Union also is not of the New Right, though they have some
overlapping membership and have cooperated on key issues,
such as opposition to the Panama Canal treaties and the U.S.-
Soviet nuclear arms accord. New Rightists and ACU generally
represent different generations. Says New Right strategist Paul
Weyrich, founder and head of the Committee for the Survival of
a Free Congress: "There is a strain between us and Establishment
Republicans. They are uncomfortable with us. Between their
leaders and our leaders exists a gap."

This gap was evident during the 1980 race for the G.O.P.
presidential nomination. The New Right's first choice was Congressman Philip Crane. And when his candidacy faltered, a significant New Right contingent, led by direct-mail strategist
Richard Viguerie, turned to John Connally. Only later did the
New Right embrace Reagan, who long had been the old guard's
candidate. The ACU had backed him for years and provided

critical help during the 1976 primaries, keeping him alive politically and making him a serious 1980 contender.

In New Right eyes, moderate Republicans like Richard Nixon
and Gerald Ford have been too ready to sacrifice principles for
power. It was, after all, Nixon who submitted a string of budget
deficits to Congress, Crane emphasized at a Heritage Foundation
lecture. And it was Nixon who imposed wage and price controls,
hiring quotas and a guaranteed income. The concessions that the
Nixon and Ford administrations made to Moscow and their almost obsessive pursuit of detente further disgust New Rightists.
Highly critical of the Nixon-Ford team, New Rightists affirm loy-
alty to neither party nor personalities, only to principles. Asked
to define these, they cite tenets with which old-guard conservatives have no quarrel: Support for the free enterprise system,
strong national defense, limited federal power and balanced budgets. But they add, with a fervor that makes the old guard wince,
the pro-family, pro-life (against abortion) and pro-religion social
issues from the traditionalist litany.

In its pre-election issue, for example, *The Moral Majority Report*
urged readers "to look at the candidates. See how they stand on
these vital issues—your home, your family, your morality and
your nation. Then mark your ballot for those candidates who
believe in America."[6] Most New Rightists would agree with Conservative Caucus National Director Howard Phillips that "virtually all of the problems facing the nation are moral." Commitment
to old-fashioned morality and patriotism is obvious at New Right
events. They typically begin with an invocation, the Pledge to the
Flag and, at times, communal recitation of the Lord's Prayer.
Grace is said at meals, even in restaurants.

There is nothing old-fashioned, however, about New Right
techniques. Here too, they contrast markedly with Establishment
conservatives and old-guard Republicans. In a videotaped pep
talk shown at Conservative Caucus field training sessions held in
most of the country's congressional districts in 1981, Phillips
says: "We have rejected the attitude of all too many conservatives
that their job is to slow down the supposedly inevitable march of
socialism and humanism—or, as some have put it, to lose as
slowly as possible. On the contrary, we believe in victory."

They also believe in exploiting electronic-age technology to
achieve this victory. More so than any of their adversaries, New
Rightists—tutored by Viguerie—have mastered the art of direct

mass mailings to get their arguments into tens of millions of households and to solicit millions of dollars in campaign contributions. They have been so astoundingly successful at this that long-established liberal/conservative fund-raising roles have been reversed. Today conservatives are the ones getting money from ordinary folk at the grass roots in a tidal wave of tiny donations, while liberals look mainly to fat cats, like labor unions and trade associations, for their five and six-digit contributions.

New Right leaders are widely envied for their proven organizational skills; without apologies, they use the commercial term "marketing" to describe their methods. Proven too is their ability to move rapidly to take advantage of situations, even if it means cutting corners. "There is a trade-off between credibility and action," notes Weyrich. "As a practitioner, I can tell you that the trade-off is on the side of action." In short order, the New Right can organize a broad-based coalition, call a press conference, mobilize a rally or summon a flood of letters, telegrams and phone calls to inundate elected officials.

While little of this is conceptually very original, never before were these response and reaction systems so carefully crafted. What did exist, moreover, was a near-monopoly of the left. Conservatives rarely systematically attempted to marshal grass-roots backing for their public policy positions. Now the New Right frequently can preempt its opponents and force liberals onto the defensive. "Power is the ability to set the agenda for debate," Phillips told the Birmingham "Understanding Politics" audience, repeating a favorite New Rightist aphorism. And challenging the left's long dominance of setting the political agenda is exactly what the New Right has been doing with remarkable success.

Putting liberals on the defensive and framing the debate are twin objectives of one of the most controversial and effective New Right groups—the National Conservative Political Action Committee, or "nick-pack" as its widely known acronym is pronounced. Headed by John (Terry) Dolan, who turned thirty as the 1980's began, and based in Arlington, Virginia, this aggressive multimillion-dollar-a-year organization has become a major political force by targeting prominent liberals for defeat. A very early campaign start and a delight in going straight for its opponent's jugular are its hallmarks.

Though NCPAC spent $2 million on fifteen commercials

boosting Reagan's candidacy in 1980, the organization is best known for its campaigns against legislators. In 1980, it took on six of the nation's key liberal senators—George McGovern, Birch Bayh, John Culver, Frank Church, Thomas Eagleton and Alan Cranston—and helped defeat the first four. For the 1982 congressional elections, Dolan in late 1981 preliminarily was targeting fifteen Democratic members of the House of Representatives, eighteen Democratic senators and four G.O.P. senators. He began firing his salvos nearly eighteen months before the polls were to open. It is no wonder that NCPAC represents what the left most hates (and fears) about the New Right. So continually and viciously excoriated is NCPAC that former Treasury Secretary William Simon quipped at a 1981 NCPAC banquet that, in just two years, Terry Dolan has gone from a nobody to a "social pariah." Unrepentant, Dolan seems to relish such distinctive notoriety. He beams broadly when he observes that "after the 1980 campaign, we were about as popular as the plague in the states where we operated." He routinely insists, moreover, that he is "not after respectability. The only thing I care about is if we're effective."

Like other New Right groups, NCPAC is of very recent vintage. It was founded in 1975, when Dolan and a couple of other politically active young conservatives concluded that there was great need for an organization to raise money for conservative candidates. The idea also made sense to Senator Jesse Helms, the North Carolina Republican and a principal New Right patron. He introduced the Dolan group to Richard Viguerie, who subsequently became both counselor and sugar daddy to NCPAC in its early years.

By 1981, the organization had mushroomed to a twenty-person staff, a sprawling suite of offices and 1979–80 revenues exceeding $7.6 million. Though federal laws limit to $10,000 the sum which any of the nation's 2,300 political action committees can contribute to help a candidate's campaign, funds independently spent to defeat a candidate are unlimited. It is this provision which NCPAC skillfully exploits, pouring great resources into attacks on carefully selected liberals. In theory, NCPAC is strictly nonpartisan, dedicated to aiding conservatives of any political party. It has not been until the campaign for the 1982 elections, however, that NCPAC actually began opposing Republicans.

These honors go to Rhode Island's John Chafee, Vermont's Robert Stafford and Connecticut's Lowell Weicker.

NCPAC's strategy is devilishly simple. It exposes incumbents' liberal voting records in a torrent of television, radio and print ads and with well-publicized news conferences and other "media events." This proves particularly devastating when liberals represent basically conservative constituents who pay little attention to how their officials vote in Washington. "What incumbents always try to do is to get away from their records, especially if they don't represent the interests of their states," Dolan told Conservative Caucus district leaders attending a post-1980 election strategy session in Washington. "This is why you don't have to lie about the people you're attacking," he continued. "The stuff these guys do in Congress is so outrageous that you don't have to lie." To which Howard Phillips, a native of Boston, added: "In Massachusetts, we have a saying: Liberals won't lie about conservatives if conservatives won't tell the truth about liberals." Telling conservative voters the truth about their liberal representatives and making them pay the price of their votes in Washington, maintains Dolan, is what NCPAC basically does. And, he could add, it does this with a raw brutality which seizes public attention and bloodies its target.

In the 1980 campaign, NCPAC hammered away continuously on such themes as burgeoning government spending, foreign policy setbacks, mounting Soviet military might and cuts in the Pentagon budget. Dolan's surveys revealed that these issues bothered voters in Idaho, South Dakota, Iowa, Indiana and the other targeted states. NCPAC raised these matters in media blitzes which blamed the problems on the incumbents. Months before they had been planning to begin their reelection campaigns, and even before some faced declared opponents, these liberals found themselves feverishly defending their records, hedging long-held positions and (with the exception of Culver) pleading that they were not nearly as liberal as NCPAC was charging. George McGovern, despite his years of voting against the Pentagon, even tried to convince voters that he had a strong pro-defense record and actually was backing the Air Force generals calling for a new manned strategic bomber.

Dolan proved unrelenting, seldom allowing an opponent to catch his breath and gain the initiative. To prevent its targets from exploiting two of their best assets, their high-profile personalities and incumbency, NCPAC kept the campaign centered on issues. Over and over, in effect, NCPAC was saying to voters: "Your representative has been giving away the store. Does he really represent you?" Using the slogan "If Bayh Wins, You Lose," NCPAC harped incessantly on the Indiana Democrat's big-spending and anti-defense record. By bringing the facts of his record to the folks back home, NCPAC blocked Bayh from employing a tactic which had served him very well in previous campaigns—camouflaging his liberalism with conservative rhetoric whenever he returned to electioneer among his Hoosier constituents.

Idaho's Frank Church received the same treatment. His dismal record on defense was ruthlessly exposed, as were his vote supporting the potentially costly government guarantee of the huge Chrysler loans and his considerable financial backing from East Coast liberals—something that did not go down very well in sagebrush country. NCPAC ads ranged from the devastatingly cute to the deadly serious. One depicted Church skipping through daisies singing, "I Love New York." Another featured retired Air Force Lieutenant General Daniel Graham, a former CIA deputy director, accusing Church of undermining U.S. intelligence capabilities when he headed the 1975 Senate investigation of the CIA. In a Viguerie-prepared mailing to Idaho voters, Church was described as "the radical . . . who singlehanded has presided over the destruction of the FBI and CIA."

Explains NCPAC's Lisa Stoltenberg: "We forced Church to go on the defensive. We were hitting hard at him almost every day—with a TV commercial, a press conference, an ad in the paper. He really panicked." It was panic which apparently drove Church, in August 1979, to surprise the Carter Administration by announcing dramatically and exaggerating the importance of a Soviet military brigade in Cuba. Overnight, it seemed, Church had undergone a political sex change, transforming him from a cooing dove to a strutting hawk. Desperately he needed to demonstrate that he was not soft on defense—despite a long Senate voting record to the contrary.

The anti-Church offensive used classic NCPAC tactics. First, voter opinion was surveyed to uncover an incumbent's vulnerabilities; these then were exploited in a two-week barrage of TV and radio commercials; after a brief lull, public opinion again was sampled to measure the ads' impact and to expose new areas of weakness; a celebrity capable of attracting media coverage, such as a retired general, was dispatched to the state to make speeches, give interviews and hold press conferences further attacking the incumbent; after another lull, a new ad salvo was fired.

High on NCPAC's 1982 list is Democrat Paul Sarbanes, a first-term senator from Maryland and one of Congress' half-dozen most liberal members. Dolan kicked off the anti-Sarbanes offensive in April 1981. The early start was intended both to soften the target and to intimidate other congressional liberals who, because of Washington's proximity to Maryland, could witness Sarbanes being mauled. "By focusing on Sarbanes," explains NCPAC's Dolan, "we put pressure on anyone else who is against Reagan's programs." Adds Thomas Edmonds, an Alexandria media consultant who produced the anti-Sarbanes commercials: "We wanted senators and congressmen to see our TV spots and imagine similar ones with their names and faces in place of Sarbanes."

The Maryland Democrat is ideal meat for the NCPAC grinder. He is much more liberal than his constituents, but they do not know it. This became clear from NCPAC's first poll. When asked what issue they associated with Sarbanes, 65 percent of the Maryland respondents could not name anything and only 4.5 percent called him a liberal. When asked which of several specific categories best described Sarbanes, 29 percent checked liberal, 17 percent moderate and 10 percent conservative; 43 percent said that they knew too little about him to make a choice. "We were amazed by the extraordinarily high 'don't knows,' " says Dolan. "We had found nothing like this during our 1980 campaigns."

NCPAC's task was clear; the "don't knows" had to be clued in. And this is what the NCPAC campaign did. "What do you know about Maryland's liberal senator, Paul Sarbanes?" asks a voice in one of NCPAC's thirty-second commercials. When a construction worker shrugs his shoulders, the voice continues, "Maybe he wants it that way. Maybe he'd like to keep his voting record secret." The commercial then points out that the National Taxpayers Union rates Sarbanes "the biggest spender in the Senate" and that he opposes Reagan's budget and tax cuts. "Now what do you think of Sarbanes," concludes the ad. "Doesn't Maryland deserve better?" Another commercial recounts Sarbanes's consistently extreme liberal stands on key economic issues and ends: "There's one good reason to replace Paul Sar-banes. His record."

After a three-week barrage of these commercials, NCPAC took another opinion sampling. It found the share of respondents identifying Sarbanes as a liberal climbing sharply. In the more revealing, open-ended question asking respondents to cite an issue that they identify with Sarbanes, many this time said that he is "a big spender" or "an opponent of Reagan." Observes Dolan: "In a sense, we have been able to create Sarbanes's image in his own state."

Though clever and tough, just how well NCPAC's tactics work is a matter of some controversy. Republican Dan Quayle, for example, publicly told NCPAC to butt out of his ultimately successful campaign against Bayh. Quayle strongly implied that NCPAC's jugular approach was creating a pro-Bayh backlash in Indiana. Political observers, however, suspect that Quayle's repudiation of NCPAC is itself a shrewd tactic; it enabled him to campaign on the high ground while NCPAC was doing his dirty work on the low ground. "Better that the voters hate our guts than the candidate's," says Dolan gamely. "After all, they don't have to vote for NCPAC."

There is little evidence, in fact, of anti-NCPAC backlashes hurting conservative candidates. To the contrary, considerable data prove NCPAC an asset. According to Lance Tarrance, a Houston-based political scientist and pollster, only 35 percent of Iowans in 1979 thought that Democrat John Culver was a liberal, despite the solidly liberal votes he had been casting in the Senate for nearly six years. Then NCPAC moved into the state. After a year-long anti-Culver campaign, the share perceiving him as a liberal doubled.

McGovern aide George Cunningham says that South Dakotans' approval of his boss plunged from 76 percent in December 1978 to 54 percent twelve months later. He blames this disastrous drop almost exclusively on NCPAC. "What is critical is the cumulative impact of its tactics," Cunningham says. Approval ratings of Church, Culver and Bayh also declined steadily during NCPAC offensives. Equally telling are the reasons respondents offered for their new negative feelings about their senators; invariably cited were the incumbent's stands on precisely those issues highlighted by NCPAC. Complains the leftist National Committee for an Effective Congress in a 1981 fund-raising appeal: "[NCPAC] threw many progressive candidates off balance—a balance they never regained."

At the same time that they attest to NCPAC's impact, liberals charge that the organization's tactics are unfair, even dirty. "Scummy" is what Church calls them. Most frequently cited is what critics call NCPAC's "negative" campaigning. It is undeniable, of course, that NCPAC hits hard, at times with karate chops. Yet it is scarcely "negative" in the manner commonly understood in American politics. Dolan's organization does not try to defame its targets by dredging up the seamy, shady sides of their personal lives—their love affairs, sexual indiscretions, drinking problems, corrupt practices or criminal ties. Such defamation is what "negative" campaigning ordinarily means, not NCPAC's almost exclusive focusing on issues, shrill as it is. When NCPAC errs, moreover, it publicly corrects the record. It even submitted ad texts to Sarbanes's staff so that it could spot inaccuracies before the commercials were broadcast.

Yet vilification of NCPAC is unabated. Foes accuse it, without offering evidence, of being linked to the John Birch Society and the Ku Klux Klan. With the launching of the antiSarbanes campaign, the chorus of outrage rose to such a pitch that *Washington Post* editorial page editor Meg Greenfield was forced to rally to NCPAC's defense, astonishing fellow liberals. "I have studied the NCPAC attacks on Sarbanes, which have been characterized as sinister and scurrilous, and come away stunned," she writes. She is stunned, she says, not by NCPAC's brutality, but because the nastiest thing which she can find NCPAC saying about Sarbanes is that he "is a liberal Democrat." This apparently means, she says, tongue-in-cheek, "that calling a fellow a big-program, big-spending liberal is the worst thing you can do to him."[7]

Strongly criticized also is NCPAC's habit of drawing up what its opponents call "hit lists." This refers, of course, to the catalogue of targeted liberal incumbents. It is hard to see, however, why NCPAC's list is so objectionable, when the environmentalists' famed list of targeted officials, labeled "the dirty dozen," is so widely applauded. Nor does there seem much difference between a NCPAC list and the National Committee for an Effective Congress fund-raising letter in which photos of sixteen conservative incumbents (including Senators William Roth, Harry Byrd and Harrison Schmitt) are crossed out by a large red X. And NCPAC does not even use the term "hit list;" it has been saddled with it by its critics. Even so, a *Seattle Times* editorial blasted NCPAC for "borrowing from the vocabulary of organized crime" and "invoking images of criminal violence."[8] The only violence of which NCPAC so far has been guilty, however, is to the careers of liberal politicians.

For New Right strategists, bringing conservative grass-roots pressure on officials is nearly as important as defeating liberals. At Birmingham and similar training sessions around the country, Howard Phillips tells eager, note-taking participants that "if Congress is the key to national policy, then the district is the key to Congress." Turning congressional districts into base camps from which conservatives can shell Washington is the main goal of Phillips's Conservative Caucus. Founded in 1974, in the wake of the Watergate-influenced elections which doomed dozens of conservative incumbents, the Caucus recruits activists for local level politics. Explains Phillips in a Caucus training videotape: "Instead of a single fixed battle in Washington, where our strength is weakest and liberal power is magnified, we seek to operate on 435 political battlefields—one in every congressional district." These operations, during a typical month in 1980, included a lecture in a California district against racial busing, a rally in Michigan against high taxes, a meeting in Nebraska opposing ratification of the Constitutional amendment giving the District of Columbia voting representatives in Congress and rallies against the SALT II treaty in Pennsylvania, Texas, Utah, Wisconsin, Virginia and Wyoming.

During its early years, the Caucus played a key role in mobilizing mass New Right opposition to the Panama Canal treaties and the U.S.-Soviet SALT II nuclear arms limitation accord. Phillips made more than 100 speeches denouncing the Canal agreements and was a principal speaker at the "Campaign to Defeat SALT II" rallies staged in all fifty states. In addition, Conservative Caucus sent out 4.5 million anti-SALT letters and collected 300,000 signatures on petitions denouncing the accord. By telephone, it monthly contacted 25,000 treaty opponents, urging them to continue their fight against SALT. Though a number of factors are responsible for stalling, perhaps permanently, SALT II's momentum, a major one is the grass-roots New Right campaign.

With a conservative occupying the White House, the Caucus has adopted a friendly, though impatient, attitude toward the

Administration. Caucus members, for example, push for deeper spending cuts and faster movement toward a balanced budget than the President originally proposed. Prodded by Phillips, they also urge elimination of the U.S.-U.S.S.R. arms control process as a central ingredient of Washington's strategic planning and call for tougher policies to counter Soviet and Cuban adventures in Latin America. Few issues are receiving more Caucus attention than what Phillips and other New Rightists enjoy calling "defunding the left"—stanching the hundreds of millions of dollars which flow from more than three dozen federal programs, such as Vista, CETA and the Youth Project straight to leftist activist groups. It has been generous taxpayer subventions, argue Phillips, Weyrich and others, which enable leftist organizations to thrive and block the traditionalist agenda. Rightist groups, on the other hand, enjoy very little, if any, federal largesse and rely for support on their own members and on private sector contributors.

That "defunding the left" is picking up support is due mainly to Howard Phillips' efforts. He is perhaps the New Right's most articulate spokesman, with a talent (some may say obsession) for relating issues to what he sees as an underlying left *vs.* right conflict. As head of the Office of Economic Opportunity in 1973, at age thirty-one, he sparked a major controversy when he tried to abolish several of the agency's costly Great Society programs. His efforts put him high on the left's "enemies list" and he has done nothing since then to get off.

Though active at times in both Republican and Democratic politics, he rejects partisanship in favor of firm ideological commitment to conservatism. He watched in horror as the Nixon Administration, though Republican, ultimately embraced liberal policies. "I discovered that we conservatives were losing the government even though we were winning elections," he told the Birmingham training session. "I decided then that we have to give our loyalties to principles and ideals rather than to parties."

An indefatigable organizer and stump speaker, Phillips visited all 435 congressional districts in 1976 (perhaps the only American ever to do so), giving four speeches a day, five days a week, as he constructed the Conservative Caucus network. "My goal was not to leave any meeting without signing up at least one volunteer to carry on," he recalls. To aid his typically politically inexperienced recruits, Phillips leaves behind an extraordinarily detailed leadership manual. In addition to providing a model charter, hints for fund raising, guidelines for "compliance with federal laws governing civic participation" and a catalogue of issues-oriented resource materials (such as the *Federal Register, Congressional Record* and *Commerce Business Daily*), the manual outlines a twenty-step formula for organizing a district in exactly 153 days. On Day 1, for example, the director is to "make a personal commitment to get the job done"; Day 9 is for setting "a realistic timetable for recruiting" local leaders; Day 82 is for announcing the steering committee's "meeting time and location"; and, at last, Day 153 is for accepting "the congratulations and gratitude of all concerned."

Some volunteers are put off by such strict, detailed accountability. Yet it is pure Phillips. When addressing prospective Conservative Caucus district directors, for instance, he routinely reels off a seemingly endless and certainly daunting laundry list of qualifications for the position. Among many other things, he asks:

"Are you thoroughly familiar with the various political organizations within the district?

"Do you have a complete list of the businesses and industries?

"Do you know the products they make and the laws and regulations which particularly concern them?

"What conservative issue groups are active locally? What trade associations, labor unions?

"Do you have a complete list of the daily and weekly newspapers, the TV and radio stations?

"Have you personally eyeballed every neighborhood, either on foot or by car?"

Through Phillips's sheer energy, Conservative Caucus chapters were humming in about 150 congressional districts by mid-1981. Its members, by and large, are solidly middle class, what once was called Middle American. At a Caucus district meeting in Charleston, South Carolina, for instance, those attending included a truck driver, retired Army colonel, insurance agent, a mid-ranking administrator at a federal agency's local office and a TV tower constructor. Several also belonged to other conservative groups, such as NCPAC, the American Security Council and Senator Jesse Helms's Congressional Club. The district chapters, to varying degrees, respond to an alert from Phillips and light grass-roots fires under their congressmen—through mail, telegrams, calls, letters to local newspapers, statements on radio call-in talk shows and, on occasion, meetings and rallies.

* * *

Training is the key to the New Right's ability to mobilize the grass roots. Says Paul Weyrich: "Training is the difference between interest and impact. The Moral Majority and other New Right mass membership groups have aroused the interest of a lot of people in key issues. Now we have to train them." Much of the effort of Weyrich's Committee for the Survival of a Free Congress is aimed at just this. The Moral Majority's Birmingham session, for instance, and those at other locations were organized by CSFC.

New Right training stresses nuts and bolts. At Birmingham, the lecture on lobbying techniques by CSFC's Connaught Marshner was studded with practical advice. "Read the other side's literature," she told the audience. "Know what their arguments are. Get on leftist mailing lists." Reasonableness and pragmatism were constant themes, hardly fitting the extremist, unbending New Right image painted by its critics. "Sometimes you have to compromise; sometimes all that you can do with your lobbying is to make a terrible bill less objectionable," she said. In dealing with legislators, she counseled, "don't sound like an emotional Bible-thumper; don't come across like a crackpot. Avoid scolding. When you write your representatives, don't scribble slogans or put stickers on the envelopes. If you do, you will be treated like a kook and no one will pay attention to what you say." Above all, she added, "Don't forget that the most useful words that you can ever say to a representative are: 'What can I do for you?'"

The New Right also trains prospective candidates. Weyrich and Dolan both run week-long schools where candidates and their staffs learn such critical campaign skills as volunteer recruitment, fund raising, survey research, voter identification, press relations and election day planning. Weyrich's program alone has trained more than 1,000 activists since 1974. New Hampshire's Gordon Humphrey attended the school when he was running for the Senate and credits it with having been "vitally important to my election."

Beyond training, CSFC has been intimately involved in more than 500 campaigns. It helps conservatives organize, raise money and develop electioneering strategies. Marc Nuttle, the widely traveled CSFC national field coordinator, has been a consultant to some 200 campaigns. He assures conservative candidates who follow his rigorous nine-month program of precinct organization that it can "make a five or ten-point difference on election day." Dozens of congressional seats, he emphasizes, are decided by margins even smaller than that. Good organization is particularly critical in primary races, where voter turnout normally is very low. Here a modest but well-run conservative campaign can defeat liberals even before they get into a general election.

Among Weyrich's most ambitious projects is coordinating the New Right groups in Washington. They are discovering, as did those business associations fighting the Consumer Protection Act, the synergystic bonus of coalescing on specific issues. Starting in the early 1970's, occasional, informal brainstorming sessions have evolved into regular, tightly structured strategy meetings of several score business, conservative and single-interest organizations. Hosting them is Coalitions for America, an umbrella organization created by Weyrich to foster coalition-building on the right.

He is well suited to midwife such an original and potentially very influential enterprise. A onetime print and broadcast journalist who arrived in Washington in 1967 as an aide to Senator Gordon Allott of Colorado, he is now widely regarded as one of the New Right's top strategists. He is extremely prolific, cofounding the Heritage Foundation, establishing CSFC and its affiliates and helping launch both the House Republican Study Committee and the Moral Majority. Probably more than any other New Right leader, Weyrich prizes ideological purity and grows quickly impatient with those tempted to settle for less. His CSFC, headquartered in a pair of renovated townhouses in a working-class neighborhood behind Washington's Union Station, has become the New Right's social agenda clearinghouse, coordinating lobbying strategies on such issues as abortion, family policies, education, homosexuality, parents' rights, pornography and drug abuse.

Dealing specifically with these issues is one of three Weyrich-sponsored coalitions. Named the Library Court Group, after the site of its 1979 inaugural session, it convenes every other week at the CSFC headquarters under Marshner's chairmanship. As the pro-traditional family movement's main coordinator and editor of the *Family Protection Report,* she stays continually in touch with many of the thirty or so organizations which attend the meetings. Gathering every second week as well is the Stanton

Group, established in 1980, whose two to three dozen participants concentrate on defense and foreign policy matters. The oldest of the three coalitions is the Kingston Group, which evolved from the original informal gatherings of the early 1970's. Its roughly fifty members convene weekly to survey economic, political and institutional affairs.

While the coalitions do not routinely reveal their participants' identities, it is commonly known that among them are leading traditionalist organizations: Eagle Forum, Conservative Caucus, Moral Majority, Heritage Foundation, American Legislative Exchange Council, right-to-life groups and pro-defense committees. Also attending the sessions are congressional staffers, administration aides and conservative writers. All have at least two characteristics in common: 1) They represent organizations with grass-roots networks or constituencies capable of affecting the public policy process; and 2) They head their organization or hold posts high enough to be able to commit them to action at the meeting.

Action indeed is the purpose of Library Court, Stanton and Kingston meetings. They are neither kaffeeklatches nor bull sessions. After the group is called to order and recites the Lord's Prayer, business zips along. Discussions typically end abruptly with the chairman saying: "Okay, this is an action item. What do we propose to do?"

A case in point is Reagan's block grant program, aimed at giving the states greater leeway in using federal funds. When the White House proposal seemed mired in Congress, Marshner put the matter on the Library Court agenda. A congressional staffer opened discussion by pointing out that liberals opposing the block grant concept were flooding Capitol Hill with grass-roots petitions. "We've got to do something to counter this," he said. For half an hour, the group discussed the political aspects of block grants. Then Marshner rapped her pencil sharply on the table and declared: "This is an action item."

There was quick agreement on a triple-pronged strategy— eighty to ninety organizations were to be recruited for a nationwide pro-block grant coalition that would issue a statement and hold a press conference to demonstrate broad-based support for the Reagan proposal; Library Court participants would mobilize their grass-roots networks to lobby congressmen on behalf of the program; a Library Court sub-group would meet with forty to fifty pro-block grant senators and representatives to plan further moves. Marshner then scanned the room for volunteers. One said that she could assign a member of her organization's staff to call across the country to recruit groups for the pro-block grant coalition. Another offered to arrange the meeting with the legislators. A third promised to organize the press conference. A CSFC staffer, taking notes of this, later called the volunteers to check on their progress.

While the Library Court block grant effort sought to generate nationwide support, the coalitions also can target selectively. The Kingston Group, for example, focused on just a handful of swing Democrats when a critical part of the Reagan economic program seemed short of votes in the House. With a bit of "educating," it was argued, these Democrats could be turned around and convinced to back the President. "We can have some of our people in their districts write letters to the local papers," said a Kingston participant. "We can probably get papers to run editorials urging the congressmen to support the measure," added another. Observing that his organization had a very active chapter in one congressman's hometown, a third offered to find out "if any of our members have worked in his campaign or know him well enough to contact him and make a personal pitch."

Much of the three coalitions' impact goes unnoticed. The groups do not seek—in fact, they shun—publicity and until very recently even denied the existence of a formal coalition structure. While they are not able to deliver on every issue and not all members support every item on the agenda, they bring unprecedented coordination to grass-roots lobbying, an asset once enjoyed exclusively by the labor unions.

Though Washington has been feeling the coalitions' heat for just a few years, their influence already is respected. Conservative officials and legislators turn to them increasingly for help in shaping policies and getting bills passed. Weyrich says that the three coalitions have been involved in hundreds of legislative matters. Labor law reform, taxpayer funding of congressional elections and the Domestic Violence Bill all have been defeated, he claims, partly because of grass-roots campaigns against them organized by the coalitions. And when the Reagan budget won its surprise 1981 victory in the House, G.O.P. Whip Trent Lott thanked "all of the Kingston Group members." Their grass-roots effort, he said, "was pivotal in this critical victory."

Indicative too of the coalitions' clout is the frequency with which cabinet members, senators and senior White House aides turn up at Library Court, Kingston and Stanton sessions and subject themselves to fairly rough grillings. When one department secretary appeared in June 1981 and remarked that he still had Carter holdovers on his staff, he was curtly asked, "Why don't you get rid of them?" When an undersecretary acknowledged at another session that his department had botched the presentation of a new policy to Congress and the public, Weyrich cut in saying, "Next time, come to us. We can help you." The senior official nodded and said, "Next time, I will."

The most important New Right coalition may be the least formal—the small circle of the movement's founding fathers. They confer frequently, dine together, visit each others' homes and enjoy each others' company. The tightest nucleus contains Phillips, Dolan, Weyrich, Viguerie, Heritage's Feulner and Morton Blackwell who, as a pied piper of conservatism, has turned countless college students into activists. On many occasions, the circle widens a bit to include Eagle Forum's Phyllis Schlafly, Senator Jesse Helms, Religious Roundtable founder Edward McAteer and Robert Billings, the Moral Majority's first executive director and later a Reagan Administration senior official.

Viguerie plays a particularly critical role in this informal coalition. His direct mail firm, which started with a list of 12,000 contributors to the 1964 Barry Goldwater campaign and now contains names of more than 4 million conservatives and 15 million other voters, has been the chief fund-raising vehicle for almost every New Right group, at least during its early years. Other New Right figures, moreover, highly value his strategic and tactical insights and personal advice. Says Phillips: "We could not have happened without Richard. The strength of his firm is much of the strength of the movement."

The founding fathers get along well, perhaps because they stem from similar soil. All of the inner circle were in their late-thirties as the 1980's began, with Dolan a half-decade younger and Viguerie a half-decade older. They are not preppies. None have blueblood pedigrees and, except for Harvard graduate Phillips, none attended elite schools. Though initiated into politics by the G.O.P., their roots do not reach to the Establishment or country club wings of the party. Instead, they are alumni of the very conservative Young Americans for Freedom (Viguerie was its first executive secretary) and the Intercollegiate Studies Institute. Jesse Helms and Paul Laxalt, predictably, are much more their idea of Republicans than George Bush and Charles Percy. "We really come from the lower middle class—from blue-collar backgrounds," says Weyrich. "I lived in a neighborhood filled with union members; all my relatives belonged to unions."

Political analysts at times describe New Rightists as populist. In some respects, the label fits. Their rhetoric blasts Big Business, for example, just about as often as it does Big Government, Big Labor and Big Bureaucracy. A populistlike sense of mission clearly propels them, as does their populist enthusiasm for grass-roots politicking. Earthy language comes easily to Dolan, who uses obscenities to shock. Weyrich shocks too, but by shifting effortlessly into a mega-moral righteousness. They clearly enjoy what they are doing—despite Phillips' perpetual permanent teeth-clenching scowl—and delight in shaking up the Republican Party apparatus by outperforming it on some issues and in some races.

Their names constantly pop up on membership lists of New Right boards and advisory committees. It is not unusual for them all to appear on the same platform, teaching and preaching at New Right conferences, rallies and workshops. In a sense, therefore, the inner circle functions as a true interlocking directorate, speeding the flow of ideas and information between groups and providing extraordinary coordination for the whole movement.

When they spot a political opportunity which they feel might be exploited by formation of a new committee or group, they help launch it by making the calls, bringing together the potential organizers and suggesting seed-money sources. At times, they have been astonishingly successful. In late 1978, for instance, Phillips, Weyrich and McAteer concluded that the vast Christian Fundamentalist community was ripe for political mobilization. At McAteer's suggestion, he and Phillips flew to Lynchburg, Virginia, in January 1979, for a luncheon meeting with Reverend Jerry Falwell, one of the nation's most popular Fundamentalist clergymen and TV preachers who had begun speaking out with increasing frequency and fervor about America's moral problems. When his guests arrived, Falwell apologetically told them that he could spare only one hour. Yet so engrossed did he become in their grim description of the state of the nation that he canceled the rest of the day's appointments. They talked through early evening, for eight hours, and sketched the outlines of a new, mass, grass-roots organization. At one point during this marathon session, Phillips suddenly observed: "There is a moral majority in this country." From this observation came the name of the New Right's most spectacular political force.

Paul Weyrich first used the name Moral Majority in public. The name clearly touches a nerve. To those tens of millions of Americans who have felt that their values are being assaulted by an aggressive minority determined to impose amoral and even immoral liberalism, the new organization's banner reassures that out there, scattered across the country, is a majority for morality. Its membership, in essence, existed before Moral Majority was formed. Little else explains its phenomenal growth.

By election day 1980, just seventeen months after its founding, the Moral Majority, Inc., had become a national household word and the subject each week of hundreds of newspaper and magazine articles. Its membership had rocketed to 2 million, was still growing and included 72,000 ministers, priests and rabbis. Though only about one-tenth of these clergymen are active Moral Majoritarians, the numbers still are staggering, for they comprise a cadre with enormous credibility and influence in their communities. They have signed up because they see Moral Majority, as its recruiting brochure states, giving "voice to the millions of decent, law-abiding, God-fearing Americans who want to do something about the moral decline of our country." It is a very new voice. For most of its members, Moral Majority is an initiation into political activity. When asked why they have joined, typically they reply that they have had no choice for they take with deadly seriousness the warning of Proverbs 29:2, the religious right's favorite scriptural passage, that "when the righteous are in authority, the people rejoice, but when the wicked beareth rule, the people mourn."

Moral Majority is not the only new conservative Christian movement dedicated to putting the "righteous in authority." The California-based Christian Voice, founded in 1978 by Fuller Theological Seminary graduate Robert Grant, has more than 30,000 clergymen on its rolls. During the 1980 election campaign, it ran television commercials in southern states accusing Jimmy Carter of supporting homosexual rights and sponsored "Christians for Reagan."

More ecumenical is the Religious Roundtable, established in

1980 by Edward McAteer, a former Colgate-Palmolive marketing executive and Conservative Caucus national field director. Its advisory board includes a sprinkling of Roman Catholic priests, mainline Protestant ministers and Jewish rabbis in addition to a large number of evangelical and Fundamentalist preachers. It was at the Roundtable's August 1980 National Affairs Briefing in Dallas, attended by about 15,000 politically concerned pious Americans, that Candidate Reagan and the religious right publicly and formally embraced. During the campaign, McAteer's organization sent copies of the G.O.P. and Democratic platforms to 35,000 clergymen, calling their attention to the sharp differences in the planks dealing with family matters. The main reason for these differences, of course, is that New Right pressure forced the Republicans to adopt strong "pro-family" positions.

By far, the dominant religious force on the right is the Moral Majority. Its name has become synonymous with the entire movement (to both its advantage and disadvantage), overshadowing all other groups. In large part, the Moral Majority's success is due to Jerry Falwell, who brings impressive credentials to the movement he agreed to head. He is articulate, intelligent and dedicated to moral revival. Above all, he is a tremendously inspiring preacher and superb organizer. From his tiny church of thirty-five souls founded in an abandoned Lynchburg pop-bottling factory in 1956, he has built the 17,000-member Thomas Road Baptist Church, the 3,000-student and accredited Liberty Baptist College, Lynchburg Academy for primary and secondary schooling, a home for alcoholics, a Bible institute and a seminary. His televised "Old-Time Gospel Hour" reaches millions of households weekly via nearly 400 stations. Since he kicked off his first "I Love America Rally" in celebration of the nation's bicentennial, he has taken this noon-time program of religious and patriotic hymns, sermons and moral exhortation to the steps of each of the fifty state capitols.

To listen to the legions of apocalyptical critics on the left, it would seem that the Moral Majority not only poses an enormous threat to American liberties and pluralism but that it substantially (and negatively) influenced the 1980 elections. Ironically Falwell and his colleagues take relatively little credit for what happened at the polls. The national organization, for example, endorsed no candidates. While the October 15, 1980 issue of the *Moral Majority Report,* mailed to 475,000 homes, featured a sample presidential ballot on its first page, no candidate preference was indicated and the Carter-Mondale ticket actually appeared ahead of Reagan-Bush. The issue's editorial emphasized that "this is the most important election in modern history," yet carefully avoided even implying a Moral Majority candidate. "It is a sacred duty to vote," is all that the editorial said. "We are encouraging as strongly as we know how, a turnout of every American voter."

The relatively few candidates supported by the Moral Majority were endorsed by state or city chapters which enjoy almost full autonomy from Lynchburg in policy matters. Alabama's Moral Majority, for example, opposed Congressman John Buchanan, a Birmingham Republican, because the group concluded that he had become too liberal, particularly on abortion. With Moral Majority backing, Gary Lee Smith beat Buchanan in the G.O.P. primary and then won the general election.

Moral Majority's major national election effort was voter registration, and Falwell claims that his organization inscribed two million new names on polling lists. At his own church, he regularly exhorted unregistered voters: "Repent of it. It is a sin." Oklahoma Moral Majority Chairman James Vineyard, pastor of Oklahoma City's Windsor Hills Baptist Church, advised his fellow preachers to tell their congregations that good Christians were good citizens and good citizens register and vote. Nearly 1,000 Tulsa and Oklahoma City churches joined Vineyard's registration drive.

In Indianapolis, Reverend Greg Dixon, Indiana Moral Majority chairman and a seminary classmate of Falwell, invited official registrars to set up tables in the foyer of his huge Indianapolis Bible Temple. As worshipers left services, they paused to register. Dixon says that 1,000 new voters signed up this way at the Bible Temple alone. "This large figure says something about the evangelical and Fundamentalist churches," observes Dixon. "Great numbers of these people had dropped out of the political process and many now are returning, hoping their voices will be heard."

Though not endorsing candidates, the Moral Majority did publicize their voting records in Congress by distributing hundreds of thousands of comparative indexes. The National Christian Action Committee's "Family Voting Index," for example, assigns a morality rating ranging from 0 to 100 to every member of Congress, based on how he or she has voted on ten specific issues. Among the Senate votes used for the index are those on the school prayer amendment, parental consent for sex education in public schools, establishment of the Department of Education, Internal Revenue Service harassment of private schools and restrictions on federal spending. To be rated favorably, senators had to vote for positions backing prayer in school, consent for sex education and budget limitations and opposing the other issues. Five senators scored a perfect 100, all Republicans: William Armstrong, Jesse Helms, Gordon Humphrey, Paul Laxalt and Richard Schweiker. At the other end of the scale were the four Republicans and nineteen Democrats with zero ratings. Among them were the most prominent liberals subsequently defeated at the polls: Birch Bayh, John Culver, Gaylord Nelson and George McGovern.

In some localities, Moral Majority chapters distributed small leaflets prepared by FaithAmerica of Scottsdale, Arizona. Instead of assigning a cumulative score, the leaflets simply indicated how candidates had voted on abortion, school prayer, forced school busing, tax deductions for contributions to churches and similar social issues. Explains Richard Osborne, Indiana Moral Majority Executive Director: "We didn't endorse anyone, only distributed material to show how they voted—such as Bayh favoring abortion. Thus, if you were for abortion, our leaflet made you think that Bayh is a great guy; but if you opposed abortion, then you just knew that Bayh is not with you." Every Moral Majoritarian, of course, almost surely ferociously opposes abortion and has strong feelings on the other voting index items. The Bayhs, McGoverns and Culvers thus are certain to suffer when such long-apathetic citizens at last begin participating in the political process.

Simply bringing Fundamentalists, especially the preachers, into this process may be the Moral Majority's most remarkable accomplishment to date. Aversion to politics, after all, long has been a Fundamentalist hallmark. Strengthening their local churches and fortifying their own commitment to Christ typically have concerned the faithful infinitely more than has reforming the community. Explains Oklahoma City's Vineyard: "Our crowd, the Fundamentalist crowd, had taken the position of— let's just pray about it rather than get involved in politics." Praying was precisely all that Falwell was doing a decade ago, when he preached against mixing pulpit and politics.

Since then, the preachers have grown alarmed by what they see as the nation's steep moral decline—a perception they form from Falwell's messages, Moral Majority training sessions, New Right workshops and Ed McAteer's Religious Roundtable. Typical is Bill Smith, minister of White's Ferry Road Church of Christ in West Monroe, Louisiana. "I was one of those saying that preachers shouldn't get into politics," he explains, "and for 180 years, we had no cause to get involved." Where to build a highway or how many trucks the fire department needs were decisions which Smith happily left to government. But now, he charges, "the government has been transgressing into our business—into the business of morals and values, into social matters." This leaves him no choice, he says, but "to get politically involved," a sentiment countless other clergymen echo.

As proselytizers by trade, Fundamentalist and evangelical ministers throw themselves with skilled zeal into organizing Moral Majority chapters. After James Vineyard and a few Oklahoma City colleagues returned from a spring 1980 Moral Majority conference in Indianapolis, inspired to battle for moral resurgence, they began culling the state's telephone books, making lists of ministers in the county seats. Eventually they persuaded at least one minister in each of the seventy-seven counties to host and invite local clergymen to a breakfast or luncheon meeting. Recalls Vineyard: "We appeared at these meetings and asked for help in putting together a state Moral Majority. We told them what we saw happening in America—the dropping morals, the blatant homosexuality, the abortions. I said to them all: 'God is going to judge this country because of what we're doing with abortion.' " Of the ten to thirty attending the sessions, half usually signed on with Vineyard.

They went back to their churches and established Moral Action Committees, which then contacted other members of the congregation and distributed Moral Majority literature. The clergymen also organized "God and Country" rallies on their county courthouse steps. At them, a Moral Majority representative described the nation's sad plight and made a pitch for members.

By early 1981, chapters were functioning in every state, politicizing habitually indifferent Christians. Ron Zelinsky, a mid-thirties optometral photographer in the Los Angeles area, is one of them. "I had never been involved in anything political," he recalls. "But I was becoming distressed by the trends in the country.

One Sunday in mid-1980, my pastor preached that good Christians must be good citizens and good citizens must know what's going on in the country." Taking the sermon to heart, Zelinsky helped found a Bible Political Awareness Group to relate Scripture to such contemporary issues as abortion, taxation, social welfare programs and corruption. After that, he joined his local Conservative Caucus and soon became its district director.

Judged by its rather tame activities, the Moral Majority seems an unlikely target for excoriation. Yet brutal rhetorical attacks continue, based mainly on misunderstanding or misinterpretation of what the organization says and does—or on deliberate misrepresentation. The most egregious distortions come, strangely enough, from those who ought to be most committed to fair play and truth. The American Civil Liberties Union, for example, without citing evidence, has run a full-page ad in major newspapers which directly states or very strongly implies that the Moral Majority 1) is against birth control (it is not), 2) wants its "religious doctrines enacted into law and imposed on everyone" (it does not), 3) says the "law should keep women in their place" (it has not), 4) is for legally punishing homosexuals (it is not) and 5) raises $1 million each week with its television program (it does not but wishes it did).

Columnists such as Mike Royko depict Falwell as a Nazi, ignoring completely the fact that the Moral Majority president has been honored by Jewish organizations in recognition of his support for Israel. And *The New York Times,* meanwhile, without verifying it, repeats the accusation that Falwell has said that God "does not hear the prayer of a Jew."[9] (Southern Baptist Convention President Bailey Smith said it; Falwell repudiated the statement months before the *Times* article.)

Distortions became so prevalent that the Moral Majority paid for ads in early 1981 simply to explain what it is *not,* a topic which Falwell has had to make the theme of speeches. In joking allusion to its unwarranted sinister image, Moral Majority Vice-President Cal Thomas started a speech to an Alabama Moral Majority meeting by saying: "Good evening, fellow fanatics. It's good to be with a group ready to take over America." To improve the organization's image, he advised the group to take reporters and editors to lunch. "If you don't show up in a white sheet or wearing a Nazi armband, you will shock them and already will be halfway there in making your points," he said only in half-jest. "Show them that you are a normal citizen, with valid, reasonable concerns."

Prompting much of the criticism of the Moral Majority seems to be a feeling that it has built its muscle by somewhat illegitimate means, in a sense by violating the rules of the American political game. Such feelings were at the heart of the charge, for example, raised often around the 1980 elections, that Jerry Falwell and the other preachers violate the constitutionally-mandated rigid separation of church and state when they speak out on political issues. For weeks, editorialists, commentators and liberals warned that the religious right was undermining a fundamental constitutional principle.

This attack eventually collapsed. For one thing, constitutional scholars began pointing out that the Bill of Rights enjoins the state from making laws respecting religion but does not bar clergymen from addressing political questions. For another thing, conservatives were quick to note that liberal and radical clerics have not been criticized (or even reprimanded) for their public, political stands in support of civil rights or against the draft. So convincing was the religious right's rebuttal that liberals ultimately had to concede the hollowness of their Church/State criticism. Said Rabbi Alexander Schindler, an unrelenting foe of the New Right: "I'm not concerned with clergy being involved in politics; I am involved too. Everyone is." Remarked the ACLU's Ira Glasser: "The Christian right is not doing anything different than did Martin Luther King, Jr., when he preached civil rights from the pulpit or than did William Sloane Coffin when he opposed the war in Vietnam."

The attacks, however, did not cease, they only shifted ground. The issue then became the voting indexes disseminated by the Moral Majority. "Moral hit lists with 'zero ratings,'" is how the American Jewish Committee's Tanenbaum indignantly put the matter. Surely this proved that Falwell and company were not playing fairly.

Yet at least a couple of dozen liberal organizations have been doing the same thing for years. The Americans for Democratic Action, for instance, has rated members of Congress since 1947. As with the "Family Issues Index," the ADA uses a 0 to 100 scale and gives candidates a "Liberal Quotient" score derived from votes in Congress. For the 1980 index, candidates won ADA points by voting for food stamps and continued government regulation of small business and against draft registration and funds for the MX missile. The index distributed by AFSCME, the public employees union, brands votes "right" or "wrong," as do the AFL-CIO and the National Education Association in their indexes. To vote against the positions backed by Ralph Nader's Congress Watch lobby, meanwhile, is to be tagged anti-consumer. The Moral Majority and the other Christian right groups are not even the only religious organizations monitoring candidates' votes; the Friends Committee on National Legislation, a Quaker group, has been doing just this since 1945.

Some critics of the Christian right argue that a number of the issues on which it rates candidates have little to do with morality or family matters. Why should the Moral Majority, it is said, care how a congressman votes on establishing the Department of Education or restricting budget growth? The same objections, however, apply to other organizations which broadly stretch the definition of what is appropriate for their indexes. The Friends, for example, include votes on the International Development Bank. For Nader's group, legislation regarding construction of a waterway running from Tennessee to the Gulf Coast is apparently a "consumer" issue, while the NEA defines "support of education" to mean voting to make the birthday of Martin Luther King, Jr., a national holiday on which federal employees receive full pay and voting against limiting federal outlays to 21 percent of the gross national product.

The Moral Majority and the smaller organizations of the Christian right thus are simply doing what other groups long have done—with one critical exception. And it is this which almost certainly is the real and root cause of the left's concerns and fears. The Moral Majority is speaking to and mobilizing a truly mass constituency in support of traditional values, and these are values alien to the contemporary American left. Howard Phillips was among the first to appreciate the enormous potential of galvinizing the preachers. Eighteen months after the Moral Majority's founding, he buoyantly exclaimed that his expectations were being fulfilled. "The religious conservative movement is the most significant movement in American politics since organized labor discovered the ballot box," he said.

The secret of Moral Majority growth turns out to be no secret at all. It is not that Falwell has been playing dirty or breaking the rules of the game. He and his preachers simply stand for and articulately advocate what vast and increasing legions of Americans want. A Moral Majority "platform," in fact, would read like a traditionalist resurgence checklist. In a signed article in the May 14, 1981, *Moral Majority Report,* Falwell sketched his organization's basic beliefs, emphasizing commitment to the "dignity of human life" (hence opposition to abortion), the "traditional monogamous family," the work ethic and a common decency which excludes pornography. Crucial too is Moral Majority's strong support of Israel; Falwell argues that America's own future could depend on how it deals with the Jewish state. Citing Genesis 12, in which God tells Abraham that "I will bless them that bless thee and curse them that curse you," Falwell explains (as he has for years) that "history proves that God deals with nations in accord with how those nations deal with Israel."

The article pleads for God-centered education to take the place of the "secular humanism" which, it states, "has become the religion of the public school system in America." This issue is of growing importance to traditionalist groups across the country as they conclude that public education has been captured by "secular humanists" who not only have driven religion from the classrooms but are substituting for it an explicitly anti-religious doctrine. It is, they maintain, a "man-centered" philosophy that undermines traditional Judeo-Christian moral teachings. Banning classroom prayer is simply one of the "secular humanist" agenda's most visible aspects. Writes Falwell: "While every American should oppose mandated prayers and the teaching of any particular religious creed in publicly funded classrooms, the return of voluntary prayer to public schools would be a first step back toward God-centered education."

A more detailed list of Moral Majority beliefs is Falwell's *Ninety-Five Theses For the 1980's,* issued in May 1980. It champions the American flag, the free enterprise system, strong national defense, a balanced budget, limited federal power, tougher treatment of criminals and removal from office of elected officials "found guilty of sexual promiscuity." One-fourth of the theses deal with family matters. Branded specifically "anti-family" are: communal living, abortion, homosexuality, polygamy, child or wife abuse, alcohol or drug abuse, pre-marital sex, incest, adultery, pornography, no-fault divorce and the Equal Rights Amendment. Thesis Number 68, meanwhile, insists that "churches and private religious schools be free from state and federal harassment." This refers to the Carter Administration's attempt to use the IRS to intimidate and even shut down private Christian schools. Many evangelical and Fundamentalist clergymen were so enraged by this that they decided, for the first time, to become politically active.

Since the 1980 elections, Moral Majority has continued growing. It is giving a high priority to training its members at sessions like that at Birmingham and to lobbying in Washington for anti-abortion measures, the Reagan economic package, tax deductions for private school tuition costs and bills permitting prayer in public classrooms. Its newsletter was going to 850,000 households by late 1981, its budget was over $4 million and it was projecting $10 million in spending for 1982. Along with several dozen other New Right and religious organizations, Moral Majority formed the Coalition for Decency to monitor television broadcasting and direct public pressure, possibly through product boycotts, on firms sponsoring programs containing excessive sex and violence.

At state levels, Moral Majority chapters have won a number of legislative victories. Oklahoma passed a law requiring that the theory of creation be taught in classrooms along with the theory of evolution; Indiana has enacted a law specifically recognizing the rights of parents to discipline their children, including by spanking (something that had been contested under prior statutes). Greg Dixon and Richard Osborne, meantime, have become frequent guests on local Indiana TV and radio interview programs and at civic and social group meetings. Osborne even has debated a homosexual rights activist on whether homosexuals are entitled to status as a legal minority.

When the Reagan budget and tax cuts were heading toward a vote in Congress, the Moral Majority's state chapters mobilized their members to write and phone their congressional representatives urging support for the President. The state groups also are working with Eagle Forum to demand that local authorities and publishers revise school textbooks to again favorably portray traditional family relationships. A bit dazed by Moral Majority's soaring influence, Osborne muses: "It is amazing how little you have to do politically to be doing a lot. This is because so few people do anything politically."

Some local groups, however, manage to embarrass Lynchburg by seeming to confirm the left's caricature of the Moral

Majority. The Maryland chapter, for example, earned statewide ridicule by campaigning against "pornographic" cookies— anatomically correct gingerbread men and women sold by an Annapolis baker. Though extremely displeased, Lynchburg could take no action against its autonomous affiliate. (The Maryland chairman ultimately broke away from the national headquarters and formed his own moral-issues group.) A self-appointed Moral Majority chairman in northern California, meanwhile, demanded the death penalty for homosexuals. An outraged Lynchburg quickly repudiated him and the proposal. Said Moral Majority National Field Director Charles Cade in a Gannett News Service interview: "Some of our people get *A* for enthusiasm, but an *F* for judgment."[10] And Ronald Godwin, Moral Majority's executive director, told the Birmingham conference that "we've made mistakes. We've made a lot of mistakes. Some of our zealous members have said things that could have been said better."

Godwin assured the group that Moral Majority learns from its mistakes. It has adjusted its rhetoric, for example, to make it less vulnerable to charges of indifference to the nation's pluralistic heritage. Seldom do Falwell, Godwin and other senior Majoritarians make a speech or give an interview without reaffirming deep commitment to American pluralism. The organization also intends to tighten control of local chapters and to recruit more minority members. Though it counts Orthodox rabbis and black Fundamentalist ministers in its ranks, most members are white Christians, mainly Protestants. Godwin publicly has invited black and Jewish leaders to meet Moral Majority halfway. "Say, fellows, call our bluff," he declared. "Test our good intentions; put the ball back in our court; and see if Moral Majority is really willing to deliver on our pledge of friendship to minorities." If it successfully expands into the nation's minority communities, Moral Majority will have created an unprecedented grass-roots organization, providing an extraordinary mass base for the New Right.

Few phenomena of modern American politics rival the New Right for the speed with which it has emerged as a significant force and the extent of its influence. Liberals, of course, can imitate some New Right methods, such as mass mailings to solicit contributions and spark support for issues and candidates. Yet Richard Viguerie probably enjoys at least a half-decade head start in mastery of mass mailing technology. Other New Right tactics also may not be easy to copy. Spotlighting voting records, for example, works well when the target is a liberal legislator representing conservative constituents. It may be equally effective against conservatives who represent liberals. But the left surely cannot count very much on harming conservatives representing conservative areas. Liberals are hardly going to score points by "exposing" Paul Laxalt's conservative record to his fellow Nevadans or Strom Thurmond's to South Carolinians or Jake Garn's to Utahans. What gives the New Right clout, in short, is a quality which the left cannot duplicate—the skill of translating the traditionalist resurgence, particularly on social matters, into political power.

While liberals puzzle how to fight back, New Rightists continue pushing ahead to broaden their base. Weyrich's CSFC, for example, has launched a project to foster coalitions of Republican and Democratic conservatives when they constitute majorities in their state assemblies. There also is a chance of this at the federal level. After the 1982 congressional elections, even without a clear-cut Republican majority, conservatives could take control of the House of Representatives if the three to four dozen conservative Democrats, known as the "boll weevils," vote with the Republicans. They could elect a conservative speaker, conservative committee chairmen and control the very powerful committee staffs.

To improve the chances of such a coalition emerging, New Right groups plan to go after liberals on their home turf—the Democratic Party. By entering and supporting conservatives in Democratic Senate and House primaries, the New Right hopes to defeat liberals before they get to the general election. Said one New Right leader at a closed-door conference in mid-1981: "The time is ripe for conservatives to take over the Democratic party." The general election then would become a contest between conservatives.

The top New Right priority remains its relationship with the Reagan White House. Though few New Rightists had experience qualifying them for cabinet-level posts, several have been appointed to second ranking positions and hundreds serve in third-and-fourth-ranking slots. This is creating a cadre of New Rightists who will have the backgrounds and experience qualifying them for very senior jobs in future administrations. Meantime, the New Right intends to maintain its pressure on Reagan, to keep him—

as it most commonly is put—"honest." To a Conservative Caucus group in December 1980, Weyrich said: "Our role is to hold the feet of those elected to the conservative fire." Several months later, NCPAC's Dolan told participants at a Religious Roundtable leadership training conference that their "responsibility with the Reagan Administration is to remind them constantly why it won."

Members of the Reagan White House welcome this. Franklyn (Lyn) Nofziger, a key presidential adviser, has assured New Rightists: "I don't mind if you criticize this President. He needs pressure from the right." The trouble is, explained Nofziger, "in this town, traditionally, most of the pressures have come from the left. You need some balance there."[11] Balance is precisely what the New Right brings.

XII

CONCLUSION: THE TRADITIONALIST CHALLENGE

KAISER ALUMINUM'S CORNELL MAIER has called it "war" when urging fellow business executives to speak out for the free enterprise system. Illinois Homemaker Rosemary Thomson talks of a massive counteroffensive against radical feminism. New Right organizer Paul Weyrich plots political strategies and tactics. And neoconservative Irving Kristol rallies fellow intellectuals to enlist in the war of ideas.

Martial terminology aptly describes what has been happening in traditionalist America. War now rages. For decades, it was a one-sided cold war in which counterculture, ultraliberal and other anti-traditionalist forces employed classic salami tactics, cutting away at traditionalist positions a slice at a time. So thin were the slices that traditionalists paid little attention to what was happening and, as historian James Hitchcock puts it, mainly "grouched."

Then pushed to the brink of patience and tolerance, frightened and angry by what they regarded as the horrible excesses of contemporary liberalism, traditionalists stopped grouching, started returning the hostile fire and turned the cold war hot. In so doing, they have been altering the balance of forces in American society and reshaping the landscape of American politics. The 1978 congressional elections, with conservative upsets in Iowa, New Hampshire and Colorado, were early signs of this. Strengthening the trend two years later were Ronald Reagan's startlingly wide victory margin, the Republican capture of the

Senate and conservative gains within both parties in the House of Representatives.

In these two elections, more than half of the Senate's most prominent liberals were replaced by aggressively conservative Republicans. Missing from their Senate seats in 1981 as the Ninety-seventh Congress convened were Iowa's Dick Clark and John Culver, South Dakota's George McGovern, Idaho's Frank Church, Washington's Warren Magnuson, Indiana's Birch Bayh, New York's Jacob Javits and Wisconsin's Gaylord Nelson. In the House, with the forty or so members of the newly formed Conservative Democratic Forum voting with Republicans on tax, budget and other critical issues, conservatives effectively have a majority. Even most of the more liberal members of both chambers seem to be less liberal now; ratings by the American Conservative Union and other organizations show Senate and House averages moving steadily to the right since the late 1970's.

Yet politics is a recent, perhaps the most recent, arena in which traditionalists are scoring points. Marxists have no monopoly on the common sense observation that a society's administrative "superstructure" reflects and responds to developments at the grass-roots "substructure." And it is at the grass roots where the battle has been raging, often little noticed, for some time. It is being fought in a number of social sectors by different armies and a variety of weapons: Illinois Power Company fighting to tell its side of a controversial story; parents demanding minimum competency standards in education; the Skousens, Schroeders and their neighbors battling for the traditional family; homemakers opposing the Equal Rights Amendment and asserting the dignity of the traditional woman; Bud Clarke and Stephen Wesley struggling to restore the basics to the school curriculum; Christians and Jews flocking back to the faith of their fathers; and businessmen and economists battling the regulatory Leviathan.

These are traditionalists, or those with traditional views in a critical sector of their lives, mounting their counteroffensive. Their success has dazed and demoralized much of American liberalism. Surveying the carnage strewn across the political battlefield in early 1981, George Cunningham, a veteran liberal activist and long-time aide to George McGovern, admitted: "Now we call ourselves 'progressives.' We don't dare use the term 'liberal.' " He tells of his meeting with a group of "old-line liberals" who wanted to "do something" to combat the conservative trend. "I almost felt like I was visiting Tito's partisans during World War II," Cunningham recalls. "They were very distressed and depressed, as if completely surrounded by the enemy. And they talked as if all their efforts of the past decades had been for naught."

Their hysterical reaction, of course, is scarcely warranted—as yet. Traditionalists are just beginning to roll back two generations of liberal measures. Liberals and liberalism are far from being decisively crushed. The great tide, however, clearly and strongly is flowing with the traditionalists. Their self-confidence and sense of momentum are increasing, along with signs that their counteroffensive is spreading to new sectors. Unabashedly conservative publications, like *The Wall Street Journal, Commentary, Human Events* and *The American Spectator* are growing in circulation and influence and have become required reading for policy-makers and analysts. *The New Republic,* long a liberal flagship, has begun steering to the right on economic matters—though it continues proclaiming a blind faith in "an aggressive role" for government in "improving the national welfare."[1] In other papers and journals, finding traditionalist arguments and ideas is getting easier. Where once liberal pundits were featured almost exclusively, today more than a dozen conservative columnists are syndicated in newspapers across the nation. Among them: George Will, M. Stanton Evans, R. Emmett Tyrrell, Jr. (the founder of *The American Spectator*), Phyllis Schlafly, William Safire and conservative veterans William F. Buckley, Jr., Patrick Buchanan and James J. Kilpatrick.

Traditionalism is breaching other major liberal strongholds. America's ethnic communities, long impregnable New Deal citadels, are questioning liberalism's once-accepted infallibility. East and South European groups have become suspicious of budget deficits, the burgeoning federal bureaucracy and a shrinking defense capability. On social issues, they oppose abortion and radical feminism and support traditional approaches to schooling and sex education. As a result, they are voting in greater percentages for Republican candidates, particularly Ronald Reagan.

This is true even for the devotedly Democratic Jewish community. According to surveys of voters leaving the polls on November 4, 1980, only 47 percent of the Jewish electorate backed Jimmy Carter, while 37 percent supported Reagan and 17 percent were for Independent John Anderson. This was the first time since at least 1928, observes Milton Himmelfarb, coeditor of *The American Jewish Yearbook*, that a majority of Jews did not vote for the Democratic presidential candidate. The Orthodox Jewish community of Brooklyn's Borough Park, meanwhile, gave an astounding 76 percent of its vote to Reagan. Orthodox Jews are recognizing common interests with the New Right on such important issues as aid to private schools and opposition to abortion, sexual permissiveness and aggressive secularism. Writes Himmelfarb: "Courts forbid the Ten Commandments to be exposed to children and then allow the children to be exposed to vile movies. For the Moral Majority, that is secular humanism. For Borough Park, it is . . . paganism."[2]

What is most remarkable, traditionalism seems to be making inroads into the nation's most overwhelmingly liberal constituency on public policy matters: blacks. When San Francisco's Institute for Contemporary Studies, in December 1980, hosted an unprecedented conference of conservative blacks, more than 100 black educators, economists, writers and professionals turned up. Some were deeply moved by the occasion. Until that moment, a number of them later said, they had felt as if they were the only black conservatives in the nation. A *Washington Post* reporter assigned to this two-day Black Alternatives Conference wrote that "the atmosphere was as if some long-ago separated tribe had come together again."[3]

Because blacks contemptuously have associated the "conservative" label with racism, they are shocked when they recognize that, in effect, they are conservatives. Typical is William Keyes, a staffer on the Joint Economic Committee of Congress. He told the *Baltimore Sun:* "I wanted to categorize myself as a liberal, but the approach to problems that I kept taking was the same as conservatives were taking."[4] Explains J. A. Parker, a Washington, D.C., black who heads his own public relations firm and founded the Lincoln Institute, a research organization concentrating on black issues: "Middle-class blacks confront many of the same issues that concern middle-class whites—inflation, quality education, high taxes, crime, national defense and employment opportunities." Economics is a major issue nudging blacks rightward. Two leading conservative black spokesmen, in fact, are economists: Hoover Institution Senior Fellow Thomas Sowell and George Mason University Professor Walter Williams. They and their colleagues stress that what blacks most need are the opportunities offered by a growing economy rather than the favors granted by a growing government.

Sowell told the Black Alternatives Conference that "the issue is not that government gives too much help to the poor. The problem is that the government creates too much harm to the poor." Rent control, the minimum wage and other measures ostensibly designed to help the impoverished, argue Sowell and Williams and their conservative associates, not only fail to fulfill their lofty promises but end up making things worse for the poor. "When we talk about rent controls, we need not be satisfied with clichés about affordable housing," Sowell said at the Conference. "We need to ask the factual question: Will there be more housing or less under rent control? When we talk about minimum wage laws, we need to ask not whether a decent wage is a good objective, but whether there will be more jobs at higher pay or no jobs and no pay for increasing numbers of people."[5] Elsewhere, Sowell has claimed that poverty could be eliminated by holding "a meeting of all the leading experts on poverty somewhere in the middle of the Pacific and not let them go home for ten years. When they came back, they would discover that there was no poverty."

What would have happened during their stay in the Pacific is that the free enterprise system, unharassed by poverty experts, would have generated sustained economic growth in which black Americans would participate and from which they would benefit. Says Parker: "In a word, the enemy of black economic progress is white liberalism, the maze of rules, regulations and debilitating welfare programs which—although they may have been motivated by high ideals—have had a wholly negative impact."[6]

Just as bad for blacks as government meddling in the economy, complain conservative blacks, are government attempts to end racial discrimination. For this reason, these conservatives, like their white colleagues, oppose busing, affirmative action and other political approaches to discrimination. Said Sowell to the San Francisco gathering: "Very often, legislation intended to help the disadvantaged in fact pays people to stay disadvantaged and penalizes them to the extent that they make an effort to rise from disadvantage." This is the case, he argues, with generous welfare payments which eliminate poor blacks' incentive to seek work.

As for affirmative action, conservative blacks fear that it creates an image of substandard mentality in those it intends to help. Special preferences, in essence, tell blacks that they are not as capable as whites and thus need not try as hard to get and hold a job. Black credentials obtained through affirmative action, moreover, will always be viewed suspiciously. Asks Clarence Thomas, a young black who was a Senate aide before joining the Reagan Administration: "Would you go to a black lawyer if you felt he was there just because he was black? Would you have your car or stereo repaired by someone if you felt he had the job just because of race and was not really qualified?"[7]

Conservative blacks do not suggest that they and fellow blacks face no problems or disadvantages. They insist, however, that these difficulties have not been helped very much by liberal theories and programs. What such measures mainly achieve is soothing white liberals' guilt over the injustice of racism. Quips Walter Williams: "I'd like to grant all white people full and general amnesty on racism so they would stop feeling guilty and stop acting like fools. Their guilt is hurting black people."[8]

Black conservatism today falls short of a full-fledged "movement." It lacks coherence and a nationally recognized structure; its potential members are just awakening to their inner conservative stirrings. But by standing up and declaring themselves conservative, several score prominent blacks at least are contesting liberalism's claim to the undivided allegiance of black America. And even in its infancy, the appearance of black conservatism confirms that the traditionalist resurgence is penetrating liberal quarters long-regarded as impregnable.

In its infancy too is the effort to challenge liberalism with one of its own favorite weapons—public interest law. In the past two decades especially, the American Civil Liberties Union, Naderite organizations and scores of other ideologically leftist, nonprofit groups of attorneys very successfully have been using the courtroom to effect their agenda. It is the judiciary, after all, which has been promulgating what traditionalists regard as some of the most heinous measures, like the right to abortion on demand, the ban on prayer and Bible reading in public schools and the recognition of children's rights over parents' rights.

When liberal groups argue in court against traditional positions, they twine themselves in the "public interest" mantle. By claiming to be altruistic advocates of what is best for the broad, unrepresented public and opponents of rich special interests, they acquire a sterling credibility which they exploit to great advantage. In truth, leftist public interest law firms represent narrow interests. Their bias runs strongly toward an expanded government role in social and economic matters and growing federal authority at the expense of the states and localities. Within the federal government, moreover, they argue continually for enhancing the power of judges and other appointed officials, which effectively reduces the role of elected officials. Almost without exception, they oppose free market approaches to problems and seek redistribution of existing wealth rather than creation of new wealth and an expanded welfare system rather than a growing economy.

For nearly two decades, liberal groups enjoyed an uncontested monopoly of the "public interest" badge. But in the mid-1970's, with funding from conservative foundations and businessmen, particularly those who were witnessing at first hand the sky-high cost imposed on the economy and their firms by government regulation, explicitly conservative nonprofit law groups began forming. They proclaimed that they too represented a "public interest," in fact a broader public interest than did the liberals. Says Raymond Momboisse, managing attorney of the Pacific Legal Foundation, the oldest of the conservative legal groups: "Who is more unrepresented than the silent, hard-working taxpayer? The little man who foots the bills for the great social experiments of a bloated bureaucracy? We represent them." Adds Harrison Fitch, legal director of the New England Legal Foundation: "Those who believe in traditional values often receive the least representation when their interests are at stake."

How dare liberal groups purport to litigate in the public interest, charge the conservatives, when their actions to block construction of a dam or power plant destroy current and future jobs for thousands of workers? And what about the extra cost of food to consumers when supplies cannot be increased because liberal legal groups successfully have argued for bans on pesticides, herbicides and fertilizers? The broad public interest in jobs and living costs, argue conservative lawyers, is ignored by Naderite and other liberal legal groups. It is specifically the defense of such essential economic interests that conservative nonprofit law groups see as their main mission. "We're going to look the Naderites, the bureaucrats and the criminals in the eye," vows Daniel Popeo, the feisty general counsel of the Washington Legal Foundation, "and we're going to tell them that we've been pushed around long enough and now we're going to start fighting back."

This counteroffensive began in 1973 on the West Coast with the creation of the Pacific Legal Foundation. Ronald Zumbrun, its president, had been a senior trial attorney for the State of California throughout the 1960's and a key architect of Governor Ronald Reagan's welfare reform program. This attempt to trim welfare costs ran into the buzz-saw opposition of leftist public interest legal groups. They entangled the state in fifteen law suits and almost defeated the proposal in court. Afterward, Zumbrun, Momboisse (a California deputy attorney general), a number of their colleagues and Ronald Reagan were determined to confront the left on its own terms in the courthouse. With a full-time staff of a dozen attorneys in Sacramento and half that number in Washington, D.C., Pacific Legal has been doing just that and winning victories.

As important, it has cloned conservative legal groups across the country. Since the late 1970's, similar though smaller offices opened in Atlanta, Boston, Philadelphia, New York City, Denver, Chicago, Kansas City and the nation's capital. Also launched were conservative legal groups concentrating on specific fields, such as the National Right to Work Legal Defense Foundation, the Center for National Labor Policy and the Chamber of Commerce's National Chamber Litigation Center. In its short history, these organizations have produced distinguished alumni. Interior Secretary James Watt, for example, headed the Denver-based Mountain States Legal Foundation, Massachusetts Governor Edward King helped found Boston's New England Legal Foundation and Missouri Governor Christopher Bond directed the Great Plains Legal Foundation in Kansas City.

Defending the free marketplace from government or special interest interference is a major task of conservative legal groups. Explains Zumbrun: "In our view, liberty and property equate. Many of our cases involve the rights of people to do what they want with their own property." Suits are filed, therefore, challenging government regulatory agencies, land use rulings, zoning laws and unreasonable environmental restrictions. Pacific Legal, for example, routinely combs the volumes of federal regulations for particularly costly and unfair rulings to challenge in court.

High on the list of such rulings are those interfering with development of energy sources. Cheap supplies of energy, safe from threats of foreign embargoes, are in the broadest public interest, argue the conservative lawyers. Thus, the New England Legal Foundation has been fighting the attempt to designate the Georges Bank as a marine sanctuary. Its lawyers protest that such a designation would prevent exploratory drilling for oil and gas in an extremely energy-poor region whose economic growth requires new energy supplies. In other areas, conservative legal groups are battling the well-organized (and well-funded) efforts to block construction of new nuclear reactors and to close down existing plants. Energy needs also are prompting suits against the Interior Department to force it to open public lands to oil exploration.

Constitutional questions rank high among the other concerns of the conservative legal organizations. The Washington Legal Foundation, for example, challenged the Carter Administration in court over its authority to terminate, without Senate approval, the U.S. treaty with Taiwan. And Mountain States Legal Foundation has been arguing in court that states have the right to change their minds and rescind their earlier ratification of the Equal Rights Amendment.

What the conservative groups especially relish is playing the cavalry, rushing in to rescue states and localities under assault from bigger governments. One of Zumbrun's favorite cases is Pacific Legal Foundation's successful battle against the Federal Environmental Protection Agency's ruling that would have forced Los Angeles to spend $250 million on a new sewage treatment plant. Objecting to the city's continued dumping of sewage sludge in a deep canyon seven miles out at sea, EPA wanted the sewage treated, instead, in a facility to be built at El Segundo. City officials were horrified by the enormous cost for what they believed a thoroughly unnecessary plant. Zumbrun's cavalry came to the rescue. Pacific Legal Foundation took the EPA to court and there, after lengthy hearings, beat the agency with one of environmentalists' favorite all-purpose weapons, the Endangered Species Act.

Pacific Legal argued that if Los Angeles stopped dumping sludge in the sea canyon, it would trigger an ecologically disastrous series of events. The anchovies which feed on the sludge, Pacific Legal pointed out compassionately, are part of the food chain of the brown pelican which is, sadly, an endangered species. Preserving the pelican thus requires the sludge which only Los Angeles provides. To make matters worse, locating the proposed sewage plant at El Segundo would dramatically alter the delicate ecological balance of that area which, regrettably, is the habitat of the El Segundo blue butterfly, another endangered species. Persuaded by this argument, the court blocked EPA's order. Pacific Legal, so far, thus has managed to save Los Angeles taxpayers $250 million—to say nothing of its public interest services to the brown pelican and blue butterfly.

A much smaller sum, but the same principle, was at risk on the other side of the continent, where the Mid-Atlantic Legal Foundation came to the aid of Bordentown, New Jersey. Although the town was taking no state funds for its welfare program, officials of the state's Department of Human Services nonetheless demanded that Bordentown comply with all state regulations governing welfare administration. Compliance would have been very costly. Bordentown would have to remodel City Hall to provide a separate waiting room for welfare applicants, create a large cash fund for welfare emergencies and hire a full-time welfare director. None of these measures, moreover, would have noticeably improved the Bordentown program. All this carried little weight with the state bureaucrats—until Mid-Atlantic, at the urging of a dozen Bordentown taxpayers, took the Department of Human Services to court. Ultimately the state relented and reluctantly agreed to allow the town to continue running its own welfare program.

Dozens of similar victories are being won each year across the nation by conservative legal groups. Where no such organizations existed as the 1970's began, by 1981 they boasted combined staffs of about seventy-five full-time attorneys and an $8 million annual budget. Even so, they remain heavily outgunned by the $50 million-a-year liberal public interest legal movement whose 110 groups field some 700 lawyers. In addition, many of the activities of the federally funded Legal Services Corporation are indistinguishable from those of the private liberal groups. (This makes Legal Services Corporation a primary target of the New Right.)

The conservative groups, however, continue to grow. Though they fail to match in size the liberal effort, they are managing to shield an increasing number of communities, individuals and businesses from capricious government actions. By going to court and arguing that the general public benefits enormously from a healthy free marketplace, the conservative groups at least are beginning to redefine and break the liberal monopoly of the extremely potent "public interest" label. They are in effect, opening another front against the left in the traditionalist counteroffensive.

How much territory will this traditionalist counteroffensive recapture? How much of the counterculture will be repealed? How many of liberalism's excesses will be redressed? These questions surely require much of the 1980's to answer. What already is certain is that the battle is going to be fierce. Though the left is shocked by and even reeling from traditionalist gains since the mid-1970's, it still has massive reserves and is far—very far—from defeated.

A traditionalist victory still faces enormous obstacles. Among the most formidable is simply the inertial force created by decades of conditioning the public to rely on government to remedy wrongs and resolve problems. When a community today faces difficulties, it reflexively looks to Washington for help. When local budgets have to be cut and services trimmed, Washington is asked to plug the gap or underwrite the endangered services. When high wage demands and production costs push symphony orchestras and opera and ballet companies deep into the red, Washington is assumed to be culture's patron of last resort, ready to subsidize the performing arts. When the handicapped and chronically poor need financial, employment or medical help, only Washington is expected to have compassion and a heart. And even when management's blunders drive major firms to the brink of bankruptcy, Washington is supposed to rush cash to the rescue.

Reliance on government, particularly federal, has become addictive and is as hard to break as any other serious addiction. This is responsible for what sociologists Seymour Martin Lipset and Everett Carll Ladd, Jr., describe as the "profound ambivalence which now characterizes public opinion and values in the U.S." Writing in *Public Opinion* magazine, they explain that Americans continue "to look to the state for answers and actions. At the same time, however, the public . . . *does* believe the government is too intrusive, too profligate, too inefficient." In sum, they conclude that there is "a strange mixture of attraction-rejection, a genuine ambivalence with regard to the state."[9]

The public's habit of looking to government for answers and help is a form of inertia, a passive resistance which traditionalist forces will have to conquer. Active resistance, meanwhile, is being mounted by groups directly challenged by traditionalists. Many of these groups richly benefit from the policies and programs enacted during recent decades. They are going to fight hard to maintain the programs. Few groups benefit as much as do bureaucrats at all levels of burgeoning government. Their influence and jobs are at stake if traditionalists manage to shift tasks from the public sector to the private. The regulator, for example, wants to keep regulating; the administrator of experimental educational programs wants to keep experimenting; the putative rehabilitator of criminals wants to keep rehabilitating; and the social engineer wants to keep on engineering. It is hardly surprising that the nation's largest teachers' union, the National Education Association, is the most bitter opponent of the back to basics movement in schooling or that the public employees' union, the American Federation of State, County and Municipal Employees, unrelentingly opposes budget and tax cuts that lead to reduced government programs and payrolls.

Their opposition is rooted mainly in self-interest. More formidable, probably, is ideologically motivated opposition, much of which is coordinated by a network of socialist or radical leftist organizations. There is, for instance, the Democratic Socialist Organizing Committee, headed by veteran socialist Michael Harrington; it works primarily within Democratic Party circles attempting to pull them to the left. (Opposing it in the party is the Coalition for a Democratic Majority, which counts several prominent neoconservatives among its members.) Leftist policy analyses and position papers, meanwhile, are churned out by Washington's Institute for Policy Studies. Since its establishment in 1965, this Marxist-leaning and often pro-Soviet center has served as the left's main think tank, marshaling a torrent of arguments antithetical to nearly every item on the traditionalist agenda. Its studies advocate price controls, government regulation of the economy, unilateral disarmament and support for Soviet-backed regimes overseas; they oppose the free enterprise system, corporations, U.S. intelligence activities and development of nuclear power.

Ideologically inspired too is the opposition to traditionalists by a number of the nation's labor union leaders who stand considerably farther to the left than their rank and file. The AFL-CIO Executive Council, for example, in August 1979 called for nationalizing the country's oil industry. National Education Association leadership not only supports increasing federal involvement in nearly every sector of society (except defense) but opposes just about every traditionalist economic, social, political and foreign policy position. Other labor proposals call for dissolving large corporations and penalizing firms which move plants or even shut down operations altogether. Some labor leaders, like William Winpisinger of the International Association of Machinists and Aerospace Workers, are avowedly socialist.

Illustrating unionist attitudes toward American capitalism is the booklet *A Working Economy For Americans,* sponsored by, among others, the NEA, United Auto Workers and the machinists' and public employees' unions. In a sweeping attack on free enterprise, the booklet states: "The private enterprise system is in need of change . . . It is long past time for the grabbing, greedy, self-interest which too often characterizes our society today to be replaced by a concern for the public interest. Yet this concern can be reduced only through governmental mechanisms."[10]

Several of the groups sponsoring this booklet also helped establish the Interchange Research Center, a Washington-based umbrella organization founded in 1978 specifically to block the ascending traditionalist influence. Interchange's membership list, in fact, reads like a Yellow Pages of anti-traditionalist activists. In addition to those cited above are the National Association of Social Workers, Women's League for Peace and Freedom, National Gay Task Force, Americans for Democratic Action and National Organization for Women. Included too are a dozen religious organizations whose administrative staffs in recent years have swung sharply left. Sociologist Peter Berger identifies what he calls the "virulent anti-Americanism that permeates Christian church agencies and seminaries."[11] Such religious groups have supported guerrilla activities in Africa, backed the Castro regime in Cuba and Cuban anti-American adventures in the Third World and vigorously opposed the free enterprise system in the U.S. and abroad. Methodist publications have called for socialism and an Episcopal tract has asserted that what America needs "is not a liberal faith, but a radical one." And an organization named

Clergy and Laity Concerned, which has close ties to the increasingly leftist National Council of Churches, openly proclaims its commitment to "join those who are angry and hate the corporate power which the U.S. presently represents."

Most formidable of the obstacles threatening the advance of traditionalism is a group which dominates some of the nation's most important power centers. Its members have a great deal to say about what young Americans are taught in colleges, how events are reported and interpreted in the press and on television (and what is designated as "news") and the options and data top government officials are given to make their decisions. Says political scientist Jeane Kirkpatrick: "They shape debate, determine agendas, define standards and propose and evaluate policies."

They are the "New Class," a name popularized by the neo-conservatives who have written extensively to warn of the dangers posed by this group. It is "new" because its numbers and power are unprecedented; it greatly overshadows, for example, what in earlier eras were the pockets of intellectuals who thrived on criticizing the American system. It is a "class" because its members, by and large, share values, outlooks and goals and make their livings in generally the same fashion, mainly by producing, gathering, packaging and marketing information. Writes Kirkpatrick: "What wealth is to the capitalist, what organization is to the old-style political boss, what manpower is to the trade unionists, words are to the New Class."[12]

Broadly speaking, its members deal full time with words and other symbols of ideas. They include first-ranking intellectuals who teach, contemplate and engage in primary research, and also those semi-intellectuals like clergymen, journalists, bureaucrats, planners, researchers, social workers and a host of others who specialize in communication. Their influence is enormous if for no other reason (and there are others) than because of the tremendous growth in their numbers. It is estimated, for example, that the knowledge industry supplies some 35 percent of the gross national product. While all levels of government employed a mere 4.2 million people in 1940, a quarter-century later this had jumped to 15 million. And where miners in 1940 outnumbered college professors 845,000 to 111,000, the ratio reversed by 1978, when there were more than 600,000 college professors

compared to only 164,000 miners. Such a turnaround illustrates
the general change between society's hard-output manufacturing
sector and its soft-output knowledge sector.

Not every knowledge specialist, of course, holds New Class
membership. Enough do, however, to set the public tone for their
professions. "While it is possible to argue that academe as a
whole does not contain a liberal majority," observes Seymour
Martin Lipset, who has surveyed exhaustively college and university faculties, "its most publicly visible segment, social science
professors at major universities, is to the far left of a profession
whose views are considerably more liberal than other segments
of American society." And though conservative professors certainly do exist, adds Lipset, they "are concentrated in the least
visible part of the academy, the lower status colleges and the
professional schools, the least politically involved group."[13]

This enormous New Class promotes views shaped greatly by
the counterculture—hostility to capitalism, rejection of economic
growth and contempt for the middle-class values of hard work,
discipline, individual restraint, deferred gratification and social
propriety. A special villain is technology, excoriated for ravaging
the environment and squandering resources. Ignored are technology's achievements and the evidence of nearly two centuries
of dynamic economic growth. Rather, the New Class acts as if the
economy were a static system capable of expanding in one sector
only at the expense of another and, in the process, consuming
vast quantities of irreplaceable resources. Right at home within
the New Class, therefore, is radical environmentalism's "Small is
Beautiful" rhetoric. Rejected entirely is the obvious counter-ar-
gument that big is not necessarily bad and that technology driven
economic growth creates more resources and wealth than it devours.

Above all, the New Class opposes capitalism and its private
enterprise corollary. On almost every issue, New Class proposals
seek to shift responsibility from the individual, family or private
group to some government agency. There is little sympathy for,
and perhaps no understanding of, society's need for capital formation, investment and the macro-efficiencies of economic competition. Not all New Class members may be aware of how
adamantly anti-capitalist they are. Yet the attitude permeates just
about everything they produce. Irving Kristol observes that the
entire American culture, particularly educational institutions, are

"unfriendly (at the least) to the commercial civilization, the bourgeois civilization, within which most of us live and work." Why else do we expect, he asks, that "when we send our sons and daughters to college . . . that by the time they are graduated they are likely to have a lower opinion of our social and economic order than when they entered. We know this from opinion poll data; we know this from our own experience. We are so used to this fact of our lives, we take it so for granted, that we fail to realize how extraordinary it is."[14]

The polling data, indeed, confirm Kristol's observations. A series of surveys conducted during the 1970's reveals jarring differences in attitudes on economic, social, foreign policy and personal matters between those whose education stopped with a high school diploma and those who studied beyond their bachelor's degree. The former group had relatively limited exposure to New Class teachers; the latter spent at least a quadrennium inside New Class-dominated institutions. Everett Carll Ladd, Jr., who has analyzed these surveys in *Public Opinion,* notes that in only three areas "did the middle to lower strata favor public expenditures more than trained college professionals and managers: To halt the rising crime rate, to respond to increasing drug addiction and to provide for the national defense."[15]

A litmus of the New Class outlook is the survey question asking whether self-fulfillment is more important than providing economic security for a family. Only 15 percent of the high school graduates say "yes," compared to 45 percent of the college post-graduates. This reflects New Class fascination with what is often called "self-actualization," an indulgence that New Class members can afford because their careers offer financial security and relative affluence. While there is nothing inherently wrong with this, of course, it prompts the New Class to view with distaste the mundane money worries of ordinary workers and impedes understanding of popular resentment over the high taxes levied to pay for generous welfare programs.

Thrift is not a New Class virtue. Two thirds of the college post-graduate group say that "saving money" is not "very important," compared to about half of the high school graduates. On whether communism is the worst form of government, three-fourths of the educated elite say "no," a response given by only 46 percent of the less educated group. When it comes to social issues, those ending formal education with high school are much

more traditional than the college post-graduates. Indeed, the
New Class champions a hedonism that respects few, if any, checks
on personal behavior so long as—to invoke a favorite New Class
rationalization—"it doesn't hurt anyone." This is evident from
other responses to the survey questions. Is homosexuality always
wrong? "No" say 57 percent of the better educated, compared to
26 percent of the high school group. Is adultery always wrong?
"No" say 51 percent of the educated elite, versus the same 26
percent of the high schoolers. And is abortion on demand okay
for married women? "Yes" say 70 percent of the elite, compared
to 43 percent of the other group.

Why is this highly educated, relatively affluent group, which
benefits more from America's riches than its less educated fellow
countrymen, so antagonistic to those values and institutions responsible for producing these riches? Speculating on this probably is best left to the burgeoning literature on the New Class. In
general, however, an important factor appears to be what Kirkpatrick describes as the intellectual's "habit of measuring institutions and practices against absolutist standards—[and thus]
reality is invariably found unsatisfactory."[16] Another factor surely
is, as Daniel Bell notes in *The Coming of Post-Industrial Society,* that
less than one fourth of the educated elite work in business of any
sort. Never having had to meet a payroll, as the adage goes, the
New Class has only limited appreciation of the cost of getting
things done and thus can blithely pursue what, in effect, are
utopian social goals.

Whatever the causes of the New Class world view, it does exist
and, through New Class-dominated channels of information,
bombards the public with anti-traditionalist arguments and senti-
ments. Nowhere is this more evident—or more threatening to
traditionalist gains—than in the news media, particularly the so-
called national elite media comprised of television's three major
networks, the nation's three leading newspapers—*The New York
Times, The Washington Post* and *The Wall Street Journal*—and two
weekly newsmagazines, *Time* and *Newsweek.* By education, professional concerns, ambitions, income and peer reinforcement, the
reporters and editors staffing these enterprises are mainly New
Class (*The Wall Street Journal* less so than the others). They identify much more with the values of Manhattan, Georgetown and
Beverly Hills than with those of Grundy Center, Iowa, or Lynchburg, Virginia. They almost all professionally inhabit the same

one-fourth square mile of midtown Manhattan, dining and drinking in the same restaurants and bars, reading the same books,
succumbing to the same fads and outraged by the same urban
problems. Headquartered literally within a dozen blocks of ele-
gant Rockefeller Center are *Time, Newsweek,* ABC, CBS, NBC, *The
New York Times,* Associated Press, United Press International, *Fortune, Business Week, People* and dozens of other media operations.
Located there too and sharing the same values are the advertising
and public relations firms which to a great extent shape America's
tastes.

New Class values act as a prism distorting how this media elite
receive and transmit data and ideas from and to Trans-Hudson
America, that vast nation beyond Manhattan. After passing
through this prism, for example, the leftists fighting in El Salvador's civil war become "guerrillas," while the rightists are branded "terrorists." It is a prism effect which also explains,
apparently, the media elite's skewed coverage of the Reagan Administration's nomination of C. Everett Koop as U.S. Surgeon
General. Reporting concentrated almost entirely on his outspoken opposition to abortion. Little was said about his professional
qualifications for the post, such as his distinguished medical career—that he had longer tenure as surgeon-in-chief of a major
hospital than anyone else in the U.S. and that he had been deco-
rated by the French government for pioneering work in pediatric
surgery.

So many similar examples exist that Stanley Rothman of
Smith College concludes, in his study "The Mass Media in Post-
Industrial Society," that "pivotal members of the elite media
share a 'paradigm,' which tells them what the world should be like
and which leads them to deal with events in certain ways." Among
other things, this paradigm dictates that:

¶ Groups calling for radical change are generally described as humanitarian. If their programs show few signs of
success, patience is urged.

¶ Groups calling for a conservative change generally are
treated as if their only conceivable motivation is narrow
self-interest or psychological malfunction.

¶ Social problems are assumed soluble by a combination
of good will and rational management. If injustice persists,
then it is not because the solutions are lacking but because

self-interested, powerful individuals and groups are block-
ing reasonable policies.

In addition, writes Rothman, the elite media evince "a gener-
alized distrust of the American military, of people who are 'overly
patriotic,' of the police and of the working-class and lower-mid-
dle-class Americans who do not share [New Class] cosmopolitan
lifestyles."[17]

Like the rest of the New Class, the media elite is hostile to or
at the least very ignorant of how the economy works. Says Leonard Theberge, head of Washington's Media Institute, which has
extensively analyzed news (particularly television) reporting:
"Sometimes it seems that journalists think that the law of supply
and demand is a statute enacted by Congress which, as such, can
be amended or even repealed." Anti-business bias may be what
prompts these journalists to give Ralph Nader, environmentalists, zero-growth advocates and other antagonists of U.S. business more coverage than the corporate executive and to treat
their views more sympathetically. In this regard, ABC-TV's handling of the story involving wire manufactured by Kaiser Aluminum and CBS-TV's feature on Illinois Power Company's nuclear
plant are much more the rule than the exception—especially with
television news. So long as it remains the rule, not only for the
elite media but also for the much broader New Class, and not only
regarding attitudes toward business but also those toward the full
range of social, economic and individual matters, an enormous
obstacle lies in the path of a traditionalist resurgence.

Traditionalists can overcome these obstacles mainly by continuing to do what they have been doing with surprising success
since the mid-1970's—speaking out on behalf of their values,
organizing and challenging the left's monopoly of the platform
setting the agendas for debate on public policy issues. Sustained
activism, however, is not easy for the traditionalist. James Hitchcock correctly notes that conservatives prefer "a life that is set-
tled, stable, placid, private" and they are reluctant "to give up too
large a part of their private lives to the demands of public activity."[18] Yet legions of traditionalists already have sacrificed huge
portions of their private lives; they will have to continue doing so
if they intend to hold and expand the ground won from the left.

As for the New Class obstacle in particular, circumventing

may prove easier than surmounting it. Rather than await fair treatment from the elite media, traditionalists can take their cases directly to the public, as Illinois Power Company, Cornell Maier, the New Right and others have been doing. Traditionalist lines of communication already are open, through direct mass mailings, newsletter networks and frequent workshops, seminars and training sessions.

On a number of fronts, traditionalists could battle more effectively. Corporations, for instance, barely take advantage of new opportunities to participate in the political process and help elect conservatives to office. To be sure, corporate political action committees (PACs) have soared in number from less than 100 in 1974 to more than 1,250 by early 1981. Yet instead of donating funds mainly to candidates who champion free enterprise, a commitment which would seem critically important to the long-term survival of American business, corporate PACs frequently use their money simply to gain access to officials. They back incumbents or play it very safe by contributing to both candidates for the same office. Labor union PACs, on the other hand, which outspend corporate groups by three or four times, almost exclusively support liberals, or at least Democrats. Current corporate PAC strategy is "short-sighted," says the University of Southern California's Center for the Study of Private Enterprise. In a handbook for corporate PACs, the Center declares: "We have the PAC instrument set up by the Congress of the U.S. We have to be out of our minds not to use it."

Businessmen could also target their philanthropy more selectively. Though routinely denounced as demonic embodiments of capitalism, major corporations continue contributing generously to those denouncing them—New Class, counterculture, radical environmentalist and other groups hostile to the free enterprise system. Finding this masochistically outrageous, former Treasury Secretary William Simon has been imploring fellow corporate executives to stop subsidizing "collectivist ideals." And Irving Kristol devotes a great deal of time to addressing businessmen, urging them to seek advice from intellectuals sympathetic to capitalism before they contribute funds to research or activist groups whose outlooks and ultimate aims are unknown. What Simon and Kristol sensibly call for is an explicit strategy of corporate philanthropy to reduce sharply the money flowing to leftist groups and increase it to conservative ones. Recipients would include think tanks and publications, basics education organizations, institutes promoting free market ideas and economic education programs, groups defending traditional family values and their frontline allies in the traditionalist counteroffensive.

Perhaps there is nothing more important for traditionalists to start doing than to see themselves as part of a broad movement. So far, the groups on the front lines have been operating mostly in isolation, focusing on one or two specific issues. Those organizing to defeat the Equal Rights Amendment, for example, typically are unaware of a neighboring group working for some other traditionalist cause, like monitoring sex education in the public schools or advocating limits on government spending. Jo Ann Gasper, founder of *The Right Woman,* explains: "I'd be invited to speak on social issues to sewing circles, Bible study groups, church groups and so forth, and one didn't know of the other's existence." Recognizing that they are part of a much greater phenomenon should encourage inter-group communication and, on occasion, cooperation.

Cooperation is needed most between the traditionalist movement's two main strata. In one stratum are those who have become activists because of their outrage at the spectacle of the U.S. economy going wrong through overregulation, huge deficits and stifling tax rates and at the spectacle of America's global position shrinking as a result of years of pinched military spending. In this group mainly are the neoconservatives, corporate executives, rightist academics, members of conservative research organizations like the American Enterprise Institute and Georgetown University's Center for Strategic and International Studies and, generally, mainline Republicans. This first stratum concerns itself mostly with the weighty matters of economic policy, foreign affairs and defense. Contrasting with it is a second stratum, those outraged at the spectacle of the nation gone wrong morally. Much more populist that the first stratum, the members of this second group have been encountered throughout this study—they are the homemakers, Moral Majoritarians, Fundamentalists and evangelicals, Christian club women and the New Right.

The two strata live, work and fight their battles independently of each other. Only rarely are their separate worlds bridged; from a distance, they eye each other, usually suspiciously. Midge Decter, the neoconservative who has written widely read critiques of radical feminism, for example, has never met Eagle Forum founder Phyllis Schlafly. A prominent Fundamentalist scholar at Wheaton College snickers at the mention of Jerry Falwell. And a senior attorney at a conservative public interest law firm turns sarcastic when discussing the New Right's Paul Weyrich or Terry Dolan. Yet when these first-stratum folks are questioned about their negative attitudes, they are unable to point to any great policy differences with the other stratum. The Wheaton theologian concedes that generally he agrees with Falwell on both Scripture and social issues. The conservative attorney cannot pinpoint any specific quarrels with New Right goals. And Decter admits to "a bad conscience" about her long-condescending view of Schlafly because, "in a sense, Phyllis Schlafly has done my dirty work for me" by getting into the trenches to fight the radical feminists.

If policy disagreements do not account for the gap between traditionalism's two camps, what does? Style, apparently. The first group simply is uncomfortable with the direct, insistent and studiedly unsophisticated manner of the social issues crowd. "He embarrasses me," finally confesses the theologian of Falwell. "They're not my kind of people," says the conservative attorney. "I used to think that they were a bunch of kooks," recalls Humboldt State University economist Jacqueline Kasun, a leading critic of "progressive" sex education curriculums. "I didn't know any of them, of course, but that was their image. And it kept me away from them for a long time. I wouldn't even read any New Right publications. I didn't want to be thought of as a fascist. Now that I'm involved with them, I see how off-base my early perceptions were."

Overcoming false perceptions and, then, opening channels of communication between the two strata could yield the traditionalist movement an enormous synergistic bonus. The social issues camp could be mobilized for grass-roots support on economic, foreign policy and defense matters, such as continued deregulation, budget and tax cuts, measures encouraging investment and productivity, bold initiatives to check Soviet adventurism and development of advanced weapons systems. In turn, backing for the social agenda by the first stratum would bring enhanced respectability to such issues as rolling back federal involvement in local education, banning abortion, endorsing voluntary prayer in schools, cracking down on pornography and pressuring broadcasters to reduce gratuitous sex and violence on television.

How actively first-stratum traditionalists have to support this social agenda is uncertain. Sympathetic statements and displays of understanding may be enough. What should end, it seems, are the hostility and ridicule with which the first group often treats the social-issues activists. While there are legitimate concerns about the priorities assigned to issues and the amount of political capital to be spent on social questions, first-stratum fears that social-issue advocacy could become a serious political liability seem unwarranted and vastly exaggerated. Opinion surveys indicate that the public already endorses much of the traditionalist social platform. A major poll released by the Connecticut Mutual Life Insurance Company in 1981 reveals that a majority of Americans back traditionalist positions on eight of ten critical social issues. When asked to signify whether a specific behavior is "morally wrong," 85 percent did so on adultery, 84 percent on use of hard drugs, 71 percent on homosexuality and engaging in sex before age sixteen, 70 percent on lesbianism, 68 percent on pornographic movies, 65 percent on abortion and 57 percent on smoking marijuana. Slightly fewer than half regarded it immoral to live with someone of the opposite sex before marriage, while 40 percent said that sex between two single people is immoral.

Other surveys find that 76 percent of the public favors "an amendment to the Constitution that would permit prayers to be said in the public schools" and 79 percent believe that human reproduction and methods of contraception should be explained in the classroom only with parental consent. There even seems widespread support for traditionalists' overall emphasis on morality. When the Gallup Organization survey for the White House Conference on Families asked respondents to list "three things most harmful to family life," 40 percent cited "decline of religious and moral values." Ranking ahead of this only were the 60 percent for "alcohol abuse" and 59 percent for "drug abuse." And most Americans even favor "religious qualifications" for the land's highest office; 53 percent say that an atheist should not be President. Though this is dramatically down from 75 percent two decades ago, it still is a majority and is significantly more than the 40 percent who say that they would vote for an atheist.[19]

Has the United States begun a new era? Certainly the evidence and examples encountered by this study's journey through traditionalist America seem convincingly to answer "yes." Since the late 1970's, attitudes and policies have been changing in ways repudiating liberalism's two-generation reign. Rejected in particular are the liberal excesses of the past decade. Attitudes have changed so profoundly in many areas that they seem certain to endure for some time. It is hard to imagine, for instance, government intervention in the economy soon finding many new champions. It is hard to imagine Americans very quickly again trusting the Soviet Union. Nor does it seem likely that there will be much new experimenting with education, indulging criminals or thumping by churches of political issues instead of Bibles. To the contrary. Feminists are learning that they have been committing political suicide by failing to show proper respect for the family; educators are exalting the virtues of the three R's; mainline Protestant denominations are trying desperately to keep their dwindling flocks by rediscovering evangelism and Scripture-based preaching; liberals are bowing before the balanced budget altar and Milton Friedman and George Gilder are finding themselves on best-seller lists. America, in sum, is heading back to basics.

Throughout the nation, appreciation is growing of conservativism's lessons—that history and tradition are better able than man to fashion man's institutions and norms, that reason has its limits and that today's generation has the solemn responsibility to convey unharmed to its heirs what it has inherited from its ancestors. Writing for a 1980 *Commentary* symposium on "Liberalism & The Jews," theologian Eugene Borowitz confesses: "Like most Jewish liberals in recent years, I have been chastened in my hopes that government can produce greater social justice. People are not as moral or rational as I once believed; professors and journalists are not as smart; and government is not only as corruptible as other American institutions but has its own proclivities for producing evil with the good."[20]

With liberals across the country similarly chastened, liberalism today looks and acts like a movement in retreat, a dynamo burned out. As the right generates a torrent of ideas, liberals huddle, confer, caucus and grope in workshops for new thoughts and concepts. But they simply are not coming. Liberalism indeed seems like a dynasty fast losing the Mandate of Heaven. On the ascendancy is traditionalism, challenging liberalism on every major front and ending the liberal monopoly of the agenda-setting process. On every critical public policy matter, liberals now must share the platform with traditionalists.

Ronald Reagan's election confirmed the traditionalist gains. The Ronald Reagan presidency could assure that his Republican party becomes the political vehicle of what may well be a traditionalist dynasty. For this, Reagan will have to demonstrate a commitment to the full traditionalist agenda—social questions as well as economic, moral issues as well as institutional. Should he fail, a restructured Democratic Party could capture the traditionalist movement, become its champion and return to power for another long reign. Lincoln once observed that the Republican party seemed to have stolen the clothes of its opposition. Democrats in this age could try to wrap themselves in traditionalism's mantle. The traditionalist movement, after all, did not begin with Ronald Reagan—and it will not end with him.

NOTES

INTRODUCTION

1. Irving Kristol, "The Adversary Culture of Intellectuals," *Encounter,* October 1979, p. 14.
2. Gertrude Himmelfarb, "What is a Liberal—Who Is a Conservative?," *Commentary,* September 1976, p. 68.
3. Everett Carll Ladd, Jr., "The New Divisions in U.S. Politics," *Fortune,* March 26, 1979, p. 89.
4. James Hitchcock, "Is Life a Spectator Sport?" *The National Review,* February 6, 1981, p. 97.
5. Daniel Bell, *Society,* January 1979, p. 17.
6. Oscar Handlin, "Liberalism and the Jews: A Symposium," *Commentary,* January 1980, pp. 39–40.
7. Robert Nisbet, "The Nemesis of Authority," *Encounter,* August 1972, p. 17.

CHAPTER I

1. Michael Kort, *The Wall Street Journal,* August 16, 1977, editorial page.
2. *U.S. News and World Report,* February 20, 1978, pp. 17–18.
3. *Saturday Review,* September 29, 1979, p. 28.

CHAPTER II

1. *The Effect of "The People on Market Street,"* Evaluative Research Department, Educational Research Council of America, July 1979, p. 72.
2. *Human Events,* February 9, 1981, p. S-5.
3. Tom Bethell, *The Wall Street Journal,* July 8, 1980, op-ed page.
4. Cited in a *Commonweal* editorial, April 11, 1980, p. 195.

CHAPTER III

1. Cited in *Regulatory Action Network,* U.S. Chamber of Commerce, December 1980, p. 10.
2. *The Wall Street Journal,* October 28, 1980, p. 1.
3. Murray Weidenbaum (Speech to Utah State University, April 17, 1980), cited in *Vital Speeches,* Vol. XLVI, No. 14, (1980), p. 421

4. See: *The New York Times*, April 13, 1980, p. 63. See also: *Regulation*, January 1981, p. 28.

5. *The Nation*, December 15, 1979, p. 626.

6. Alfred Kahn, cited in *Regulatory Action Network*, November 1980, p. S-2.

7. See: *Regulatory Action Network*, July 1980, last page.

8. *Perspective on National Issues*, U.S. Chamber of Commerce, March 1980. See also: *Regulatory Action Network*, July 1980.

9. Paul Johnson, *Regulation*, June 1980, pp. 16–17.

10. *Risk-Benefit-Cost Background Report*, NAM Risk-Benefit-Cost Scoping Study Steering Committee, June 1980, p. 21.

11. Ibid., pp. 6–8.

12. *Public Opinion*, September 1980, p. 11.

13. *The New York Times*, January 8, 1981, p. B6

14. "Consumer Attitudes Toward Government Taxation and Spending," U.S. Chamber Survey Center, Economic Policy Division, U.S. Chamber of Commerce, September 3, 1980, p. 2.

15. Milton Friedman, *National Tax Limitation Committee News*, Winter 1979, p. 5.

16. *The New York Times*, March 25, 1980, p. B11.

17. Cited by *Newsweek*, November 19, 1979, p. 23.

18. Robert Lucas, *Competition*, The Council for a Competitive Economy, August 1980, p. 8.

19. Cited in *The Public Interest*, Spring 1979, p. 115.

20. Cited by *Forbes*, October 1, 1979, p. 52.

21. *Public Opinion*, June 1980, p. 38.

22. Seymour Martin Lipset and William Schneider, *Public Opinion*, February 1979, p. 10

CHAPTER IV

1. Kenneth Strike, *Educational Leadership*, November 1977, p. 94.

2. Ibid., p. 98.

3. Willard Wirtz et al, *Report of the Advisory Panel on the Scholastic Aptitude Test Score Decline*, College Entrance Examination Board, New York, 1977, pp. 5, 37–38.

4. *Change*, November 1979, p. 39.

5. *Today's Education*, May 1980, p. 216. See also: *America*, July 8, 1980, p. 12.

6. *The New York Times*, October 30, 1979, p. C4

7. Jackson Toby, *The Public Interest*, Winter 1980, p. 29.

8. Ibid., pp. 31–32.

9. SAT Panel Report, 1977, pp. 30–31.

10. Paul Copperman, *The Literacy Hoax*. New York: Morrow Quill, 1979, p. 65.

11. See: William Gorth, "A Study of Minimum Competency Testing Programs," for the Office of Testing, Assessment and Evaluation, National Institute of Education, December 1979, p. 7.

12. *Time*, July 30, 1979, p. 66. See also: Gorth, *op. cit.*, pp. 15, 18, and *Development of the Florida Statewide Assessment Program: A Chronology from 1971*, State of Florida, Department of Education, 1981.

13. Introduction by Chris Pipho, Robert Frahm and Jimmie Covington, *What's Happening in Minimum Competency Testing*. Bloomington, Indiana: Phi Delta Kappa, 1979, p. 6.

14. *The New York Times*, July 8, 1980, p. C4.

15. Barbara Lerner, "Minimum Competence and Maximum Choice" (Paper presented at AERA Annual Meeting, April 11, 1979).

16. Russell Vlaanderen, "Trends in Competency-Based Teacher Certification," (Denver, CO: Education Commission of the States, October 1980).

17. *California Monitor of Education*, September 1979, p. 3.

18. "A Statistical Report on U.S. Catholic Schools 1979–1980," National Catholic Education Association Data Bank.

19. *Educational Digest*, March 1978, p. 31.

20. Peter Skerry, *The Public Interest*, Fall 1980, p. 27.

21. Cited in *Persuasion at Work*, Rockford Institute, Rockford, Illinois, January 1979, p. 3.

22. *Compact*, Spring 1980, p. 25.

23. William Hazard, "The Flight from the Public Schools," (Paper presented at Annual Meeting of the Education Commission of the States, July 31, 1980), pp. 12–13.

24. Cited in *GEM Newsletter*, Project on General Education Models, July 1979, p. 6.

25. Arvo Juola, "Grade Inflation in Higher Education—1979. Is It Over?" Learning and Evaluation Service, Michigan State University, pp. 4, 6–7.

CHAPTER V

1. White House Conference on Families, *Listening to America's Families: Action for the 80's*, The Report to the President, Congress and Families of the Nation, October 1980, p. 9.

2. *Christianity Today*, May 29, 1980, p. 911.

3. Felix Berardo, *Journal of Marriage and the Family*, November 1980, p. 724.

4. See: Ibid., p. 907. See also: *Society*, January 1981, p. 56.

5. Berardo, *op. cit.*, p. 726.

6. Allan Carlson, *The Public Interest*, Winter 1980, p. 77.

7. See: *Christianity Today*, May 25, 1979, p. 909. See also: *The Nation*, November 17, 1979, p. 498.

8. Carlson, *op. cit.*, p. 74.

9. Cited by *Family Protection Report*, October 1980, pp. 11–12.

10. Bruce Hafen, *American Bar Association Journal*, October 1977, pp. 1386–1387.

11. Ibid., p. 1387.

12. See: *California Monitor of Education*, February 1980 and subsequent issues.

13. Jacqueline Kasun, *The Public Interest*, Winter 1980, p. 135.

14. Ibid., pp. 133–134.

15. *Newsweek*, May 15, 1978, p. 83.

16. *Journal of Marriage and the Family*, November 1980, p. 974.

17. White House Conference on Families, *op cit.*, p. 181.

18. Ibid., p. 180.

19. Nathan Glazer, *Commentary*, March 1978, p. 49.

CHAPTER VI

1. Betty Friedan, "Feminism's Next Step," *The New York Times Magazine*, July 5, 1981, p. 14.

2. *The Phyllis Schlafly Report*, November 1972, pp. 3–4.

3. Cited by *Saturday Review of Education*, March 1973.

4. Robin Morgan (WITCH—Women's International Terrorists' Conspiracy for Hell), cited by *Arkansas Gazette*, August 30, 1977. See also: *The Nation*, November 17, 1980, cover and pp. 497–498.

5. *The Nation*, November 17, 1980, cover and pp. 497–498.

6. Friedan, *op. cit.*

7. *The Daily Illini*, April 25, 1981.

8. *The Nation*, November 17, 1980, cover and pp. 497–498.

9. Andrew Hacker, *Harper's*, September 1980, p. 11.

10. Jean Bethke Elshtain, *The Nation*, April 5, 1980, p. 392.

11. U.S., Congress, Senate, *Congressional Record*, Vol. 123, No. 157, (October 3, 1977), p. S16204.

12. Ibid., p. S16205–S16206.

13. Yankelovich, Skelly and White for the American Council of Life Insurance. Cited by *Public Opinion*, January 1980, p. 34.

14. *The 1980 Virginia Slims American Women's Opinion Poll*, conducted by the Roper Organization, 1980, p. 44.

15. *Today's American Woman: How the Public Sees Her,* prepared for the President's Advisory Committee for Women by the Public Agenda Foundation, September 1980, p. 45.

16. Ibid., p. 10.

17. Carol Felsenthal, *The Sweetheart of the Silent Majority* (New York: Doubleday, 1981), pp. 2, 3, 5.

18. Ibid., p. 322.

19. *The Phyllis Schlafly Report,* November 1972.

20. Boyd Packer, *The Ensign,* March 1977, p. 7.

21. See: Juli Loesch, "Pro-Life, Pro-ERA," *America,* December 9, 1978, pp. 435–436.

22. *Des Moines Register,* November 20, 1980, op-ed page.

23. Harris Poll of April 28, 1977; ICPSR Election Study of 1976; Gallup Poll 1974.

24. Friedan, *op. cit.*

CHAPTER VII

1. *Christianity Today,* May 23, 1980, p. 46.

2. Joseph Fichter, *Commonweal,* March 17, 1978, pp. 169–170.

3. Richard Lovelace, *Christian Century,* March 18, 1981, p. 296. See also: Dean Hoge, "Social Factors Influencing Youth Ministry," 1980 (From a book in preparation), p. 21.

4. *Public Opinion,* March 1979, p. 39.

5. *Christianity Today,* May 2, 1980, p. 23 and December 21, 1979, p. 14. See also: *Public Opinion,* March 1979, p. 36, and George Gallup, Jr., and David Poling, *The Search for America's Faith* (Nashville: Abingdon Press, 1980), p. 51.

6. *The New York Times,* November 11, 1979.

7. Martin Marty, *Christian Century,* January 2, 1980, p. 4.

8. Gallup and Poling, *op. cit.,* p. 10.

9. See: Dean Hoge and David Roozen, eds., *Understanding Church Growth and Decline 1950–1978* (New York: The Pilgrim Press, 1979), p. 341.

10. Ibid.

11. John Shelby Spong, *Christian Century,* January 3, 1979, p. 12.

12. D. Keith Mano, *The National Review,* July 20, 1979, p. 931.

13. *Christianity Today,* December 20, 1979, p. 14.

14. *Christianity Today,* May 2, 1980, p. 25.

15. See: *Christian Century,* July 2, 1980, p. 691.

16. Ibid., p. 692.

17. *Christianity Today,* November 2, 1979; p. 29.

18. See: Joel Carpenter, *Church History,* March 1980, pp. 70–71.

19. *Adweek,* February 9, 1981, p. 1. See also: *America,* April 7, 1979, p. 271, and *Time,* February 4, 1980, pp. 64–65.

20. Gallup and Poling, *op. cit.,* pp. 79–81.

21. William Fore, *Christian Century,* January 7, 1981, pp. 29–30.

22. *Christianity Today,* February 6, 1981, p. 15.

23. James Wall, *Christian Century,* February 4, 1981, p. 91.

24. "Affirm the Good News," (Resolution adopted by the 189th General Assembly of the United Presbyterian Church in the USA, 1977) pp. 1–10.

25. Cited by *Publishers Weekly,* February 15, 1980, p. 54.

26. David Glanz and Egon Mayer, "The Quality of Jewish Life," *Forum,* No. 35, pp. 126–127.

27. *Public Opinion,* May 1979, p. 37.

CHAPTER VIII

1. *Time,* March 23, 1981, p. 22.

2. Cited by *The New York Times,* February 9, 1981, p. D10.

3. Arthur Stinchcombe et al., *Crime and Punishment—Changing Attitudes in America* (San Francisco: Jossey-Bass, 1980), p. 50.

4. James Bagley, "Why Illinois Adopted Determinate Sentencing," *Judicature*, March 1979, p. 391.

5. Stinchcombe, *op. cit.*, p. 31. See also: *Public Opinion*, November 1980, p. 31.

6. Cited by David Fogel, *We Are the Living Proof* (Cincinnati: Anderson, 1975), pp. 5–8. See also: Walter Berns, *For Capital Punishment* (New York: Basic Books, 1979), p. 44.

7. Cited by Walter Kaufman, "Retribution and the Ethics of Punishment," *Assessing the Criminal: Restitution, Retribution and the Legal Process* (Cambridge, MA: Ballinger Books, 1977), p. 223.

8. See: Stinchcombe, *op. cit.*, p. 28. See also: *Sourcebook of Criminal Justice Statistics—1979*, Law Enforcement Assistance Administration, U.S. Department of Justice, p. 293, and ABC/*The Washington Post* Poll, May 1981.

9. Law Enforcement Assistance Administration, U.S. Department of Justice, *op. cit.*, pp. 294–295.

10. Elizabeth Taylor, "In Search of Equity: The Oregon Parole Matrix," *Federal Probation*, March 1979, p. 57.

11. Cited in Berns, *op. cit.*, p. 76.

12. See: *Hofstra Law Review*, Fall 1978, p. 31.

13. Robert Martinson, "What Works—Questions and Answers About Prison Reform," *The Public Interest*, Spring 1974.

14. See: James Q. Wilson, "What Works Revisited: New Findings on Crime Rehabilitation," *The Public Interest*, Fall 1980.

15. Adult Corrections Subcommittee, *Summary of the Report to the Illinois House Judiciary II Committee by the Subcommittee on Adult Corrections*, June 24, 1976, p. 4.

16. David Fogel, "Justice, Not Therapy: A New Mission for Corrections," *Judicature*, March 1979, p. 378.

17. *The New York Times*, February 9, 1981, p. D10.

18. See: *Hofstra Law Review*, Winter 1979, p. 363.

19. Isaac Ehrlich, "The Deterrence Effect of Capital Punishment," *American Economic Review*, June 1975, p. 398. See also: Berns, *op. cit.*, p. 98.

20. Berns, *op. cit.*, p. 136.

21. Roberta C. Cronin and Blair B. Bourque, *National Evaluation Program Phase I Assessment of Victim/Witness Assistance Projects: Summary Report*, prepared for the Law Enforcement Assistance Administration (Washington, D.C.: American Institutes for Research, May 1980), p. 2.

22. Bronson LaFollette, *Wisconsin Victim/Witness Assistance Program: Program Guidelines*, (Report distributed by the Wisconsin Department of Justice), November 11, 1980, p. 1.

23. *Snyder* v. *Massachusetts*, 291 U.S. 97, 122 (1934).

24. *Stein* v. *New York*, 346 U.S. 156, 197 (1953).

25. Carol Holliday Blew and Robert H. Rosenblum, *An Exemplary Project: Witness Information Service; Peoria, Illinois*, National Institute for Justice, U.S. Department of Justice, August 1980, p. 24.

26. Robert Reiff, *The Invisible Victim: The Criminal Justice System's Forgotten Responsibility* (New York: Basic Books, 1979), p. 37.

27. William McDonald, "The Role of the Victim in America," *Assessing the Criminal: Restitution, Retribution and the Legal Process*, (Cambridge, MA: Ballinger Books, 1977), p. 299.

28. Ibid., p. 295.

CHAPTER IX

1. See: *Change*, November 1979, p. 2.

2. *The Wall Street Journal*, May 14, 1981, p. 22.

3. *Christianity Today*, February 15, 1980, p. 56.

4. Arthur Levine, *When Dreams and Heroes Died: A Portrait of Today's College Student* (San Francisco: Jossey-Bass, 1980), p. 7.

5. Kenneth Keniston, "Heads and Seekers: Drugs on Campus, Counter-Cultures and American Society," *American Scholar*, Winter 1968, pp. 109–110.

6. Levine, *op. cit.*, pp. 64–65.

7. Dean Hoge, "Social Factors Influencing Youth Ministry in the 1980s," 1980, p. 38.

8. Ibid. See also: Dean Hoge, Cynthia Luna and David Miller, "Trends in College Students' Values Between 1952 and 1979: A Return of the Fifties?" 1981 (From a book in preparation), Table 7.

9. Joseph Katz, "The New and Old Lives of Men and Women Undergraduates," ed. Carole Leland, *Men and Women Learning Together: A Study of College Students in the Late 70s;* (Providence, RI: Brown University Press, 1980), p. 145.

10. *The National Review*, November 23, 1979, pp. 1483–1491.

11. *Religion in America: 1979–1980*, Princeton Religion Research Center, p. 57.

12. See: Louis Filler, *Vanguards and Followers: Youth in the American Tradition* (Chicago: Nelson-Hall, 1978) p. 170. See also: *Character*, November 1979, p. 2, and Levine, *op. cit.*, p. 5.

13. Levine, *op. cit.*, pp. xv–xvi.

14. Ibid., pp. 41–42.

15. Hoge et al., *op. cit.*, Table 3.

16. Philip Hastings and Dean Hoge, "Religious Trends Among College Students: 1948–1979," 1980 (From a book in preparation), pp. 12, 14, Table 2.

17. *The National Review*, November 23, 1979, p. 1490.

18. *Religion in America: 1979–1980*, Princeton Religion Research Center, pp. 63–65.

19. Cited in *Bride's Eye*, October 1980, p. 3.

20. *Bride's Research Report*, October 1979, p. 2.

21. *Money*, June 1980, p. 88.

22. Hastings and Hoge, *op. cit.*, p. 1.

CHAPTER X

1. See: *The Heritage Lectures: Objections to Conservatism*, The Heritage Foundation, 1981, p. 4.

2. Emily Yoffe, "Brookings and AEI," *The Washington Journalism Review*, November 1980, p. 33.

3. Peter Stone, "Conservative Brain Trust," *The New York Times Magazine*, May 10, 1981.

4. *Human Events*, January 10, 1981, p. 30.

5. Daniel Bell, *Cultural Contradictions of Capitalism* (New York: Basic Books, paperback edition, 1978), p. xi.

6. Irving Kristol, *Public Opinion*, October 1979, p. 51.

7. *The National Review*, June 26, 1981, p. 726.

8. Kristol, *op. cit.*, p. 52.

9. Daniel Bell, *Society*, January 1979, p. 17.

10. Norman Podhoretz, *Breaking Ranks* (New York: Harper and Row, 1979), p. 320.

11. Irving Kristol, "Capitalism, Socialism and Democracy," *Commentary*, April 1978, pp. 53–54.

12. Irving Kristol, *Public Opinion*, October 1979, p. 51.

13. The Heritage Foundation, *op. cit.*, p. 12.

CHAPTER XI

1. Cited in *The Washington Post*, May 22, 1981, p. C2.

2. William Raspberry, "Have We Become Too Tolerant?" *The Washington Post*, November 26, 1980, p. A17.

3. Cited by *Conservative Digest*, December 1980, p. 13.

4. George McGovern, Fund-raising letter for Americans for Common Sense, 1981.

5. Cited in *The Washington Post*, May 22, 1981, p. C2.

6. *The Moral Majority Report*, October 15, 1980, p. 2.

7. Meg Greenfield, *The Washington Post*, May 13, 1981, editorial page.

8. *Seattle Times*, June 5, 1981, editorial page.

9. *The New York Times*, March 26, 1981, p. B14.

10. Gannett News Service, "The New Right," March 1981, Part IV, p. 23.

11. Cited in *The Christian Science Monitor*, May 12, 1981, p. 6.

CHAPTER XII

1. *The New Republic*, January 20, 1979, p. 13.
2. Milton Himmelfarb, "Are Jews Becoming Republican?" *Commentary*, August 1981, p. 30.
3. *The Washington Post*, December 15, 1980, p. A8.
4. *Baltimore Sun*, June 21, 1981, p. A1.
5. Bernard E. Anderson, et al., *The Fairmont Papers: Black Alternatives Conference*, (San Francisco: Institute for Contemporary Studies, 1981), pp. 6–7.
6. *The National Review*, April 17, 1981, p. 416.
7. *National Journal*, March 14, 1981, p. 438.
8. *Baltimore Sun*, June 21, 1981, p. A1.
9. Everett Carll Ladd, Jr., and Seymour Martin Lipset, "Anatomy of a Decade," *Public Opinion*, January 1980, pp. 3–4.
10. *A Working Economy for Americans*, Working Economy (Box 19530, Washington, D.C. 20036), 1977, p. 21.
11. Peter Berger, "The Class Struggle in American Religion," *Christian Century*, February 25, 1981, p. 194.
12. Jeane J. Kirkpatrick, "Politics and the New Class," *Society*, January 1979, p. 43.
13. Seymour Martin Lipset, "The New Class and the Professoriate," *Society*, January 1979, p. 34.
14. Irving Kristol, "The Adversary Culture of Intellectuals," *Encounter*, October 1979, p. 5.
15. Everett Carll Ladd, Jr., "The New Lines Are Drawn: Class and Ideology in America," *Public Opinion*, July 1978, pp. 50–52.
16. Kirkpatrick, *op. cit.*, p. 45.
17. Stanley Rothman, "The Mass Media in Post-Industrial Society," *The Third Century: America As a Post-Industrial Society*, ed. Seymour Martin Lipset (Stanford, Ca.: Hoover Institution Press, 1979), pp. 363–364.
18. James Hitchcock, *The National Review*, February 6, 1981, p. 97.
19. Cited by Burton Yale Pines, "A Majority for Morality?" *Public Opinion*, April 1981, pp. 46–47.

BIBLIOGRAPHICAL NOTE

For the reader seeking additional information about the traditionalist resurgence and its roots, a starting point is the sizable literature on American conservativism. Among the earliest and most important are Russell Kirk's seminal *The Conservative Mind* (1953) and Clinton Rossiter's *Conservatism in America* (1955). Significantly influencing all conservative American thought since World War II have been Friedrich Hayek, *The Road to Serfdom* (1944) and Richard M. Weaver, *Ideas Have Consequences* (1948).

Recent important works reflecting or analyzing the right include George Nash, *The Conservative Intellectual Movement in America / Since 1945* (1976); James Roberts, *The Conservative Decade: Emerging Leaders of the 1980's* (1980); Richard Viguerie *The New Right: We're Ready to Lead* (1981); George Gilder, *Wealth and Poverty* (1981) and Bruce Bartlett, *Reaganomics*.

A number of periodicals regularly analyze issues from a conservative perspective. The most important are: American Enterprise Institute publications, *The American Spectator, Chronicles of Culture, Commentary, Conservative Digest*, Heritage Foundation publications, *Human Events, The National Review, The New Right Report, Persuasion at Work, Public Interest, The Wall Street Journal* editorial page, *The Weyrich Report*. Conservative views are also frequently found in *Encounter*.

Very valuable for gauging those current social and intellectual trends particularly relevant to the growing traditionalism are: *American Demographics, Compact, Christian Century, Christianity Today, Journal of Marriage and the Family, Public Opinion*, studies by the Princeton

Religion Research Center and *Regulation*. The most important programs in the burgeoning economic education movement are listed in *Contract: A Directory of Business and Economic Education Programs*, compiled by the U.S. Chamber of Commerce and *Free Enterprise Resource Index*, by the Free Enterprise Institute of Ada, Michigan.

The best sources for what is happening within the traditionalist community are the bulletins and newsletters of traditionalist organizations; many of these are available by subscription at modest cost. The most informative are: *ACU Education and Research Institute Newsletter* (American Conservative Union, Washington); *AIM Report* (Accuracy in Media, Washington); *Business and the Media* (Media Institute, Washington); *California Monitor of Education* (Betty Arras, Alamo, California); *The Communicator* (Georgia State University Chair of Private Enterprise, Atlanta); *Competition* (Council for a Competitive Economy, Washington); *Dollars and Sense* (National Taxpayers Union, Washington); *Eagle Forum* (Alton, Illinois); *Education Update* (Heritage Foundation); *Family Protection Report* (Free Congress Research and Education Foundation, Washington); *Foundation for Teaching Economics Newsletter* (Foundation for Teaching Economics, San Francisco); *GEM Newsletter* (Project on General Education Models, Washington); *Insider Newsletter* (Heritage Foundation); *Moral Majority Report* (Lynchburg, Virginia); *National Tax Limitation Committee News* (National Tax Limitation Committee, Washington); *Pathfinder* (Center for Education and Research in Free Enterprise, Texas A & M University); *Perspective on National Issues* (National Association of Manufacturers, Washington); *The Phyllis Schlafly Report* (Alton, Illinois); *Private Enterprise* (University of Southern California Center for the Study of Private Enterprise); *Pro-Family Forum Newsletter* (Fort Worth, Texas); and *Regulatory Action Network* (U.S. Chamber of Commerce, Washington).

INDEX

Abortion, 136–140, 142, 150, 155, 227, 303, 324
  women's liberation movement and, 156, 160, 161, 163, 165, 170, 175
Abzug, Bella, 159
Advertising, 33–38, 41–49
  advocacy, 33–38, 42, 62, 83
Alchian, Armen, 58
Allen, Brian, 119–120, 124
Allison, Grady, 201
Allott, Gordon, 290
Alperovitz, Gar, 250, 255
American Bar Association, 60, 209, 219
American Broadcasting Company (ABC), 41–44, 265, 266, 326
American Civil Liberties Union (ACLU), 22, 275, 300, 313
American Conservative Union (ACU), 277–278, 309
American Enterprise Institute (AEI), 32, 75, 82, 132, 247–259, 271, 328
American Federation of State, County and Municipal Employees (AFSCME), 96, 302, 319
American Legislative Exchange Council, 264, 265, 276, 291
American Security Council, 267, 288
Americans for Democratic Action (ADA), 301–302, 320
Anderson, John, 311
Armerding, Hudson, 197
Armstrong, James, 202, 203
Armstrong, William, 298
Armstrong Cork Company, 51, 71
Arras, Betty, 141
Astin, Alexander, 228–230

Bagley, James, 210
Bakker, Jim, 200
Baldwin, Jean, 174
Banfield, Edward, 246
Barlow, F. G., 75
Barr, Noreen, 177–178
Basics education movement, 110–129
Bayh, Birch, 276, 280, 282, 284, 298, 309
Becker, Richard, 198
Bell, Daniel, 22, 267, 268, 269, 324
Berardo, Felix, 133
Berger, Peter, 268, 320
Berkeley Barb, The, 226, 232, 233
Berns, Walter, 211–212, 220
Bethell, Tom, 64
Billings, Robert, 144, 293
Billings, William, 136
Blacks, 151, 268, 305, 311–313
  education and, 107, 117, 124
Blackwell, Morton, 293
Blodgett, Mindy, 234
Bond, Christopher, 315
Boren, David, 137–138
Bork, Robert, 255
Borowitz, Eugene, 331
Bowes, Jane, 156
Bright, Bill, 192–193
Broder, David, 13–14, 275
Brookings Institution, 246, 249, 254, 255
Brooks, James, 63
Brown, Holmes, 57–58
Brozen, Yale, 70
Brunsdale, Anne, 251
Bryant, Winston, 150

Buchanan, John, 297
Buchanan, Mary, 176
Buchanan, Patrick, 310
Buckley, William F., Jr., 270, 277, 310
Burger, Chief Justice, 209, 219
Burian, Denise, 110–112
Burke, Edmund, 19, 131
Burke, Fred, 108
Burns, Arthur, 254, 259
Business Roundtable, 51–52, 84
  on comparative risk assessment, 80
  on the Consumer Protection Act, 72, 73
  on government aid to business, 97
  power of, 85
Butcher, Willard, 31
Byrd, Harry, 285

Cade, Charles, 305
California Monitor of Education, 115–116, 132, 141
Cameron, Karen, 165, 166, 169, 176
Campus Crusade for Christ, 192–193
Capital gains taxes, 36–38, 83, 87
Capital punishment, 211–212. 220, 305
Cardinal Ritter Prep High School, 117–121, 124
Cardozo, Justice Benjamin, 221
Carlson, Allan, 135–136
Carlton Group, 83–85
Carnegie Foundation, 124, 125, 228, 230, 246
Carr, George, 107–108
Carter, Jimmy, 13, 24, 68, 75, 111, 137, 159, 169, 172, 276, 295, 310
  on the family, 142–143
  on regulations, 80
  tax reform by, 36–38, 82–83
Carter Administration, 17, 80, 266, 282, 304
Carty, James, 75, 81
Catholicism, 183–191, 204–206, 238
  education and, 117–124
  the family and, 130, 153
Censorship, 41–44
Center for the Study of Government Regulations, 251–252, 257
Center for the Study of Private Enterprise, 55, 56, 60, 327
Central Illinois Public Service Company, 51, 53
Central Intelligence Agency (CIA), 24, 66, 265, 282
Children's rights, 138–139
Christian Century, 189, 200, 201
Christian Women's National Concerns, 165–166, 169, 176
Christianity Today, 63, 183, 191, 193, 228
Chrysler Corporation, 97, 266, 282

Church, Frank, 13, 276, 280, 282, 284, 285, 309
Ciuba, Monsignor Edward, 205
Clark, David, 198–199
Clark, Dick, 150, 309
Clark, Wallace, 115, 116, 309
Clarke, Elizabeth, 173–174, 176
Cobb, Stephen, 106, 108
Coffin, William Sloane, 301
Columbia Broadcasting System (CBS), 39, 44–49, 54, 64, 265, 327
  censorship charges against, 40, 41
Commentary, 269, 270, 310, 331
Committee for the Survival of a Free Congress (CSFC), 132, 276, 277, 289–290, 306
Communism, 54, 231, 267, 270
Conservative Caucus, 20, 131, 132, 276, 278, 281, 286–288, 291, 300
Consumer Protection Act (CPA), 66–75, 77, 82, 83, 84, 290
  major opponents to, 72–75
Continental Group, 53, 57–58
Coors, Joseph, 53, 247, 260
Coors Industries, 53–54
Copperman, Paul, 103–104
Council of Economic Advisers, 32, 69
Crane, Philip, 277, 278
Crime, 79, 209–225
  class X category, 216–217
  liberalism and, 210, 213–214, 225
  protection against, 209–210, 220–225
  rehabilitation and, 213–214, 217–220, 224–225
Crutchfield, Charles, 38–40, 60
Cuba, 282, 287, 300
Culver, John, 276, 280, 281, 284, 298, 309
Cunningham, George, 276, 284, 309–310

Dart, Justin, 51–52
Dart & Kraft, 51–52, 54, 56–57, 62
De Tocqueville, Alexis, 184, 274
Deakins, Harold, 44–48
DeCrow, Karen, 167–168
Decter, Midge, 268, 269, 271, 328–329
Denton, Jeremiah, 275
Detrick, Ralph and Mary, 153
Divorce, 132–135, 151
Dixon, Greg, 297, 304
Dolan, John, 279–285, 289, 293, 294, 307, 329
Domestic Violence Bill, 137–138, 292
Dow Chemical Company, 48, 53, 54, 55, 233, 247
Drug abuse, 26, 165–166, 227, 323, 330
Durkin, John, 276
Dylan, Bob, 183, 184

Eagle Forum, 16, 131, 141, 147,
   162–167, 173, 176–178, 276, 291,
   304
Eagleton, Thomas, 136–137, 280
Eakin, J. Thomas, 235, 237–238
Economic education, 50–65
   effectiveness of, 55–59
   propaganda aspect of, 56, 57
   in the school system, 57–62
      chairs for, 60–61
   starting a program of, 54–55
Edmonds, Thomas, 283
Education, 99–129, 323–324
   the basics education movement,
      110–129
   Blacks and, 107, 117, 124
   competency exams, 104–108, 110
   cost of, 99–100
   current trends in, 226–241
      statistics on, 228–230, 236–237
   liberalism and, 106, 128
   public vs. private schools, 110–111,
      122
   religion and, 117–124, 195–199,
      236–239
   restructuring in, 102–104
   sex, 139–142, 163, 176
   student achievement, 99–101,
      110–111, 125–127
   teacher certification standards, 109
   television and, 127, 129
   violence in the schools, 102
   See also Economic education
El Salvador, 226, 234, 325
Elitism, 122, 123, 125
Elshtain, Jean Bethke, 158–159, 167,
   178
Energy, 21, 32, 34–35, 41, 69, 70, 316,
   320
Environmentalists, 59, 62, 326
Equal Employment Opportunity Act
   (1972), 70, 169
Equal Rights Amendment (ERA), 18, 25,
   89, 149, 155, 156, 160–178, 207,
   303, 309, 328
   basic objections to, 169–171
Erb, Richard, 259
Ervin, Sam, Jr., 171
Evangelism, 185, 191–204
Evans, M. Stanton, 24, 270, 310
Exxon Corporation, 40, 60

Fairness Doctrine, 41, 173
Falwell, Jerry, 16, 131, 194, 200, 274,
   276, 294, 296–305, 329
Family, the, 130–154
   government and, 130–132, 137–138,
      142–143, 154
   liberalism and, 131, 137, 149

religion and, 130, 135–136, 153
statistics on, 133–134
Family Life America God (FLAG), 131,
   138–139, 145, 148–150, 162
Family Protection Act, 131, 150–151
Family Protection Report, 16, 132, 162,
   290
Federal Bureau of Investigation (FBI),
   24, 66, 282
Federal Register, 68, 79, 288
Feldstein, Martin, 93
Fellner, William, 255
Felsenthal, Carol, 167
Feulner, Edwin, 253, 260, 261, 263, 293
Fichter, Joseph, 184
Fitch, Harrison, 314
Fogel, David, 214, 215, 219
Ford, Gerald, 169, 276, 278
Fordham, Jim and Andrea, 159
Fore, William, 200–201
Fosdick, Harry Emerson, 199
France, 37, 184, 231, 232
Free enterprise concept, 31–65, 247–248
   government regulations and, 51,
      53–54
   television's hostility and, 41–49, 63–64
Friedan, Betty, 135, 156, 158, 178
Friedman, Milton, 54, 86, 88–89, 92,
   254, 255, 331
Fuller, Charles, 199
Fuller, Ted, 38, 39–40
Fundamentalists, 17, 185, 193–195, 277,
   294, 298–299, 305

Gabler, Mel and Norma, 176–177
Gaff, Jerry, 125–126
Galbraith, John Kenneth, 63
Gallup, George, Jr., 154, 187, 200, 205,
   228
Gallup polls, 83, 153–154, 175, 184,
   191, 193, 207, 231–232, 237, 330
Garn, Jake, 306
Gas industry, 32, 34–35, 69
Gasper, Jo Ann, 132, 155–157, 162–163,
   165, 178, 179, 328
General Motors Corporation, 40, 64
Georgetown University, 235, 266
Gergen, David, 259
Gilbert, Father Edward, 205, 206
Gilder, George, 23, 331
Glanz, David, 207
Glasser, Ira, 275, 301
Glazer, Nathan, 154, 156, 268, 269
Godwin, Ronald, 305
Goldwater, Barry, 167, **293**
Goldwin, Robert, 255
Gornick, Vivian, 158
Government
   deregulation of, 75–77, 249–254

Government (cont'd)
  expansion of activity of, 68–71
  the family and, 130–132, 137–138,
    142–143, 154
  inflation and, 32, 54, 64, 78, 261–262
  Keynesianism and, 90–96
  public relations programs of, 96
  rational expectations economics and,
    95–96
  regulations by, 36–38, 53–54, 59,
    66–75, 248–254
    changes in, 67–68
    cost of, 69–70
    free enterprise concept and, 51,
      53–54
    major opponents to, 72–75
    paper work and, 79–80
    productivity and, 70–71
    public disenchantment with, 97–98
    trade-offs and, 79–81
  regulatory reform, 77–81
  reliance on, 318–319
  rising cost of, 52, 54
Grace, J. Peter, 36–38
Graham, Billy, 196, 200
Graham, Daniel, 282
Grant, Robert, 295
Grassley, Charles, 275
Gray, Dennis, 109–110, 128–129
Greenfield, Meg, 285
Guthrie, Arlo, 183, 184
Gutman, Jonathan, 56–57

Haberler, Gottfried, 255
Hacker, Andrew, 159
Hafen, Bruce, 138, 139
Haig, Alexander, 262
Handlin, Oscar, 23, 25
Harpers, 64, 132
Harrington, Michael, 319
Harvard University, 71, 93, 125, 264
Hastings, Philip, 236, 241
Hatch, Orrin, 137
Hawkins, Paula, 176
Hayek, Friedrich, 92, 93
Health care, 52, 65
Heilbroner, Robert, 63
Heller, Walter, 94
Helms, Jesse, 131, 160, 280, 288, 293,
    294, 298
Henry, Carl, 196
Heritage Foundation, 132, 246, 247,
    252–254, 259–264, 271, 290, 291
Herndon, James, 102
Hill, Reuben, 134
Himmelfarb, Gertrude, 19
Himmelfarb, Milton, 311
Hines, Emmett, 71–72, 74
Hitchcock, James, 21, 308, 326

Hobbs, Lottie Beth, 144, 156, 165, 178
Hoge, Dean, 187–188, 230–231, 236,
    241
Holmes, Arthur, 227
Holt, John, 102, 127
Holtzman, Elizabeth, 176
Homosexuality, 140–141, 151, 153, 161,
    165, 169, 227, 268, 269, 295, 303,
    305, 324, 330
  religion and, 197, 207
Hook, Sidney, 254
Hooks, Ben, 268
Hoover Institution, 247, 254, 264, 311
Hornbeck, David, 100
Humbard, Rex, 200
Humphrey, Gordon, 137, 289, 298
Hunt, Carolyn, 105
Hunt, James, 99, 104, 105
Hurwicz, Leonid, 94, 96

Iacocca, Lee, 97
Illinois Power Company, 16, 40, 44–49,
    62, 309, 326, 327
Income taxes, personal, 82, 85, 87
Inflation, 52, 54, 86, 89
  government and, 32, 54, 64, 78,
    261–262
  productivity and, 71
  taxes and, 82
Institute for Contemporary Studies, 265,
    311
Institute for Policy Studies, 246, 319
International Women's Year (IWY),
    143–145, 155, 159–166, 178

Jackson, Jesse, 268
Japan, 37, 64, 231, 232
Javits, Jacob, 309
Jefferson, Thomas, 211
Jepsen, Roger, 150–151
John Paul II, Pope, 204, 205
Johnson, Paul, 78–79
Johnson, Thomas, 249–250, 256
Joint Council on Economic Education,
    51, 57, 58
Jorgensen, Dale, 93
Joseph, Jeffrey, 77
Journal of Marriage and the Family, 133,
    152–153
Judaism, 122, 172, 184–186, 206–207,
    236–239, 305, 310–311, 331
  the family and, 130, 135–136, 153
Juola, Arvo, 126

Kahn, Alfred, 75, 76
Kaiser Aluminum and Chemical
    Corporation, 31, 32, 40–44, 62, 65,
    89, 326
Kannensohn, Michael, 212

Kareken, John, 94
Kasun, Jacqueline, 140, 329
Katz, Joseph, 231
Kelley, Dean, 188, 274
Kemp, Jack, 90
Keniston, Kenneth, 230
Kennedy, Edward, 75, 137
Kennedy, James, 276–277
Kennedy, John F., 94
Kent, Calvin, 50, 61
Keyes, William, 311
Keynes, John Maynard, 90, 92, 96
Keynesianism, 90–96
Kidder, Priscilla, 240
Kilpatrick, James J., 310
King, Edward, 87, 315
King, Martin Luther, Jr., 301, 302
Kingston Group, 291–293
Kirk, Russell, 246, 271
Kirkpatrick, Jeane, 258, 259, 268, 321, 324
Kissinger, Henry, 266
Kohl, Herbert, 102
Kolb, Erwin, 202
Koop, C. Everett, 325
Korb, Lawrence, 259
Kort, Michael, 32
Kosters, Marvin, 250, 251, 252
Kozol, Jonathan, 102
Kristol, Irving, 16, 18, 248, 255, 260–271, 308, 322–323, 327

Labouré High School, 117–119
Ladd, Everett, Jr., 20, 318–319, 323
Laffer, Arthur, 55, 90
LaFollette, Bronson, 221
LaForce, J. Clayburn, 50–51
LaHaye, Beverly, 156
Laird, Melvin, 257
Latshaw, William, 35, 36
Laxalt, Paul, 131, 150, 294, 298, 306
Lee, William, 40
Lefever, Ernest, 265
Leifer, Daniel, 238
Lesbianism, 189, 330
  women's liberation movement and, 155, 159–161, 166
Levine, Arthur, 228, 230, 233, 236
Liberalism, 15, 21–27, 59, 63, 76, 91, 229, 255, 268–271, 309–310, 327, 331
  business and, 89–90
  crime and, 210, 213–214, 225
  education and, 106, 128
  the family and, 131, 137, 149
  New Right and, 274–276, 279–285, 305
  religion and, 203–207
Library Court Group, 290–293

Lindberg, James, 57
Lipset, Seymour Martin, 97–98, 258, 268, 318–319, 322
Loewenwarter, Paul, 44, 46
Lott, Trent, 292
Lougee, Carolyn, 126
Lovelace, Richard, 184
Lucas, Robert, 91–92, 95, 96

McAteer, Edward, 132, 293–294, 296, 299
McDonald, William, 223, 224
McGavran, Donald, 187
McGovern, George, 255, 276, 280, 281, 298, 309
McGraw, Onalee, 132, 144
McIntyre, Thomas, 150
McKevitt, James, 74
Macklin, Eleanor, 134–135
Madden, Father Lawrence, 235, 238
Maier, Cornell, 31, 40–44, 62, 65, 89, 308, 327
Mandate for Leadership, 252–254, 260
Mano, D. Keith, 189, 276, 309
Marshner, Connaught, 16, 132, 140, 144, 146, 148, 150, 151, 289–292
Martinson, Robert, 219
Marty, Martin, 186
Marxism, 24, 63, 135, 160, 234, 246, 309, 319
Mason, H. Marc, 115
Massa, Cliff, 67
Massachusetts Institute of Technology (MIT), 93, 264
Matijevich, John, 174
Mayer, Egon, 206, 207
Meany, George, 172
Media Institute, 48, 64, 265, 326
Meese, Edwin, III, 265
Meiselman, David, 247
Mescon, Michael, 60
Michigan State University, 71, 74–75, 126
Mikulski, Barbara, 137
Miller, James, III, 251, 259
Millett, Kate, 135
Minnesota, University of, 93–96
Minuchin, Salvador, 152
Mitchell, Jeri, 120
Mobil Oil Corporation, 34–35, 40
Momboisse, Raymond, 314, 315
Moody, Dwight, 195
Mooneyham, H. Lamarr, 139
Moral Majority, 15, 18, 131, 137, 139, 144, 194, 207, 273–276, 289–291, 295–305
Moral Majority Report, The, 278, 296–297, 303
Morgan, Robert, 276

Motion pictures, 53, 54, 56, 58–59, 267
  religion and, 195, 197
Motley, John, 75, 84
Moynihan, Daniel Patrick, 21, 268, 269
Myers, Charles, 61
Myers, Henry, Jr., 116

Nader, Ralph, 57, 74, 255, 302, 326
Nash, George, 246
Nation, The, 72, 159
National Association of Manufacturers,
  51, 55, 67, 72–75, 80–81, 84, 97
National Broadcasting Company (NBC),
  34–35, 41, 42, 265, 325
National Conservative Political Action
  Committee (NCPAC), 276, 279–286,
  288, 307
National Council of Churches, 63, 200,
  201, 321
National Education Association (NEA),
  109, 123, 302, 319, 320
National Federation of Independent
  Business (NFIB), 72–75, 84
National Gay Task Force, 144, 320
National Organization for Women
  (NOW), 145, 161, 163, 172, 320
National Pro-Family Coalition, 144, 146,
  148, 149
National Review, The, 189, 231, 237, 277
National Tax Limitation Committee, 86,
  88–89, 264
National Taxpayers Union (NTU), 86,
  88, 283
Nelson, Gaylord, 255, 276, 298, 309
Nevin, John, 64
New Class, 270, 321–327
New Deal, 96–97, 270, 310
New Republic, The, 269, 310
New Right, 18, 150, 245, 273–307, 329
  grass-roots campaign of, 286–295
  liberalism and, 274–276, 279–285,
  305
  radio and, 282, 304
  Reagan and, 275–280, 283, 284, 296,
  306–307
  religion and, 274–275, 305
  television and, 282–284, 304
New York Times, The, 34, 90, 185, 300,
  324, 325
New York Times Magazine, The, 156, 158,
  178, 250
Newsweek, 35, 152, 324, 325
Nickles, Don, 275
Nisbet, Robert, 26–27, 246, 255
Nitze, Paul, 267
Nixon, Richard, 91, 278
Nofziger, Franklyn, 307
Novak, Michael, 19, 132, 255, 256,
  258–259, 268, 269

Nuclear energy, 44–49, 236, 286
Nuttle, Marc, 289–290

Occupational Safety and Health
  Administration (OSHA), 68–70, 75,
  77–78, 257
Oil industry, 21, 32, 34–35, 320
Oreffice, Paul, 53
Osborne, Richard, 298, 304

Packer, Boyd, 170
Parker, J. A., 311, 312
Pasch, Sam, 240
Pfund, Lee, 198
Phillips, Howard, 132, 278, 279, 281,
  286–288, 293–295, 302
Phyllis Schlafly Report, 162, 166, 168, 169
Podhoretz, Norman, 268, 269, 271
Poe, Randall, 33
Poling, David, 187, 200
Popeo, Daniel, 314–315
Postman, Neil, 127–128
Pound, Roscoe, 255
Prescott, Edward, 94
Priester, Helen, 160
Pritchett, Ballard, 203
Profit, 32, 33, 53, 55, 57
Proposition 13, 85, 86–87
Protestantism, 172, 183–204, 236–238
  education and, 121–124
  the family and, 135–136, 153
Public Interest, The, 122, 135, 268, 269
Public Opinion, 97–98, 318, 323

Quayle, Dan, 284

Radio, 42, 48, 62, 96, 252, 256
  New Right and, 282, 304
  religion and, 185, 192, 199, 200
Rand Corporation, 108, 254
Ranney, Austin, 255
Ranney, Joan, 113
Raspberry, William, 274
Reagan, Ronald, 13–15, 62, 89–91, 96,
  111, 131, 147, 177, 251, 259, 308,
  310–311, 315, 332
  block grant program, 291–292
  New Right and, 275–280, 283, 284,
  296, 306–307
  tax reform by, 36, 38, 82, 85, 87, 90,
  261, 263, 283
Reagan Administration, 31, 67, 69, 98,
  144, 252, 254, 258, 260, 262, 325
Reasoner, Harry, 44–47
Reiff, Robert, 223
Reisman, Bernard, 206
Religion, 63, 183–208, 248–249
  education and, 117–124, 195–199,
  236–239

the family and, 130, 135–136, 153
homosexuality and, 197, 207
liberalism and, 203–207
motion pictures and, 195, 197
New Right and, 274–275, 305
radio and, 185, 192, 199, 200
statistics on, 184–187, 193
television and, 185, 192, 195–201,
    294
women's liberation movement and,
    158, 161, 166, 169–172, 189
Religious Roundtable, 132, 207, 276,
    295–296, 299
Resource Bank, 262–264
Reverski, Robert, 122–124
Rhodes, Steven, 52
Rhody, Ronald, 41
Rice, Charles, 144
Right to Life, 147, 163
Right Woman, The, 132, 162–163, 328
Ritter, Joseph Cardinal, 119
Roberts, Oral, 200
Roberts, Paul Craig, 90, 254
Robertson, M. G., 194, 198, 200
Robison, James, 200
Roof, Wade, 185
Roselle, Charles, 237, 238
Rosovsky, Henry, 125, 126
Rossiter, Clinton, 246
Rostow, Eugene, 267
Roth, William, 90, 285
Rothman, Stanley, 325–326
Rowe, Howard, 46–48
Royko, Mike, 300
Russell, Norma, 161
Ryor, John, 123

Safire, William, 310
Samuelson, Paul, 92–93
Sanjuan, Pedro, 258
Sarbanes, Paul, 283–284
Sargent, Thomas, 94–96
Say, Jean Baptiste, 90, 93
Schindler, Rabbi Alexander, 274–275,
    301
Schlafly, Phyllis, 16, 131, 141–142,
    146–148, 156, 157, 166–169,
    172–174, 177, 178, 293, 310,
    329
Schlesinger, Arthur, Jr., 63
Schlesinger, James, 266
Schmertz, Herbert, 34, 35
Schmitt, Harrison, 285
Schneider, William, 97–98
Schroeder, Mary and George, 148–149,
    152
Schuller, David, 204
Schuller, Robert, 199–200
Schwartz, George, 74–75

Schweiker, Richard, 298
Scott, Eva, 160
Seable, Mrs. Stephen, 115–116
Sells, Ray, 16, 190, 201
Sethi, S. Prakash, 36, 37
Sex education, 139–142, 163, 176
Shafer, Carl, 54, 55–56
Sheen, Bishop Fulton, 199
Shetler, Douglas, 58
Simon, William, 97, 280, 327
Sims, Christopher, 94
Skerry, Peter, 122
Skousen, Sam and Beth, 16, 143,
    146–148, 152
Smart, S. Bruce, Jr., 53
Smeal, Eleanor, 172–173
Smith, Adam, 92–93
Smith, Bailey, 188, 194, 300
Smith, Bill, 299
Smith, Gary Lee, 297
Smith, Roger B., 64
Smith, Timothy, 203, 204
SmithKline Corporation, 35, 247
Social Security, 52, 70, 257
Socialism, 54, 59, 63, 258, 259, 320
Solarz, Stephen, 90
Sowell, Thomas, 311–312
Spong, John Shelby, 189
Stafford, Robert, 281
Stanton Group, 290–291, 293
Stapleton, Jean, 155, 172
Stein, Ben, 63
Stein, Herbert, 32, 254
Steinem, Gloria, 158, 166
Steinglass, Peter, 152
Stoltenberg, Lisa, 282
Stop-ERA, 15, 146, 147, 167, 169, 173
    174, 176, 177
Strike, Kenneth, 100
Sullivan, Kathleen, 177
Supply-side economics, 90–98
Swaggart, Jimmy, 199
Symms, Steve, 275

Tabbush, Victor, 59
Tanenbaum, Rabbi Marc, 63, 274, 301
Tarrance, Lance, 284
Taxes, 54, 81–89
    capital gains, 36–38, 83, 87
    inflation and, 82
    investment and, 35–36
    Keynesianism and, 90–96
    organizations combating, 85–90
    personal income, 82, 85, 87
    reform of
        by Carter, 36–38, 82–83
        by Reagan, 36, 38, 82, 85, 87, 90,
            261, 263, 283
    statistics on, 37, 68

Taylor, Elizabeth, 213
Television, 33, 38–49, 96, 99, 105, 155,
    252, 256, 267, 324
    advocacy advertising on, 34–35, 42
    censorship charges against, 41–44
    education and, 127, 129
    hostility to business, 40–49, 63–64
    New Right and, 282–284, 304
    the public interest issue and, 41–49
    religion and, 185, 192, 195–201, 294
    unbalanced reporting by, 44–49, 54
Teller, Edward, 254
Theberge, Leonard, 326
Thomas, Cal, 300–301
Thomas, Clarence, 313
Thomas, John, 84
Thompson, James, 172, 216–217
Thomson, Rosemary, 16, 156, 161, 163,
    308
Thurmond, Strom, 306
Time, 209, 324, 325
Toben, Sister Jacqueline, 119
Truitt, Michael and Cheryl, 183, 184
Truluck, Phillip, 261, 271
Tucker, Jim Guy, 131, 143
Ture, Norman, 90, 254
Tyrrell, R. Emmett, Jr., 310

Union of Soviet Socialist Republics
    (U.S.S.R.), 21, 24, 25, 262, 263,
    266–270, 277, 278, 281, 282, 286,
    287, 319, 329, 331
Unions, 55, 56, 109, 327
U.S. Chamber of Commerce, 38, 39, 55,
    58, 72–74, 77, 84
U.S. Constitution, 24, 88–89, 171, 209,
    224, 258, 330
U.S. Supreme Court, 75–76, 136, 209,
    221, 224, 259

Van Andel, Jay, 53
Van Deerlin, Lionel, 42
Vaughn, Christine, 85
Vietnam War, 183, 189, 232, 233, 235
Viguerie, Richard, 277, 278, 280, 282,
    293–294
Vineyard, James, 298, 299
Vlaanderen, Russell, 109

W. R. Grace and Company, 36–38, 83
Wall, James, 201
Wall Street Journal, The, 70, 101, 227,
    268, 269, 310, 324
Wallace, Mike, 39
Wallace, Neil, 94–95
Wanniski, Jude, 90
Washington Post, 13, 266, 285, 311, 324
Watt, James, 254, 315
Wattenberg, Ben, 255
Weaver, Richard, 246
Weicker, Lowell, 281
Weidenbaum, Murray, 69, 70, 251, 259
Welfare, 270–271, 312, 315
Wesley, Stephen, 16, 118–121, 309
Weyrich, Paul, 132, 260, 277, 279, 287,
    289, 290, 293, 294, 306, 307, 308,
    329
Wharton, Clifton, 129
Wheaton College, 196–198, 277
White, Frank, 150
White, Harold, 238–239
White House Conference on Families
    (WHCF), 131, 142–151, 156, 163,
    176
Wilcke, Richard, 266
Will, George, 310
Williams, Walter, 311–312, 313
Williams College, 236–237
Wilson, James Q., 218, 255
Wilson, Woodrow, 126
Winpisinger, William, 320
Winter, Thomas, 270
Wisconsin, University of, 60, 233–235
Wise, Arthur, 108
Wise, Stephen, 199
Women's liberation movement, 135,
    143, 145, 155–179, 331
    abortion and, 156, 160, 161, 163,
    165, 170, 175
    lesbianism and, 155, 159–161, 166
    religion and, 158, 161, 166, 169–172,
    189

Young, Andrew, 24

Zelinsky, Ron, 299–300
Zumbrun, Ronald, 315, 316